Apple Training Series

Mac OS X
Server Essentials
v10.6

Arek Dreyer with Ben Greisler

Apple
Certified

Apple Training Series: Mac OS X Server Essentials v10.6
Arek Dreyer with Ben Greisler
Copyright © 2010 by Apple Inc.

Published by Peachpit Press. For information on Peachpit Press books, contact:
Peachpit Press
1249 Eighth Street
Berkeley, CA 94710
510/524-2178
510/524-2221 (fax)
www.peachpit.com

To report errors, please send a note to errata@peachpit.com.
Peachpit Press is a division of Pearson Education.

Apple Training Series Editor: Rebecca Freed
Production Editor: Danielle Foster
Project Editor: Kim Saccio-Kent
Copyeditors: Rachel Fudge and Marla Miyashiro
Tech Editor: David Colville
Apple Editor: John Signa
Proofreader: Darren Meiss
Compositor: Danielle Foster
Indexer: Valerie Perry
Cover design: Mimi Heft
Cover illustrator: Kent Oberheu

ISBN 13: 978-0-321-63533-4
ISBN 10:   0-321-63533-7

9 8 7 6 5 4 3 2

Printed and bound in the United States of America

Acknowledgments

Arek Dreyer

Thanks to my lovely wife, Heather Jagman, for her support while I tried to meet deadlines for this book.

Thanks to Schoun Regan, David Pugh, and other authors of earlier versions of this material, Simon Wheatley for working on the exercises and slides associated with this version of the course, and David Colville for excellent technical editing suggestions.

Thanks to Becca Freed, Kim Saccio-Kent, and Danielle Foster at Peachpit for making the impossible possible. Thanks to Ben for joining in and for picking up my slack.

Thanks to Tip Lovingood at TechIt, Geordie Korper at GroupLogic, Charles Edge at 318, and the following people at Apple, for their help: Jason Deraleau, Michael Dhaliwal, André LaBranche, Timo Perfitt, Mike Reed, Joel Rennich, John Signa, and Josh Wisenbaker.

Finally, thanks to the Mac OS X Server community for always striving to better serve their users.

Ben Greisler

Without the support and patience of my wife, Ronit Greisler, and my children, Galee and Noam, I would have never been able to get through this project.

Thanks to Arek for bringing me into this project and trusting me to support his efforts.

Thanks to all the people from Apple and Peachpit whom Arek has already thanked, for they have been a tremendous help.

Thanks to Ståle Bjørdal, Ken Holden, Ed Marczak, and Josh Perlman for reality checks.

Thanks to my clients, students, and colleagues who encourage me to become a better consultant, trainer, and member of the OS X ecosystem. Without them, this would have been an empty effort.

Contents at a Glance

Contents

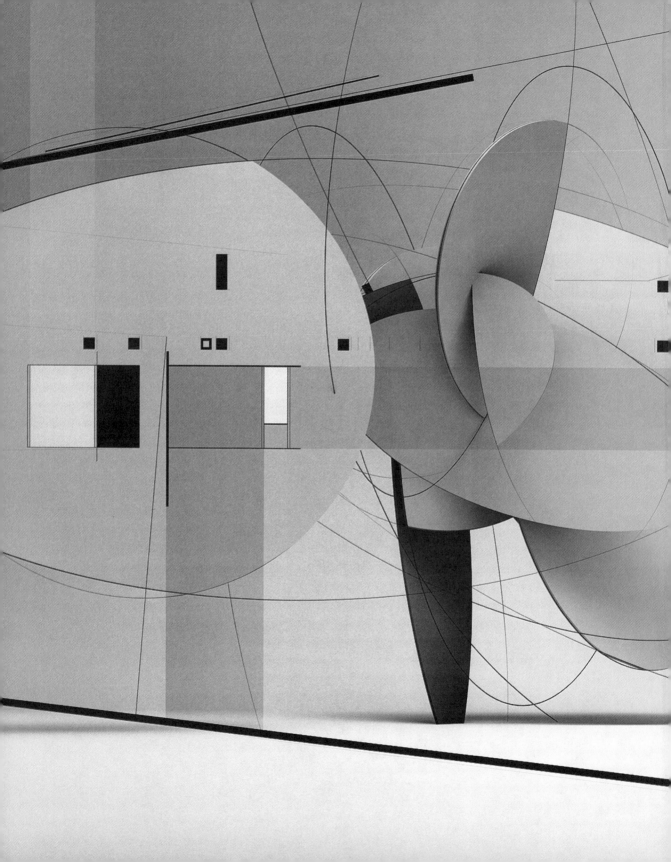

Getting Started

This book is based on the same criteria used for Apple's official training course, Mac OS X Server Essentials 10.6, an in-depth exploration of Mac OS X Server v10.6. This book serves as a self-paced tour of the breadth of functionality of Mac OS X Server and the best methods for effectively supporting users of Mac OS X Server systems.

The primary goal of this book is to prepare technical coordinators and entry-level system administrators for the tasks demanded of them by Mac OS X Server; you will learn how to install and configure Mac OS X Server to provide network-based services, such as file sharing, authentication, and collaboration services. To become truly proficient, you need to learn the theory behind the tools you will use. For example, not only will you learn how to use Workgroup Manager—the tool for managing preferences for users, groups, and computer accounts and lists—but you will also learn about the ideas behind preference management, how to think about policies and control of resources, and how to set up preference and policy management to support your environment.

You will learn to develop processes to help you understand and work with the complexity of your system as it grows. Even a single Mac OS X Server computer can grow into a very complicated system, and creating documentation and charts can help you develop processes so that additions and modifications can integrate harmoniously with your existing system.

This book assumes that you have some knowledge of Mac OS X, because Mac OS X Server is built on top of Mac OS X. Therefore, basic navigation, troubleshooting, and networking are all similar regardless of whether the operating system is Mac OS X or Mac OS X Server. The main differences you will encounter focus on the services provided with Mac OS X Server. For example, user creation is managed very differently in Mac OS X Server than in Mac OS X. While Windows file sharing and user management services are included in Mac OS X, Mac OS X Server adds a rich interface to configure and monitor these services. This book will therefore concentrate on the features that are unique to Mac OS X Server. When working through this book, a basic understanding and knowledge of Mac OS X is preferred, including troubleshooting the operating system. Refer to *Apple Training Series: Mac OS X Support Essentials v10.6* from Peachpit Press if you need to develop a solid working knowledge of Mac OS X.

Unless otherwise specified, all references to Mac OS X and Mac OS X Server refer to version 10.6.0, which was the most current version available at the time of writing. Due to subsequent upgrades, some screen shots, features, and procedures may be slightly different from those presented on these pages.

Learning Methodology

This book is based on lectures and exercises provided to students attending Mac OS X Server Essentials 10.6, a four-day, hands-on course designed to give technical coordinators and entry-level system administrators the skills, tools, and knowledge to implement and maintain a network that uses Mac OS X Server. For consistency, this book follows the basic structure of the course material, but you may complete it at your own pace.

The exercises contained within this book are designed to let you explore and learn the tools necessary to manage Mac OS X Server. They move along in a predictable fashion, starting with the installation and setup of Mac OS X Server and moving to more advanced topics such as multiprotocol file sharing, using access control lists, and permitting Mac OS X Server to be a centralized storage center for user information and authentica-

tion via LDAP and Password Server, and to become a Kerberos Key Distribution Center (KDC). If you already have a Mac OS X Server set up, you can skip ahead to some of the later exercises in the book, provided you understand the change in IP addressing from the examples to your server and are not running your server as a production server.

This book serves as an introduction to Mac OS X Server and is not meant to be a definitive reference. Because Mac OS X and Mac OS X Server contain several open source initiatives, it is impossible to include all the possibilities and permutations here. First-time users of Mac OS X Server and users of other server operating systems who are migrating to Mac OS X Server have the most to gain from this book; still others who are upgrading from previous versions of Mac OS X Server will also find this book a valuable resource.

Mac OS X Server is by no means difficult to set up and configure, but how you use Mac OS X Server should be planned out in advance. Accordingly, this book is divided into five sections:

▶ Chapter 1 covers planning, installation, and initial configuration of Mac OS X Server, and contains an introduction to the various administration tools.

▶ Chapters 2 and 3 define authentication and authorization, various types of access control, and Open Directory and the vast functionality it can provide.

▶ Chapter 4 covers the various file-sharing protocols—AFP, SMB, FTP, and NFS— and introduces the concept of sharing files and associating share points with users and groups.

▶ Chapters 5, 6, and 7 focus on setting up collaboration services such as mail, web, wiki, calendaring, and instant messaging.

▶ Chapters 8 and 9 teach you to manage user preferences, create a network startup disk, and deploy disk images.

Chapter Structure

Each chapter begins by listing the learning goals for the chapter and providing an estimate of time needed to complete the chapter. The explanatory material is augmented with hands-on exercises essential to developing your skills. If you lack the equipment necessary to complete a given exercise, you are still encouraged to read the step-by-step instructions and examine the screen shots to understand the procedures demonstrated.

WARNING ▶ The initial exercise in this book requires you to reformat a volume on which you will install Mac OS X Server. All data on this volume will be erased. Once past that point, the majority of the exercises in this book are designed to be non-destructive if followed correctly. However, some of the exercises are disruptive; for example, they may turn off or on certain network services. Other exercises, if performed incorrectly, could result in data loss or corruption to some basic services, possibly even erasing a disk or volume of a computer connected to the network on which Mac OS X Server resides. Thus, it is recommended that you run through the exercises on a Mac OS X Server computer that is not critical to your work or connected to a production network. This is also true of the Mac OS X computer you will use in these exercises. Please back up all your data if you choose to use a production computer for either the Mac OS X Server and/or the Mac OS X computers. Instructions are given for restoring your services to their preset state, but reasonable caution is recommended. Apple, Inc. and Peachpit Press are not responsible for any data loss or any damage to any equipment that occurs as a direct or indirect result of following the procedures described in this book.

You'll also find resources that provide ancillary information throughout the chapters. These resources are merely for your edification, and are not essential for the coursework or certification.

Each chapter closes with a list of relevant Apple Knowledge Base articles and recommended documents related to the topic of the chapter. Mac OS X Server documentation (http://www.apple.com/server/macosx/resources/) and Knowledge Base articles (http://www.apple.com/support) are free resources that contain the very latest technical information on all of Apple's hardware and software products. We strongly encourage you to read the suggested documents and search the Knowledge Base for answers to any problems you encounter.

Finally, at the end of each chapter is a short chapter review that recaps the material you've learned. You can refer to various Apple resources, such as the Knowledge Base, Mac OS X Server documentation, as well as the chapters themselves, to help you answer these questions.

System Requirements

This book assumes a basic level of familiarity with Mac OS X. All references to Mac OS X and Mac OS X Server refer to v10.6, unless otherwise stated.

Here's what you will need to complete the lessons in this book:

▶ Two Macintosh computers, one with Mac OS X v10.6 installed and one on which to install Mac OS X Server v10.6

▶ A USB or FireWire storage device for transferring files from one computer to the other

▶ An Ethernet switch to keep the two computers connected via a small private local network

▶ Two Ethernet network cables for connecting both computers to the switch

▶ Optionally, two additional computers, one on which to install Mac OS X Server v10.6 and configure as an Open Directory replica, and one on which to install Mac OS X Server v10.6 and bind to your Open Directory server

Apple Certification

After reading this book, you may wish to take the Mac OS X Support Server 10.6 Exam to earn the Apple Certified Technical Coordinator 10.6 certification. This is the second level of Apple's certification program for Mac OS X professionals, which includes:

▶ Apple Certified Support Professional 10.6 (ACSP)—Ideal for help desk personnel, service technicians, technical coordinators, and others who support Mac OS X customers over the phone or who perform Mac OS X troubleshooting and support in schools and businesses. This certification verifies an understanding of Mac OS X core functionality and an ability to configure key services, perform basic troubleshooting, and assist end users with essential Mac OS X capabilities. To receive this certification, you must pass the Mac OS X Support Essentials 10.6 Exam. This book is designed to provide you with the knowledge and skills to pass that exam.

▶ Apple Certified Technical Coordinator 10.6 (ACTC)—This certification is intended for Mac OS X technical coordinators and entry-level system administrators tasked with maintaining a modest network of computers using Mac OS X Server. Since the ACTC certification addresses both the support of Mac OS X clients and the core functionality and use of Mac OS X Server, the learning curve is correspondingly longer and more intensive than that for the ACSP certification, which addresses solely

Mac OS X client support. This certification is not intended for high-end system administrators or engineers, but may be an excellent step to take on an intended career path to system administration. This certification requires passing both the Mac OS X Support Essentials 10.6 Exam and Mac OS X Server Essentials 10.6 Exam.

NOTE ▶ Although all of the questions in the Mac OS X Server Essentials 10.6 exam are based on material in this book, simply reading it will not adequately prepare you for the exam. Apple recommends that before taking the exam you spend time setting up, configuring, and troubleshooting Mac OS X Server. You should also download and review the Skills Assessment Guide, which lists the exam objectives, the total number of items, the number of items per section, the required score to pass, and how to register. A 10-item sample test is also available for download. Items on the sample test are similar in style to items on the certification exam, though they may vary in difficulty level. To download the Skills Assessment Guide and sample test, visit http://training.apple.com/itpro/snow201

▶ Apple Certified System Administrator 10.6 (ACSA)—This certification verifies an in-depth knowledge of Apple technical architecture and an ability to install and configure computers; architect and maintain networks; enable, customize, tune, and troubleshoot a wide range of services; and integrate Mac OS X, Mac OS X Server, and other Apple technologies within a multiplatform networked environment. The ACSA certification is intended for full-time professional system administrators and engineers who manage medium-to-large networks of systems in complex multiplatform deployments. ACSA 10.6 certification requires passing the Mac OS X Server Essentials 10.6 Exam, Mac OS X Directory Services 10.6 Exam, Mac OS X Deployment 10.6 Exam, and Mac OS X Security and Mobility 10.6 Exam.

▶ Mac OS X 10.6 certification offerings now include new Specialist certifications for the ACSA-level Directory Services, Deployment, and Security and Mobility exams.

▶ Apple hardware service technician certifications are ideal for people interested in becoming Macintosh repair technicians, but also worthwhile for help desk personnel at schools and businesses, and for Macintosh consultants and others needing an in-depth understanding of how Apple systems operate:

▶ Apple Certified Macintosh Technician (ACMT)—This certification verifies the ability to perform basic troubleshooting and repair of both desktop and portable Macintosh systems, such as iMac and MacBook Pro. ACMT certification requires passing the Apple Macintosh Service exam and the Mac OS X Troubleshooting Exam.

About the Apple Training Series

Apple Training Series: Mac OS X Server Essentials v10.6 is part of the official training series for Apple products developed by experts in the field and certified by Apple. The chapters are designed to let you learn at your own pace. You can progress through the book from beginning to end, or dive right into the chapters that interest you most.

For those who prefer to learn in an instructor-led setting, Apple also offers training courses at Apple Authorized Training Centers worldwide. These courses are taught by Apple Certified Trainers, and they balance concepts and lectures with hands-on labs and exercises. Apple Authorized Training Centers have been carefully selected and have met Apple's highest standards in all areas, including facilities, instructors, course delivery, and infrastructure. The goal of the program is to offer Apple customers, from beginners to the most seasoned professionals, the highest-quality training experience.

To find an Authorized Training Center near you, please visit http://training.apple.com.

1

Time	This chapter takes approximately three hours to complete.
Goals	Configure your Mac OS X computer so that you can follow the exercises in this book
	Install the Mac OS X Server software
	Configure the initial setup of Mac OS X Server
	Save your configuration settings

Chapter 1
Installing and Configuring Mac OS X Server

You can divide working with Mac OS X Server into three phases:

1. Planning and installation: Plan how the server will be set up, verify and configure the hardware, and install the server software.

2. Initial configuration: Use Server Admin and Server Assistant to perform the initial Mac OS X Server configuration. You can also use the Network preferences pane to update the interface configurations, including increasing performance by combining multiple Ethernet interfaces to act as one.

3. Maintenance: After the server is running, use utilities such as Server Admin and Workgroup Manager to perform ongoing server and account maintenance.

This chapter begins with the first two phases, installation and initial configuration. Then it introduces the tools that you will use throughout the rest of this book to manage your server.

Preparing to Install Mac OS X Server

Installation of Mac OS X Server should be done in two steps:

1   Before you install the software, take the time to evaluate the server needs of your organization and the Mac OS X Server hardware requirements.

2   Then use the Mac OS X Server Install Disc to install the operating system, server applications, and utilities.

We will not be covering the upgrade process in this book. Upgrading from an existing version of Mac OS X Server is an option available to administrators. It is always best practice to back up any existing setup prior to running the upgrade so you can restore should anything go wrong.

> **NOTE ▶** Updating the server software should be a planned event. Always run updates on a test system before rolling out into production. In some cases, third-party solutions have not continued to operate smoothly with the new software. You should preflight the update in isolation first and roll out the update once you have tested your implementation.

Mac OS X Server can be installed using either of two methods: locally, while you are sitting at the server, or remotely, from another computer on the network (ideally, this will be a Mac OS X computer on your local network). Because both Mac OS X and Mac OS X Server—when booted from the Install Disc—use Bonjour, Internet Protocol (IP) address differences are not a problem. Once the software is installed, configuration can take place as long as both computers are on the same physical network. This configuration can also be done either locally or remotely. Because a local installation and configuration does not force you to authenticate, you will be doing a remote installation in this chapter as if the server were in a server room or network closet down the hall from you, without a video monitor to rely on. You should already have a Mac OS X computer running Mac OS X v10.6 and have downloaded and installed the latest software updates. You will also want to install the Mac OS X Server Admin Tools. These tools, which can be either downloaded from the Apple Support webpage or obtained from the Mac OS X Server Install Disc, are what make the remote installation, configuration, and administration of Mac OS X Server possible. They require at least 226.1 megabytes (MB) of free disk space to be installed.

NOTE ▶ Mac OS X v10.6 Server Administration software will not run on a computer running Mac OS X v10.5 or earlier.

Also, be sure you install the Server Admin Tools on the computer that you will be using to configure the remote install. Do not merely copy the tools from another computer, because you won't necessarily get all the required files.

To install the Mac OS X Server Admin Tools on Mac OS X:

1 Log in to your Mac OS X v10.6 computer, and insert the Mac OS X Server Install Disc or download the Server Admin Tools from Apple's website.

2 Open the disc and install the package named ServerAdministrationSoftware.mpkg located inside the Other Installs folder, or install the package you downloaded from Apple's website. You do not need to restart.

3 Once the software is installed, you can locate the Server Admin Tools inside the /Applications/Server folder. The following tools are installed:

iCal Server Utility   Podcast Composer   Server Admin

Server Monitor   Server Preferences   System Image Utility

Workgroup Manager   Xgrid Admin

You will be introduced to Server Preferences, but you will use Server Admin and Workgroup Manager in this first chapter to install and perform the initial configuration of Mac OS X Server v10.6.

Configuring Mac OS X

After installing the Mac OS X Server Admin Tools, you'll want to set a network location for the chapters in this book so you can quickly refer back to them from any other network location. You will also be changing your computer name to make it easier to follow the examples in this book. Make sure your Mac OS X computer is up and running and plugged into an Ethernet switch. The computer that will be the Mac OS X Server should also be plugged into this switch.

> **NOTE ▶** In order to use Server Admin with the DNS (Domain Name System) name of your server for these exercises, configure the DNS server as 10.1.17.1.

1   If not already logged in, log in to your Mac OS X computer and open System Preferences.

2   Select the Sharing preferences pane and change the computer name to XSE-CLIENT (we are using *XSE* to stand for *Mac OS X Server Essentials*—the name of this book). You can change it back anytime you want.

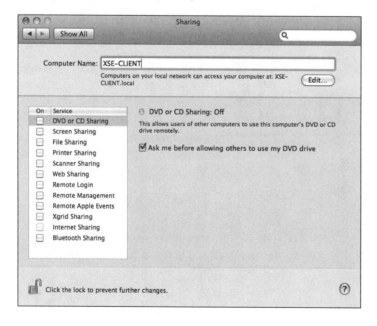

3 Click Show All and select the Network preferences pane.

4 Choose Edit Locations from the Locations pop-up menu, create a new location, and name it XSE Book. Click Done to dismiss the Locations pane.

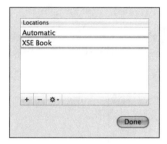

5 Use the Services Action pop-up menu (labeled with a gear and a down arrow) to make all the interfaces except Ethernet inactive.

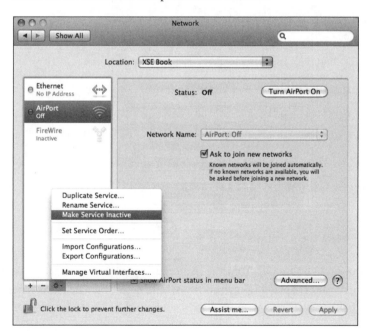

6   Select Ethernet from the list on the left. In the pane to the right, choose Using DHCP from the Configure IPv4 pop-up menu if not already selected.

You should be getting a self-assigned address at this point, but since Mac OS X runs Bonjour, this will not currently be a problem.

7   In the DNS Server field, enter the IP address of your DNS service. This chapter assumes that you have only one client and one server, so enter the IP address that you will assign to your server: 10.1.17.1.

8   Click Show All and select the Accounts preferences pane.

9   Select Login Options and choose Off from the "Automatic login" pop-up menu, select "Name and password" for "Display login window as," and select the checkbox labeled "Show fast user switching menu as: Name."

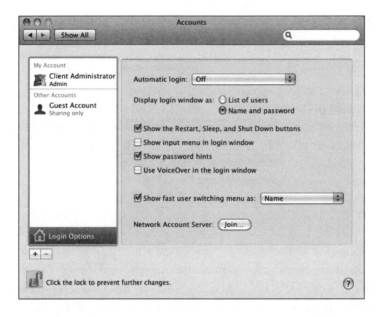

10 For these chapters, you may also want to change your Energy Saver preferences pane settings to have your Mac OS X computer never go to sleep.

11 Close the System Preferences window, which quits System Preferences.

Evaluating Mac OS X Server Requirements

All desktop Mac computers are supported by Mac OS X Server v10.6, provided they meet the following requirements. Although Mac OS X Server can be installed on a portable Mac computer, Apple does not support or recommend this configuration.

Minimum Hardware Requirements

The basic installation requirements are as follows:

▶ An Apple desktop computer with an Intel processor

▶ 2 gigabytes (GB) of RAM

▶ At least 10 GB of available disk space

You do not need a keyboard or display. As you will see later in this chapter, you can install Mac OS X Server using an administrator computer or another server.

Additional Hardware Considerations

Typical considerations when choosing server systems include network and system performance, disk space, and RAM.

Networking

Be sure to consider the speed of the network interface when making a server hardware decision. Many of Apple's products support Gigabit Ethernet. You can also combine two Ethernet interfaces to act as one, to double your aggregate network throughput for services such as Apple file sharing.

Computer Speed

Although Mac OS X Server is supported on a wide variety of Mac computers, not all of them may meet your needs. For a server that will provide services for only a few people, a Mac mini might be suitable. For workgroups, you should use a Mac Pro. For demanding server environments, you might consider using an Xserve. Apple's Xserve is a 1U rackmount server that offers the ability to stack 42 Mac OS X Server systems in a typical server rack with dual Gigabit Ethernet interfaces, Lights Out Management capabilities, and optional redundant power supplies.

> **NOTE** ▶ Intel Xserve and Mac Pro computers have special hardware (a PMU timer) that is used to automatically restart the computer in the event of an operating-system freeze. All Mac computers running Mac OS X v10.5 and later have a setting in the Energy Saver pane of System Preferences to "Start up automatically after a power failure." These two features help ensure that Mac OS X Server on appropriate hardware stays up and running.

Planning Your Mac OS X Server Deployment

A server administrator should follow certain steps when setting up Mac OS X Server. The first step is to review your organization's server needs. Will the server be used mainly for web services; podcasting and QuickTime streaming; iCal, Address Book, and wiki services; file and print services; or something else? Will it be a dedicated server or will it have multiple uses?

When deciding how to use your Mac OS X Server, you might want to study the extensive planning document that is included with the documentation you get when you purchase Mac OS X Server.

NOTE ▶ Mac OS X Server v10.6 can be initially configured in three separate ways to manage users and groups: "Create Users and Groups," "Import Users and Groups," or "Configure Manually." Depending on which you choose, the setup panes vary. Subsequently, not all the fields in Table 1.1 may have entries.

After reviewing the intended uses of the server, and before you install and set up Mac OS X Server, fill out the Mac OS X Server Installation & Setup Worksheet document that comes with your copy of Mac OS X Server and with the Mac OS X Server Admin Tools.

Installing Mac OS X Server

When you boot from the Mac OS X Server Install Disc, an array of utilities is available to you when you click past the initial installation main language pane:

- ▶ Startup Disk
- ▶ Reset Password
- ▶ Firmware Password Utility
- ▶ RAID Utility (if you have a hardware RAID card installed)
- ▶ Disk Utility
- ▶ Terminal
- ▶ System Profiler
- ▶ Network Utility

You can also choose Restore System From Backup to restore from a Time Machine backup.

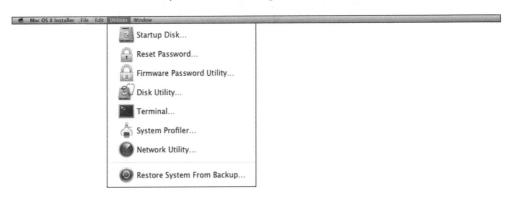

Verifying System Requirements

Before you install Mac OS X Server, you should confirm the hardware requirements listed previously in this chapter. To do so, start up the Mac or Xserve from the Mac OS X Server Install Disc and choose System Profiler from the Utilities menu.

When the System Profiler application opens, you can check the CPU type and speed and the amount of RAM and locate the hardware serial number and Ethernet MAC address in the Hardware Overview window.

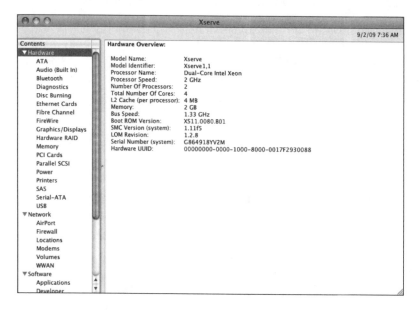

Then check available disk space from the ATA, SAS, or Serial-ATA contents list, depending on the type of hard drive(s) you have installed in your computer.

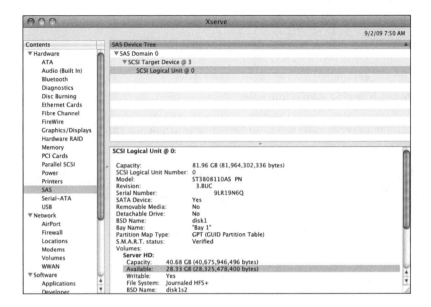

Formatting/Partitioning Drives

After you have confirmed that your computer meets the hardware requirements, you can begin making decisions surrounding the devices and subsequent formatting of those devices prior to actually installing the software.

Like System Profiler, Disk Utility is also located under the Utilities menu when booted from the Mac OS X Server Install Disc. Using this utility, you can divide the hard disk into one or more partitions. Doing so allows you to first choose a partition scheme for your disk. Your choices are as follows:

▶ GUID Partition Table—Used to start up Intel-based Mac computers

▶ Apple Partition Map—Used to start up PowerPC-based Mac computers

▶ Master Boot Record—Used to start up DOS and Windows-based computers

> **NOTE ▶** In order to install Mac OS X Server on a volume, that volume's disk must have the GUID Partition Table.

Once you choose a partition scheme, you can divide your disk into as many as 16 logical drives, each with its own format. Each logical drive is called a partition. Once you format a partition, it becomes a volume. Read *Mac OS X Support Essentials v10.6* for further information about the available volume formats.

In order to install Mac OS X Server v10.6 on a volume, it must have one of the two following journaled formats:

▶   Mac OS X Extended (Journaled)

▶   Mac OS X Extended (Case-Sensitive/Journaled)

Unless you have a compelling reason to use Case-Sensitive/Journaled format, use Mac OS X Extended (Journaled).

You can use the other, nonjournaled formats for data partitions, but journaling eliminates the need for a lengthy disk check on a volume after a power outage or other failure.

> **MORE INFO** ▶ For more information about journaling, see *Mac OS X: About file system journaling* at http://support.apple.com/kb/HT2355.
>
> To read about moving your HFS+ journal to a separate disk in order to increase disk performance, see *Mac OS X Server v10.6: Moving an HFS+ Journal to a different volume* at http://support.apple.com/kb/HT3790.

By using separate partitions, you can segregate your data from the operating system; in order to help you accomplish this, Server Assistant gives you the option of storing service data on a separate volume. Having the operating system on its own volume conserves space by keeping user and service files and data from filling up the boot volume. In case you need to perform a clean install of Mac OS X Server at a later time, you can erase the entire boot volume and install the operating system without touching the data on the other volumes. Having multiple partitions does not increase speed, but installing multiple drives may increase server performance. Simply select your hard disk, choose the number of partitions from the partition scheme menu, and choose the following for each partition:

▶   Name of partition—Using lowercase alphanumeric characters and removing spaces in volume names may help reduce troubleshooting of share points later down the road.

▶   Format of partition—See the previous list for various acceptable Mac OS X Server partition formats.

▶   Size of partition—Again, Mac OS X Server requires at least 10 GB of available disk space for installation.

Before you click the Apply button, remember: *All previous data on the disk may be erased!*

Installing the operating system on one drive and installing additional drives to store user data and system service data can reduce connection times to the operating system and to data. If you add the second drive on a separate bus, the server can read and write to each of those buses independently.

RAID (Redundant Array of Independent Disks)

If you have multiple drives of the same size and bus type, another option is to install Mac OS X Server on a volume on a software or hardware RAID set to potentially speed up throughput on your server and avoid downtime.

If you have an Apple hardware RAID card, you can use RAID Utility to create a RAID set, and then create a volume or volumes on that RAID set. The hardware RAID card supports striping (RAID 0), mirroring (RAID 1), and striping with parity (RAID 5).

If you do not have a hardware RAID card, you can use Disk Utility to create a software mirrored RAID set (RAID 1) and format that mirror with a volume. See *Mac OS X Support Essentials* for more information about software RAID.

Do not install Mac OS X Server on a software or hardware striped RAID set (RAID 0) because if one hard drive fails, the entire RAID set fails also.

> **NOTE** ▶ RAID is not a substitute for backup. It does not protect against your accidentally erasing a file or folder, nor does it protect against file corruption.

You begin the installation of Mac OS X Server v10.6 from a volume containing the Mac OS X Server Install Disc (on DVD or an image on a volume), by starting up directly from the Mac OS X Server Install Disc. If you have purchased a new Xserve, the server software is already installed, so you can proceed directly to the configuration. If you've already started up your server from the internal drive, insert the Mac OS X Server Install DVD and run the Install Mac OS X Server program. After you authenticate, the server reboots from the disc and proceeds with the installation process, starting with the selection of a language, and then prompting you for initial information. It then proceeds uninterrupted until it completes the installation.

Local vs. Remote Installation

You can choose to install Mac OS X Server sitting locally in front of the computer on which you are installing the server software, or you can choose to install the software remotely. If you decide on the latter, you must have network access to the computer.

Installing Locally

Local initial installation information that requires your input or response includes:

▶ Welcome/Read Me information

▶ License agreement

▶ Destination drive for server software

▶ Installation type—default install or customized

A default install installs the following packages:

▶ Essential System Software

▶ Essential Server Software

▶ Server Administration Software

A default install also installs the following packages, but if you choose to customize the local installation, you will be able to disable them:

▶ Language Translations—for French, German, and Japanese

▶ Printer Support—from various printer manufacturers

▶ X11—used to run applications in the X11 windowing system

▶ Rosetta—for running PowerPC-based applications with your Intel-based Mac

Installing Remotely

When you install Mac OS X Server v10.6 on Apple's Xserve systems, there are additional items to consider. For example, Xserve is designed to be run "headless" (with no monitor) and with multiple Xserve systems installed on a server rack. Performing a local installation in this situation would require attaching a monitor and keyboard to each Xserve, so a more convenient method may be remote installation using Server Admin.

In order to perform a remote install, you need to gather information from your target server. You will use this information to:

▶   Identify and locate the target server—with the MAC address

▶   Authenticate to the server—normally with the hardware serial number

You can find this information on the label attached to the box of every Mac and Xserve sold. Also, every Mac has a label with this information attached to the computer itself. Finally, every Intel Xserve has an information system information tab at the rear of the computer that you can pull out and view.

At your computer that is booted from the Mac OS X Server Install Disc, repeat the method of opening System Profiler—similar to when you confirmed your hardware requirements—and click Network in the sidebar to obtain the Ethernet (MAC) address(es).

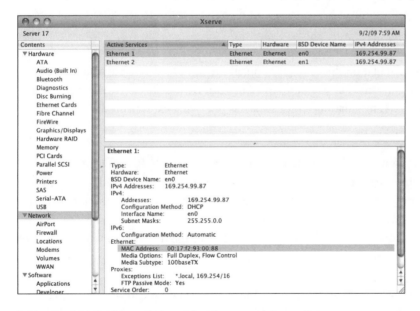

Write the MAC address(es) and hardware serial number on your server worksheet if you have not already done so. You may also want to record your server's current IP address, whether it was self-assigned or provided by a DHCP service.

In normal situations, to authenticate to your server, you will use the first eight characters of your target server's hardware serial number. However, if the remote server is an Intel Xserve that has no serial number after its main logic board was replaced, the password is System S. Other computers with no serial number after a main logic board was replaced will have the password 12345678. The password is case sensitive. Finally, if you are configuring an upgraded server, the password will be the password of the root user account from the previous version of Mac OS X Server.

From any Mac OS X v10.6 computer with Server Admin Tools installed, you can use Server Admin and Server Assistant to install Mac OS X Server v10.6 on a remote computer that is started up from the Mac OS X Server Install Disc.

> **NOTE** ▶ In order to access Server Assistant, first open Server Admin (located in /Applications/Server), and then choose Server Assistant from the Server menu. Alternatively, you can open Server Assistant directly; it is located in /System/Library/CoreServices.

Running a remote installation does not give you all the options that are available locally without additional software. For example, you can't run Disk Utility or RAID Admin, and you can't customize the installation options such as removing extra print drivers and language translations.

> **NOTE** ▶ You can use Apple Remote Desktop or third-party VNC software to connect to the computer started up from the Mac OS X Server Install DVD and take control of the keyboard and mouse, just as if you were sitting in front of the computer. This enables you to use the applications and tools under the Utilities menu. *Leave the user name blank* for connecting to the computer, and enter the first eight characters of the hardware serial number for the password.

Server Assistant will search for and display all the computers on the local subnet that are started up from a Mac OS X Server Install DVD. You will now need to know the MAC address of your target computer to be able to choose it from the list of network computers if more than one computer is started up from a Mac OS X Server Install Disc. When Server Assistant contacts the target computer, you are asked for a password.

You need the following pieces of information in order to remotely install Mac OS X Server on a Mac:

▶   IP address, Bonjour name, or DNS name of the Mac

▶   Password for remote install, usually from the serial number of the Mac

There are a few ways to obtain the IP address acquired by a computer booted from the Mac OS X Server Install Disc. One method is to use the Bonjour discovery features of Server Admin and Server Assistant. Another method is to open System Profiler from the Utilities menu on the target computer, and then click Network in the System Profiler sidebar, as described earlier. As stated previously, the password is usually the first eight characters of the hardware serial number.

What if your Mac does not have the ability to use an installation DVD? You can use other methods for remote installation. These include the following:

▶   Connect an external optical drive to the Xserve system via a FireWire or USB cable.

▶   Use an optical drive on a computer in target disk mode connected to the Xserve system via a FireWire cable.

▶   Start the Xserve in target disk mode and use another computer to install the server software on the Xserve system's mounted volume.

▶   Use another server with NetBoot services enabled to perform a network installation with a NetInstall image. As you will learn later, a server can be set up to install software onto other computers. This is extremely useful when you are setting up several servers—you can create one installation image and have it quickly replicated onto multiple computers.

Installer Issues

You can view the Installer log file during the installation process by choosing Installer Log from the Window menu. When you do so, a separate window appears at the bottom of the screen, allowing you to view three types of events within the log file:

▶   Show Errors Only

▶   Show Errors and Progress

▶   Show All Logs

You also have the option of saving the log file to a separate volume, such as an attached USB or FireWire device, and the option of sending the log to Apple with your email address and comments.

You should keep the installer log open on the computer on which Mac OS X Server is being installed to verify a successful install. Should the install fail for some reason, either select Show Errors Only from the menu on the left or select Show All Logs and use the Filter field to search for keywords such as *fail*, *error*, *unable*, and *warning* that may indicate why the installation was not successful.

Installing Mac OS X Server Remotely

Remote installation and management is often a headache for system administrators. Mac OS X Server is designed to be easy to install and configure in remote installations or headless environments. You will use your computer running Mac OS X v10.6 to install Mac OS X Server on your server computer. You need to have Mac OS X Server connected via Ethernet to a network switch; your computer with Mac OS X should be on the same subnet.

> **NOTE** ▶ As of the current writing, you need to have DHCP service available on the subnet; otherwise, you will not be able to perform a remote installation. In this case, perform a local installation by skipping steps 3–9 below.

1   Write down the MAC address(es) and hardware serial number (both can be found using System Profiler) of the computer on which Mac OS X Server is to be installed, or use the method discussed previously to obtain this information using the Mac OS X Server Install Disc.

2   Start up the target computer from the Mac OS X Server Install Disc by holding down the C key, just as you would to do a local install; afterward do not touch the keyboard or mouse of the computer on which Mac OS X Server is to be installed. Everything else will be done remotely.

As discussed at the end of the "Installing Remotely" section, you can use other methods, such as booting from a NetInstall image or using an image of the Install Disc on a FireWire or USB drive, to boot from the Mac OS X Server Install Disc.

3 On your computer running Mac OS X v10.6 with the Server Admin Tools for v10.6 installed, open Server Admin (found in /Applications/Server).

4 Click Cancel if you are prompted to provide a server address and authentication information.

5 In Server Admin's left SERVERS column, click Ready for Install.

6 In Server Admin's right column, select the computer on which you will install Mac OS X Server.

If several computers are displayed, note that the MAC address of each computer is shown; you can use this to find your target server.

If your target server is not on the list, click Refresh in the lower-left corner of Server Admin. If it is still not listed, from the Server menu, choose Install Remote Server.

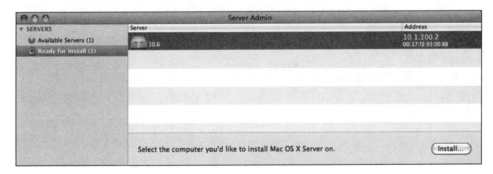

7 Click Install in the lower-right corner, near the text "Select the computer you'd like to install Mac OS X Server on." This opens Server Assistant.

8 Confirm that your target computer is displayed in the Address field of Server Assistant's Destination pane. If it isn't, enter the DNS name or IP address in the Address field.

9 In the Serial Number field of Server Assistant's Destination pane, enter the password for your computer. It is usually the first eight characters (case sensitive) of the hardware serial number, or in the case of a replaced main logic board, it may be "System S" for an Xserve or "12345678" for other Mac computers. Click Continue.

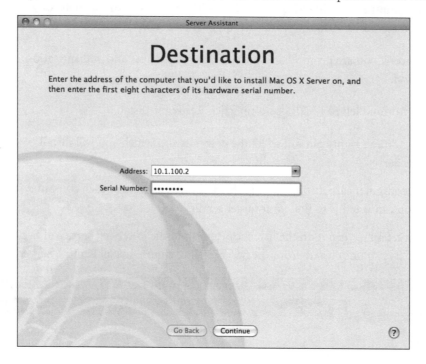

10 Choose the appropriate language for you, and click Continue.

11 Read the Important Information pane, and click Continue.

12 Agree to the license agreement.

13 Select the disk or volume onto which Mac OS X Server will be installed.

If the target disk or volume will not support Mac OS X Server, you may see a notice that you must use Disk Utility to prepare the volume before you can install Mac OS X Server on that volume. The target disk must have the GUID Partition Table instead of the Apple Partition Map.

If an earlier version of Mac OS X Server is installed on the volume you choose, you will be notified that you can either erase the volume or upgrade, which preserves files, user accounts, and other server information.

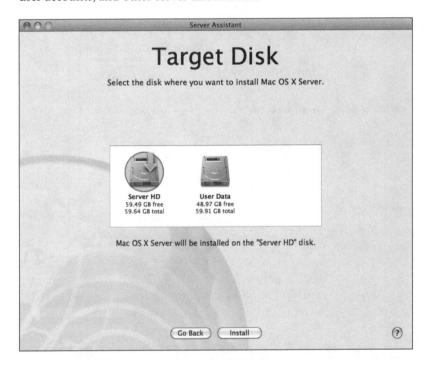

14 With the appropriate target volume selected, click Install. Your Mac OS X Server computer will now install the necessary software and automatically restart your server.

NOTE ▶ Once you click Install to start the remote install, do not allow anyone to touch the mouse or keyboard of your target server; it is possible to start the installation process directly at the server even after you start a remote install. The end result would be a failed install.

15 After the installation completes, the target computer restarts with Mac OS X Server ready to be configured. If you click More Options, this brings you to a Server Assistant Welcome pane, where you have three choices: "Install Mac OS X Server remotely," "Set up Mac OS X Server remotely," and "Prepare and save information for automatic setup."

Instead, click Quit, which quits Server Assistant and returns you to Server Admin.

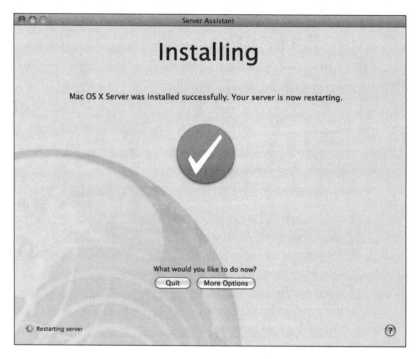

Initial Mac OS X Server Configuration

If you did a local installation, upon completion of the installation a Welcome pane appears, prompting you to create a valid server configuration. In Mac OS X Server v10.6, initial configuration is completed using Server Assistant, which runs both as an installation assistant and, following a successful installation of Mac OS X Server, as a separate application used to install and configure remote computers. In each case, Server Assistant uses slightly different steps. It is Server Assistant that is used to configure the administrator account, computer names, network interfaces, and server configuration type. This makes the setup and configuration processes go quickly, provided you have already planned the configuration of your server.

Mac OS X Server v10.6 can be configured automatically using a configuration file generated by Server Assistant (which you can open from the Server Admin application). The generated configuration file can be stored on another mounted volume, such as an iPod, USB or FireWire storage device, or CD/DVD.

In order to make your configuration file available to a Mac OS X Server that is waiting at the Welcome pane to be configured, you must place it in a folder named Auto Server Setup at the root of any volume accessible to the server. The configuration file is generally named AutoServerSetup.plist, but you can name it whatever you like, as long as the filename ends in .plist.

When you save the configuration file, you have two choices:

▶   "Apply this profile to any server"

▶   "Apply this profile only if any of the following conditions are true"

You can set conditions based on the following elements:

▶   Serial number

▶   MAC address

▶   IP address

▶   DNS name

For example, you can set the condition that the serial number starts with G86 and the MAC address ends in 88.

Additionally, you can encrypt the configuration file with a passphrase. In order to use the file, you would do either of the following:

▶   Provide the passphrase interactively at the server.

▶   Place the passphrase in a clear text file with a filename suffix of .pass; this file should be in the same folder as the configuration file.

If a configuration file is in a folder named Auto Server Setup at the root of any accessible volume, and the server matches the conditions specified in the configuration file, Mac OS X Server will locate the file and automatically configure itself based on the settings in the configuration file. Later in this chapter you will save just such a server configuration file.

Choosing Setup Options

When using Server Assistant to set up a remote server, you are asked to select the destination computer and to authenticate again using the first eight characters of the hardware serial number (see the section "Installing Remotely" for special cases involving the password).

Local setup does not require these authentication steps. At this point, both local and remote installations are similar, in that you now decide on how you want your server to be configured initially. You have three options to configure users and groups:

▶   Create Users and Groups

▶   Import Users and Groups

▶   Configure Manually

Choosing one of these options will affect which panes appear later in the setup process. The Create Users and Groups option is useful for a novice Mac OS X Server administrator and requires little background on how Mac OS X Server functions. In this configuration, the server is configured as an Open Directory master where user and group information will be stored and shared with client computers. This configuration is useful when you want to manage users and groups independently for a small organization.

The Import Users and Groups option is useful when you already have users and groups defined on another server, but you want to use the various services offered by Mac OS X Server. In this configuration, Open Directory on the server is configured to connect to an Open Directory or Active Directory server where user and group records are stored. This configuration is intended for environments where the server supports a group or department that is part of a larger organization.

The Configure Manually option may be appropriate if you want more control over how services are set up. This option does automatically configure your server to run a DNS service for itself (if you do not specify another DNS service and assign your Mac OS X Server an IP address), and you will have the ability to bind your server to another directory server or make your server a directory server during initial setup.

Because the "Create Users and Groups" and "Import Users and Groups" options do not set up user accounts for a scenario with network home folders, you will choose Configure Manually for the exercises in this book.

MORE INFO ▶ The "Create Users and Groups" and "Import Users and Groups" options configure Mac OS X Server to advertise its services to Mac OS X v10.6 computers. This allows users to quickly set up their Macs to use services offered by your server. See Chapter 7, "Managing Users' Computers," in the Getting Started document for more information.

Table 1.1 shows which panes are available during each configuration.

Table 1.1   Mac OS X Setup Panes per Configuration

	Create Users and Groups	Import Users and Groups	Configure Manually
Auto Server Setup Configuration File Found	✔	✔	✔
Welcome	✔	✔	✔
Destination (remote install only)	✔	✔	✔
Language (remote install only)	✔	✔	✔
Keyboard	✔	✔	✔
Serial Number	✔	✔	✔
Transfer an Existing Server	✔	✔	✔
Registration Information	✔	✔	✔
Additional Requested Information	✔	✔	✔
Time Zone and Network Time Server	✔	✔	✔
Date & Time (if not using Network Time Server)	✔	✔	✔
Administrator Account, SSH, and Remote Management	✔	✔	✔
Internet Gateway (depending on active network ports)	✔	✔	✔

Table 1.1   Mac OS X Setup Panes per Configuration (continued)

	Create Users and Groups	Import Users and Groups	Configure Manually
Network Address Information	✔	✔	✔
TCP/IP Information per MAC Address	✔	✔	✔
Network Names	✔	✔	✔
How to Manage Users and Groups	✔	✔	✔
Connect to a Directory Server		✔	✔
Set Up an Open Directory Master			✔
Select Services to Enable and set Service Data Location	✔	✔	✱
Client Time Machine Backup	✔	┼	┼
Mail Options	✦	✦	✦
Review and Save Settings	✔	✔	✔

✱   Displayed only if you select the "Connect to a directory server" or "Set up an Open Directory master" checkboxes.

┼   Displayed only if you select the File Sharing checkbox in the Services pane.

✦   Displayed only if you select the Mail checkbox in the Services pane.

Services Questionnaire

After the Serial Number pane and a registration pane appear, you are presented with a pane titled "A Few More Questions," which asks how the server will be used, what type of clients the server will support, and what services the server will host.

Mac OS X Server provides a wide range of services. These services can be started at startup time to make sure they are available without administrator intervention. However, if you do not need a service, leave it off to reduce overhead and increase security.

With an initial installation, it is best not to enable any services during the installation process. Some services require proper supporting services, such as DNS or DHCP, to be running and configured correctly. It is likely that none of the services will be configured exactly to your liking just by turning them on. It is best practice to always configure and thoroughly test your services before enabling them to start automatically.

When you select a checkbox in this pane, it does not actually enable the service, it only indicates your interest in the service.

Table 1.2 shows what services are automatically enabled based on the type of server configuration you chose earlier.

Table 1.2   Default Enabled Services per Configuration

	Create Users and Groups	Import Users and Groups	Configure Manually
File and printer sharing	✔	✔	
Web and application hosting	✔	✔	
Mail services	✔	✔	
Directory services and authentication	✔	✔	
Calendaring and collaboration	✔		
Instant messaging	✔		
Podcast and media streaming			
Network services			
Client management			
Computational clustering			
Digital asset management			
Rendering and media encoding			
Database hosting			
Other			

Time and Time Zone Information

You are asked to specify the time zone where the server will be located and to choose whether or not this server will use another server running the Network Time Protocol (NTP). It is important to note that if you are planning to handle authentication through Kerberos or are connecting this server to another server running Kerberos, synchronizing time to avoid time drift is paramount. This is because by default, a Kerberos authentication scheme does not permit time skew greater than five minutes between itself and computers requesting authentication.

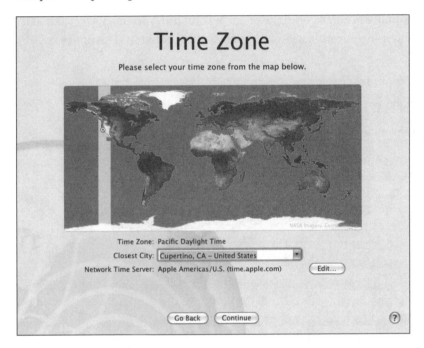

Administrator Account

After the registration information and questionnaire panes, you are asked to enter initial account information. The first account that is created on Mac OS X Server v10.6 is a local administrator account. However, the System Administrator account (root) is activated as well.

The password for System Administrator (root) is the same as the password for this initial local administrator account, but they are not synchronized. If either the administrator's or the System Administrator's (root's) password is changed, the change does not affect the other account's password.

Having the System Administrator (root) account active when Mac OS X Server is set up allows a system administrator to log in as root and gain unrestricted access to all contents of all mounted volumes via either the command line or the Finder. However, it has security implications, as anyone who knows the initial local administrator password can potentially gain the same unrestricted access. Therefore, you should change the root user's password after you have completed your initial configuration of Mac OS X Server with the steps under "Accounts Preferences" in the section "Using Tools" later in this chapter.

You have the opportunity to enable or disable remote login using Secure Shell (SSH) and remote management using screen sharing and Apple Remote Desktop. This applies only for administrators.

TIP Password Assistant is available in this pane to help you select a more secure password; just click the key button.

Configure Xsan

If Server Assistant detects an Apple Fibre Channel card, you have the opportunity to configure your server as an Xsan metadata controller as part of your initial server setup.

NOTE ▶ Xsan is not covered in this reference guide. Unless you have a copy of your Xsan installation media and understand the ramifications of choosing "Configure as Xsan Metadata Controller," choose "Don't configure Xsan now."

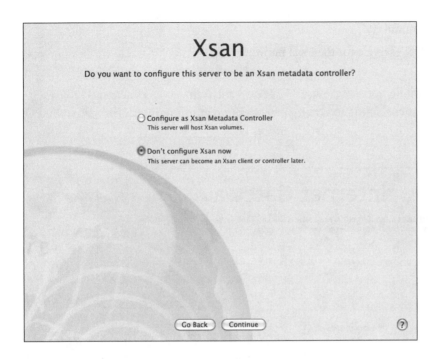

Internet Gateway

If you have at least two active Ethernet ports, you will have the opportunity to select the "Configure this server as an Internet gateway" checkbox. If you enable this option, Server Assistant configures the Firewall and NAT services. In order for Server Assistant to successfully configure your server as a gateway, the following conditions must be met:

▶ One Ethernet port must have a public IP address (as opposed to a private IP address in the 10.0.0.0/8, 172.16.0.0/12, or 192.168.0.0/16 range).

▶ Another Ethernet port must be connected to a private network switch or hub.

If you enable the Internet gateway, Server Assistant automatically:

▶ Assigns the internal Ethernet port the IP address 192.168.1.1

▶ Enables the DHCP service with a scope of 192.168.1.100 through 192.168.1.199

▶ Enables the NAT service to share your server's Internet connection with computers on the local network

▶   Enables the firewall

▶   Enables the DNS service for the local network

> **NOTE** ▶ If you do not want to use 192.168.1.1 for your server's internal IP address, you should not enable the Internet-gateway option at this point; rather, you should configure and enable the associated services later.

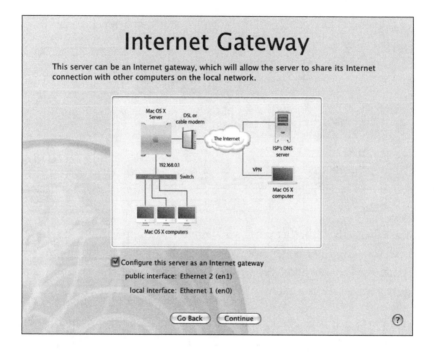

Network Addressing

After setting the initial administrator account, you are prompted to choose whether your server will keep its current network configuration (set to DHCP by default) or whether you will manually set up each interface. If a DHCP server is not present on your network, a self-allocated Bonjour address starting with 169.254 will appear.

It is highly recommended that you choose a manual address for your servers, because dynamic addressing will reduce the number of services you can offer, and most services require a statically assigned address.

Apple servers can use multiple interfaces for network access. Examples include computers with AirPort cards installed, Xserve systems with dual Gigabit Ethernet, and Mac OS X Server computers with four-interface Ethernet cards.

Server Assistant displays any interfaces it finds, so the administrator can select whether TCP/IP should be enabled for each interface. You are prompted for detailed configuration information for each selected interface on subsequent panes.

The figure below shows how each Ethernet interface is displayed for configuration in Server Assistant. Each interface has its own IP settings—for hosting different server services or dividing the amount of traffic supported over any one interface, including the ability to disable IPv6 and set your Ethernet interface to match the speed of your switch, should the need arise. You can also manually configure multiple interfaces or reconfigure network information later using the Network pane of System Preferences.

NOTE ▶ If no existing DNS service can be found for your server, DNS services will be configured automatically, only for your server's host name and IP address.

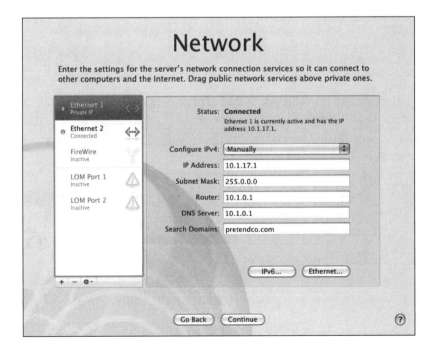

NOTE ▶ In the Network pane of System Preferences, you can also create multiple settings for a single interface. (To do so, you select the interface, and then click the Duplicate button.) This option is useful for assigning multiple IP addresses to the same Ethernet interface. One use of this is to host multiple websites, with unique IP addresses and unique webpages, from a single server with only one Ethernet interface. This configuration may require modifying DNS entries.

Lights Out Management

On Intel Xserves, you also have the ability to connect to your server and manage rudimentary tasks via the Ethernet interfaces. In order to use Lights Out Management (LOM) to remotely start up, reboot, and shut down your Intel Xserve, you are required to give this configuration a separate IP address per interface (interfaces are called *channels*) and a different user name and password (the password must be between 8 and 20 characters).

Note that the user name and password for LOM are in no way related to any system users you have. Be careful that the IP address you configure for LOM is not the same as the IP address you have previously given any of the interfaces. Refer to the Xserve documentation for more information on Lights Out Management.

NOTE ▶ On the Xserve (Early 2009), LOM can be configured only on a single port. Server Assistant will set up LOM on the Built-in Ethernet 1 port; the port can be changed later in Server Monitor.

Network Names

After setting the initial administrator account and network settings, you are prompted to provide unique names for your computer:

▶ The Primary DNS Name is a unique name for a server, historically referred to as the fully qualified domain name, or FQDN. Some services on Mac OS X Server either require a working FQDN or will work better if one is available. If Server Assistant does not detect the DNS name you specify here from a DNS service, Server Assistant automatically configures DNS service on your Mac OS X Server to provide a forward DNS record for your primary DNS name and a reverse DNS record for your IP address. This ensures that your directory service is set up correctly, if applicable. Be sure to have an active network connection, even if it is only to a network switch that doesn't have anything else connected to it.

▶ The Computer Name is used by clients who use the Apple Filing Protocol (AFP) to access AFP share points and print services on the server. The Computer Name can contain spaces, but the Primary DNS Name cannot. Mac OS X users will see this name in the Shared section of the Finder sidebar if your Mac OS X Server offers file- or screen-sharing services.

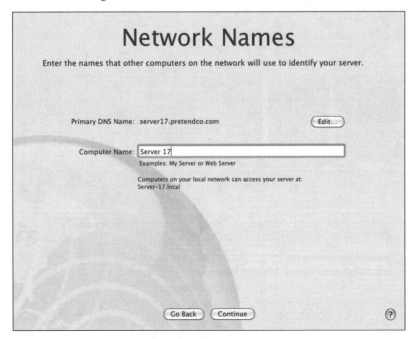

Managing Users and Groups

In the Users and Groups pane, you specify how you will manage users and groups on this Mac OS X Server. The choice you make here will determine which additional panes you will see throughout the rest of the initial server configuration process.

If you select "Create Users and Groups" or "Import Users and Groups," Server Assistant will automatically create an Open Directory master for you. The directory administrator name will be Directory Administrator, the short name diradmin, the UID 1000, and the password the same password that you set for your local administrator account.

If you select Configure Manually you will later have the option to create an Open Directory master, with the ability to modify some attributes of the Directory Administrator account. See the upcoming section, "Directory Services."

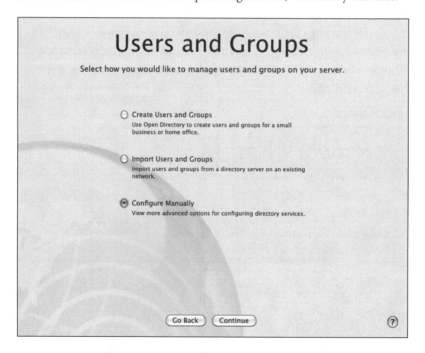

Import from a Directory Service (Only If You Select "Import Users and Groups")

If you already have an Open Directory or Active Directory server configured to permit user, group, and computer information to be used for authentication purposes on your network, select "Connect to a directory server." This option "binds" your server to some other authentication server.

If you selected "Import Users and Groups," you *must* connect to a directory server at this point. If you specify an Active Directory server, you must provide credentials for a user authorized to bind to Active Directory. If you specify an Open Directory server, you can either bind anonymously or provide credentials for any user in that directory. The name and password in the figure below are the credentials for a directory administrator for another server's directory service.

> **NOTE ►** If you set up a server with the choice "Import Users and Groups" on an isolated network that does not have access to the target directory server, Server Assistant will not allow you to continue with the setup until you successfully connect to a directory server or you click Go Back.

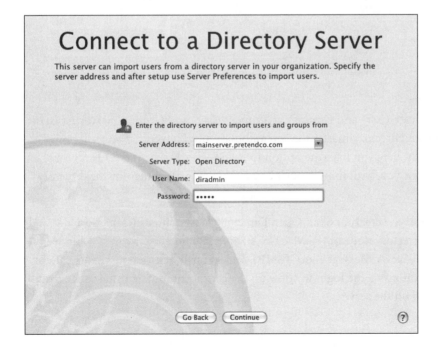

If you select Configure Manually, you can specify a server in the same way, as shown in the preceding figure, or click Continue to skip this pane. You will always have the option of configuring directory usage after you complete the initial server configuration.

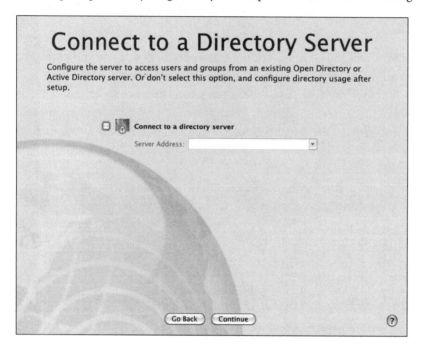

Directory Services

If you selected "Create Users and Groups" or "Import Users and Groups," Server Assistant configures an Open Directory master for you automatically. However, if you selected Configure Manually, here you have the option to have Server Assistant create an Open Directory master for you, with limited flexibility in changing attributes for the directory administrator.

If you do not enable the creation of an Open Directory master, user information is stored only in the local directory node of the Mac OS X Server. Remote users can still connect to services via AFP, Server Message Block (SMB), and so forth, but remote clients cannot sign in to user accounts via the login window on their local computers using user account information stored on the server.

You also have the ability to set automatic restrictions to services by users and groups. See "Controlling Access to Your Server" in the next chapter for more information about service access control lists (SACLs). If you select the "Restrict individual and group access to services" checkbox, any users and groups that you create with Workgroup Manager will automatically have no access to certain services offered by your Mac OS X Server. However, as the figure below states, users that you add with Server Preferences will initially be granted access to services.

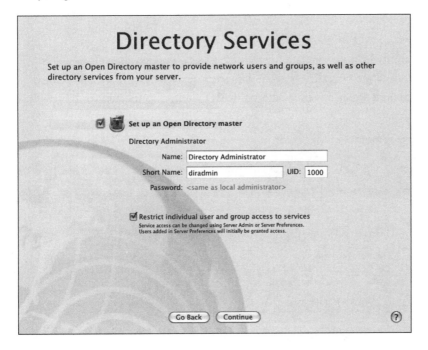

Select Services

You have the opportunity to select which basic services to enable if you:

▶ Choose to create users and groups

▶ Choose to import users and groups

▶ Choose to configure manually *and* create an Open Directory master

In the Services pane, you can enable or disable each of the following basic services:

- ▶ File Sharing
- ▶ Address Book
- ▶ Calendar
- ▶ Instant Messaging
- ▶ Mail
- ▶ Web

You also have the ability to store the data for these services on a separate volume. This allows you to easily separate operating-system data from service data; you may decide to store service data on a direct-attached external RAID volume connected via Fibre Channel, for example.

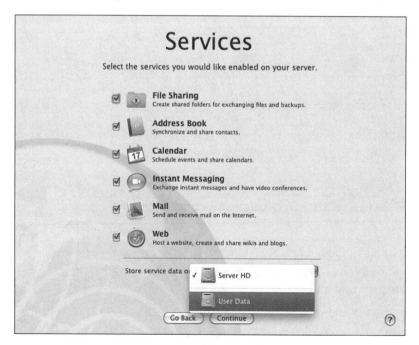

Client Time Machine Backup

You can provide a network repository for Mac OS X Time Machine backups. In the Client Backup pane, select the option and select a volume on which Mac OS X Server will store these Time Machine backups.

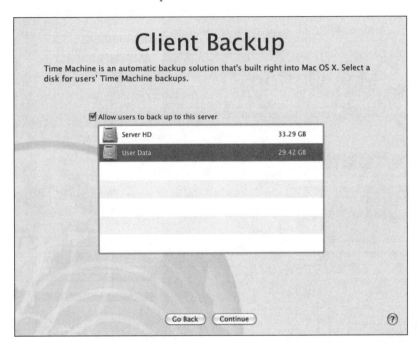

Mail Options

If you chose to enable the Mail service, you can send all outgoing mail through another mail service. When you use Server Preferences to create a new user, the server automatically sends an email message to this new user with information about the server's DNS name and an explanation of the services that the server provides. You can customize the text that is sent to users along with the standard information.

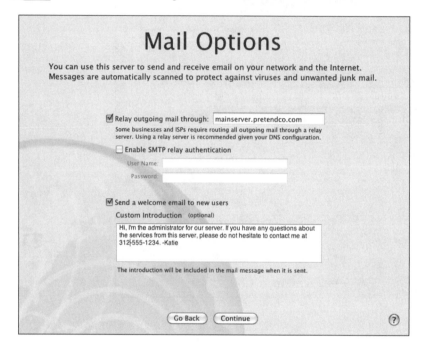

Review Settings

Finally, setup concludes with the Review pane. Review your information by scrolling through the pane. You *can* apply the settings you have just configured; however, for this book you will be saving your configuration first, so do *not* click the Set Up button immediately when finished with the following exercise.

After you click Set Up, your server begins to configure itself based on your previous choices throughout the setup process and subsequently restarts.

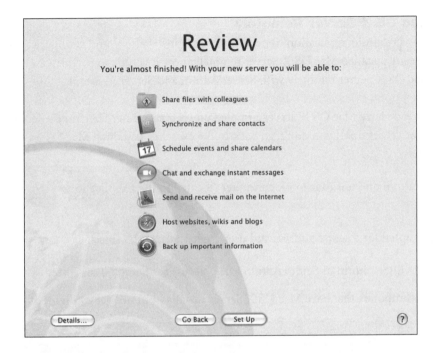

Upgrading Mac OS X Server

Upgrading from an earlier version of Mac OS X Server to Mac OS X Server v10.6 involves careful planning and testing, and it should not be undertaken lightly.

If you install Mac OS X Server on a volume that contains an earlier version of Mac OS X Server (v10.4.11 or any version of v10.5), Server Assistant will prompt you for the language and serial number, and then it will upgrade your server and prompt you to reboot. Server Admin will not allow you to do any other server configuration during this phase.

Setting Up Mac OS X Server Remotely

You can use the Server Admin application to perform remote installations and configurations. You have already installed Mac OS X Server remotely; now it is time to perform an initial setup of Mac OS X Server remotely with Server Admin and Server Assistant.

1 You should already have Mac OS X Server installed on your computer from an earlier exercise but not yet set up. If you don't, go back to the exercise "Installing Mac OS X Server Remotely."

2 Open Server Admin on your Mac OS X computer (located in the /Applications/ Server folder).

3 If you are prompted for a server address and user credentials, click Cancel.

4 In the left SERVERS column of Server Admin, click "Ready for Setup," if it is listed.

This contains computers that have Mac OS X Server installed but not yet configured.

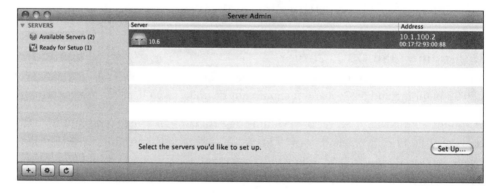

NOTE ► As of the current writing, if you do not have DHCP available on your subnet, "Ready for Setup" will not appear. However, your server will appear in the list of Available Servers with a Bonjour host name based on its model and MAC address, along with its IP address. Make a note of the current IP address and use that in step 7.

5 Locate your server in the right pane of Server Admin; each available server is listed with its current IP address and MAC address. If you have more than one server ready for setup on your network, use the MAC address to differentiate between available servers.

If your target server does not show up in the list of servers ready for setup, choose Set Up Remote Server from the Server menu and click Add. This opens Server Assistant.

Otherwise, select your server in the right pane, and then click Set Up. This opens Server Assistant.

6   If your target server appeared in the list of servers ready to be set up, select your server and click Authenticate.

If your target server did not appear in the list of servers ready to be set up, click Add.

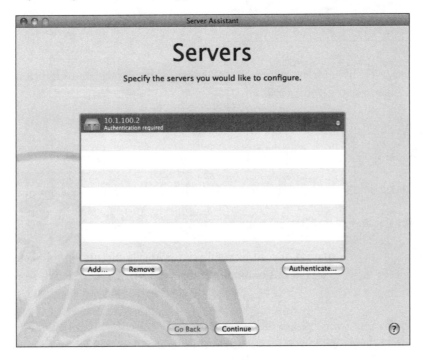

7   Confirm or enter your target server's IP address or Bonjour address, which is usually based on the type of computer, a dash, and the MAC address of the computer (followed by .local).

In either case, enter the password for your server. It is usually the first eight characters (case sensitive) of the hardware serial number, or in the case of a replaced main logic board, it may be "System S" for an Xserve or "12345678" for other computers. If you installed Mac OS X Server on a volume with an earlier version of Mac OS X Server, the password is the previous root password.

Click OK to attempt to authenticate.

8   Your target server should now be listed as authenticated by a green status indicator. Click Continue to set up your server.

9   Select your region and click Continue.

10   Select an appropriate keyboard layout and click Continue.

11   Enter a valid serial number and registration information, and then click Continue.

12   In the "Transfer an Existing Server" pane, select "Set up a new server."

13   Enter registration information to your liking. Because you should not be connected to the Internet for the exercises in this book, this information will not be sent to Apple. Click Continue.

14   Because you are not connected to the Internet for these exercises, do not enter any information in the A Few More Questions pane; otherwise, you will get an error when Mac OS X Server attempts to send this information to Apple. Click Continue.

15   Set the appropriate time zone.

16   Because you are not connected to the Internet for these exercises, disable the Network Time Server. Click the Edit button, deselect "Use network time server," and then click OK to dismiss the Network Time Server pane.

17 Confirm that Network Time Server is set to None, and then click Continue.

18 Set the date and time, and then click Continue.

19 Set your local administrator long name, short name, and password. Reenter your password.

Enter Local Administrator as the long name, ladmin as the short name, and ladmin as the password. It is good practice to choose a strong password for your local administrator account.

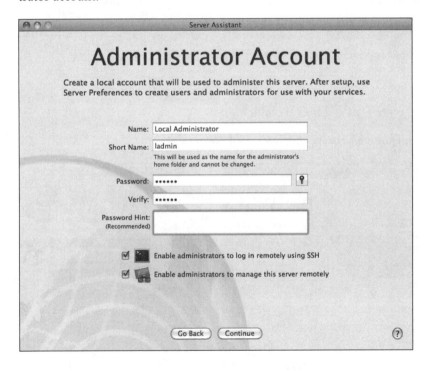

20 Leave the two remote-administration options selected and click Continue.

21 If you have an Apple Fibre Channel host bus adapter installed, select "Don't configure Xsan now" and click Continue.

22 If you are prompted, leave the Internet gateway disabled and click Continue.

23 In the Network pane, if you have more than one Ethernet interface, leave only the first Ethernet interface enabled. To disable any additional interfaces, select that interface, and from the Action menu, choose Make Service Inactive.

24 Because you do not have another computer to act as a router or gateway in these exercises, you will specify your server's IP address as the router address, which will cause a warning message to appear.

Choose Manually from the Configure IPv4 pop-up menu, enter the following information for the first built-in Ethernet port, and then click Continue:

▶   IP Address: 10.1.17.1

▶   Subnet Mask: 255.255.0.0

▶   Router: 10.1.17.1

▶   DNS Server: [Leave this field blank for now]

▶   Search Domains: [Leave this field blank for now]

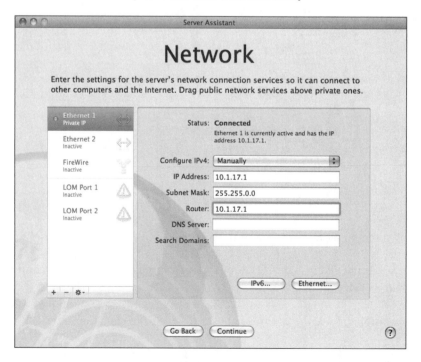

25 Click Ignore at the warning "The IP address and router are the same. The IP address for 'Ethernet 1' is not reachable because it is the same as the router address."

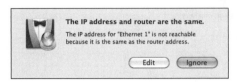

26 Enter server17.pretendco.com for the Primary DNS Name and Server 17 for the Computer Name. Server 17 is the name that Mac OS X computers will see in the Shared section of the Finder's sidebar if your server offers file- or screen-sharing services.

If your server received information about DNS service from a DHCP service, and that DNS service has a DNS record for the IP address you assigned, the Primary DNS Name field will be automatically entered.

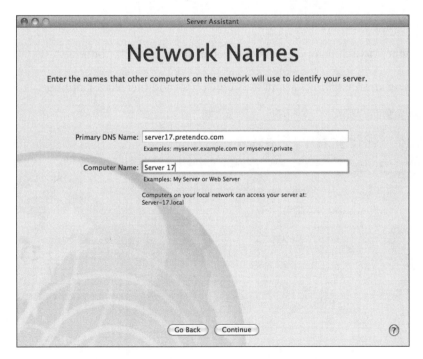

27 In the Users and Groups pane, select Configure Manually, and then click Continue.

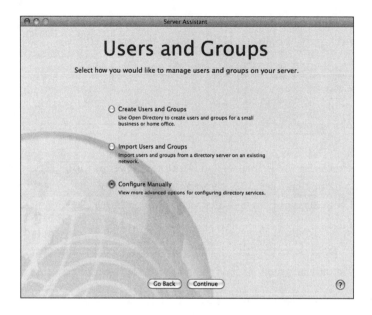

28 Leave "Connect to a directory server" deselected, and then click Continue.

29 Leave "Set up an Open Directory master" deselected, and then click Continue.

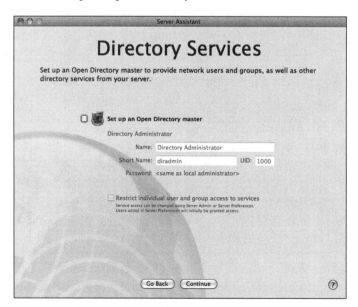

30 You are now at the Review pane. Do *not* click the Set Up button. Instead, leave your Mac OS X Server at this Review pane.

You will save an Auto Server Setup file and use it in the next exercise.

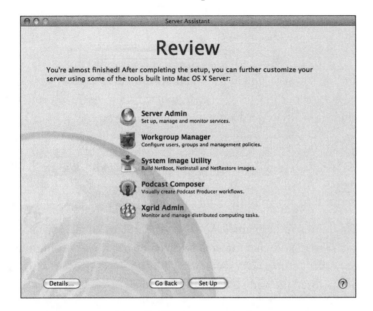

Generating Auto Server Setup Configuration Data

Rather than immediately setting up your server with the information you entered with Server Assistant, you can also generate and save the configuration data in an Auto Server Setup profile for later use.

There are three ways to create an Auto Server Setup profile that you can use later to automatically configure your Mac OS X Server:

▶ When running Server Assistant at the server itself or remotely, in the Review pane, click Details.

▶ Open Server Admin, and from the Server menu, choose Create Auto Server Setup Profile.

▶ Open Server Assistant from /System/Library/CoreServices, and then choose Create Auto Server.

Then proceed to choose the configuration options for the target server in the subsequent panes.

From Server Assistant, you have two choices:

▶ Save Setup Profile

▶ Save Summary

If you click Save Summary, you can save a plain text file that summarizes the various settings you specified. It does not include any passwords. You may find it useful to copy this information later and include it in whatever documentation system you use.

In order to create a file that Server Assistant uses to automatically configure a server, click Save Setup Profile. This creates an XML formatted file with the suffix .plist that contains all the settings you specified in Server Assistant. AutoServerSetup.plist is the default name of the file, but you can change it to any valid filename, as long as .plist is the file extension.

The XML file should be placed in a folder named Auto Server Setup on any available volume mounted on the target server. Note that the default filename has no spaces but that this folder must have Auto Server Setup as its exact name. When Server Assistant starts, it looks for such a folder and enclosed file and automatically configures the server.

When saving the Auto Server Setup profile, you have the option of encrypting the file with a passphrase. This is important if you cannot ensure the security of this file, because without a passphrase, the XML file is stored as clear text, permitting any user to view its contents—the exact configuration of your server, including the administrator password. You can supply the passphrase to Server Assistant by typing it in locally at the server itself, or by placing the passphrase in clear text in a .pass file with the same name as the Auto Server Setup profile in the Auto Server Setup folder (which needs to be at the root of any available volume in order to be seen by Server Assistant).

Because you have not configured your server yet, you will save this file for later use in case you want to try this chapter again. Saving the file enables you to manually install a fresh copy of Mac OS X Server, and then have it automatically configured based on the settings you have configured here.

Save Your Settings and Automatically Configure Your Server

You will now save all the settings from all the steps you just completed as a single file, enabling you to configure this server identically should you want to reformat or reinstall the server software.

1 You should still have Server Assistant open at the Review pane from the last exercise. If you don't, go back to the exercise "Setting Up Mac OS X Server Remotely," which ends at the Review pane.

In the Confirm Settings pane, click Details.

2 Scroll through the list of various settings.

Click Save Setup Profile.

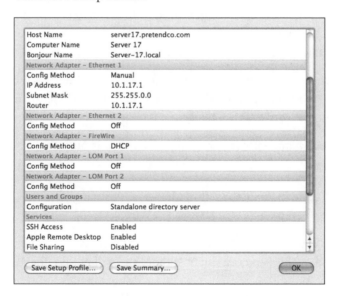

3 Because the Auto Server Setup profile contains a password, you will practice saving and using this file with encryption.

From the Encryption pop-up menu, choose Passphrase Encrypted, and specify the password apple (of course, you should not use such a simple password outside of this exercise).

Click Save to open the Save dialog.

Save your Auto Server Setup profile in a folder named "Auto Server Setup" at the root of any volume on the computer you would like to set up and it will be applied the next time you install Mac OS X Server.

◉ Apply this profile to any server
◯ Apply this profile only if any of the following conditions are true:

    (Serial number ⇕) (is ⇕) [   ]   ⊕

Encryption: [Passphrase Encrypted   ⇕]
Passphrase: [•••••   ]

This file will require a passphrase to unlock. Server Assistant will prompt for the passphrase, or it can be applied by placing a ".pass" file with the same name as the Auto Server Setup profile in the "Auto Server Setup" folder at the root of any volume.

(Cancel) (**Save**)

4   At the Save As dialog, you will create a new folder called Auto Server Setup. Because you are doing this remotely, you will be saving the configuration file to your local Mac OS X computer or attached USB or FireWire device.

       Connect a USB or FireWire disk to your Mac OS X computer. Create a folder at the root of this external disk, and name it `Auto Server Setup`. Note that the folder name must have spaces between the words.

       Save the file with the default name AutoServerSetup.plist inside this Auto Server Setup folder.

5   Do not click the Set Up button to apply the settings in Server Assistant; you will instead use the Auto Server Setup file on the USB or FireWire device.

       Close the Server Assistant Review pane; otherwise, your Mac OS X Server will be in a state of being configured by this Server Assistant session, and will not use the Auto Server Setup profile.

6   Look at the monitor connected to your Mac OS X Server, and notice that it is at the Welcome pane. This will change when the server finds the Auto Server Setup file.

7   Unmount and remove the USB or FireWire device from your Mac OS X v10.6 computer, and then connect it to your server.

8   At your server, supply the passphrase and click Complete Setup.

9   If Server Assistant does not start configuring your server, click Configure Now.

Using Tools

After you have installed Mac OS X Server and performed the initial setup, the administrator account you specified will be automatically logged in at the server. Be sure to read Mac OS X Server Next Steps.pdf, which is on that administrator's desktop, and contains suggestions and information specific to your server's configuration. You will use a few utilities to perform additional configuration and maintenance of your server. This section introduces eight key utilities:

▶   Server Preferences

▶   Workgroup Manager

▶   Server Admin

▶   Accounts preferences

▶   Network preferences

▶   Software Update

▶   Server Monitor

▶   Server Status Dashboard widget

Later chapters will introduce additional utilities, such as iCal Server Utility, System Image Utility, and Ticket Viewer.

> **NOTE ▶** You can run Mac OS X Server Admin Tools v10.6 only on Mac OS X v10.6 or later.

Server Preferences

You can change basic service and system settings and add users and groups with Server Preferences.

The settings are for:

- ▶ File sharing
- ▶ Address Book service
- ▶ iCal (calendaring) service
- ▶ iChat service
- ▶ Mail service
- ▶ Web service
- ▶ VPN (virtual private network) service

You can also view server information, view system and secure log files, show usage graphs, and manage Time Machine settings and Security (Firewall) settings.

When you use Server Preferences to create a new user, you have the ability to enable or disable access to basic services for that user.

Workgroup Manager

With Workgroup Manager, you can administer users, groups, computers, and computer groups and perform client management. Account information can be entered individually or imported from a compatible file. There are two ways to use Workgroup Manager, depending on whether you spend most of your time working with one server or several. If you work with a single server most of the time, authenticate when you open Workgroup Manager.

> **NOTE** ▶ We cover Workgroup Manager only briefly in this chapter. It is covered in greater detail throughout the book.

To work with Workgroup Manager:

1   From your server, click the Workgroup Manager icon in the Dock. Or, from your Mac OS X computer, open Workgroup Manager, which is located in the /Applications/Server folder.

2   In the Address field, enter the IP address or use the existing local name (or DNS name if the network is set up for DNS in a production environment) of the server, or click Browse to select from a list of servers on your local network. You will use server17. pretendco.com for this book. Click Connect.

> **NOTE** ▶ If you administer several different servers and work with different directory domains (directories will be discussed in Chapter 3, "Using Open Directory"), open Workgroup Manager without authenticating. To do so, click Cancel in the Workgroup Manager Connect pane and choose View Directories from the Server menu. You will have read-only access to information displayed in Workgroup Manager for directories you have access to. To make changes, click the lock icon to authenticate as an administrator.

3 After you authenticate, a dialog appears, notifying you that you will be working in the local directory, one that is not visible to others in your network. Click OK, and the Accounts pane appears with lists of users, user groups, computers, and computer groups in the server's local directory domain. The following options are available:

▶ Click the Server Admin icon in the toolbar to open Server Admin.

▶ Click the Accounts icon in the toolbar to administer users, user groups, computers, or computer groups.

▶ Click the Preferences icon in the toolbar to work with preferences for managed accounts.

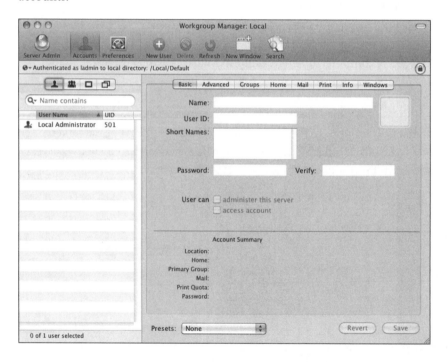

Server Admin

With Server Admin, you can configure and monitor services running on Mac OS X Server systems. You also use Server Admin to set up and manage share points, such as folders, or other volumes.

> **NOTE ▶** We cover Server Admin only briefly in this chapter. It is covered in greater detail throughout the book.

Selecting a Server

1   From your server, click the Server Admin icon in the Dock. Or, from your Mac OS X v10.6 computer, open Server Admin, which is located in the /Applications/Server folder (you previously installed the Server Admin Tools on your Mac OS X v10.6 computer).

2   In the Address field, enter the IP address or use the existing local host name (or DNS name if the network is set up for DNS in a production environment) of the server. Since Server Assistant set up a DNS record specifically for your server and modified the Network preference to use itself as a DNS server, use the DNS name server17. pretendco.com.

3   Authenticate as your local administrator. In this case, enter the user name (Local Administrator) and password (1admin) you supplied earlier in Server Assistant.

4   Click Connect.

5   Since you did not choose to start any services earlier in the setup process, you will be presented with a pane alerting you that there are no services running. Click the Cancel button.

6   Click SERVERS in the upper-left corner of Server Admin.

The SERVERS list contains a list of available servers (discovered via Bonjour services discovery), any servers ready for install, any servers ready for setup, all the servers you're connected to (in this case, just your server at the moment), and, optionally, the services available on each server. To add a server to the window, click the Add (+) button in the bar at the bottom of the window and authenticate to the server. To remove a server from the list, select it, click the Action pop-up menu (labeled with a gear and a down arrow), and choose Remove Server.

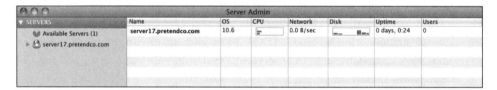

If you select your server from the list on the left, you will be able to interact with your server directly. If, however, you click directly on the word *SERVERS* in the window, you will be able to view statistics on all the connected servers, such as the name, operating-system version, CPU usage, network throughput, disk usage, uptime, and number of connected users. Double-clicking the disk usage icon will bring up a pane showing the percentage of CPU usage, network traffic, and disk space being used for all mounted volumes.

Working with General Settings

To work with the general settings for a server, select the server in the SERVERS list and use the buttons at the top of the window:

1   Click Overview to view information about the server. You can view hardware information, server software version information, services running, and in the Status section, the number of connected users and uptime.

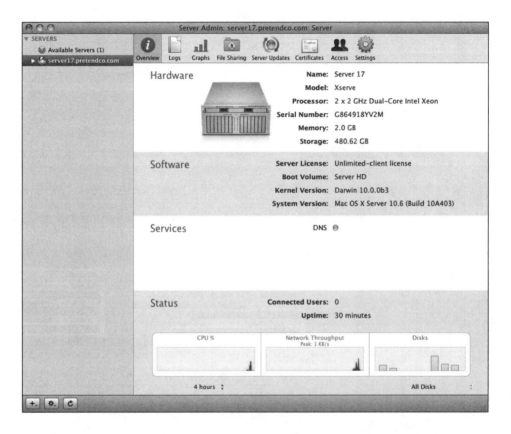

2   Click Logs to view the system log, kernel log, security log, or software update log.

3   Click Graphs to view a graphical history of server CPU and network activity.

Once Graphs is selected, you can choose to view network traffic and CPU usage over varying lengths of time (past day; 1, 2, 4, 6, 12, and 24 hours; 2, 3, 5, and 7 days; and the past week) by selecting either option from the pop-up menu at the bottom of the window.

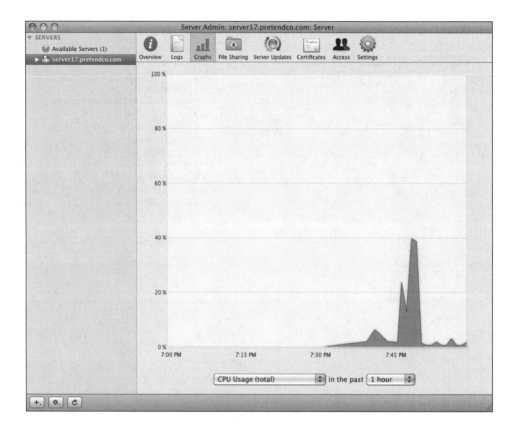

4   Click File Sharing to view all mounted volumes, preset share points, user and group permissions, and quotas on share points. You can also browse a volume hierarchy and set up new share points. You will use this file-sharing function of Server Admin in Chapter 2, "Authenticating and Authorizing Accounts."

5   Click Server Updates to use Software Update to remotely update the server's software.

6   Click Certificates to view the default certificate generated when Mac OS X Server v10.6 is set up or to create and manage your own certificates.

7 Click Access to restrict who can access the server's various services and who can administer and monitor those services. You will use this to manage service access control lists (SACLs) in the next chapter.

8 Click Settings, and then click the General tab to enable or disable various protocols and services and to view the serial number information.

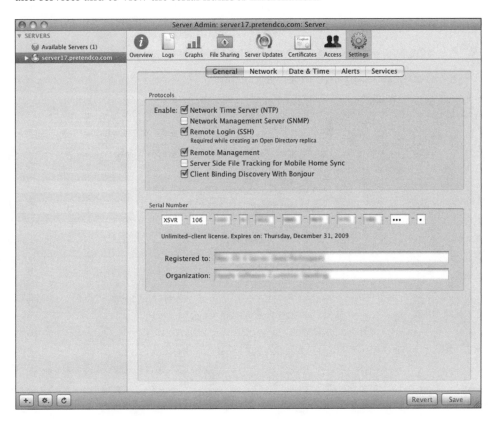

9 Click the Network tab to see the computer name, local host name, and network interface information. The computer name is what Mac OS X computers will see in the sidebar if your server offers file- or screen-sharing services.

10 Click the Date & Time tab to control whether you use the Network Time Server, which is important if you are in a Kerberos environment. You can also set the time zone here.

11 Click the Alerts tab to configure the sending of an email to a specified address when one of three criteria is met:

▶ A disk has less than x percent of free space, where x is determined by you.

▶ New software updates are available for the server.

▶ A certificate is expired or about to expire.

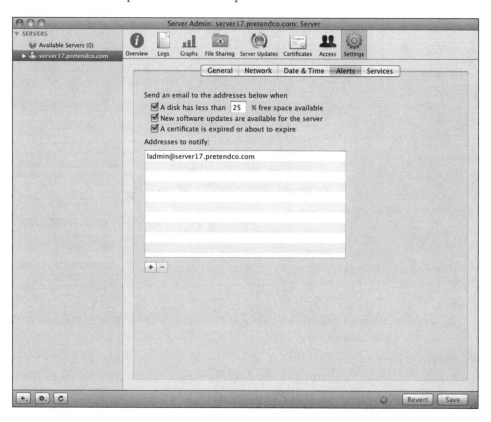

12 Click the Services tab to select various services your server will offer.

Working with Services

To work with a particular service on a server, enable the checkbox next to the service, and then click the Save button at the bottom of the window.

Next, click the disclosure triangle beside the server to reveal the list of services offered by the server, and then click the service. Use the buttons at the top of the window to manage the service's settings and to display status information, including logs and graphs.

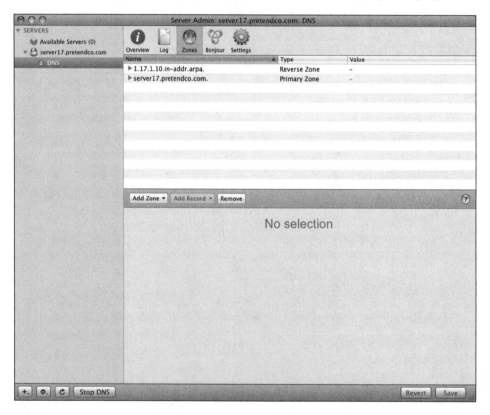

To start or stop a service, select the service (rather than the server entry) under your server, and then click Start *Service Name* or Stop *Service Name* at the bottom left of Server Admin. You can also use the Server menu and choose Start Service, Stop Service, or Soft Restart service, depending on the service.

You can have Server Admin have several windows open at once by choosing New Server Admin Window from the Server menu, and you can be connected to several servers simultaneously by clicking the Add (+) button at the bottom of the window and choosing Add Server. Table 1.3 defines the Mac OS X Server services.

Table 1.3 Mac OS X Server Services List

Service	Function
Address Book	Shared contacts service
AFP	File sharing for Macs
DHCP	Distributes IP address and associated information
DNS	Maps IP addresses to names
Firewall	Protects ports against attacks
FTP	File sharing for most computers
iCal	Calendaring service for users and groups
iChat	iChat service for users and groups
Mail	Mail service
Mobile Access	Provides secure proxied access to private Mail, Web, and iCal services without requiring a VPN
MySQL	Database service using MySQL
NAT	Network Address Translation
NetBoot	Network booting and installing service
NFS	File sharing for most computers
Open Directory	Shared directory and authentication service
Podcast Producer	Automates and shares processing of podcast creation
Print	Offers print services
Push notification	Notifies a client if the client has received an event invitation or new email message
QuickTime Streaming Player	Streams media for access via webpage or QuickTime
RADIUS	Strict authentication for remote access to server

Table 1.3   Mac OS X Server Services List (continued)

Service	Function
SMB	File sharing for Windows and Macs
Software Update	Offers Apple software updates stored locally
VPN	Virtual private network service
Web	Creates and manages multiple websites
Xgrid	Manages processing jobs across a grid of Macs

When you select certain services, such as Podcast Producer, mail, and RADIUS, and then click Overview for that service, there is a Configure *Service Name* button available.

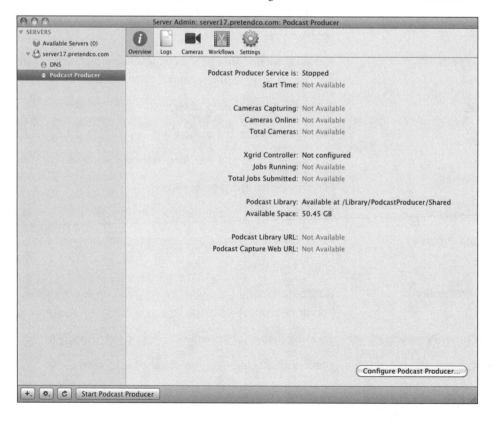

When you click that Configure *Service Name* button, a new window opens and presents a step-by-step assistant that helps you through the setup of that service.

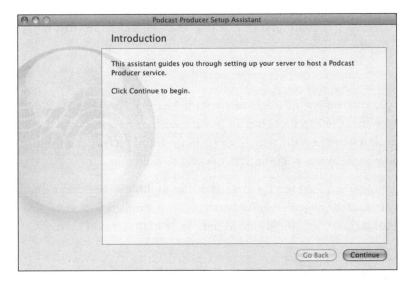

Exporting and Importing Settings

You can export (and subsequently import) both service settings and your server settings by choosing Server > Export > Service Settings and/or Server > Export > Server Admin Preferences. When exporting your Server Admin preferences, you can save the single file anywhere you choose. When saving service settings, you are presented with a dialog showing all the currently running services. You simply select the checkbox next to the services whose settings you want to save, and then click OK. Find a location suitable for saving those preferences, and save them.

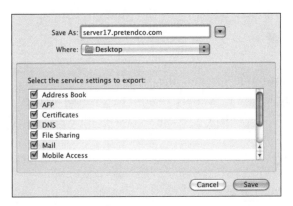

Conversely, when you are ready to import a service setting, simply locate the appropriate file and choose Server > Import in Server Admin.

> **NOTE** ▶ If importing the DNS settings does not have any visible effect the first time, try importing DNS settings again.

Enabling Screen Sharing

Using Server Admin, you can control the screen of a remote Mac OS X Server v10.6. You must first connect and authenticate to the server so you can see the Overview window and other various services windows. Select the remote server in the list of servers, and from the Server menu, choose Share Server's Screen. This opens screen sharing.

An authentication pane appears, asking you for that server's local administrator user name and password. Once you enter the information requested and click Connect, a new window appears, allowing you to take control of the keyboard and mouse of that remote server.

> **NOTE** ▶ The Name field automatically contains the name of the user you are currently logged in as. You need to use credentials for an administrative user on the computer you are attempting to control with screen sharing, as shown in the figure above.

Accounts Preferences

As discussed in the earlier section "Administrator Account," the password you specified for the initial local administrator account is used to set the password for the root account. You can change this password with Directory Utility, which you can access through Accounts preferences or find in /System/Library/CoreServices. Change the root user's password with the following steps:

1   Open the Accounts pane of System Preferences.

2 Select Login Options.

3 Click Edit (or click Join).

4 Click Open Directory Utility.

5 From Directory Utility's Edit menu, choose Change Root Password.

Software Update

After installation and setup are complete, you can update your server locally or remotely. Locally, you would use the Software Update Preferences pane of System Preferences or select Software Update from the Apple menu. You should choose to show the details of the updates and select which updates you want to install, or you can choose to install all updates. Next, authenticate as a local administrator to begin the update process.

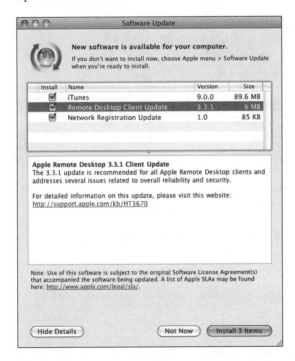

Alternatively, you can run Software Update remotely by using the Server Admin tool to update your Mac OS X Server. Software Update uses the server's Internet connection to check for the latest software updates for the server. You can also have Server Admin alert you to the presence of software updates by setting an email address and clicking the checkbox requesting notification of such updates. This is done under the Settings tab of Server Admin. Regardless of the method, Software Update provides updates for both the base Mac OS X operating system and Mac OS X Server.

NOTE ▶ Plan for software updates. As updates to the server software become available from Apple, you will want to apply them to your servers. This should be done carefully. Your installation may contain third-party software or custom installations that have not been fully qualified with the updated software. Always preflight updates on nonproduction servers before rolling out the changes. Updates from Apple are important and will add value to your implementation. You should evaluate the updates according to your customers' needs and apply them when appropriate—not just because they are available.

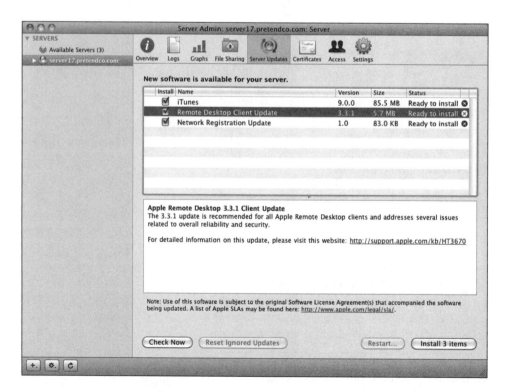

Server Monitor

You can use Server Monitor to remotely restart, power off, and power on Xserves.

You can also use Server Monitor to monitor various statistics of your server:

▶ General server information

▶ Drive status

▶ Power information

▶ Network activity

▶ Temperature and blower statistics

▶ Memory configuration and health

▶ Security lock information

You can configure Server Monitor to send email notifications to specific email addresses if the status of various server components changes.

When using Server Monitor on an Intel-based Xserve, it is important to configure the Lights Out Management (LOM) IP address(es) and administrative user name and password. You can configure the LOM only at the server itself (or with screen sharing or Apple Remote Desktop).

Server Status Dashboard Widget

The Server Status Dashboard widget permits an administrator to monitor several aspects of your server. It is installed on Mac OS X Server and on any Mac OS X v10.6 Mac that has Server Admin Tools v10.6 installed. The Server Status widget will monitor:

▶ Various services and their status

▶ CPU utilization

▶ Network load

▶ Disk usage

The Server Status Dashboard widget is installed along with all the other Server Admin tools, although it does not appear in the /Applications/Server folder.

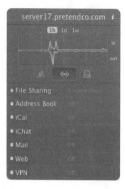

To use the Server Status Dashboard widget:

1 Activate Dashboard by clicking the Dashboard icon in the Dock (or by pressing the Dashboard button on your keyboard).

2 Click the plus button in the lower-left corner.

3 Select the Server Status widget from the list at the bottom of the screen.

4 Once the Server Status widget appears, enter your server's IP address or DNS name and local administrator's credentials, and then click Done.

Once you are connected, you will see three icons across the middle of the widget, and clicking each one will reveal (in order from left to right) CPU utilization, network activity, and free disk space. Clicking each icon will update the graphic above the icons with the relevant information for your server. Moving your mouse over the graphic will show used and free totals for disk usage and permits you to change the view of network activity and CPU usage over time (last hour, last day, last week).

You can also open a second widget and connect to the same server should you want to monitor more than one item simultaneously, such as the percentage of disk space (used and free) and network activity.

Troubleshooting

For troubleshooting during installation, you can display the installer log, as discussed earlier in this chapter. This is most useful when an installation does not complete correctly. In that case, rerun the installation with the log file showing so that you can identify where the problem occurred and compare it to a successful installation's log file.

If you use Server Assistant to create an automatic configuration file, as we did in this chapter, be sure to delete the file from the volumes or drives available to the server after the server has been set up. Otherwise, if you need to repurpose the server after you reinstall the server software, the server will be automatically configured using the old configuration data.

> **NOTE ▶** One common problem found in server installations is incompatibility with third-party hardware and software configurations. Many times bad third-party RAM has caused problems. Isolate the changes to your system when you run into problems. Keep the variables to a minimum.

What You've Learned

▶   Mac OS X Server requires a desktop computer with an Intel processor, 2 GB of RAM, and at least 10 GB of available disk space.

▶   The Mac OS X Server Assistant guides you through the initial configuration of your server.

▶   You can install and configure Mac OS X Server v10.6 remotely using a variety of tools, such as Server Assistant and Server Admin.

▶   Link aggregation enables you to improve performance by combining two or more Ethernet ports and having them act as one.

▶   Apple provides updates to Mac OS X Server through the Software Update service. To ensure that your system is up to date, run Software Update on a regular basis.

▶   You use Server Preferences to manage users and groups, including settings and access to a basic set of Mac OS X Server services.

▶   You use Server Admin to configure and monitor Mac OS X Server services and share points.

▶   You use Workgroup Manager to manage users, groups, computers, and computer groups and to manage preferences.

▶   You can use the Server Status widget to monitor the state of various services, disk usage, and CPU and network use over time.

References

The following documents provide more information about installing Mac OS X Server. All of these and more are available at http://www.apple.com/server/macosx/resources/.

Mac OS X Server Administration Guides

Installation & Setup Worksheet

Getting Started

Upgrading and Migrating

Command-Line Administration

Apple Knowledge Base Documents

You can check for new and updated Knowledge Base documents at http://www.apple.com/support/.

Document HT1822, *Mac OS X Server: Admin Tools compatibility information*

Document HT1310, *Startup Manager: How to select a startup volume*

Document HT3508, *Xserve (Late 2006 or later): How to configure Server Monitor to access Xserve*

Document HT2773, *Xserve (Late 2006 and later): Configuring Lights-Out Management (LOM)*

Chapter Review

1. What are the minimum hardware requirements for installing Mac OS X Server v10.6?

2. What information must you collect before installing Mac OS X Server?

3. What are three things that the Server Assistant application can be used to do?

4. In what formats can Server Assistant save setup information, and what is each format used for?

5. What tool should be used to keep Mac OS X Server up-to-date with the latest versions of software?

Answers

1. The minimum requirements are:
    ▶   A desktop Mac computer with an Intel processor
    ▶   2 GB of RAM (more for high-demand servers running multiple services)
    ▶   10 GB of available disk space

2. Hardware serial number and MAC address(es) of the computer, administrator name and password, computer name, TCP/IP configuration, and how you will manage users and groups.

3. Server Assistant can be used to install Mac OS X Server v10.6 on a remote server, to set up a remote Mac OS X Server v10.6 system, and to save and encrypt setup information for a Mac OS X Server v10.6 server in a configuration file.

4. Server Assistant can save setup information in the following formats:
    ▶   Text file—Used as a description of the setup (just a reference).
    ▶   XML file—Can be placed in a folder named Auto Server Setup at the root of any volume mounted on the target server to automatically configure that server.

5. Software Update (in System Preferences) or the Software Update pane of Server Admin.

2

Time

This chapter takes approximately three hours to complete.

Goals

Configure Mac OS X Server to control access to an account

Configure Mac OS X Server to control access to files and folders based on local user accounts and groups

Define authentication and authorization as they are used in Mac OS X Server

Use Server Admin to configure share points and permissions

Use Workgroup Manager to create local user accounts and groups

Use Server Admin and Workgroup Manager to create administrators

Understand and implement file-system and service ACLs in Mac OS X Server

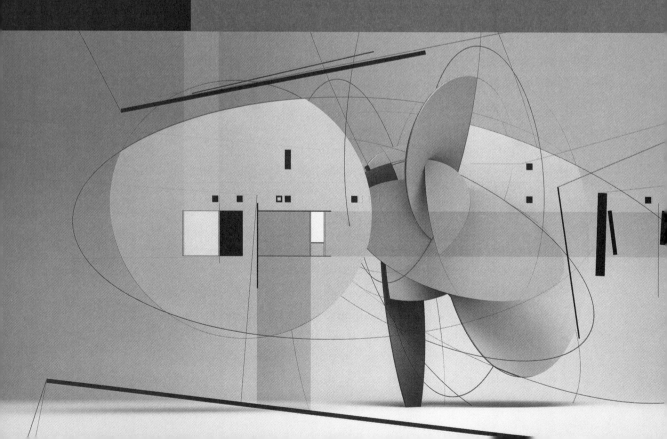

Chapter **2**

Authenticating and Authorizing Accounts

Authentication is the process by which a person identifies *which user account he or she wants to use on the system*. This is similar to, but slightly different from, saying that authentication is how a person proves his or her identity to a system. The distinction is useful because multiple people may share the same user name and password, or one person may have multiple user accounts on the same system. In each case, the person supplies user account *credentials* (which usually consist of a name and a password) to identify the user account the person wants to use, and if the supplied credentials are valid, the person successfully authenticates. While there are other methods of authenticating a user account, such as smart cards or voice print, the combination of name and password is the most common (and is assumed for this chapter).

Authorization is the process that determines what an authenticated user account is *allowed to do* on the system.

In this chapter you will learn how file permissions, access control lists (ACLs), and service ACLs (SACLs) control access to files and services. You will use Workgroup Manager to configure local user and group accounts, and use Server Admin to manage access to files and services.

Managing Server Access

When configuring any server for access by users, you'll need to determine what services the server will provide and what levels of user access to assign. For many of the services this book will cover, such as file sharing, you will need to create specific user accounts on your server.

When considering the creation of user accounts, you'll want to determine how to best set up your users, how to organize them into groups that match the needs of your organization, and how to best maintain this information over time. As with any service or information technology task, the best approach is to thoroughly plan your requirements and approach before starting to implement a solution.

Authentication and Authorization in Action

Authentication occurs in many different contexts in Mac OS X and Mac OS X Server, but it most commonly involves using a login window. For example, when you start up a Mac OS X computer, you may have to enter a user name and password in an initial login window before being allowed to use the system at all.

Another example occurs when you attempt to connect to a network file service, whether via AFP or SMB.

A user must authenticate before accessing these services, even if logging in just as a guest user. Depending on what he or she is trying to access, the user may or may not get feedback on whether *the user typed the wrong password* (authentication) or *the user is not allowed access to the service* (authorization). For instance, if you type a wrong password at the login window, the login window will simply shake and return you to the login window. However, if you do not have authorization to log in at a computer, even if the user name and password are correct, the login window will simply shake and return to the login window in this case as well. The user experience is the same, despite the different reasons for the user not being able to access a service.

Here is a window that indicates that either authentication or authorization failed:

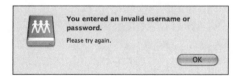

And here is a window that indicates that even though the *authentication* may have succeeded, the *authorization* failed:

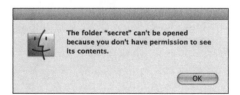

Creating and Administering User and Administrator Server Accounts

A number of tools are available to create and administer user and group accounts. The Accounts pane of System Preferences on Mac OS X Server is just like Mac OS X's Accounts pane of System Preferences—you use it to define local users and perform very basic administration of local groups. However, System Preferences does not have a remote mode; you have to use tools such as screen sharing or Apple Remote Desktop to remotely administer System Preferences on a remote Mac OS X Server.

This chapter focuses on using Server Admin and Workgroup Manager to remotely manage local user and group accounts, and to remotely manage access to the services Mac OS X Server provides.

Like Mac OS X, Mac OS X Server stores local user and group accounts in the local directory domain or local directory node. You will see this referred to as *Local/Default* in Workgroup Manager.

Server Preferences is another tool to manage users, but it manages *network* users, a topic covered in Chapter 3, "Using Open Directory."

To administer a server with Server Preferences, Server Admin, or Workgroup Manager, you must authenticate as an administrator (or a user that has limited administrative privileges) using those applications. This is required whether you use those applications at the server locally or remotely from another computer.

NOTE ▶ When you select the checkbox labeled "Remember this password in my key-chain," you store your credentials in your keychain. This means that the next time you attempt to access this service, if your keychain is unlocked, you will not be prompted to authenticate, or your user name and password may be entered automatically, depending on the tool and service. See Mac OS X Support Essentials, Chapter 2, "User Accounts," for information about the keychain.

Using Workgroup Manager for Configuring User Accounts

To grant a person specific permissions on Mac OS X Server, you must set up a user account for that person. Workgroup Manager is the primary tool you will use in this chapter for creating and configuring user accounts on Mac OS X Server. You will use Workgroup Manager to create *network* user accounts in the next chapter.

Standard *local* user accounts on Mac OS X enable a person to access files and applications local to that computer. Similarly, local user accounts on Mac OS X Server permit users who log in locally (at the server) to access files or services (such as mail and print services) that are located on the server, but they also give remote users access to server volumes and associated files. When you use another computer, you can use a server's local user account to remotely access various services offered by that server, but you cannot use it at another computer's login window to log in to that computer (unless that other computer also has that local user account defined in its local directory domain, a complication you should avoid by using a centralized directory, which is covered in the next chapter).

Here are some examples of Mac OS X Server user account settings:

▶ Name

▶ UNIX user ID (UID)

▶ Short names

▶ User password type (shadow hash, crypt, open directory)

▶ Home folder location

▶ User address information

▶   Mail settings

▶   Print settings

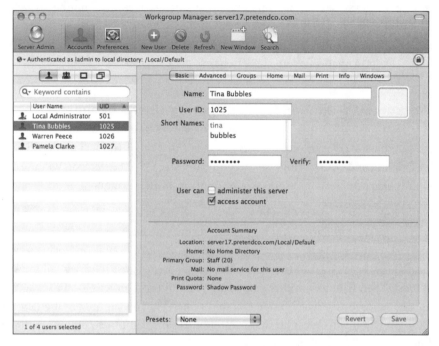

A user account's *name* is also known as a *long name* or *full name*; it is common practice to use a person's full name, with the first letter of each name capitalized, and a space between each word in the name. The name can contain no more than 255 bytes, so character sets that occupy multiple bytes per character have a lower maximum number of characters.

A user account's *short name* is an abbreviated name, usually consisting of all lower-case characters. A user can authenticate using the name or short name. Mac OS X and Mac OS X Server use a user's first short name when creating a home folder for that user. Carefully consider the first short name before assigning it, because it is not a trivial task to change a user's short name. You are not permitted to use the space character in a user's initial short name; it can contain only the following characters:

▶   a through z

▶   A through Z

- ▶ 0 through 9
- ▶ _ (underscore)
- ▶ - (hyphen)
- ▶ . (period)

You can assign multiple short names to a single user account. This allows a user to have a different email name without having to change the initial short name. To create an additional short name, double-click the blank entry at the bottom of the Short Names list, and then enter an additional short name.

In the Basic pane, the user ID (UID) is a numerical value that the system uses to differentiate one user from another. Though users gain access to the system with a name or short name, each name is associated with a UID, and that's what the operating system primarily cares about. When you create a new user, Workgroup Manager automatically assigns it a UID with an unused number, starting with 1024, but you can change it to any unique number from 500 through 2,147,483,647. Do not modify or delete user accounts with UIDs between 0 and 100; they are reserved for system use, and they will not appear in the login window. Workgroup Manager does not display user accounts with a UID of less than 500 unless you choose View > Show System Records.

Note that when two users are logged in with different names and passwords but with the same UID access documents and folders, the system will consider them to be the same owner. Because of this, the system will provide both users with the same access to documents and folders, a situation you should avoid. If you attempt to create two users with the same UID in Workgroup Manager, you'll have to confirm that you really want to do that.

Workgroup Manager has other uses besides managing user accounts. You can also use it to manage group, computer, and computer group accounts. A group account is a collection of user accounts. A computer account identifies a particular computer, and you can assign a computer account to be a member of one or more computer group accounts. As you will see in Chapter 9, "Managing Accounts," you can apply policy management to user accounts, group accounts, computer accounts, and computer group accounts.

> **NOTE** ▶ It is common to drop the word *account* from the terms *user account, group account, computer account*, and *computer group account*.

Using Workgroup Manager for Configuring Administrator Accounts

An administrator account is a special type of user account on Mac OS X Server that enables the user to administer the server. A user with an administrator account can create, edit, and delete user accounts, as well as modify the settings of various running services on the Mac OS X server where the administrator account exists. The administrator uses Server Preferences to perform basic account and service management, Server Admin to configure advanced service settings, and Workgroup Manager to edit users, groups, and account preferences.

To give a user the ability to administer the server, designate that user as an administrator: Select the "User can administer this server" checkbox in the Basic pane in Workgroup Manager, as shown in the figure below.

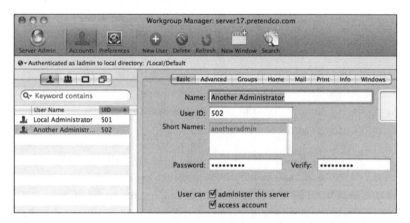

When you make a user account an administrator, under the hood, the operating system makes that user account a member of the local group account called Administrators (short group name admin).

> **MORE INFO ▶** For network user accounts, there is a Privileges pane that contains an option for "Administration capabilities," which controls the authorization for that user account to modify the shared directory domain. You will learn about that in Chapter 3, "Using Open Directory."

In the section "Limiting Administration Capabilities" you will learn how to use Server Admin to delegate to nonadministrative users the ability to administer or monitor services with Server Admin, without making them a member of the admin group.

Configuring Local User Accounts

Mac OS X Server maintains a list of local user accounts for managing access to resources, such as files when running as a file server. You should already be familiar with using the Accounts pane of System Preferences. You will use the Workgroup Manager utility to add three sample local users to your server computer. Additionally, to demonstrate the ability to import and export users with Workgroup Manager, you will export these users, delete them, and then reimport them.

NOTE ▶ During this entire chapter, you will be using your Mac OS X computer to configure your Mac OS X Server computer. This demonstrates that you can perform server configuration from any computer with Mac OS X v10.6 that has network access to your server computer. You will also be authenticating to Workgroup Manager with your Local Administrator account credentials.

Add Users

Follow these steps to add three users to your Mac OS X server:

1   On your Mac OS X client computer, open Workgroup Manager and connect to your Mac OS X server as Local Administrator.

Because the local node can be used for authentication only to resources resident on the server, you will be notified that your directory node is not visible to the network. You will learn about directory services in Chapter 3, "Using Open Directory."

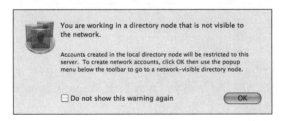

2   Click OK to dismiss the directory node notification.

3   Click Accounts in the toolbar.

4   Click the Users button above the accounts list.

5   Ensure that the current administrator account is selected and visible.

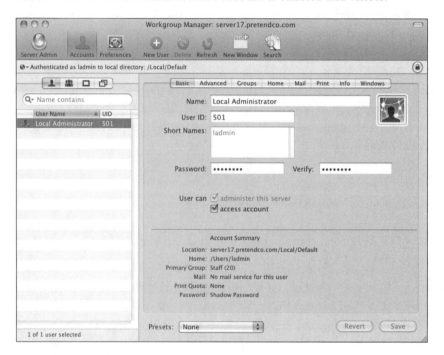

6   Click New User in the toolbar.

7   Click OK when you get the message that "New users may not have access to services." This is a warning that SACLs may be in effect, and you may have to specifically grant access to services for this new user.

You can enable the "Do not show this warning again" if you wish.

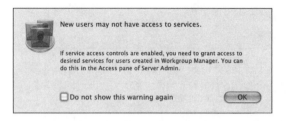

8 In the Basic pane, enter the following information for the first new user. Note that Workgroup Manager automatically generates the first short name based on the Name field, and you must double-click that automatically generated short name in order to change it, although once you click Save, you cannot change the new user's first short name.

▶ Name: `Tina Bubbles`

▶ Short Names: `tina`

▶ Password: `tina`

▶ Verify: `tina`

Of course, do not use such an insecure password in a non-lab environment.

9 Leave the other settings at their default values (including leaving Presets, at the bottom of the window, set to None), and be sure you don't select "User can administer this server."

10 Double-click the second line (the empty one below "tina") in the Short Names field to add another short name.

11 Enter `bubbles`, and then click Save.

The new user name appears in the list of users on the left side of the Workgroup Manager window. You should also see that the first short name is now dimmed, indicating that it cannot be changed after you clicked Save. Notice that the name and the alternate short names *can* be edited after this point.

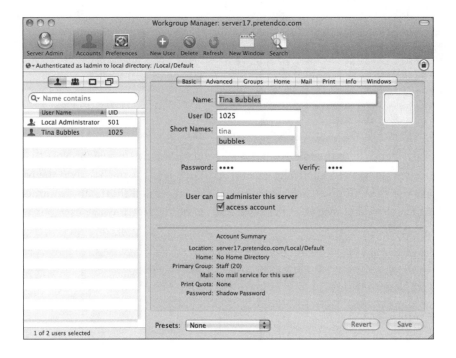

12 Add a second user, Warren Peece, by clicking the New User button and entering the
following values:

▶ Name: Warren Peece

▶ Short Names: warren

▶ Password: warren

▶ Verify: warren

Leave the other settings at their default values.

13 Click Save.

14 Create a third user with default values except for the following fields:

▶ Name: Pamela Clarke

▶ Short Names: pamela

► Password: pamela

► Verify: pamela

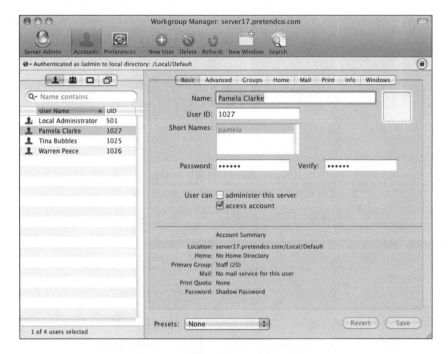

15 Select the existing Local Administrator account from the list of current users.

Note that the administrator account has the checkbox labeled "User can administer this server" selected. You cannot change this checkbox because you are currently accessing Workgroup Manager as that user; you cannot remove administrative privileges for the currently authenticated user.

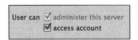

Now compare the new accounts with the Local Administrator account, and notice that the checkbox labeled "User can administer this server" is selected on Local Administrator and not on the others. When you create new users, they are not automatically administrators. You must select the appropriate checkbox to allow them to be administrators.

Configure Comments and Keywords

During the setup of accounts, you can configure advanced features such as comments and keywords in each account. These features are useful for organizing users or searching for particular users based on something other than name or user ID. This provides for a more realistic search pattern should you need to specify a range of users without actually adding them to a specific group.

1   Select Tina Bubbles from the list of users.

2   Click Advanced.

3   In the Comment field, enter Employee# 408081.

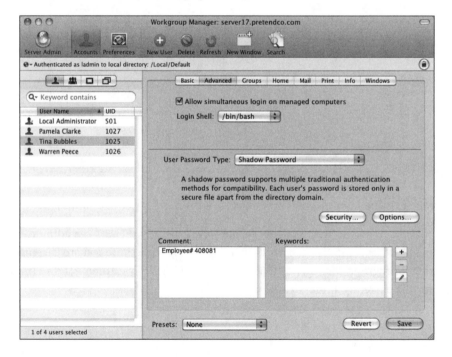

4   Click the Add (+) button next to the Keywords field.

5   In the pane that appears, click Edit Keywords.

6 In the "Manage available keywords" pane that appears next, click the Add (+) button.

7 In the text field, enter Manager.

8 Click the Add (+) button again.

9 In the second text field, enter Marketing.

10 Click the Add (+) button again to add a third keyword: Engineering.

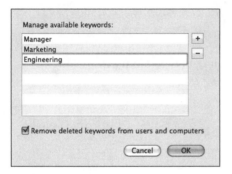

11 Click OK to save the new keywords and return to the "Select the keywords to add to tina" pane.

12 Select Manager and click OK to add the Manager keyword to the Tina Bubbles user account.

13 Click Save to save the changes to the user account.

14 Click the Add (+) button again, and add the Marketing keyword to the Tina Bubbles account. Click Save.

15 Select Warren Peece from the accounts list, click the Add (+) button, and add the Manager and Engineering keywords to the Warren Peece user account.

16 Add Employee# 410103 to the Comment field for the Warren Peece user account, and click Save.

The users should now have the following keywords:

▶ Tina Bubbles: Manager, Marketing

▶ Warren Peece: Manager, Engineering

▶ Pamela Clarke: [none]

The users should now have the following values in their Comment fields:

▶ Tina Bubbles: Employee# 408081

▶ Warren Peece: Employee# 410103

▶ Pamela Clarke: [none]

17 Click the Search (magnifying glass) pop-up menu above the accounts list, and choose Keyword Contains.

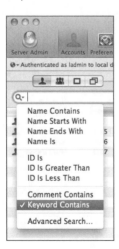

18 In the search field, enter Manager.

Only the Tina Bubbles and Warren Peece accounts appear in the user list.

19 In the search field above the list of users, choose Keyword Contains and enter Eng.

Warren Peece is now the only user listed, because you added the Engineering keyword only to the Warren Peece account.

20 In the search field, choose Comment Contains and enter 408.

Only Tina Bubbles is listed in the accounts list, because her account's comment contains "408" in her employee number.

21 Click the cancel button in the search field to display all users.

TIP ▶ To construct more-advanced search queries, you can use the Search button in the toolbar, or click the Search pop-up menu above the accounts list and choose Advanced Search.

NOTE ▶ The Comments and Keywords fields are not related to the groups that a user is a member of, they are only used as examples in this chapter.

Exporting and Importing Users and Groups

You can create user accounts individually, or you can import them from a properly formatted file. The file could be created on your own, created with a third-party tool, restored from another server, or restored from a backup of the current server. To back up and restore user and group accounts from a Mac OS X Server computer, use the Export and Import commands in Workgroup Manager.

To back up user and group accounts defined in Workgroup Manager, first select the accounts you want to export, choose the Export command from the Server menu, and then specify a name and location for the resulting file.

User passwords are *never* exported, so anytime you export and then later import users from a file, you will need to set their passwords after you import the users.

NOTE ▶ You must export each category of accounts separately; you must export users, and then user groups, and then computers, and then computer groups if you want to export all your accounts. The Export function saves only the accounts selected in the current Workgroup Manager view.

To restore user or group accounts using Workgroup Manager, use the Import command from the Server menu. In the Import dialog, choose "Ignore new record" from the Duplicate Handling pop-up menu. This setting will skip any records if a user with that UID already exists on your server. This prevents you from damaging or overwriting any existing accounts.

You do not want to export your Local Administrator account. Because the Local Administrator user ID is 501, and the other users have user IDs starting with 1024, you will sort the list of users by their user IDs to make it easier to separate the Local Administrator account from the rest of the user accounts. By default, Workgroup Manager displays the list of users by User Name in alphabetical order.

Use the following steps to export your user accounts, delete them, and then import them. Because user passwords are not exported, you will also assign passwords again.

1   In Workgroup Manager, click the word *UID* in the UID column to sort the user list from low UID to high UID.

2   Select the user accounts Tina Bubbles, Warren Peece, and Pamela Clarke. Do not select the Local Administrator account for this export.

You can select and deselect multiple users by using the Command or Shift key while making your selection.

3   Choose Server > Export.

4   In the Save As window, specify the filename Chapter2Users, press Command-Shift-D to navigate to your desktop, and then click Export.

5   In Workgroup Manager, with Tina Bubbles, Warren Peece, and Pamela Clarke still selected, click Delete in the toolbar.

6   When you are asked "Delete selected users?" confirm by clicking Delete.

7   Confirm that Workgroup Manager lists only one user, Local Administrator.

8   Choose Server > Import.

9   In the Import Users pane, navigate to select the file you just exported, Chapter2Users.

Leave all the settings at their default values.

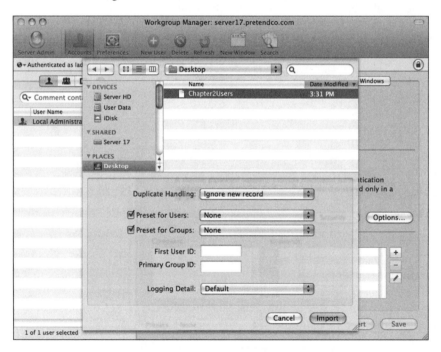

10   Click Import.

The users you previously exported and deleted are imported. Because passwords are not included in the users' import file, you need to set a password for each user account.

11   In the list of users, select Tina Bubbles.

12 Click the Basic button to display the Basic pane for Tina Bubbles.

13 Enter the Tina Bubbles password (tina) in the Password and Verify fields, and then click Save.

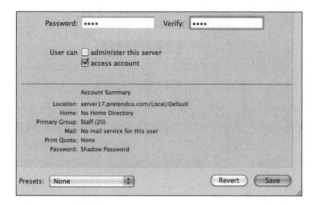

14 Just as you reassigned the password for Tina Bubbles, reassign each other user account password so that it's the user account's short name. Of course, you should always use secure passwords in a production environment.

15 Confirm that the user account information you specified in the Comment and Keywords fields was correctly imported.

In the search field, choose Keyword Contains and enter Manager.

The user accounts for Tina Bubbles and Warren Peece should be the only user accounts displayed, since they are the only accounts with the Manager keyword.

16 Click the cancel button in the search field to display all user accounts.

Promoting a User to an Administrator

As mentioned before, you use the Workgroup Manager application to define a user as an administrator. Follow these steps to configure one of your existing user accounts as an administrator:

1 With Workgroup Manager on your Mac OS X computer, select the Tina Bubbles user account.

2   In the Basic pane, select the checkbox labeled "User can administer this server."

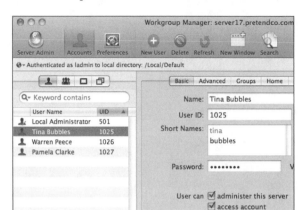

3   Click Save.

You'll notice that after an account is set as an administrator, the icon next to the user's name has a pencil to indicate that the user can edit server settings.

Confirm That the User Is an Administrator

Test the new administrator access as the user you just promoted to an administrator.

1   Close the main Workgroup Manager window.

2   Choose Server > Connect.

3   Deselect the "Remember this password in my keychain" checkbox.

4   Connect to your server. Rather than using the credentials for ladmin, use the credentials for Tina Bubbles (short name: tina; password: tina).

5 If you see the warning that you are working in the local node, click OK.

6 Look closely at the text next to the globe icon, underneath Workgroup Manager's toolbar.

You should see that though you were previously connected as ladmin, you are now "Authenticated as tina to local directory: /Local/Default."

7 Still authenticated as Tina Bubbles, create another local user account:

▶ Name: Mike Smith

▶ Short Names: mike

▶ Password: mike

▶ Verify: mike

Remove a User's Administrative Status
Make Tina Bubbles a nonadministrative user.

1 Click the lock. Note the text "Not authenticated" next to the globe icon.

2 Close the Workgroup Manager window.

3   Choose Server > Connect, and connect to your server as ladmin.

4   Select the user Tina Bubbles, click to deselect the checkbox labeled "User can administer this server," and then click Save.

> **NOTE ▶** The group called admin is special; any user in this group is a local administrator. You can use any Local Administrator credentials to access secure system preferences like the Accounts and Security panes of System Preferences, among other privileges. Be careful about which users you assign as part of the local group admin.

Working with Group Accounts in Workgroup Manager

Group accounts are closely associated with user accounts on Mac OS X Server. Group accounts enable administrators to quickly assign a set of permissions to multiple users. Mac OS X allows an easy way to change group assignments and permissions through the Get Info command, and also provides a simple interface for creating small groups using the Accounts preferences pane. With servers, however, you usually want to have many more groups with many more members.

To create a group on Mac OS X Server, open Workgroup Manager, simply click New Group in the toolbar, and enter a name for the group. There are additional options for the group, but they are not required for the group to be functional.

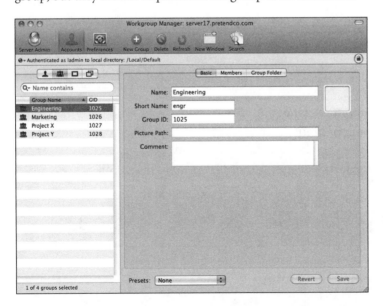

User names and group names can contain non-Roman characters. Depending on the character set, you may have as few as 64 characters available for the long name. If you are using exclusively Roman characters in your user names, you can safely use 255 characters. Short names for user accounts and group accounts must consist of no more than 255 Roman characters.

Groups can also be nested in other groups, which allows a more natural way to represent users in an organization.

Working with User Accounts and Group IDs

Every user has a single primary group ID (GID). The system stores the user's primary GID in the underlying user account record. All other group membership information is stored in the underlying group records, *rather than in the underlying user account* itself.

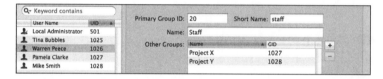

Using Workgroup Manager, you can remove a user from a group either by editing the Other Groups field in the user account or by editing the group account. However, you cannot change a user's primary group ID by these methods. Users who are members of a group by virtue of their primary group ID appear in italics in the group membership list. This is your indication that you can't remove them from the group account as you normally would—by selecting the user and clicking the Remove (–) button. Instead, you have to edit the primary GID in the user account.

In this example, the user account Lillian Gilbreth's primary GID is 1025, the Engineering group.

When you look at the member list of the Engineering group, the Lillian Gilbreth user account is listed in italics.

You cannot remove Lillian Gilbreth from the list of members because her primary GID is the GID of the Engineering group.

Creating Groups with Workgroup Manager

You'll use Workgroup Manager to create and manage local groups.

1   In Workgroup Manager on your Mac OS X computer, connect to your server as ladmin.

2   Click Accounts in the toolbar.

3   Click the Groups button.

4   In the toolbar, click New Group to create a new group.

5   Enter the following information for the first new group:

   ▶   Name: Engineering

   ▶   Short Name: engr

6   Leave all other fields at their default values, and click Save.

7   Create a second group:

▶   Name: `Marketing`

▶   Short Name: `mktg`

8   Leave all other fields at their default values, and click Save.

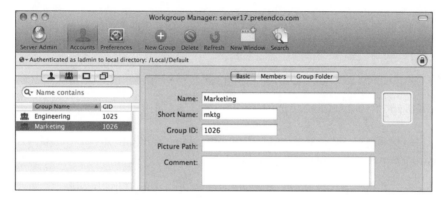

Now create two more groups, Project X and Project Y:

9   Create a group for the Project X team:

▶   Name: `Project X`

▶   Short Name: `projectx`

10   Leave all other fields at their default values, and click Save.

11   Create another group, this time for the Project Y team:

▶   Name: `Project Y`

▶   Short Name: `projecty`

12   Leave all other fields at their default values, and click Save.

Associating Users with Groups

Now that you have created four groups, you need to assign to them the users you previously created. You will do this using two different methods: adding users to a group and adding group membership to a user account.

Adding Users to Groups

The most common approach for populating groups with users is to select a group and add one or more users to it. On your server, you will select a group, and then add users to the group based on keywords.

1   Select the Marketing group from the list of groups.

2   In the Members pane, click the Add (+) button to the right of the Members list.

   The Users and Groups drawer appears.

3   From the pop-up menu in the search field in the Users and Groups drawer, choose Keyword Contains and enter Mar.

   This locates all the users with the Marketing keyword—only Tina Bubbles.

   NOTE ▶ Searches are case insensitive, and they search both the list of long names and the list of short names.

4   Select the displayed user in the drawer and drag it to the Members list.

   You should now see the user listed in the Members area for the Marketing group.

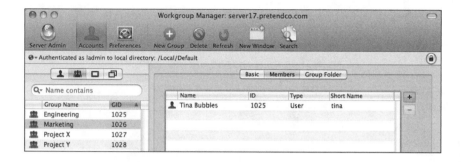

5 Click Save.

Adding Group Membership to a User Account

While you could easily use the process in the previous section to add Warren Peece to the Project X and Project Y groups, try an alternative approach by adding the groups to the Warren Peece account.

1 Click the Users button, and then select Warren Peece from the account list.

2 Click Groups.

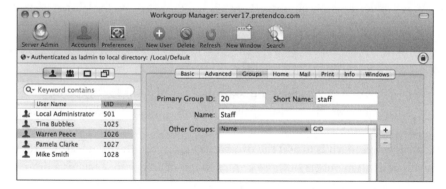

3 Click the Add (+) button.

The Groups drawer appears, displaying the list of available group accounts.

4   Select the Project X group, and drag it from the Groups drawer to the Other Groups list.

Notice that as you drag the group, the pointer changes from an arrow to a plus sign. This indicates that you are adding this group to the text field.

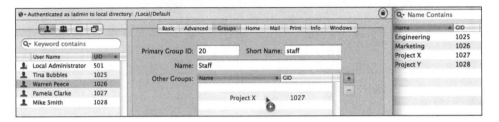

5   Click Save.

You have now successfully added Warren Peece as a member of the Project X group. However, Warren Peece also needs access to Project Y.

6   Add the Project Y group to the user account of Warren Peece. Remember that while it seems like you modified this user's account record, you really modified the group account records.

You have just added multiple groups—Project X and Project Y—to the Warren Peece user account.

Adding Groups to Groups

Let's say you need a group that enables you to control permissions for the entire Engineering department, which consists of two divisions, Project X and Project Y. You could populate the Engineering group with all the individual engineering user accounts. However, an easier approach is to add the two project groups to the Engineering group. This effectively adds all members of those groups to the main group, which is a more efficient way to manage groups than in previous versions of Mac OS X Server.

1   Click the Groups button, and select the Engineering group from the list of groups.

2   In the Members pane, click the Add (+) button to open the Users and Groups drawer.

3 In the Users and Groups drawer, click the Groups button.

4 Drag the Project X and Project Y groups to the Members list.

5 Click Save.

You have now added both users and groups to your server, as well as groups to groups.

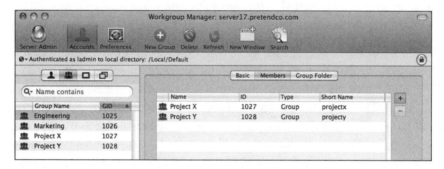

Controlling Access Through Server Accounts

Authorization is used throughout Mac OS X and Mac OS X Server. The most common example is usually transparent to the user: Every time a user accesses a file, the computer checks file permissions against the user's account information to see if the user is authorized to use the file. In Mac OS X and Mac OS X Server, owner and group permissions are associated with every file, folder, and application.

When accessing a file server, you typically have to authenticate, and then you see a choice of valid share points available to mount. When you navigate inside a mounted share point, folders' badges (small icons displayed on or under the folder icon) show whether you are authorized for read/write, read-only, write-only, or no access for that folder.

When connecting to a server with Server Admin or Workgroup Manager, after you authenticate, your user name will be checked to see if it is authorized to perform administrative functions. Additionally, authorization checks are made anytime a user tries connecting to any service, such as the Podcast Producer service, on your server, to see if the user is allowed to use that service.

Using Authorization on Mac OS X Server

Portable Operating System Interface (POSIX) permissions are the permissions that have been used on Mac OS X and Mac OS X Server since day one. They are still used on both Mac OS X and Mac OS X Server, and they exist for every file and every folder on the file system. POSIX permissions are the traditional UNIX-style permissions that enable you to apply read, write, and execute permissions for three groups of users: the owner, the group, and all other users. The initial permissions that you see in the Get Info window of Mac OS X are POSIX permissions.

Before Mac OS X v10.4, POSIX permissions were the only way to control file access on Mac OS X Server. Mac OS X Server v10.4 built on the Mac OS X heritage of using POSIX permissions, but it added the ability to define complex access rules that are not possible with standard POSIX permissions. This was done with access control lists (ACLs). ACLs are supported on disks formatted as Mac OS Extended volumes. They are stored in the file system itself, using extended attributes that have always existed in Mac OS Extended file systems but had been unused. This is how ACLs are supported without reformatting the volume to a new file-system format. In Mac OS X Server v10.6, ACL support is enabled by default.

For users accessing the server over the network, ACLs are supported for AFP, SMB, and NFS protocol connections. ACLs are also compatible with ACLs from the Windows world, thus providing a better user experience when accessing Mac OS X Server from Windows clients, since users expect a granular level of permissions settings. These access permissions can be set to support a rich organizational workflow where user permissions need to vary widely as a document gets passed among different authors and reviewers. If you use the Get Info window of Mac OS X to add additional permissions for local users or groups for a local file, they will be added using ACLs.

Even though the concept of ACLs is moderately new to Mac administrators, ACLs are familiar to Windows administrators. This makes the introduction of Mac OS X Server into a Windows environment easier to implement.

Reviewing POSIX Permissions

Every file and folder in Mac OS X has ownership and permissions information that defines the privileges available for that file or folder. Ownership includes configuring both an owner and a group, while permissions includes setting specific access settings for the owner, the group, and everyone else, commonly referred to as "other."

NOTE ▶ The Finder displays this category as "everyone," and Server Admin displays this category as "Others."

When set from the Finder, these permissions can be Read & Write, Read only, Write only (Drop Box), and No Access. When set from the command line, there are a few more possibilities. When you change the ownership or permissions of an item using a command-line interface, the changes are reflected in the Info (or Inspector) window for that item. Likewise, when you change the permissions in the Info window, the changes can be seen when displaying the item in a command-line interface.

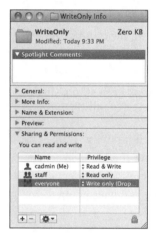

In the example figure, the *d* in front of the permissions indicates that the file is a folder (*d* stands for *directory*). The permissions for the owner, rwx, correspond to Read & Write in the Info window for that folder. The permissions for the group, r-x, correspond to "Read only" in the Info window, while the everyone permissions of -wx, highlighted in the Terminal window, mean that everyone else can write to the folder but can't read it. The x, or execute, permission on a file identifies a program that can be run. For a folder, the execute permission determines whether the folder can be searched. To access a file in a folder, you must have execute permission for each folder from the root folder down to and including the folder containing the file.

NOTE ▶ Folders and files usually default to having the everyone/other permissions set to read-only. Although this sounds secure, keep in mind that your server may have Guest Access enabled, which may permit any computer that can reach your server to read those files.

In POSIX, the user ID associated with the file or folder defines permissions ownership. If the numeric UID of the file or folder matches the UID defined in the user account, that user is considered the owner of the file or folder. Group access is determined similarly: Each file or folder has a group ID associated with it. Each group account has a numeric GID. If the user's primary GID matches the GID of the file or folder, or if the user is a member of a group with a GID that matches the GID of the file or folder, the user has access as defined in the group permissions settings.

POSIX Permissions Limitations

As a simple example of setting access permissions, suppose you have a school district that is configuring a shared math folder (named Math Files) on its server. The district's administrators want to allow math teachers to read, write, and delete math files, and to allow any math student to read the same files. Ideally, they would like to set the Math Files folder so that only math students, not all students, are allowed to see it. This example would be difficult to support with standard POSIX privileges, as you would be limited to a single group to control privileges.

There are a couple of approaches to this problem, yet each has its limitations. In the first method, you assign the Math_Teachers group to the folder and give the Math_Teachers group read and write access. Then you prevent math students from writing by assigning read-only access to Others. The problem with this scenario is that you have granted read access to everyone in the school for the Math Files folder.

Another approach is to consolidate the math users—teachers and students—into a group called Math Department. You can give this group access and deny access to everyone else. This solves the problem of the entire school accessing the Math Files folder, but you have introduced a new problem: Since the students and teachers are combined into a single group—Math Department—students and teachers have identical access privileges, and you want students to read only, not to write. You've lost that granularity. You could probably create two subfolders with different group access permissions for math students and math teachers, but what if you wanted even finer control? Maybe non–math teachers should have read-only access similar to that of math students.

You get the point: You must work around limitations in the permissions system rather than using the permissions system to naturally express the access and workflow that exists in the organization. Luckily, the access control system in Mac OS X Server helps you find a natural way—ACLs—to set up and enforce access permissions.

Setting POSIX Permissions with Server Admin

If you have an empty volume available on your server, name it User Data for the rest of this book.

If you do not have an empty volume available, share your server's screen, log in, and use Disk Utility to create an extra partition for these exercises.

1   On your client computer, open Server Admin, connect to your server as ladmin, select your server in the source list, and choose Server > Share Server's Screen.

2   Authenticate as ladmin to share the screen of your server.

3   At the login window at your server, log in as ladmin.

4   Open Disk Utility from the /Applications/Utilities/ folder.

5   Select your server's hard drive from the source list, and click Partition.

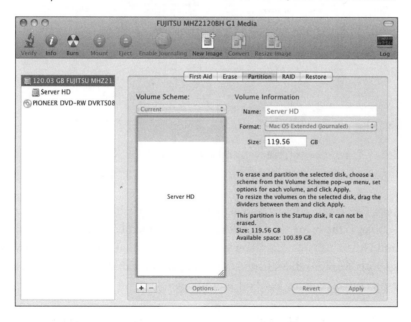

6 Click the Add (+) button below the Volume Scheme list to add a second partition. This creates a second partition of roughly 50 percent of your server's hard drive capacity.

7 Select the second partition, and then name it User Data.

8 Click Apply to start the process.

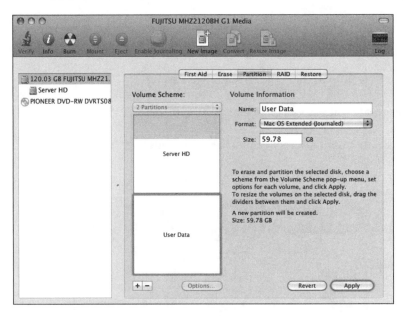

9 Quit Disk Utility, log out of your server, and on your Mac OS X computer, quit screen sharing.

In the following exercise, create a folder and assign POSIX ownership and permissions such that Tina Bubbles is the owner and can read and write, members of Project X can read and write, and Others has no access. You will demonstrate that there are several ways to change settings with Workgroup Manager. For example, you can drag a user or group to change ownership, or you can use the Edit button.

1 Using Server Admin on your Mac OS X computer, connect to your Mac OS X server as ladmin.

2 Click File Sharing in the toolbar.

3 Click Volumes.

4 Click Browse.

5 Select the User Data volume.

6 Click New Folder and name the new folder POSIX.

7 Choose View > Show Users & Groups. This opens a Users & Groups window similar to Workgroup Manager's drawer for users and groups.

8 Drag Tina Bubbles from the Users & Groups window to the User field in the Permissions table. The Permissions table appears below the word *POSIX*, and is made up of the User field, the Group field, and the Other field. In the figure below, ladmin is displayed in the User field, and staff is displayed in the Group field.

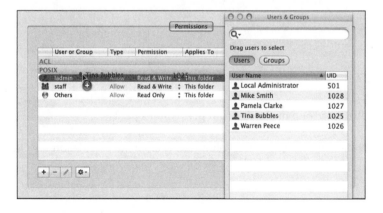

9 Close the Users & Groups window.

10 In the Group field of the Permissions table, select the staff group.

11 Click Edit (the pencil button).

12 Enter projectx to change the group associated with this folder to the Project X group. You must specify the short name of the group in this field. Leave the checkboxes selected for Read and Write. This grants the members of Project X Read & Write permissions for this folder.

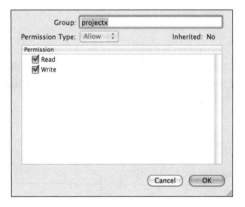

13 Click OK to dismiss the group ownership and permissions pane.

14 Use the pop-up menus in the Permission column to change the permission for Others from Read Only to No Access.

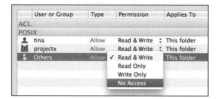

15 Click Save.

As in Mac OS X, when a user attempts to access a file or folder, the user account is compared with the file or folder's owner and group. If the user account is the owner, the permissions assigned to the owner are enforced, and the permissions for the group and everyone are ignored for that account. If the user account is not the owner but is a member of the group, group permissions are enforced. If the account is neither the owner nor a member of the group, everyone's permissions are enforced.

> **MORE INFO** ▶ In an "owner-only delete" scenario such as what may exist in a shared temporary scratch space, an authorized user has read/write access to the file, but only the owner can delete it. This option, known as the sticky bit, can be set only at the command line via *chmod +t*.

Setting ACLs

In both the client and server versions of Mac OS X v10.6, ACLs are enabled by default.

> **TIP** ▶ In the unlikely event that you are unable to assign ACLs to a particular volume, you may need to enable ACLs with the *fsaclctl* command in the Terminal utility.

Setting ACLs with Server Admin

In Mac OS X Server v10.4, you needed to use Workgroup Manager to set file-system ACLs, but in v10.5 and v10.6, you use Server Admin. Managing the ACL is similar to POSIX permissions management except that you drag accounts to the ACL section of the Permissions table instead of the POSIX section of the Permissions table, and a much larger range of permissions types is available.

Use the following steps to create a new folder and to add one access control entry (ACE) to that folder's ACL:

1   Using Server Admin on your Mac OS X computer, connect to your Mac OS X server as ladmin.

2   Click File Sharing in the toolbar.

3   Click Volumes.

4   Select the User Data volume.

5   Click New Folder and name the new folder ACLTest1.

6   Select the ACLTest1 folder.

7   Click the Add (+) button to open the Users & Groups window.

8   Drag Warren Peece to the ACL list.

   If there are currently no entries in the ACL list, you'll just see a blue line appear between the ACL and POSIX lists as you're dragging the user or group.

9   Use the pop-up menu in the Permission column to change the permission for Warren Peece from Read to Full Control.

10 Click Save.

Determining User Access to a Folder

ACLs can grow complex in a large organization. Judicious use of group membership should help clarify which users have access to which items, but you may still find yourself unsure of who has access to a given folder. The Effective Permissions Inspector will tell you exactly what access a particular user has to the selected folder. Use the following steps to use the Effective Permissions Inspector:

1   Using Server Admin on your Mac OS X computer, connect to your Mac OS X server as ladmin.

2   Click File Sharing in the toolbar, click Volumes, and then click Browse.

3   Select the User Data volume, and select the ACLTest1 folder.

4   From the Action menu, choose Show Effective Permissions Inspector.

5   If the Users & Groups window is not already displayed, choose View > Show Users & Groups.

6   Drag a user from the Users & Groups window to the Effective Permissions Inspector. You can drop the user anywhere in the Effective Permissions Inspector window.

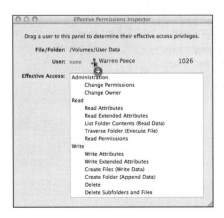

7   Click Save.

Look at the resulting values for each type of permission. A checkmark means that particular permission is allowed for that user, and the absence of a checkmark means that particular permission is denied for that user.

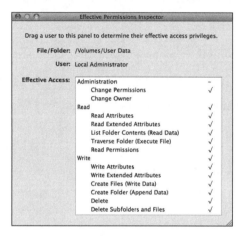

Distinguishing the Use of UID, GID, and GUID

You have learned that POSIX owners and groups are determined by user and group IDs. Because UIDs and GIDs are simple integers, it is possible for users to have duplicate user IDs. Usually this is an error, but sometimes an administrator will want the POSIX UID to be identical on two separate users.

ACLs are much more complex and require a unique identification of a user or group. For this purpose, every user and group has a globally unique ID (GUID). This is not exposed in Workgroup Manager or Server Preferences because there should be no reason to change it. Every time a user is created, a new 128-bit number (for example, 835E78F0-7808-4758-8C92-CF8AB428B99B) is generated, based on the clock time and other information, when the user is created. In this way, users and groups are virtually guaranteed unique identification in ACLs.

TIP "I can't see the files I should see" can be a common complaint from users who access a complex server. The next time you hear this, use the Effective Permissions Inspector to investigate the permissions that user has.

ACL Workflow Examples

When working with ACLs, it is important that you plan your setup properly to avoid conflicting permissions settings, such as having a user be a member of two groups, one with read permissions on a folder and one with no access permissions on the same folder. These types of conflicts can occur if you do not plan your ACL permissions models well.

Multiple Groups

The POSIX permissions work well in a single desktop mode such as Mac OS X. Yet when the system becomes more complex, such as in corporate or enterprise environments, the POSIX model does not scale well.

Complex workflows might require more than just the User, Group, and Others classes available with POSIX. In particular, having a single group is very limiting. The POSIX owner must be an individual user account (it can't be a group), and granting permission to Others usually opens up the files to a wider audience than you want. ACLs permit multiple groups assigned to a folder, each with a unique permissions setting. This is a common requirement in any environment that has multiple groups collaborating on a single project. Imagine a production environment that has writers, graphics editors, copy editors, and production editors. Different groups work on the same file at different points during the project. Because ACLs can assign different permissions to multiple groups, you must carefully plan what your group structure is going to look like to avoid any confusion.

Each group would have specific permissions for each folder. For instance, a user in the Writers group can put a document in the Submissions folder and can read and write to that file while in that folder. However, the Copy Editors group can only read the files in the folder. Users in the Production Staff and Graphics Editors groups are specifically denied any read or write access to the Submissions folder.

Also, users in the Writers group are allowed to move the document into the Editors folder but are denied permission to read what is in the folder. Users in the Copy Editors group have read permissions and are allowed the specific write permissions of creating folders or files within the Editors folder, so they can make a copy of the document within the folder. Users in the Graphics Editors group have read permissions as well but are allowed only write attributes to the document; they cannot create new files within the Editors folder. Users in the Production Staff group can read the files.

Finally, users in the Production Staff group can copy the document into the Production folder and can read and modify any documents in that folder. Users in the Writers group are specifically denied permission to read or write to the Production folder or any documents in the folder. Users in the two editor groups have all the read permissions but can write only extended attributes.

Nested Groups

In addition to assigning multiple groups to a single folder, Mac OS X Server allows groups to contain other groups. Your Writers group may be broken down further into yet other groups based on the types of articles they write, such as features or columns.

If ACLs permit multiple groups assigned to a folder, you might wonder why nesting groups are required. For example, why assign the Writers to the Submissions folder instead of directly assigning access to the three smaller groups (Feature Writers, Staff Writers, and Ad Copy Writers)? The effect would be the same.

Breaking groups down into subgroups can make your access easier to understand as an administrator. But if you need to come back to your server a month later and give all your writers access to a new folder, you would have to recall the organizational details of your groups. Are you going to remember that to grant all writers access, you need to assign the Feature Writers, Staff Writers, and Ad Copy Writers groups to the new folder? With an all-inclusive group such as Writers, your job is simpler.

You can use nested groups to reflect the structure of your organization. We used a publishing example, but another example is a school: A grade level could be a group, which contains the individual classes of students.

While nested groups are powerful, they should be used with care. If you build a deep, complex hierarchy, you may find that access is harder—rather than easier—to understand. Mirroring your organizational structure is usually safe and useful. However, be wary of ad hoc groups that don't relate to any external structure. They may be a quick way to give access to some users, but later on may make it more difficult to understand your access.

Inheritance

Another feature of ACLs is *inheritance*: When you create an ACE for a folder, from that point on, when a user creates a new item in that folder, the operating system assigns that same ACE to the new item. In other words, the ACE is inherited. For each ACE in the folder's ACL, you can control how that ACE is inherited; when you edit an ACE, you can enable or disable each of the following checkboxes. By default, all four "Applies to" options are enabled:

► This folder: This ACE applies to this folder.

► Child folders: This ACE will be assigned to new folders inside this folder, but not necessarily to new folders that are created inside the child folders of this folder, unless "All descendants" is also selected.

► Child files: This ACE will be assigned to new files inside this folder, but not necessarily to files that are inside the child folders of this folder, unless "All descendants" is also selected.

► All descendants: This makes the two preceding options apply to items in an infinite level of nested folders in this folder.

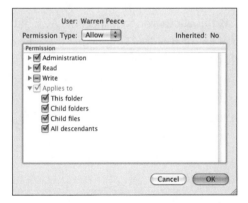

Note that in the figure above for this ACE, the pane displays the text "Inherited: No". This indicates that this ACE is not inherited *from* a parent folder, rather it is an explicit ACE defined for this folder. Also note that all four options for inheritance are enabled, in the "Applies to" entry.

When an ACE is *inherited* from a folder, it appears dimmed in Server Admin, as shown in the figure below for the ACE for Warren Peece.

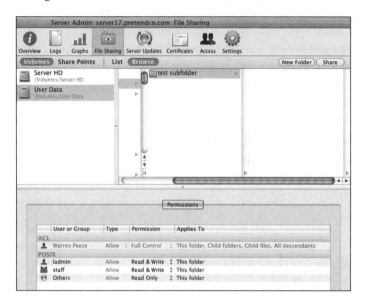

Although you can double-click an inherited ACE, this allows you to inspect the ACE but not to edit it. The following figure is an illustration of an inherited ACE; note that the pane contains the text, "Inherited: Yes" to indicate that this ACE is *inherited from* a parent folder.

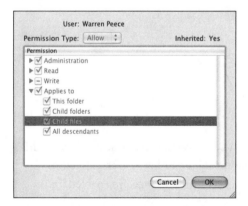

Before you change the inheritance rules for an ACE, be sure to thoroughly test how your changes affect your workflow.

POSIX Permissions vs. ACL Settings

ACLs provide you with the ability to set a finer grain of control over access settings that are compatible with the Windows environment. Seventeen additional settings can be made on a folder (or share point) from inside Server Admin. This allows a richer set of capabilities to be defined for read and write access as well as for administrative control (such as who can change permissions on or ownership of a folder). In Server Admin, these settings are enabled on folders, not individual files, although files can obtain these permissions through inheritance. This folder-level control lets you have a finer level of management, without having to worry about administering permissions for thousands or millions of individual files.

The POSIX settings available in the Finder are limited to Read & Write, Read Only, Write Only, and None. The following dialog displays the ACL settings available from Server Admin; this is displayed if you choose Custom from the Permission pop-up menu in an ACE:

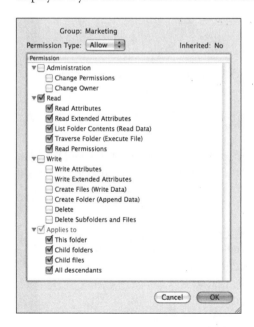

NOTE ▶ When using Server Admin to manage ACLs, access control settings are made on a container basis for either folders or share points, not on individual files themselves. Individual files obtain their respective ACL settings from their containing folder.

The inheritance configuration determines where the ACL settings are propagated to, such as to the folder itself, any files or folders one level down, or to files or folders descendant from this folder. While the initial inheritance setting applies only for files and folders created afterward, you can propagate these settings manually to apply them to enclosed files or folders.

ACLs on a file or folder do not change when you *move it from one folder to another on the same volume*. In this situation, the file or folder is not copied and deleted. Instead, there is a change to the pointer to where the file or folder is located. If you *move between volumes*, a copy and delete does occur and the file or folder inherits the ACLs from the new enclosing folder.

How File-System ACLs Work

When you use Server Admin to define ACLs, you are creating individual access control entries (ACEs). These entries and lists are specific to a file-system location and are set on container objects—either share points or folders. Each ACE contains the following information:

▶   User or group associated with this entry

▶   Type of entry (Allow or Deny)

▶   Permissions (Full Control, Read & Write, Read, Write, or Custom, along with inheritance settings)

The order of entries is important because lists are evaluated top to bottom by Mac OS X Server.

Allow and deny matches work differently for ACLs. Allow matches are cumulative for all matches that apply to a user, whether from user or group matches. Deny matches apply on the first match.

POSIX and ACL Rules of Precedence

When a user attempts to perform an action that requires authorization (read a file, or create a folder), Mac OS X Server will allow this action only if the user has permission for that action. Here is how Mac OS X Server combines POSIX and ACLs when there is a request for a specific action:

1.   If there is no ACL, POSIX rules apply.

2.   If there is an ACL, the order of the ACEs matters. You should use Server Admin's Action pop-up menu (labeled with a gear and a down arrow) and choose Sort Access

Control List Canonically to have Mac OS X Server sort the ACEs in a consistent and predictable way.

3. When evaluating an ACL, Mac OS X Server evaluates the first ACE in the list and continues on to the next ACE *until it finds an ACE that matches the permission required for the requested action*, whether that permission is Allow or Deny. Even if a *deny* ACE exists in an ACL, if a similar *allow* ACE is listed first, the allow ACE is the one that is used, because it is listed first. This is why it is so important to use the Sort Access Control List Canonically command.

4. A POSIX permission that is restrictive does not override an ACE that specifically allows a permission.

5. If no ACE applies to the permission required for the requested action, the POSIX permissions apply.

For example, if Warren Peece attempts to create a folder, the requested permission is Create Folder. Each ACE is evaluated until there is an ACE that either allows or denies Create Folder for Warren Peece or a group that Warren Peece belongs to.

Even though this is an unlikely scenario, it illustrates the combination of an ACL and POSIX permissions: If a folder has an ACE that allows Warren Peece full control, but the POSIX permission defines Warren Peece as the owner with no access, Warren Peece effectively has full control. The ACE is evaluated before the POSIX permissions.

As another example, consider a folder with an ACL that has a single ACE that allows Tina Bubbles read permission, and the folder's POSIX permission defines Tina Bubbles as the owner with read and write permission. When Tina Bubbles attempts to create a file in that folder, there is no ACE that specifically addresses the Create Folder request, so no ACE applies to that request, so the POSIX permissions apply, and Tina Bubbles can create the file.

Allow Access Is Cumulative

In the following diagram, assume that algebra tutors are algebra students, and that all algebra students are students. The folder has three entries in the ACL:

▶   All students can read the contents of the folder (inherited from the parent).

▶   Algebra students can write to the folder.

▶   Algebra tutors can administer the folder.

All students in the school can see the selected folder and files inside that folder. Algebra students have write access by virtue of their membership in the Algebra Students group, but they also have read access by virtue of their membership in the All Students group. Thus, algebra students have read/write access. Algebra tutors, who are algebra students, can read, write, and make administrative changes, such as change permissions or ownership.

Notice that inherited permissions have to be considered for the cumulative Allow access. Algebra students and algebra tutors can read by virtue of being in the All Students group. If that is not what you intended, you could remove inherited privileges from the folder using Workgroup Manager.

Now suppose that inside the Math folder is a folder containing student evaluations. It is important that no student gain access to this folder or its contents. Notice that because of inheritance, students would normally have read access to the folder. In order to keep students out of this folder, you can place a deny access control on the folder for the All Students group. This deny access control should be placed above the allow access controls, since access control entries are evaluated from top to bottom.

The deny access at the top overrides all other access controls on the folder for the specified group. Even though algebra tutors have a read access ACE (from their membership in the All Students group), a write access ACE (from their membership in the Algebra Students group), and an admin access ACE (from their membership in the Algebra Tutors group), the deny access—which applies to all students—overrides all these ACEs because it is placed at the top of the list, and no student can access this folder.

Group Membership and ACLs

Using ACLs to control access to server resources can be extremely valuable, as long as care is taken up front to organize your user and group accounts appropriately. The recommended way to approach this management is to take advantage of using smaller groups to correctly mimic the needs of your organization, including nesting groups within groups. Use these group accounts to manage access on a more granular basis.

You could address your classroom situation by creating a single group for all teachers, which is made up two groups: Staff Teachers and Student Teachers. You could then manage staff and student teachers independently and assign access rights as needed. Over time, if a student teacher becomes a full-time teacher, you can simply move the student teacher's account into the Staff Teachers group. This enables you to continue managing access on a group/organizational basis, instead of dealing with access entries for individual teachers, which can get quite unwieldy.

Access Control Configuration

In this section you will create a folder hierarchy and a means of controlling access to facilitate the workflow of the users and groups on your server. Using only file-system ACLs, you will follow the path of an example project from development to review. You will discover that the ability to manipulate a file can be determined by where the file is located in the system, rather than by who created or owns the specific file.

It is important to note that changes take effect only when you save. It is good practice to save your work frequently.

To properly configure your server, you will need to understand the intended workflow of your users. Here is the scenario: You have set up two groups, Engineering and Marketing, and each group needs different access to files at different times during a project.

Members of Engineering need to create files and folders in a Development folder. Members of Marketing need to copy items from the Development folder to the Reviewed folder, and then edit files in the Reviewed folder. Members of Engineering should not be able to edit files in the Reviewed folder, but they need to be able to see the folders and files.

For this exercise you will be adding a new group to this equation: a Contractors group, for contract employees that need access to some but not all files. Because all the contract employees work on engineering projects, they should generally get the same access as the other engineers. You will make the Contractors group a member of the Engineering group. However, there are some projects that the members of Contractors cannot see. You will create a Secret folder for the members of the Engineering group. You will use POSIX permissions to deny access to Others, and you will create an ACE to deny read and write access for the Contractors group.

You need two main folders, Development and Reviewed.

The Development folder should allow:

▶ Engineering to read and write

▶ Marketing to read only

The Reviewed folder should allow:

▶ Marketing to read and write

▶ Engineering to read only

Additionally, the Secret folder in the Development folder should allow:

▶ Engineering to read and write

▶ Marketing to have no access

▶ Contractors to have no access

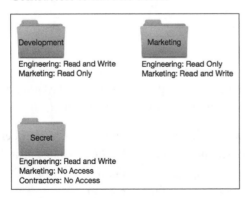

If you have been doing all the exercises in the book so far, the following will be true:

▶ Warren Peece is a member of the Project X and Project Y groups.

▶ Tina Bubbles is a member of the Marketing group.

▶ The groups Project X and Project Y are members of the Engineering group, so Warren Peece is effectively a member of the Engineering group.

Create the Folder Structure

In the example being used in this chapter, the folder structure is project based, not department based. As a document reaches a particular milestone, it will be moved from one location to another. You will create project folders and assign ACLs for those folders to control workflow. This may be different from the way you managed documents with POSIX permissions.

The first step is to create a project folder hierarchy. You can create the folders in the Finder, but you can also use Server Admin, which enables you to create folders on your server remotely without having physical access to it.

1 On your client computer, open Server Admin and connect to your server as ladmin.

2 Click the File Sharing button in Server Admin's toolbar.

The main window displays the volumes or current share points (either as a list or in a column browse view) and the owner and groups assigned to them, as well as their access permissions.

3 Click Volumes, followed by Browse.

This view enables you to navigate the local hard drive and set permissions on folders not contained within a share point.

4 In the left column, click the startup volume.

In this example, the name of the volume is Server HD.

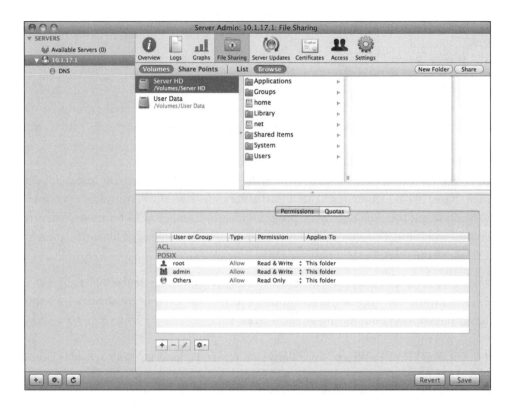

5   Click the Shared Items folder in the list of folders.

6   Click the New Folder button in the upper-right corner of the window.

This creates a new folder within the Shared Items folder.

NOTE ▸ The New Folder button creates folders inside the currently selected folder. Be sure to select the appropriate folder before you click New Folder.

7   In the "Name of new folder" field, enter `Project Phantom`, and then click Create.

8   Select the Project Phantom folder, click the Share button in the upper-right corner, and then click Save to make this folder a share point.

9   Select the folder you just created, Project Phantom, and click New Folder. Name the new folder `Development`.

10   Create another folder inside the Project Phantom folder, and name it `Reviewed`.

11   Create a folder inside the Development folder, and name it `Secret`.

12   Use the scroller and the resize control to resize the columns so you can see more folders horizontally, and confirm that you have created the folders as shown in the figure below.

Prepare Users and Groups

As mentioned before, in addition to using the existing Marketing and Engineering groups, you need to create an additional group for this exercise: Contractors. Make Mike Smith a member of the Contractors group.

1 Return to Workgroup Manager, and reconnect to your server if you are no longer connected to it.

2 Click Accounts in the toolbar, click the Groups button, and create a new group called Contractors. When creating the group, just use the default settings.

3 Add Mike Smith as a member of the Contractors group.

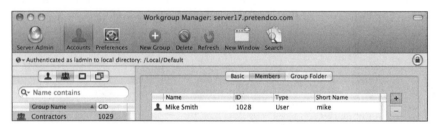

4 Add the Contractors group as a member of the Engineering group.

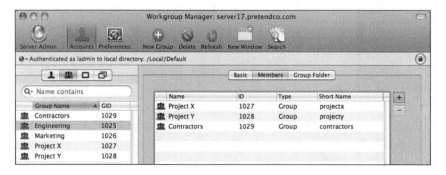

Now that you have created the folder structure, you need to assign group ownership and permissions for each of the folders. Start with the POSIX permissions and set No Access for Others. This will make it so that only the root user and members of the wheel group have access to the Development and Reviewed folders (the wheel group is a system group that the root user is a member of). You do not need to change the POSIX permissions for the Secret folder, because unless you make the Secret folder a share point, users who do not have read permission to the Development folder will not be able to navigate to the Secret folder.

Set Ownership and Permissions for the Development and Reviewed Folders

1   Return to the Server Admin application, and reconnect to your server if you are no longer connected.

2   Click File Sharing in the toolbar, and select the Development folder. You'll have to navigate to it inside the Project Phantom share if you closed your window earlier.

The rows in the Permissions table show that the Development folder is currently owned by root, and wheel is the group assigned to this folder.

3   Click the Permissions pop-up menu for the Others row, choose No Access, and then click Save.

4   For the Reviewed folder, set the Permissions for Others to No Access.

Configure the Access Control Lists for the Development Folders

1   Select the Development folder inside the Project Phantom share.

2   Click the Add (+) button to open the Users & Groups window, click Groups, and drag the Engineering group to the ACL list in the Permissions pane.

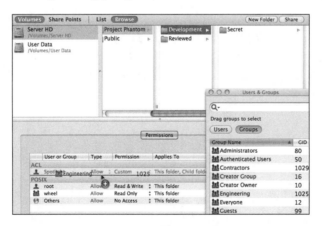

3   Before you click Save, note that Server Admin displays the group's short name in the ACL section of the Permissions table.

Click Save.

Note that after you click Save, in the Permissions table, Server Admin displays the group's *name* in the ACL section, but the group's *short name* in the POSIX section.

4 Select the Engineering entry in the ACL and, in the Permission column, choose Read & Write.

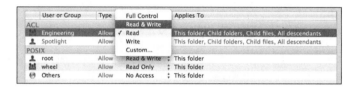

5 From the Users & Groups window, drag the Marketing group into the ACL. Click Save.

Note that the default permission for the new ACE for Marketing is Read. Leave the Marketing ACE at its default.

6 From the Action pop-up menu, choose Sort Access Control List Canonically, and then click Save to save the ACL change.

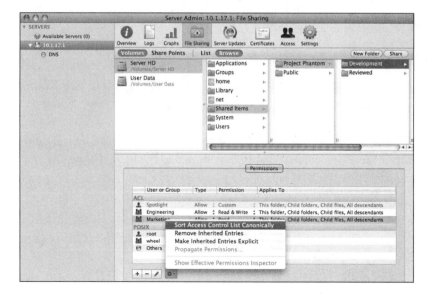

7 Confirm that your ACL appears as shown in the figure below.

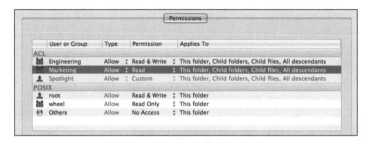

Set the permissions for the Secret folder so that the Engineering group can read and write, but the Contractors and Marketing groups have no access.

Because you created the Secret folder before you configured the ACL for its parent folder (Development), the Secret folder has the default ACL (by default, the boot volume has an ACE to allow the Spotlight process to List Folder Contents and Traverse Folder). Configure the POSIX permissions and the ACL to allow the Engineering group to read and write, but deny access for the Contractors and Marketing groups.

1 In Server Admin, select the Secret folder.

2 Configure the POSIX permissions for Others to be No Access.

3 Add an ACE to allow the Engineering group Read & Write access.

4 Add an ACE to deny the Contractors group any access at all. In the Type column for the Contractors ACE, choose Deny, and click Save.

5 From the Action pop-up menu, choose Sort Access Control List Canonically, and then click Save. Your Secret folder should appear as shown in the figure below.

Use the Effective Permissions Inspector to confirm access for various users to the Secret folder.

1   Select the Secret folder.

2   From the Action pop-up menu, choose Show Effective Permissions Inspector.

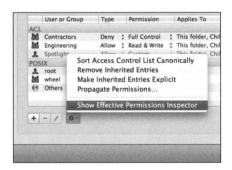

3   If the Users & Groups window is not visible, choose View > Show Users & Groups.

4   Drag Warren Peece into the Effective Permissions Inspector.

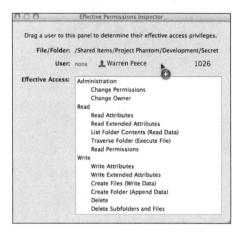

5   Confirm that Warren Peece has a checkmark next to all the Read and Write entries as shown in the figure below.

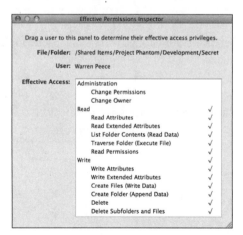

6   Drag Mike Smith into the Effective Permissions Inspector. Mike is a member of the Contractors group, which has a deny ACE for this folder. Confirm that Mike cannot read or write in the folder.

7   Drag Tina Bubbles into the Effective Permissions Inspector. Confirm that Tina
Bubbles cannot read or write in the folder. Even though you did not create an ACE for
Marketing or for Tina Bubbles, her access is set by the POSIX permissions; she isn't the
owner or in the group, so she gets the permissions set for Others, which is "No Access."

8   Close the Effective Permissions Inspector.

Set the Access and Permissions for the Reviewed Folder

Just as you did for the Development folder, you must set the access controls for the Reviewed
folder. You should already have set the POSIX permissions for Others to No Access.

1   In Server Admin, select the Reviewed folder.

2   Click the Groups button in the Users & Groups window, and drag the Marketing
group to the ACL in the Permissions pane.

3   Select the mktg ACE, and set Permission to Read & Write.

4   Drag the Engineering group to the ACL. By default, this gives the Engineering group
read access only.

5   Click Save.

6   From the Action pop-up menu, choose Sort Access Control List Canonically.

The permissions for the Reviewed folder should look like the figure below.

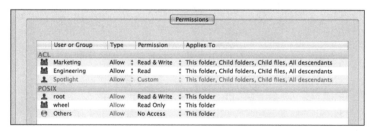

Turn On the AFP Service

Now that you've created a share point, you need to start the AFP service if it's not running already.

1 In Server Admin, click the Add (+) button in the lower-left corner, and choose Add Service from the pop-up menu.

2 Select the AFP checkbox and click Save.

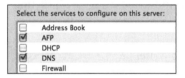

3 If necessary to display the list of services your server offers, click the triangle at the left of your server in the Servers list.

4 Select the AFP service.

5 Click Start AFP.

6 Quit Server Admin.

Watch the Workflow

You have now configured the server with the proper folders and appropriate users and groups. You will now create and edit a few documents and observe how POSIX permissions and ACLs affect various users' access to folders and files during a normal workflow. Follow the numbered steps below to accomplish the following tasks:

▶ Connect to the file service as Warren Peece, and create a document in the Development folder. Create another document in the Secret folder. Confirm that Warren Peece cannot create a document in the Reviewed folder, and then eject the AFP volume.

▶ Connect to the file service as Mike Smith, and edit the document in the Development folder. Confirm that Mike Smith has no access to the Secret folder, and read-only access to the Reviewed folder. Eject the AFP volume.

▶ Connect to the file service as Tina Bubbles. Confirm that Tina Bubbles cannot edit a document directly in the Development folder, but she can copy the file into the Reviewed folder. Eject the AFP volume.

▶ Connect to the file service as Pamela Clarke, who is not in the Engineering, Marketing, or Contractors group. Confirm that she cannot access the Development and Reviewed folders.

1 From the client computer, choose Go > Connect to Server, and enter afp://10.1.17.1.

2 Deselect the checkbox labeled "Remember this password in my keychain."

3 Authenticate as warren (password: warren).

4 Select the Project Phantom share point, and then click OK.

5 Open TextEdit from the /Applications folder.

6 Using TextEdit, type some text into the default Untitled document, and then choose File > Save.

7 Click the disclosure button to reveal more options in the Save As dialog.

8 Click the List View button as shown in this figure:

9   Enter Engineering Spec in the Save As field.

10 Select your server in the Save As sidebar.

11 Click Project Phantom to open that share point, and then click the Development folder.

12 Click Save to save Engineering Spec in the Development folder, and then close the TextEdit document.

13 Create a new TextEdit document, and save it with the filename XYZ in the Secrets folder.

14 Open a new Finder window, select your server in the sidebar, and double-click Project Phantom.

15 In the View control in the toolbar, click the List View button.

16 Click each folder's disclosure triangle to reveal its contents.

You should now have a document named Engineering Spec in the Development folder and one named XYZ in the Secret folder, as shown below.

In the figure below, the "do not edit" icon in the lower-left corner of the Project Phantom window reflects the fact that you do not have write permissions to the root of the Project Phantom share point.

17 Attempt to drag the Engineering Spec document into the Reviewed folder. The Finder should not allow this action, because you are connected to the volume as Warren Peece, and Warren Peece is not a member of the Marketing group, which has write access to the Reviewed folder.

18 Click the Eject button next to your server in the Finder's sidebar to eject the volume as Warren Peece.

19 Mount the Project Phantom volume as Mike Smith (password: `mike`), a member of the Contractors group.

20 Open the Engineering Spec document, add some text, choose File > Save, and then quit TextEdit.

21 In the Finder, confirm that you cannot open the Secret folder.

22 Confirm that you cannot drag the Engineering Spec document into the Reviewed folder.

23 Eject the Project Phantom volume as Mike Smith.

24 Mount the Project Phantom volume as Tina Bubbles (password: `tina`).

25 Confirm that you cannot access the Secret folder.

26 Open the Engineering Spec document, and modify it by adding some text.

27 Confirm that you cannot save the document. You should get a message saying that the document could not be saved.

28 Save the document in the Reviewed folder instead.

Choose File > Save As, change the filename to `Engineering Spec reviewed`, navigate to the Reviewed folder, and click Save.

29 Quit TextEdit.

30 Eject the Project Phantom volume as Tina Bubbles.

31 Mount the Project Phantom volume as Warren Peece (password: `warren`).

32 Confirm that you cannot save any changes to the "Engineering Spec reviewed" document in the Reviewed folder.

33 Eject the Project Phantom volume as Warren Peece.

34 Mount the Project Phantom volume as Pamela Clarke (password: `pamela`).

35 Confirm that you cannot access either folder in the Project Phantom share point.

36 Eject the Project Phantom volume as Pamela Clarke.

Clean Up Folders on the Server

You have created the Project Phantom folder and viewed how the workflow can occur when documents are moved from folder to folder. You can now remove the folder from the server.

1 On your client computer, open Server Admin and connect to your server.

2 Click File Sharing in the toolbar, and then click Share Points.

3 Select the Project Phantom share point, click the Unshare button in the upper-right corner, and click Save.

4 Choose Server > Share Server's Screen.

5 Authenticate as ladmin for screen sharing.

6 If you are not already logged in as ladmin at your server, log in as ladmin (password: ladmin).

7 With the Finder, drag the Project Phantom folder to the Trash, and then choose Finder > Empty Trash.

Authenticate as ladmin when prompted to do so.

8 Log out as ladmin on your server.

Controlling Access to Your Server

In addition to file-system ACLs, Mac OS X Server also supports service ACLs, or SACLs, which are separate from file-system ACLs in implementation and purpose, despite the similar name. Service ACLs enable you to define who has access to specific services on Mac OS X Server. You could use SACLs to allow all users to log in via AFP connections, but restrict Secure Shell (SSH) connections to administrators.

SACLs are stored simply through membership in a specially named group. For example, the SSH SACL is controlled by membership in the group named com.apple.access_ssh. Once you configure SACLs, it's possible that you may see similarly named groups on your system. In most circumstances, you should leave those groups alone and instead use the Server Admin application to define SACLs as explained in the specific service chapters throughout this book. To modify SACLs, you need to have administrative rights on the server.

Configuring Service ACLs

As with files, you can configure SACLs for individual users, groups, or a mix of both. Similarly, you may find that long-term administration will be easier if you assign SACLs based on organizational roles assigned to groups rather than to individual people. This will make it much easier when there are changes within your organization, because you will need to change only group membership rather than individual file and service permissions for each person.

1   Make sure you do not have any AFP volumes mounted. If your server's entry in the Finder's sidebar displays an Eject button, click that button.

2   Open Server Admin and connect as ladmin.

3   Select your server in the left column.

4   Click Access in the toolbar.

5   Select "For selected services below," and select AFP.

6   Select "Allow only users and groups below."

7   Click the Add (+) button near the bottom to open the Users & Groups window.

8 Click Groups in the Users & Groups window.

9 Select the Marketing group, and drag it into the list of allowed users and groups.

10 Click Save.

11 In the Finder, try making an AFP connection to your server as Mike Smith (password: `mike`).

Because Mike Smith is not in the Marketing group, you should see a failure when try-ing to authenticate. This error will look like a normal password failure, even if you type the password correctly.

12 Back in Server Admin, add the Engineering group to the list of allowed users and groups.

13 Click Save.

14 Try connecting to your server as Mike Smith (password: `mike`) again.

Because Mike Smith is in the Contractors group, and the Contractors group is in the Engineering group, you should be presented with a list of available share points this time.

15 Click Cancel to dismiss the list of available share points, or eject the volume if you selected a share point.

Granting Different Access for Different Services

In many cases, you may want to offer different groups different access to the server. For example, you may want to give most of your groups access to the AFP service, while giving only the Engineering and Administrators groups access to the SSH service.

1   In Server Admin, click Access, click Services, and select the SSH service.

2   Drag the Engineering group and the Administrators group into the list of allowed users and groups.

3   Click Save.

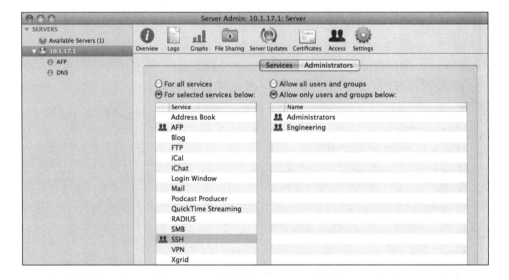

You'll notice that when you're specifying different access for specific services that services with controlled access have an icon next to their names, while the other services don't have an icon. If a service isn't listed as having access restricted to a list of users, that service is open to everyone. You may want to restrict those other services as a security measure, unless you truly do want them open to everyone.

Limiting Administration Capabilities

There are often situations where you want to grant a group of users only partial administration abilities. These are cases where the roles of your organization might require a group of users to be able to do something that requires administrator privileges, but you don't feel comfortable granting full administrator rights to those users. An example of this situation may be in a school environment. You may have a group of students responsible for monitoring your services. Another group may be responsible for managing the access control of your Podcast Producer users and the list of allowed computers for your NetBoot service. Using the limited administrator features, you can configure access as described in the following steps while not granting access to the entire server.

1   Open the Server Admin application.

2   Click the name of your server in the left column.

3   Click Access in the toolbar.

4   Click Administrators.

5   Click the Add (+) button to open the Users & Groups window.

6   Drag the Contractors group into the list of users allowed to administer or monitor.

7   Click Save.

You'll notice that the permission defaults to Monitor. This means that in addition to anyone defined as an administrator in Workgroup Manager, anyone in the Contractors group can monitor, but not change, all the services on your server.

You may also want to grant a different group of users administrative rights.

8   Drag the Engineering group into the list of users allowed to administer or monitor.

9   Change the pop-up menu option next to the Engineering group from Monitor to Administer.

10   Click Save.

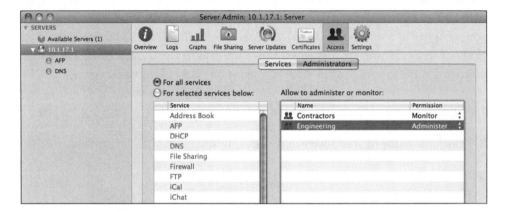

This will allow members of the Engineering group access to make changes to any of the services as well as keep the ability for any member of the Contractors group to monitor all the services. In many cases, you will find that even that access is too broad, though, and you may want to restrict access to only certain services for those groups.

11   Select "For selected services below."

12   Select Firewall.

13   Drag the Contractors group to the list of users allowed to administer or monitor.

14   Drag the Engineering group to the list of users allowed to administer or monitor.

15   In the Permission pop-up next to Engineering, change Permission to Administer.

16 Click Save.

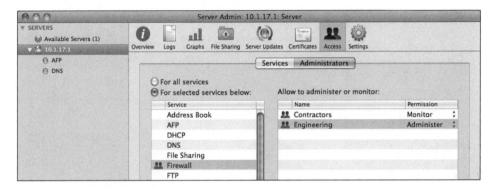

This configuration will grant only contractors extra access to monitor the Firewall service (such as logs), and will grant members of the Engineering group access to make changes to the firewall configuration. Any other service will require the user to be a total server administrator.

Clean Up Authorization on Your Server

For the rest of this book, we'll want the server returned to a state where all the users can connect and only administrators have administrative access. Follow these steps to open your server access back up to everyone:

1 Open Server Admin.

2 Click Access.

3 Click Services.

4 Select "For all services."

5 Select "Allow all users and groups."

6 Ensure that the list of allowed users and groups is empty. If there are any entries, select them and click the Remove (–) button.

7   Click Save.

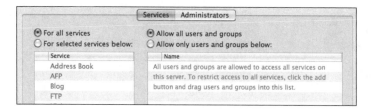

8   Click Administrators.

9   Select "For all services."

10   Ensure that the list of users and groups is empty. If there are any entries, select them and click the Remove (–) button.

11   Click Save.

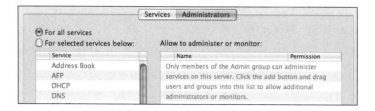

Troubleshooting

File-system ACLs can be very confusing and can get out of hand very quickly. Keep it simple by managing permissions by groups rather than by individuals where possible. If someone doesn't have the access to a file or folder that you think they should have, be sure to use the Effective Permissions Inspector in Server Admin to evaluate the permissions they have on an object. When crafting an ACL, choose Sort Access Control List Canonically to have Mac OS X Server automatically sort the ACEs in a way that is logical and consistent. For service ACLs, it can be somewhat confusing if users are trying to connect to a service for which they don't have permission. Despite the fact that they have typed their password correctly, they may see an error message indicating that they haven't. It may be useful to have users try to authenticate to a service that they do have access to so you can confirm that their password isn't the problem.

What You've Learned

▶ Authentication gets a user into the server. Authorization determines what the user can do after getting in.

▶ User accounts for Mac OS X Server are created in Workgroup Manager. You can configure two types of accounts with Workgroup Manager: user and administrator. An administrator account is the same as a user account except it has the authority to administer the server.

▶ Group accounts enable administrators to quickly assign a set of permissions to multiple users. You create and manage group accounts in Workgroup Manager. You can add users to groups and group membership to user accounts.

▶ You use Server Admin to create share points and to assign permissions to the share points.

▶ Mac OS X Server includes support for access control lists (ACLs), which provide a higher granularity for setting permissions. These ACLs are compatible with ACLs from the Windows world and work in addition to the standard POSIX (UNIX) permissions found on Mac OS X.

▶ Mac OS X Server includes support for service ACLs (SACLs), which limit access for certain services to specified users or groups.

▶ Mac OS X Server allows you to assign specific administrative permissions for services (administer or monitor) to users and groups, without adding them to the admin group.

References

The following documents provide more information about accounts, POSIX permissions, ACLs, and SACLS with Mac OS X Server. All these and more are available at http://www.apple.com/server/macosx/resources/.

Mac OS X Server Administration Guides

File Server Administration

User Management

Upgrading and Migrating

Apple Knowledge Base Documents

You can check for new and updated Knowledge Base documents at http://www.apple.com/support/.

Chapter Review

1. Describe the difference between authentication and authorization, and give an example of each.

2. What is the difference between user and administrator accounts on both Mac OS X and Mac OS X Server?

3. What application can you use to configure Mac OS X Server user and group settings?

4. What tool can you use to change ownership and permissions on Mac OS X?

5. What application can you use to configure share points for Mac OS X Server?

6. What application can you use to configure permissions for folders, including POSIX ownership and permissions as well as ACLs?

7. What is the difference between service ACLs and limited administrator settings?

Answers

1. Authentication is the process by which the system requires you to provide information before it allows you to access a specific account. An example is entering a name and password while connecting to an Apple file server. Authorization refers to the process by which permissions are used to regulate a user's access to specific resources, such as files and share points, once the user has been successfully authenticated.

2. User accounts provide basic access to a computer or server, whereas administrator accounts allow a person to administer the computer. On Mac OS X, an administrator account is typically used for changing settings or adding new software. On Mac OS X Server, an administrator account is typically used for changing settings on the server computer itself, usually through Server Preferences, Server Admin, or Workgroup Manager.

3. You can use Server Preferences or Workgroup Manager to configure Mac OS X Server user and group settings.

4. You can use Server Preferences or Get Info in the Finder to change ownership and permissions on Mac OS X.

5. You can use Server Preferences or Server Admin to configure share points for Mac OS X Server.

6. You can use Server Admin to configure permissions for folders, including POSIX ownership and permissions as well as ACLs.

7. Service ACLs determine which users are allowed to utilize a given service, whereas limited administrator settings control which nonadministrative users can monitor or change a service.

3

Time   This chapter takes approximately four hours to complete.

Goals   Understand the four Open Directory server roles you can configure on
Mac OS X Server

Configure Mac OS X Server as an Open Directory server with Server
Assistant, Server Preferences, and Server Admin

Use the Accounts preference to bind a Mac OS X computer to an
Open Directory server

Locate and identify Open Directory–related log files

Examine the contents of an Open Directory archive and restore
those contents

Describe authentication types

Understand basic Kerberos infrastructure

Chapter **3**

Using Open Directory

This chapter describes how using a directory service can help you manage users and resources on your network. You will learn about the features of Apple's Open Directory services and how these services can be integrated with other directory services in a mixed environment. You will also learn how to set up and manage directories and user accounts with Server Preferences, Server Admin, and Workgroup Manager. Finally, you will become familiar with common Open Directory services issues and learn how to resolve them.

Open Directory is extremely versatile when dealing with a variety of other directory services, such as Active Directory, eDirectory, and Network Information Service (NIS). This chapter deals with a Mac OS X Server–to–Mac OS X directory service scenario; the book *Mac OS X Directory Services v10.6* has more information about mixed-platform directory service scenarios.

If you have two extra Mac OS X Server computers, you can follow the exercises to use one as an Open Directory replica and the other as a server connected to the Open Directory replica. If you do not have extra servers, simply read through those exercises.

Introducing Directory Services Concepts

Giving a user multiple user accounts on different computers can cause problems. For instance, if each computer in a network has its own authentication database, a user might have to remember a different password for each computer. Even if you assign the user the same password on every computer, the information can become inconsistent over time, because the user may change a password in one location but forget to do so in another. You can solve this problem by using a single source of identification and authentication information.

Directory services provide this central repository for information about the computers, applications, and users in an organization. With directory services, you can maintain consistent information about all the users—such as their names, passwords, and preferences—as well as about printers and other network resources. You can maintain this information in a single location rather than on individual computers.

For example, once you *bind* Mac OS X computers to an Open Directory service (to bind is to configure one computer to use the directory services offered by another), users can freely log in to any bound Mac OS X computer and have their session managed based on who they are, what group they belong to, what computer they logged in at, and what computer group the computer belongs to. Using a shared directory service also permits a user's home folder to be located on another server and to be mounted automatically on whatever computer the user logs in to, as long as that computer is bound to the shared directory.

What Is Open Directory?

Open Directory is the extensible directory-services architecture that is built into Mac OS X and Mac OS X Server. Open Directory acts as an intermediary between directories (which store information about users and resources) and the applications and system software processes that want to use the information.

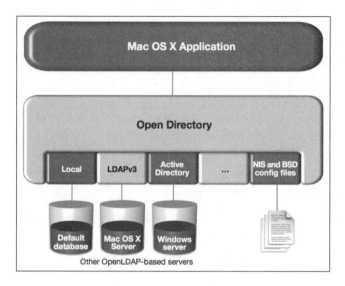

The Open Directory service is actually a set of services on Mac OS X Server that provide identification, authentication, and client management.

Many services on Mac OS X require information from Open Directory services to function. Open Directory services can securely store and validate the passwords of users who want to log in to client computers on your network or use other network resources that require authentication. You can also use Open Directory services to enforce policies such as password expiration and minimum length and to manage user preferences.

You can use Open Directory services to provide authentication to Windows users for login, file services, print service, and other Windows services that Mac OS X Server provides. Open Directory uses Samba 3, which allows an Open Directory server to function as a Windows primary domain controller (PDC) or backup domain controller (BDC).

Overview of Open Directory Service Components

Open Directory provides a centralized source for identification and authentication. For identification, Open Directory uses OpenLDAP, an open source implementation of the Lightweight Directory Access Protocol (LDAP), a standard protocol used for accessing directory service data. Open Directory uses LDAPv3 to provide read and write access to the directory data.

> **MORE INFO** ▶ While LDAP was used in Mac OS X Server v10.3 and v10.4 for its shared database, earlier versions of Mac OS X and Mac OS X Server used the NetInfo system-configuration database service for local and shared directory services. Starting with Mac OS X v10.5, NetInfo has been replaced with flat (text) files.

The Open Directory service leverages other open source technologies, such as Kerberos and LDAP, and combines them with powerful server-administration tools to deliver robust directory and authentication services that are easy to set up and manage. Because there are no per-seat or per-user license fees, Open Directory can scale to the needs of an organization without adding high costs to an IT budget.

After you bind a Mac OS X computer to use an Open Directory server, the computer running Mac OS X or Mac OS X Server automatically gets access to network resources, including user authentication services, network home folders, share points, and preferences.

Confirming DNS Records

In order to provide the full range of Open Directory services, your Mac OS X server must have forward and reverse DNS records available before you create an Open Directory master. Additionally, the computer you use with Server Admin must also have a DNS record available for its IP address.

Confirming DNS Records for Mac OS X Server

You can use Mac OS X Server's changeip command to make changes to your server's host name or IP address or to confirm that your server's host name and primary IP address match the available DNS records. Before making a server an Open Directory master or replica, you should use the changeip command to confirm that your server's host name and primary IP address have appropriate DNS records available.

If you set up Mac OS X Server in an environment *with* a DNS record available for the IP address you assigned to your server during setup, Server Assistant does not set up or start the DNS service. However, if you set up Mac OS X Server in an environment *without* a DNS record available for the IP address you assigned to your server during setup, Server Assistant creates the appropriate DNS zones and records for its host name and IP address, and then starts the DNS service.

NOTE ▶ See the section "Preparing DNS Records" at the end of this chapter if your environment does not have DNS records for the computers you will use in the exercises for this chapter, and you would like to configure your server to provide the appropriate DNS records.

The exercises in this book assume that your Mac OS X administrative computer has access to the DNS records of your Mac OS X servers, and the exercise steps instruct you to use the fully qualified domain names (FQDNs) of your servers (like server17.pretendco.com). You can use your servers' Bonjour names (for example, Server-17.local), but it is a good idea to always use the FQDN with the server tools; if there are problems with the availability of DNS records, you are more likely to notice them while using the tools and to take the time to address and resolve the DNS issues before continuing.

MORE INFO ▶ See Chapter 7, "Network Configuration," in the book *Apple Training Series: Mac OS X Support Essentials v10.6* for information on using Network Utility to confirm DNS records.

Use changeip to confirm that your server has appropriate DNS records available:

1   On your client computer, open Server Admin, connect to your server (server17.pretendco.com) as ladmin, select your server in the source list, and choose Server > Share Server's Screen.

2   Authenticate as ladmin to share the screen of your server.

3   At the login window of your server, log in as ladmin (password: ladmin).

4   Open Terminal (in /Applications/Utilities).

5   Enter the command sudo changeip -checkhostname and press Return.

6 Enter your password (ladmin) if necessary.

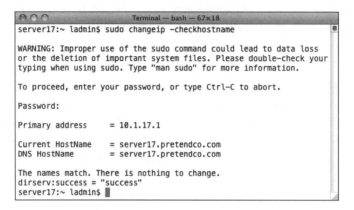

```
server17:~ ladmin$ sudo changeip -checkhostname

WARNING: Improper use of the sudo command could lead to data loss
or the deletion of important system files. Please double-check your
typing when using sudo. Type "man sudo" for more information.

To proceed, enter your password, or type Ctrl-C to abort.

Password:

Primary address     = 10.1.17.1

Current HostName    = server17.pretendco.com
DNS HostName        = server17.pretendco.com

The names match. There is nothing to change.
dirserv:success = "success"
server17:~ ladmin$
```

7 Confirm that the result of the changeip command is "The names match. There is nothing to change." If you get any other result, see the section "Preparing DNS Records" at the end of this chapter.

8 On your Mac OS X server, quit Terminal.

9 On your Mac OS X computer, quit screen sharing.

Configuring Open Directory Services

There are a number of ways to configure Mac OS X Server to offer Open Directory services. How do you choose which method to use? It depends on your needs. The following three sections address each tool you can use to configure your Mac OS X server to provide Open Directory services:

▶ Server Assistant

▶ Server Preferences

▶ Server Admin

Configuring Open Directory Services with Server Assistant

If you want Mac OS X Server to provide directory services as well as a standard set of collaboration services, you may decide to have Server Assistant configure your Open Directory master automatically during your initial setup of Mac OS X Server. If you choose "Create Users and Groups" or "Import Users and Groups," Server Assistant configures your shared directory for you. You don't choose the Directory Administrator short name, UID, or even password; Server Assistant uses the short name diradmin, the UID 1000, and the password that you specified for your initial Local Administrator account.

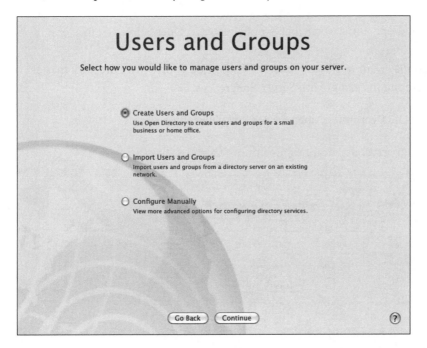

If you choose "Import Users and Groups," in addition to configuring your Mac OS X server as an Open Directory master, Server Assistant prompts you to specify another directory service to bind to.

If you choose "Configure Manually," you have the option of having Server Assistant set up an Open Directory master. You have the ability to specify the name, short name, and UID of the directory administrator, but the password for the Directory Administrator user account will be the password you assign to the first administrator account you define in Server Assistant.

Configuring Open Directory Services with Server Preferences

If you chose "Configure Manually" when using Server Assistant during your initial setup of Mac OS X Server, you can use Server Preferences to quickly set up your Mac OS X server as an Open Directory master.

Like Server Assistant's "Create Users and Groups" and "Import Users and Groups," Server Preferences uses the following for the Directory Administrator user account: the short name diradmin, UID 1000, and the password of the Local Administrator account you use to authenticate.

This exercise is valid only for a server that is not already an Open Directory master.

NOTE ▸ You may want to skip this exercise and set up your Open Directory master with Server Admin instead of with Server Preferences.

1   On your Mac OS X computer, open Server Preferences.

2   Connect to your server as Local Administrator (`ladmin`).

3   Click Users.

4   Because Server Preferences is designed to manage *network* accounts, not *local* accounts, you see a message that this server is not set up to manage users and groups.

Do *not* click Set Up if want to use Server Admin to set up your server as an Open Directory master. Server Admin gives you more flexibility—for instance, you can choose the password to assign to the Directory Administrator user account.

If you do want to use Server Preferences to set up an Open Directory master, click Set Up to set up your server as an Open Directory master; you will then skip the exercise of setting up an Open Directory master with Server Admin.

5   Click OK when asked to confirm that you are sure you want to host users and groups on this server.

Your server is now an Open Directory master. Server Preferences displays the empty list of network user accounts.

6   Quit Server Preferences.

Configuring Open Directory Services with Server Admin

If you require more options than Server Assistant and Server Preferences offer, you should use Server Admin to configure Mac OS X Server to provide Open Directory services. You can set up Mac OS X Server's Open Directory services in four ways using Server Admin:

▶ As a standalone server—The server does not provide directory information to other computers or get directory information from an existing system. The local directory can't be shared.

▶ As a server connected to a directory system—You can set up the server to provide services that require user accounts and authentication, such as file and mail services, but use accounts that are set up on another server.

▶ As an Open Directory replica—A server hosts a replicated version of a directory. The replica is synchronized with the master periodically.

▶ As an Open Directory master—A server can provide directory information and authentication information to other systems.

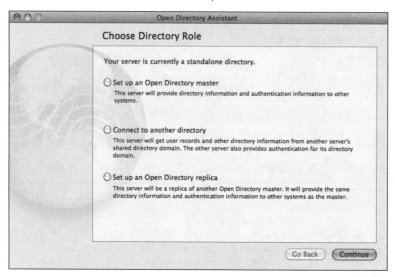

As you plan directory services for your network, consider the need to share user and resource information among multiple Mac OS X computers. If the need is low, little directory planning is necessary; everything can be accessed from a local server directory. However, if you want to share information among computers, you need to set up at least one Open Directory server (an Open Directory master). If you want to provide high avail-ability of directory services, you should set up at least one additional Mac OS X server to be an Open Directory replica.

Configuring an Open Directory Master with Server Admin

Instead of binding Mac OS X Server to another server for directory services, you can set it up to host a shared LDAP directory, Password Server, and Kerberos Key Distribution Center (KDC), providing directory information and authentication services to other systems. Use the following steps with Server Admin to configure your server to be an Open Directory master. If you already configured an Open Directory master with Server Assistant or Server Preferences, simply read through these steps.

In order for Server Admin to consistently display your DNS name rather than your IP address throughout the process of setting up an Open Directory master, use the DNS name rather than the IP address when using Server Admin.

1   On your Mac OS X computer, open Server Admin and connect to your server (server17.pretendco.com) as ladmin (password: `ladmin`).

2   If Open Directory does not appear in the list of services, click the Add (+) button and choose Add Service from the pop-up menu.

3   In the list of available services, select the Open Directory checkbox and click Save.

4   Select the Open Directory service, and then click Settings.

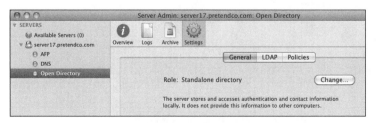

5   Click Change to open Open Directory Assistant.

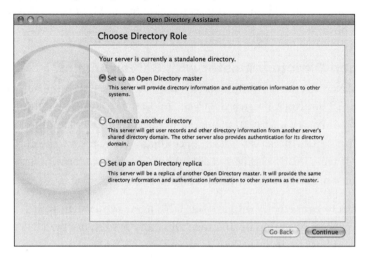

6   Select "Set up an Open Directory master," and click Continue.

7   When setting up the new Directory Administrator account, you have the ability to change the name, short name, and user ID. For this exercise, leave the defaults.

For this exercise, use the password diradmin and click Continue.

Of course, you should use a secure password in a production environment.

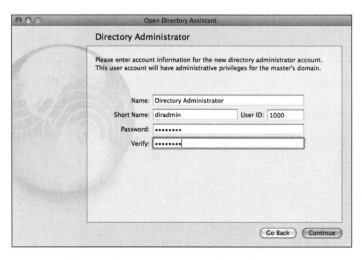

8 Verify that the automatically generated values for the Kerberos Realm and the LDAP Search Base fields match those in the following figure.

These values are somewhat arbitrary, but they are based on your server's host name, and you should leave them at the suggested defaults unless you have a compelling reason to do otherwise. Do not change these values for this exercise.

If either field references "local," quit Open Directory Assistant and recheck your DNS records.

Open Directory Assistant generates a Kerberos realm and an LDAP search base from your server's DNS name. You are allowed to change these values, but it keeps things predictable if you leave them at their defaults.

Click Continue to accept these values.

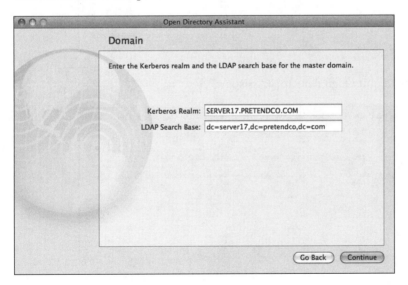

9 Click Continue at the Confirm Settings window.

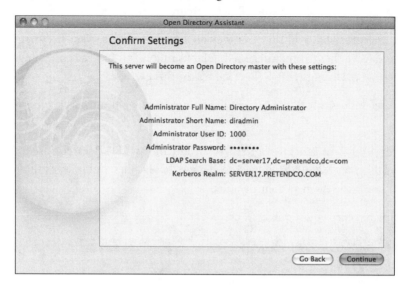

10 Click Done to quit Open Directory Assistant.

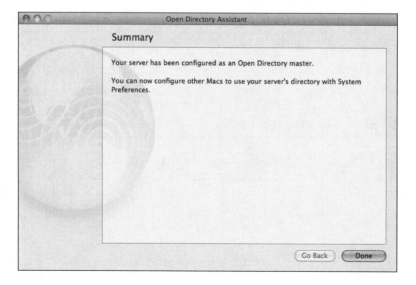

11 Click Overview in the toolbar. You should see that the three services—LDAP Server, Password Server, and Kerberos—are running.

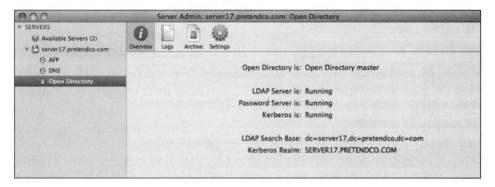

Once you have set up your server to be an Open Directory master, you can configure other computers on your network to access the server's directory services.

> **NOTE** ▶ Once you have added accounts to the Open Directory shared domain on your server, do not change the Open Directory role setting. If you do, you will lose all your account information and orphan your users' data.

To recap, you began with a local database for your local users. That database still exists. The administrator of that database is ladmin. You have now created a secondary, shared LDAP database. The administrator of that database is (by default) diradmin. Each database is separate, and managing either one requires different authentication. You have also created a Password Server database to store LDAP user passwords, as well as a Kerberos Key Distribution Center (KDC). You will learn about those later in this chapter.

Configuring an Open Directory Replica

If you already have an Open Directory master server set up, you can configure at least one more Mac OS X server as a directory *replica* to provide the same directory information and authentication information as the master. The replica server hosts a copy of the master's LDAP directory, its Password Server authentication database, and its Kerberos KDC. When authentication data is transferred from the master to any replica, that data is encrypted as it is copied over.

You can use replicas to scale your directory infrastructure and improve search-and-retrieval time on distributed networks, and to provide high availability of Open Directory services. Replication also protects against network outages, because client systems can use any replica in your organization.

Like Mac OS X Server v10.5, v10.6 lets you create nested replicas—that is, replicas of replicas. One master can have up to 32 replicas, and those replicas can have 32 replicas each; one master plus 32 replicas plus 32 × 32 replicas of those replicas totals 1057 Open Directory servers for a single Open Directory domain. Nesting replicas is accomplished by joining one replica to your Open Directory master, and then joining other replicas to that first replica.

The following figure has one Open Directory master and one replica that is also a *relay*, a replica that in turn has at least one replica. There are also three replicas that are simply replicas in the figure.

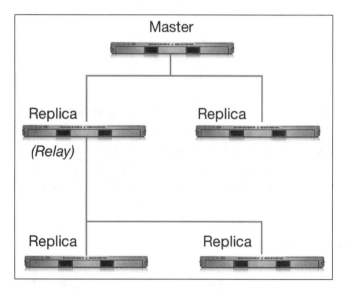

Configure Your Server to Host a Replica of an Open Directory Master

In this section you will step through the process of hosting a replica of your Mac OS X server Open Directory master. If you have only one Mac OS X server and one Mac OS X client, you can read through this exercise but not perform the steps. This exercise assumes that you have another Mac OS X server at 10.1.18.1 that you want to configure as a replica of 10.1.17.1, and that forward and reverse DNS records are available for both servers, available to your Mac OS X computer and both servers.

> **NOTE ▸** You can set up a second server to use as an Open Directory replica by following the same setup instructions as in Chapter 1, "Installing and Configuring Mac OS X Server," except you should use 10.1.18.1 as the IP address and Server 18 as the computer name.
>
> See the section "Preparing DNS Records" at the end of this chapter to set up your Server 17 to host DNS records for the host name server18.pretendco.com and the IP address 10.1.18.1.

Use the following steps to confirm the DNS records for the server that you will promote to an Open Directory replica:

1 On your client computer, open Server Admin, connect to your server (server18.pretendco.com) as ladmin, select your server in the source list, and choose Server > Share Server's Screen.

2 Authenticate as ladmin to share the screen of your server.

3 At the login window of your server, log in as ladmin (password: `ladmin`).

4 Open Terminal (in /Applications/Utilities).

5 Enter the command `sudo changeip -checkhostname` and press Return.

6 Enter your password (`ladmin`) if necessary.

7 Confirm that the result of the `changeip` command is "The names match. There is nothing to change." If you get any other result, see the section "Preparing DNS Records" at the end of this chapter.

8   On your Mac OS X server, quit Terminal.

9   On your Mac OS X computer, quit screen sharing.

Use the following steps to promote your Mac OS X server to an Open Directory replica:

1   On your Mac OS X computer, open Server Admin and connect to server18.pretendco. com as ladmin (password: ladmin).

2   Add the Open Directory service to the list of services. Select Open Directory.

3   Click Settings in the toolbar, click General, and click the Change button to open Open Directory Assistant, just as you did when you created an Open Directory master.

> **NOTE ▸** You can't create a replica if you do not have an Open Directory master on your network.

> If this server is already an Open Directory master, the current LDAP database will be emptied of all its contents.

4   Once Open Directory Assistant opens, select "Set up an Open Directory replica" in the list and click Continue.

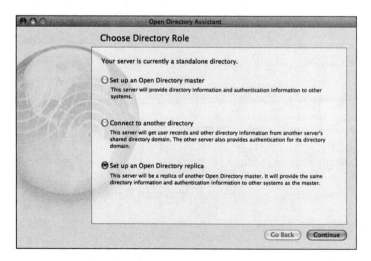

5 Configure the replica with the following parameters. Be sure to use the DNS name of the Open Directory master (as opposed to the IP address or Bonjour name).

▶ IP address or FQDN of the Open Directory master: `server17.pretendco.com`

▶ Root password on Open Directory master: `ladmin`

▶ Domain administrator's short name: `diradmin`

▶ Domain administrator's password: `diradmin`

NOTE ▶ It is important that you know the root password of the Open Directory master, because initial information is passed using this account.

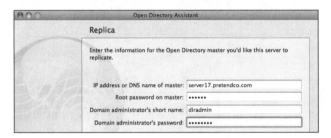

6 Click Continue.

7 Click Continue at the Confirm Settings window.

8 Click Done at the Summary window.

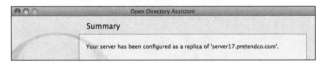

9   In Server Admin, note that the Replica Status pane is empty. This is because it lists *servers that are a replica of this server.*

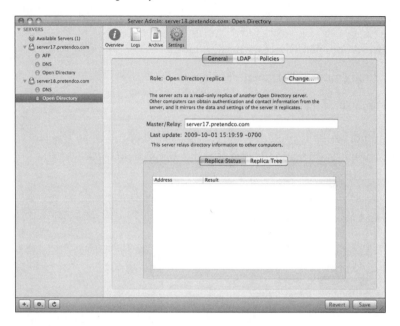

10   Click Replica Tree. Note that this reflects the fact that server17.pretendco.com is an Open Directory master and server18.pretendco.com is an Open Directory replica of server17.pretendco.com.

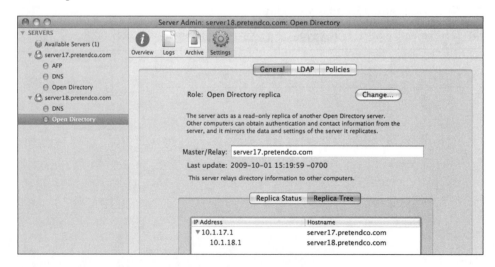

11 In Server Admin click Overview.

Note that your server is now an Open Directory replica and offers all three services: LDAP Server, Password Server, and Kerberos.

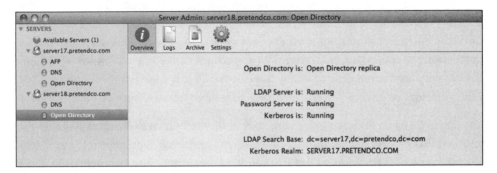

NOTE ▶ When you use Workgroup Manager to edit the shared directory, it is displayed as /LDAPv3/127.0.0.1 regardless of the address of the server that you connect to with Workgroup Manager.

Once you have set up your server to be an Open Directory replica, other computers can connect to it as needed automatically. The Open Directory master will update replicas automatically.

Once a single replica has been established, other Mac OS X servers can be set up as replicas of replicas. This increases the redundancy and potentially improves the performance of the entire Open Directory structure.

TIP Because replication uses timestamps, it is best to use NTP to synchronize the clocks on all Open Directory masters, replicas, and servers using existing masters. You use Server Admin to enable NTP services as well as to specify an NTP server to use.

Connecting Mac OS X Server to an Existing Open Directory Service

If you intend to set up multiple servers, it would be extremely inefficient to populate each server with the same user accounts. Instead, you can bind your Mac OS X server to another directory system. In this role, the server gets authentication, user information, and other directory information from some other server's directory service. This way, users can authenticate to your Mac OS X server with an account defined in your server's local directory, or with an account defined in any directory node that your server is bound to. The other directory node could be an Open Directory or an Active Directory directory service.

You can use System Preferences or Directory Utility to bind your Mac OS X server to another directory service. In order to use System Preferences, you need to be able to log in at the server's login window, but you can use Directory Utility remotely from another Mac OS X or Mac OS X Server computer.

Binding with System Preferences

You can configure your server to obtain directory services from an existing Open Directory server just like you would for a Mac OS X computer: Use System Preferences. This exercise assumes:

▶ You have a replica configured at 10.1.18.1 from the previous exercise.

▶ You have a third server that you set up with the same instructions that you used in Chapter 1, "Installing and Configuring Mac OS X Server," except you used 10.1.19.1 as the IP address and Server 19 as the computer name.

▶ You will configure a standalone Mac OS X server at 10.1.19.1 to bind to the replica at 10.1.18.1.

▶ You have forward and reverse DNS records available for these servers.

If you do not meet these requirements, you can read through this exercise but not complete it.

1   On your Mac OS X computer, open Server Admin, connect to the server you want to bind, and authenticate as ladmin (password: ladmin).

2   In the server list, select the server you want to bind.

3 Choose Server > Share Server's Screen.

4 Authenticate as ladmin for screen sharing.

5 On your Mac OS X server, open System Preferences and open the Accounts preference.

6 Click Login Options.

7 Click Join.

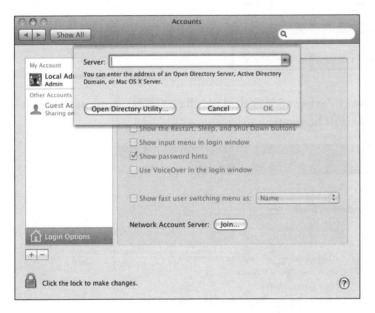

8 Enter the DNS name or IP address of an Open Directory server (server18.pretendco.com), and click OK.

9 Authenticate as a local administrator when prompted.

10 In order to create a computer account and join the Kerberos realm, enter a network user's credentials. At this time, the only network user is Directory Administrator, so enter diradmin for the user name and diradmin for the password.

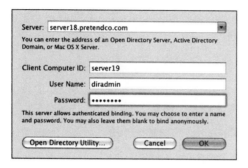

11 Note that the Network Account Server field now has the DNS name of the Open Directory server you just bound to.

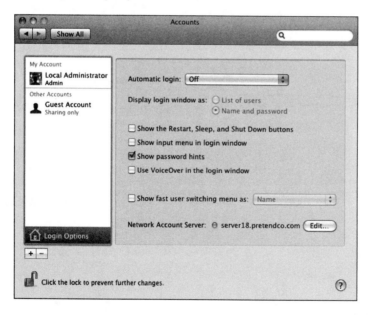

12 Close the Accounts preference.

13 Log out as ladmin on Server 19.

14 On your Mac OS X computer, quit screen sharing.

Confirming the Bind with Directory Utility

You can still use Directory Utility instead of System Preferences; in fact, the Accounts preference offers a shortcut to Directory Utility, which now is located in /System/Library/ CoreServices. Directory Utility offers a little more control than the Join button of the Accounts preference, and it allows you to control a remote computer from Mac OS X or Mac OS X Server, so you do not need to rely on screen sharing being available.

Use the following exercise to open Directory Utility on Mac OS X, but connect to Mac OS X Server and confirm the settings for directory use.

This exercise assumes that you have a replica at 10.1.18.1, that you are configuring a standalone Mac OS X server at 10.1.19.1 to bind to the replica at 10.1.18.1, and that you have forward and reverse DNS records available for these servers. If you have only one Mac OS X server and one Mac OS X client computer, you can read through this exercise but not complete it.

1   On your Mac OS X computer, open Server Admin, connect to server19.pretendco.com, and authenticate as ladmin (password: `ladmin`).

2   In the server list, select server19.pretendco.com, and click the disclosure triangle to display the list of offered services.

3   If Open Directory does not appear in the list of services, click the Add (+) button and choose Add Service from the pop-up menu. In the list of available services, select the Open Directory checkbox and click Save.

4   Select the Open Directory service for server19.pretendco.com.

5   Click Settings, and then click General.

Server Admin states that the role is "Connected to another directory."

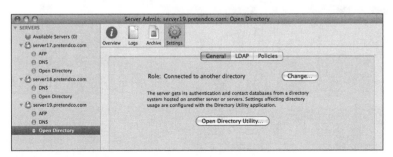

6   You will use Directory Utility to confirm the bind settings.

Click Open Directory Utility.

7   You need to use Directory Utility to connect to your server and configure the directory services that your server uses.

Choose File > Connect.

8   Enter the following information to authenticate to the remote server:

Address: server19.pretendco.com

User Name: ladmin

Password: ladmin

9   Click Services in the toolbar.

10 Select LDAPv3.

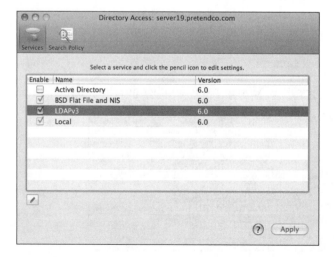

11 Click the Edit button (a pencil) to inspect the settings.

12 Note that the configuration name is based on the server's DNS name. The DNS name of the server that you bound to is listed in the middle column.

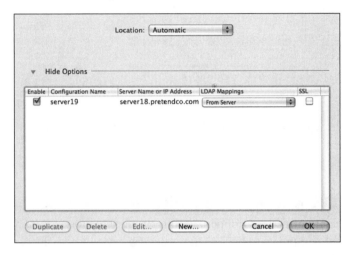

13 Click OK to dismiss the LDAP server listing.

14 Click Search Policy in the toolbar.

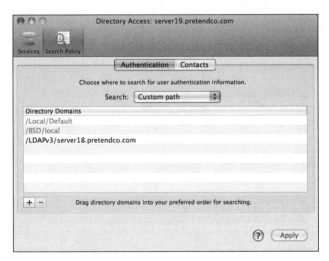

15 Confirm that the Open Directory server is listed. It will be listed starting with /LDAPv3/, followed by its IP address or DNS name.

16 Quit Directory Utility. If prompted, do not save any changes—you simply used Directory Utility to inspect settings.

17 Quit Server Admin.

You have now used Directory Utility from Mac OS X to connect to a remote server and inspect settings remotely.

If you are simply reading through the exercises for lack of extra servers, you should resume doing the exercises at this point.

Connecting Mac OS X to an Open Directory Service

Once you have an Open Directory master (and perhaps one or more replicas) set up, you must also configure the *client* computers to bind to the directory service. On each client computer, you use System Preferences to specify a server that hosts an Open Directory service, or use Directory Utility to create an LDAP configuration that has the address and search path for an Open Directory server.

You will now configure your Mac OS X computer to use authentication services from your Mac OS X server. You already configured a shared directory, and your Mac OS X computers must be able to see the shared directory in order to authenticate against it. Any client bound to the Open Directory service can authenticate users using the data in the shared directory.

Bind Mac OS X to Your Open Directory Service

In order for your Mac OS X computer to take advantage of your server's Open Directory services, you need to bind it to an Open Directory server. In an environment with many Open Directory replicas, you may consider binding Mac OS X to a replica, which leaves the Open Directory master free to communicate with the replicas.

You can use the Accounts preference, or you can use Directory Utility if you need more-advanced binding options.

Use the Accounts Preference to Bind

In the following steps, you will use System Preferences to bind your Mac OS X computer to your Open Directory master. You bind Mac OS X in a way similar to the way you bound Mac OS X Server: with the Accounts preference. However, because your Mac OS X computer will not be offering services that will allow users to use Kerberos for authentication, you may not be prompted to provide authentication to configure trusted binding.

1 On your Mac OS X computer, open System Preferences and open the Accounts preference.

2 Click Login Options.

3 Click Join.

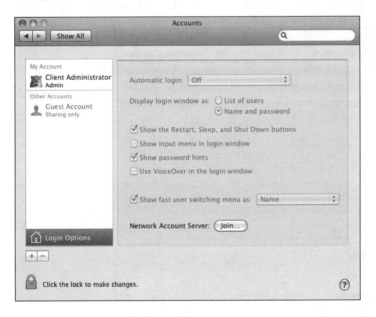

4 Enter the FQDN of your Open Directory replica, server18.pretendco.com (if you have only an Open Directory master, use this instead: server17.pretendco.com), and then click OK.

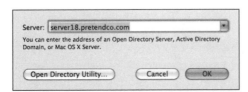

5 Authenticate as a local administrator when prompted (user name: Client Administrator and password: `cadmin`).

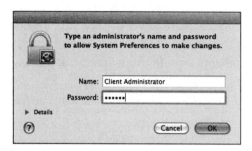

6 Confirm that the Login Options pane displays your Open Directory server.

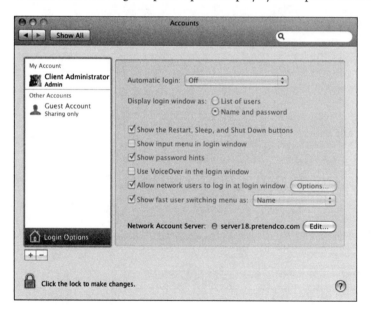

7 Close the Accounts preference.

Managing Network User Accounts

Once you have created shared LDAP directories, you need to populate them with information. User account information is probably the most important type of information you can store in a directory. User accounts that are stored in a shared directory are accessible to all the computers that search that directory; those accounts are referred to as *network user accounts* or simply *network users*.

There are two main tools for managing network user accounts: Server Preferences and Workgroup Manager. Server Preferences offers basic management of users and services. Workgroup Manager offers more-advanced editing, but Server Preferences is more integrated with the services offered by Mac OS X Server, especially the collaboration services. After exploring the services in the rest of the chapters of this book, carefully evaluate which tool you will use to manage network user accounts: Server Preferences or Workgroup Manager.

Using Server Preferences to Manage Network User Accounts

You can use the Server Preferences application for configuring network user and group accounts if you configure Mac OS X Server with any of the following options:

▶ Create Users and Groups

▶ Import Users and Groups

▶ Configure Manually, and at some point later set up an Open Directory master

Server Preferences gives you the basic options for account management, including the account details, contact information, services that user is authorized to use, and groups to which a user belongs.

When you create a user with Server Preferences, the application automatically creates a network group account named Workgroup, and automatically adds users that you create with Server Preferences to that group.

NOTE ▶ When you create network user accounts outside of Server Preferences, such as with Workgroup Manager, those users are not automatically added to the group named Workgroup. Therefore, you may decide to use Server Preferences only, or Workgroup Manager only, to create network user accounts.

Because the user-related options are generally self-explanatory when using Server Preferences, for the remainder of this chapter, the focus will be on Workgroup Manager and Server Admin.

Using Workgroup Manager to Manage Network User Accounts

To create user accounts, you can use Workgroup Manager. You have already used Workgroup Manager to create local accounts, but you can also use it to create network accounts. If you click the small globe icon at the upper left of the Accounts pane below the Server Admin button in the toolbar, you can choose a directory from a pop-up menu. This enables you to create user accounts in different directories. Use the Basic pane to create an account, and then use the other panes to set the account's attributes, such as login shell.

> **NOTE** ▶ If you are creating user accounts that other computers will use, make sure you have chosen a shared directory from the directory pop-up menu before you create the account. Workgroup Manager will display a warning whenever you start to add accounts to the local directory; this will help prevent you from accidentally creating an account in the local directory instead of in a shared one.

> **NOTE** ▶ You can also add users and/or groups from one directory to groups from another directory. This increases the flexibility of your system and servers but makes it easy to create an overly complex model across directory servers. Always be sure you know which directory you are editing before making changes.

You can use Workgroup Manager to configure both local and network user accounts. Workgroup Manager is essentially a directory editor.

Use the following steps to verify the configuration and verify that Workgroup Manager can see both databases:

1   Open Workgroup Manager on your Mac OS X computer, and connect to your server computer using the following settings:

   ▶   Address: server17.pretendco.com

   ▶   User Name: ladmin

   ▶   Password: ladmin

NOTE ▶ If you previously stored the password in the keychain, the password field gets automatically populated, and for security reasons, shows eight characters regardless of how many characters are actually in the password.

2   If the text next to the globe icon does not indicate the shared directory /LDAPv3/127.0.0.1, click the globe icon to display the Directory Node pop-up menu, and choose Other.

3   In the "Select a directory" pane that opens, select LDAPv3, select 127.0.0.1, and click OK.

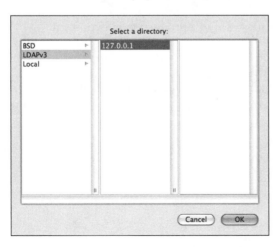

4 Because you authenticated as Local Administrator, not Directory Administrator, you cannot edit the shared directory. You must authenticate with the Directory Administrator credentials.

Click the lock icon on the right under the toolbar, and authenticate as diradmin (password: `diradmin`). For now, leave the option to remember the password in the keychain deselected.

5 In the left pane of the Workgroup Manager window, click the Users button, and then click New User in the toolbar.

6 At the message "New users may not have access to services," select the checkbox to not display the message again, and click OK.

7 Enter the following values:

▶ Name: `Student One`

▶ Short Names: `student1`

▶ Password: `network`

Of course, you should use a secure password in a production environment.

8 Click Save.

You have just created a user account in your shared directory domain. Student One is listed in Workgroup Manager's account list. The only other user currently in the shared LDAP directory is Directory Administrator.

9 Create four more users and give them the following long names, short names, and passwords:

▶ `Student Two, student2, network`

▶ `Student Three, student3, network`

▶ Student Four, student4, network

▶ Student Five, student5, network

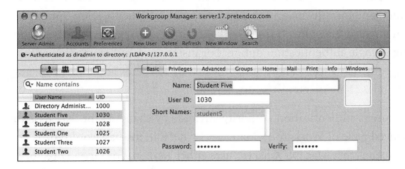

Using Authentication Methods on Mac OS X Server

For authenticating users whose accounts are stored in directories on Mac OS X Server, Open Directory offers a variety of options, including Kerberos and the many authentication methods that network services require. Open Directory can authenticate users by using:

▶ Single sign-on with the Kerberos KDC built in to Mac OS X Server

▶ A password stored securely in the Open Directory Password Server database

▶ A password stored as several hashes—including LAN Manager; NTLMv1 and NTLMv2 (NT LAN Manager); and Microsoft Challenge Handshake Authentication Protocol (MS-CHAPv2), used for VPN—in a file that only the root user can access

▶ An older crypt password stored directly in the user's account, for backward compatibility with legacy systems

▶ Local-only accounts, in which a shadow password is used, stored in a location accessible only by root

In addition, Open Directory lets you set up a password policy that affects all users (except administrators), as well as specific password policies for each user, such as automatic password expiration and minimum password length. (Password policies do not apply to crypt passwords.) Even though Mac OS X Server supports all these different authentication methods, you should not use all the methods. Crypt password support, for example, is provided for backward compatibility with older computers, but using crypt passwords is not as secure as using Open Directory Password Server.

Configuring User Authentication

To authenticate a user, Open Directory first must determine which authentication option to use: Kerberos, Open Directory Password Server, shadow password, or crypt password. The user's account contains information that specifies which authentication option to use. This information is called the *authentication authority attribute*. The attribute is not limited to specifying a single authentication option. For instance, an authentication authority attribute could specify that a user can be authenticated by Kerberos and Open Directory Password Server.

You can change a user's authentication authority attribute by changing the user password type in the Advanced pane of Workgroup Manager. By default, the password type is Open Directory, which means that Mac OS X Server uses either Kerberos or Open Directory Password Server. Open Directory passwords are stored securely in a separate database, not in the user account.

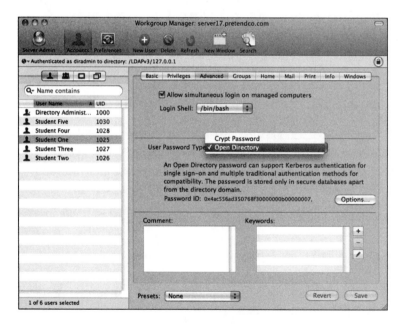

A user's account might not contain an authentication authority attribute. If a user's account contains no authentication authority attribute, Mac OS X Server assumes that a crypt password is stored in the user's account. For example, user accounts created using Mac OS X v10.1 and earlier contain a crypt password but not an authentication authority attribute.

NOTE ▶ Crypt passwords are inherently less secure because they are stored in the directory database and are subject to dictionary attacks. Configure a user account to use a crypt password only if you need to provide compatibility with a computer running Mac OS X v10.1 or earlier.

TIP ▶ If you are using a server that was upgraded from an earlier version of Mac OS X Server, you should examine the password type for all the user records stored on the server. If any records are still using a crypt password, you should upgrade the password type for the account to Open Directory.

Disabling a User Account

If you want to prevent a user from logging in, you can temporarily disable that user by using Workgroup Manager to remove access to his or her account. Doing so does not delete the user, nor does it change his or her UNIX user ID or any other information. Nor does it delete any of the user's settings, preferences, or files created by that user. It simply prevents that user from authenticating and gaining access to the server via any method.

1   Open Workgroup Manager and select the directory where the account that you want to disable resides. Generally, you will disable network user accounts, but you can also disable local user accounts.

2   Click the Accounts button, select the account, click the Basic tab, and deselect the "access account" checkbox.

3   Save the changes.

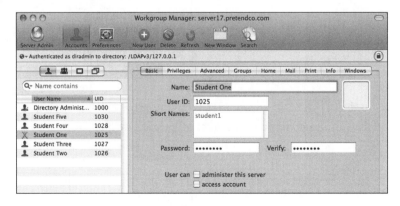

NOTE ▶ When a user account is disabled, you will see a red X through the user's icon in the list of users.

Setting Account Password Policies

Once you create new users, it is useful to establish password policies for their network accounts. (There is more on setting these policies later in this chapter.) Should the users change their passwords next time they log in? Should there be a minimum password length? You can use Workgroup Manager to establish these and other policies for your users. They can apply to just one user or to all users. Password policies applied with Workgroup Manager are called *user account settings* and are set for each user by clicking the Advanced button, and then clicking the Options button.

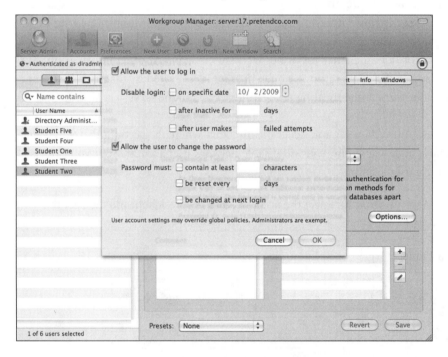

TIP ▶ Per-user policies can be set for more than one user by selecting more users prior to clicking the Advanced tab and subsequent Options button.

Password policies applied with Server Admin are called *global policies*. In Mac OS X Server, user account settings may override global policies. Administrators are exempt from both types of policies. You will learn how to set global policies later in this chapter.

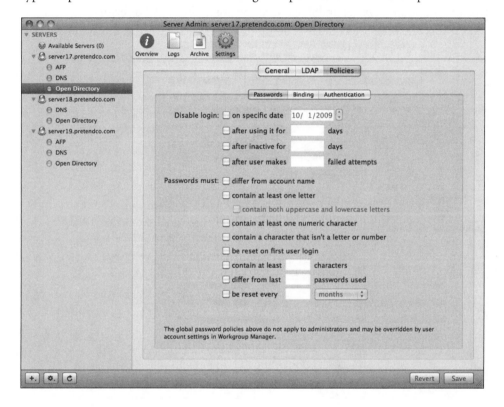

Set User Account Settings (Per-User Password Policies)

You will now set policies on a per-user basis, as opposed to a global basis.

1 Open Workgroup Manager and make sure you are in the LDAP directory (/LDAPv3/127.0.0.1). Select the user accounts you created earlier in this chapter, and click the Advanced tab.

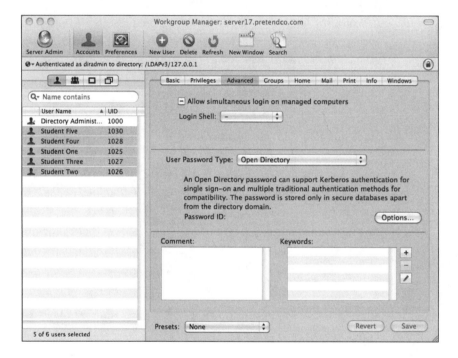

2 Click the Options button.

3 Select the following checkboxes:

▶ Disable login on specific date

▶ Allow the user to change the password

▶ Password must contain at least *N* characters

▶ Password must be changed at next login

"Allow the user to log in" and "Allow the user to change the password" will already be selected.

4   In the "Disable login on specific date" field, enter some date in the future.

5   In the "Password must contain at least *N* characters" field, enter 8.

The next time any of the highlighted users logs in, he or she will need to change his or her password; the password will need to be at least eight characters long; and the account will be disabled on the date you chose.

NOTE ▶ You will notice when you choose more than one user that dashes appear in all checkboxes. Clicking a dash changes it to a checkbox, indicating that the selection is now set for all highlighted users.

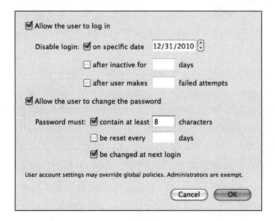

6   Click OK, and then click Save.

Set Single User Account Settings
Now perhaps you want to have only one of those users not be able to change his or her password, as in the case with a novice user.

1   Select one of your users (Student One), click the Advanced tab if it's not already selected, and click the Options button.

2   Edit the checkboxes to disallow all options under the criteria for password, and deselect the checkbox allowing the user to change his or her password.

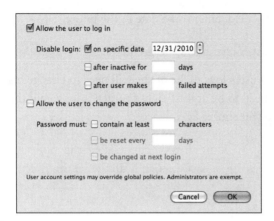

3   Click OK, and then click Save.

Now this user can't change his or her password, and it is still set to expire on a given date.

TIP There are two places to deny access to a specific user account: the Basic pane and the Advanced pane. Changing the settings in the Basic pane will automatically affect the Advanced settings, but changing the data in the Advanced pane will not affect the Basic settings. If you want to deny access to a specific user account, make sure that settings in both the Basic and Advanced panes are configured appropriately. Be sure to save changes so that the new settings will be written to the directory.

Test User Account Policies

You will now use your Mac OS X computer to test these policies.

1   On your Mac OS X computer, use Server Admin to ensure that on server17.pretendco. com, AFP service is running and there are no SACLs that restrict access to the AFP service.

2   On your Mac OS X computer, switch to the Finder and ensure that you do not have any network volumes mounted.

If the Eject button is displayed next to your server in the sidebar of the Finder, click that button.

3   Choose Go > Connect to Server.

4   Enter afp://server17.pretendco.com.

5   Attempt to authenticate as student1 (password: network).

6   You are prompted to enter a new password because you selected the checkbox "Password must be changed at next login" for this network user account.

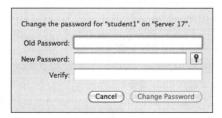

7   Enter 1234567 in the New Password and Verify fields, and then click Change Password.

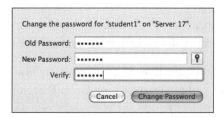

8   Click OK at the message that your password does not meet the policy enforced by the server.

9   Enter student1student1 in the New Password and Verify fields, and then click Change Password.

This should be a valid new password.

10   Since you entered a valid new password, you should see a list of share points.

Click Cancel. You do not need to mount any share points.

You successfully changed your password. This can be confirmed by watching the Password Service Server Log in Server Admin. (Directory-related log files will be covered toward the end of this chapter.)

Setting Global Password Policies

Open Directory enforces per-user and global password policies. For example, a user's password policy can specify a password expiration interval. If the user is logging in and Open Directory discovers that the user's password has expired, the user must replace the expired password. Open Directory can then authenticate the user.

Password policies can disable a user account on a certain date, after a number of days, after a period of inactivity, or after a number of failed login attempts. Password policies can also require passwords to be a minimum length, contain at least one letter, contain at least one numeral, be mixed case, contain a character that is neither a number nor a letter, differ from the account name, differ from recent passwords, or be changed periodically.

Open Directory applies the same password policy rules to Password Server and Kerberos. Password policies do not affect administrator accounts. Administrators are exempt from password policies because they can change the policies at will. In addition, enforcing password policies on administrators would subject them to denial-of-service attacks.

Kerberos and Open Directory Password Server maintain password policies separately. Mac OS X Server synchronizes the Kerberos password policy rules with Open Directory Password Server password policy rules.

After global password policies are put into effect, they are enforced only for users who change their password, or users you create or import. For instance, an existing user with the password "wayne" will not be required to change his password, even though you may have required more than eight characters and required the password to be different from the short name. This is because Wayne's account and password existed prior to the establishment of the global policy. In this case, it is best to require the user to change his password at the next login, thus forcing him to make his password conform to the recently set global password policies.

1   Open Server Admin if it's not already open. Select your Open Directory master, and then select Open Directory from the list of services on the left.

2   Click Settings in the toolbar, click Policies, and then click Passwords.

3   Choose your own criteria for when to disable the login, choose what parameters every user's password must meet, and click Save. Your settings may be different from what is shown in the figure below.

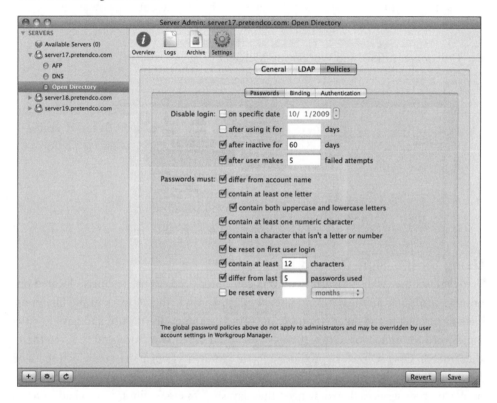

4   Use the steps from the previous exercise "Set Single User Account Settings" to require Student One to change the password at the next login.

5   Use the steps from the previous exercise "Test User Account Policies" to attempt to connect to the AFP service as student1, in order to be prompted to change student1's password (which you should have set to student1student1).

Attempt to specify a new password that does not match the global options you set in step 3, and confirm your global password policy settings.

If you successfully changed student1's password, do not mount a network volume, in order to keep the rest of the exercises simple.

6   In Server Admin, deselect all the checkboxes you just selected so that these options will not interfere with the rest of the exercises, and then click Save.

7   Use the Basic tab in Workgroup Manager to change student1's password to the same password your other network users have: network.

8   Quit Server Admin and Workgroup Manager.

> **TIP** It is important to obtain your organization's password policies if known prior to setting these options. If you miss certain criteria that are required by your organization and all users have been imported and have passwords set, changing these parameters may require users to change their passwords again to conform to the newer standards.

> **NOTE** ▸ Because you don't have home directories set at this point, you will be unable to test these policies at the login window.

Using Single Sign-On and Kerberos

Frequently, a user who is logged in on one computer needs to use resources located on another computer on the network. Users typically browse the network in the Finder and click to connect to the other computer. It would be a nuisance for users to have to enter a password for each connection. If you've deployed Open Directory, you've saved them that trouble. Open Directory provides a feature known as *single sign-on*, which relies on Kerberos. Single sign-on essentially means that when users log in, they automatically have access to other services they may need that day, such as email, file servers, chat servers, and VPN connectivity, without entering another password.

Defining Kerberos Terms

There are three main players in a complete Kerberos transaction:

▸   The user

▸   The service that the user is interested in accessing

▸   The KDC (Key Distribution Center), which is responsible for mediating between the user and the service, creating and routing secure tickets, and generally supplying the authentication mechanism

Within Kerberos there are different *realms* (specific databases or authentication domains). Each realm contains the authentication information for users and services, called Kerberos *principals.* For example, if you have a user with a long name of John Significant and a short name of johnsig on a KDC with the realm of SERVER17.PRETENDCO.COM, the user principal would be johnsig@SERVER17.PRETENDCO.COM. By convention, realms use all uppercase characters.

For a service to take advantage of Kerberos, it must be *Kerberized* (modified to work with Kerberos), which means that it can defer authentication of its users to a KDC. Not only can Mac OS X Server provide a KDC when configured to host a shared LDAP directory, but it can also provide several Kerberized services. An example of a service principal would be afpserver/server17.pretendco.com@SERVER17.PRETENDCO.COM.

Finally, Kerberos enables you to keep a list of users in a single database called the KDC, which is configured on Mac OS X Server once an Open Directory master has been created. When a network user logs in on a Mac OS X v10.2 or later client computer, that computer negotiates with the KDC. If the user provides the correct user name and password, the KDC provides an initial ticket called a Ticket Granting Ticket (TGT), which enables the user to subsequently ask for service tickets so he or she may connect to other servers and services on the network for the duration of the login session. During that time, the user can access any network service that has been Kerberized, without seeing a password dialog.

Kerberos is one of the components of Open Directory. The reason a user's password is stored in both the Password Server database and the Kerberos principal database is to allow users to authenticate to services that are not Kerberized. However, users must enter a password every time they access those services. Open Directory uses Password Server to provide support for those authentication protocols.

Because Kerberos is an open standard, Open Directory on Mac OS X Server can be easily integrated into an existing Kerberos network. You can set up your Mac OS X computers to use an existing KDC for authentication.

One security aspect to using Kerberos is that the tickets are time sensitive. Kerberos requires that the computers on your network be synchronized to within five minutes by default. Configure your Mac OS X computers and your servers to use NTP, and synchronize to the same time server so this doesn't become an issue that prevents you from getting Kerberos tickets.

Examining Kerberos Tickets

Even though you do not have a home folder at this point, you can examine your
Kerberos ticket.

1   Log in to your Mac OS X computer as cadmin if you are not already logged in
as cadmin.

2   Navigate to /System/Library/CoreServices and open Ticket Viewer.

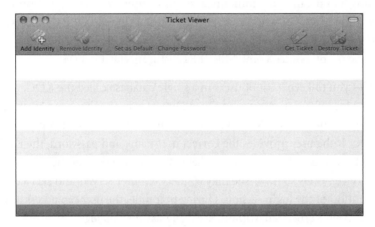

3   Click Add Identity to obtain a new Kerberos ticket.

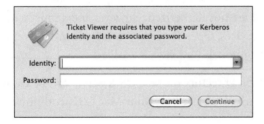

4   Enter the short name and password that you entered earlier in Workgroup Manager
(student1, network), and click Continue.

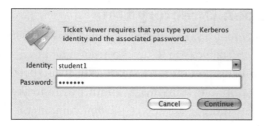

5   You should now see an entry for a valid Kerberos ticket, including its expiration date and time.

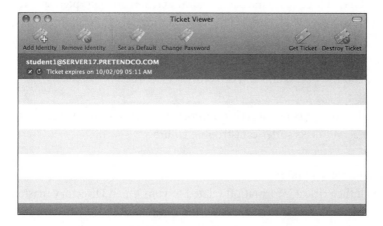

6   Click Destroy Ticket so your ticket will not interfere with any other exercises.

7   Quit Ticket Viewer.

Notice that even though you logged in at the login window as cadmin, you were able to get a Kerberos ticket as another user. This is because you authenticated *locally* to your Mac OS X computer as cadmin, but you authenticated against the Open Directory service for your network user account with Ticket Viewer.

Archiving and Restoring Open Directory Data

Once your Open Directory master (and any replicas) has been established, it is advisable to archive all your Open Directory data. This enables you to quickly recover all LDAP user information, passwords, and computer configuration information quickly. It also permits you to transfer the Open Directory service from one computer to another by restoring the Open Directory information, provided that the IP address of the new computer is the same as the old one.

Understanding the Archival Structure

When you archive the Open Directory data, Server Admin creates an encrypted sparse disk image and stores it wherever you choose. The items archived include all three major components of Open Directory masters—the LDAP database, the Password Server database, and the Kerberos Key Distribution Center—along with the local database and passwords, the local KDC, and the host name and directory service files.

NOTE ▶ It is wise to store or copy this critical information to another device for safekeeping in case the server disks suffer catastrophic failure.

Archiving the Open Directory Master

You will now archive all the critical information related to your Open Directory master.

1   Open Server Admin if it is not already open. Select your Open Directory master, and select Open Directory in the service list on the left.

2   Click the Archive button in the toolbar.

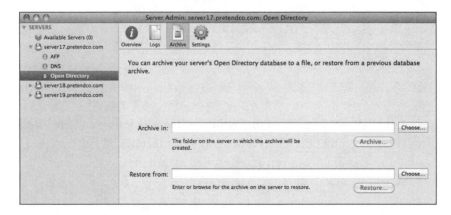

3   Click the Choose button next to the "Archive in" field. Navigate to the location where you want to save the archive disk image. For this exercise, navigate to */your boot volume*/Users/ladmin/Desktop.

The location you choose will be relative to the server you are connected to with Server Admin, not the Mac OS X computer that you use to open Server Admin.

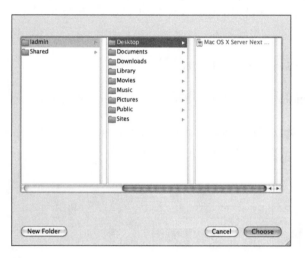

4   Click Choose to choose the location.

5   Click Archive to actually create the archive.

6   Enter the archive name Chapter3Archive and the password archivepass.

7   Click OK.

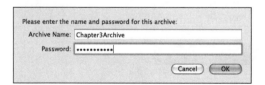

NOTE ▶ It is crucial that you give the archive a useful name, such as one containing the date of archival. Also, there is no password verification field, so enter your password carefully and check to ensure that the Caps Lock key is intentionally either enabled or disabled.

You can now view the progress bar during the archival process. Once the progress bar disappears, the process is complete.

The archive of your server's Open Directory databases won't do you much good if you just leave it on your server's hard drive and that hard drive becomes unavailable. However, for now, leave it there so you can use it to restore the Open Directory databases in an upcoming exercise. Use the following steps to copy the archive to your Mac OS X computer in order to inspect it:

1 On your Mac OS X computer, switch to the Finder.

2 If you don't have a Finder window open, choose File > New Finder Window.

3 Select the server that is your Open Directory master in the sidebar. Note that it appears as its computer name, not the DNS name or IP address.

4 Click Connect As.

5 Because you saved the archive on ladmin's desktop, authenticate as ladmin (password: ladmin) and click Connect.

6 In the Finder, double-click the ladmin folder, and then open the Desktop folder.

7 Drag Chapter3Archive.sparseimage to your local desktop.

8 Click the Eject button next to Server 17 in the sidebar, and close the Finder window.

9 Open your local copy of Chapter3Archive.sparseimage.

10 Enter the password archivepass. Leave the checkbox deselected for "Remember password in my keychain," and click OK to open the encrypted disk image.

11 Open the ldap_bk volume and confirm that it is populated with files. You do not need to understand the contents of the files at this time.

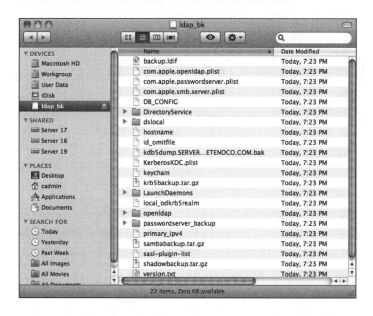

12 Eject the ldap_bk volume.

Restoring Directory Data to the Open Directory Master

Once Open Directory data has been archived, it can be restored just as easily. In this exercise you will change your Mac OS X server from an Open Directory master to a standalone server—you will destroy the Open Directory databases, simulating a catastrophic loss of your Mac OS X server. If you ever need to start from scratch for any reason, simply install Mac OS X Server with the same IP address and DNS name as your old Open Directory master, configure a fresh new Open Directory master, and then restore from your archive. This exercise gives you a taste of how the process works.

1   Quit Workgroup Manager if it is open, and open Server Admin.

2   Select your Open Directory master (server17.pretendco.com), and then select Open Directory in the service list. Click Settings, and then click General.

3   Change the role of the server from an Open Directory master to a standalone server using the Change button, which opens Open Directory Assistant.

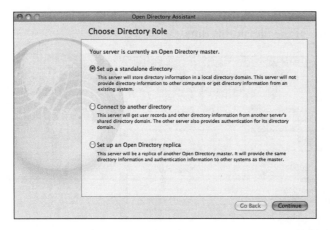

4   Select "Set up a standalone directory" and click Continue three times to remove the LDAP database, Password Server database, and Kerberos KDC—all of which constitute the Open Directory master. Click Done to close Open Directory Assistant.

You now have no LDAP database and, consequently, no users in that database.

5   Click the Change button to open Open Directory Assistant again, select "Set up an Open Directory Master," and click Continue.

6 Select the defaults for UNIX user ID and short name, enter the same password you used when you first set up the Open Directory master (the password was the same as the short name, diradmin), and click Continue.

7 Accept the defaults for the Kerberos KDC and LDAP information, and click Continue two more times.

8 Click Done to close Open Directory Assistant, and then verify in Server Admin that the role is an Open Directory master.

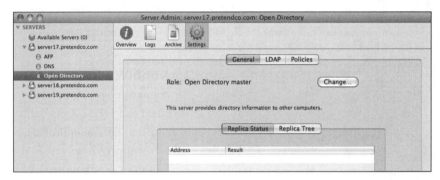

9 Click the Archive button in the toolbar, and enter the path of the encrypted sparse image in the "Restore from" field: /Users/ladmin/Desktop/Chapter3Archive.sparseimage.

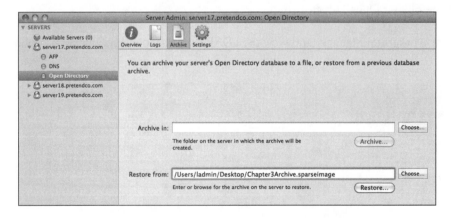

10 Click Restore.

11 When prompted to restore or merge, click Restore.

12 Enter the password for the encrypted sparse disk image (archivepass), and then click OK.

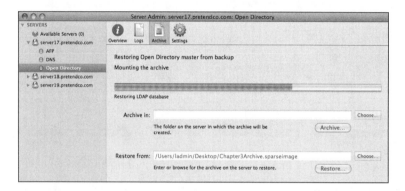

Other than a progress bar, there is no indication that you successfully completed a restore of your Open Directory data.

13 Open Workgroup Manager and view the LDAP database to ensure that all users have been restored.

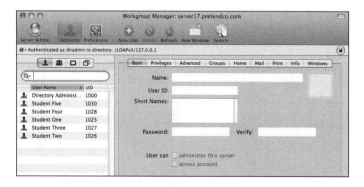

You have now successfully restored Open Directory data to your Mac OS X server.

NOTE ▶ Although you can back up an Open Directory replica, there is no real need to do so. In fact, restoring a replica can be dangerous, because it puts an outdated copy of the account information on the network. Because a replica is a copy of the master, the master effectively backs up the replica. If a replica develops a problem, you can just change its role to standalone server. Then you can set up that server as though it were a brand-new server, with a new host name, and set it up as a replica of the same master as before.

Troubleshooting

Because Open Directory includes several services, there are several log files used for tracking status and errors. You can use Server Admin to view status information and logs for Open Directory services. For example, you can use the password-service logs to monitor failed login attempts for suspicious activity, or use the Open Directory logs to see all failed authentication attempts, including the IP addresses that generate them. Review the logs periodically to determine whether there are numerous failed tries for the same password ID, which would indicate that somebody might be generating login guesses. It is therefore imperative that you understand where to look first when troubleshooting Open Directory issues.

Accessing Open Directory Log Files

Generally, the first place to look when Open Directory issues arise is the log files. Recall that Open Directory comprises three main components: the LDAP database, the Password Server database, and the Kerberos Key Distribution Center. Mac OS X Server's Server Admin tool allows for easy viewing of all server-related Open Directory log files with respect to these three components.

The main log files are:

▶ Directory Services Server Log

▶ Directory Services Error Log

▶ Configuration Log

▶ Kerberos Administration Log

▶ Kerberos Server Log

▶ LDAP Log

▶ Password Service Server Log

► Password Service Error Log

► Password Service Replication Log

To access these log files:

1 Open Server Admin. Select server17.pretendco.com and select Open Directory in the service list on the left.

2 Select the Logs icon from the toolbar, and then choose the Password Service Server Log from the pop-up menu at the bottom of the window.

3 Enter the word student1 in the search field at the upper right of the window to confirm that student1's password was changed in an earlier exercise.

Interpreting log files can be a difficult task, and you may need the help of a more experienced system administrator. You can email the appropriate log file to the administrator. To find out where in the system the log file is stored, choose the log file from the View pop-up menu in Server Admin. The path to the log file will be displayed below the toolbar.

Troubleshooting Directory Services

If Mac OS X or Mac OS X Server experiences a startup delay and a message about LDAP or directory services appears above the progress bar, the computer could be trying to access an LDAP directory that is not available on your network.

There are several ways to begin troubleshooting when you are unable to connect to a directory service. These include the following:

► Use Login Options in the Accounts preference to confirm that the network server is available.

► Use Directory Utility to make sure the LDAP and other configurations are correct.

▶ Use the Network pane of System Preferences to make sure the computer's network location and other network settings are correct.

▶ Inspect the physical network connection for faults.

If you can't modify the password of a user whose password is authenticated by Open Directory, or if you can't modify a user account to use Open Directory authentication, one of two things might be wrong:

▶ You might not be authenticated as that particular directory administrator.

▶ Your administrator user account might not be configured for Open Directory authentication. If you have upgraded from an earlier version of Mac OS X Server, the account might have a crypt or shadow password rather than an Open Directory password.

Troubleshooting Kerberos

When a user or service that uses Kerberos experiences authentication failures, try these techniques:

▶ Ensure that the DNS service you use is resolving addresses correctly. This is especially important at the time you are promoting a server to Open Directory master. If the DNS doesn't resolve addresses correctly, the incorrect address will be written to the Kerberos configuration files. Kerberos tickets won't be usable.

▶ Kerberos authentication is based on encrypted timestamps. If there's more than a five-minute difference between the KDC, client, and service computers, authentication may fail. Make sure that the clocks for all computers are synchronized using the NTP service of Mac OS X Server or another network time server.

▶ Make sure that Kerberos authentication is enabled for the service in question.

▶ Refer to the password-service and password-error logs for information that can help you solve problems. You can sometimes detect incorrect setup information, such as wrong configuration filenames, using the logs.

▶ View the user's Kerberos ticket. Kerberos tickets are visible in the Ticket Viewer application, which is found in /System/Library/CoreServices.

Preparing DNS Records (Optional)

NOTE ▶ Skip this section if you already have the appropriate DNS records available in your environment.

Open Directory services rely on forward and reverse DNS records for the computers hosting Open Directory services. You can use the exercises in this section to have your Mac OS X server provide a common set of DNS records for the servers you will use to complete the exercises in this chapter.

In this section you will prepare a DNS zone, create appropriate DNS records, and configure your Mac OS X computer to use this newly updated DNS service so you can get on with the task of configuring Open Directory services.

If you configure your Mac OS X computer to use the DNS service hosted by your Mac OS X server, you may experience delays with Server Admin, because there are not yet DNS records for your Mac OS X computer.

Configuring DNS to Support Multiple Open Directory Servers

If no DNS records are available when you initially set up Mac OS X Server, Server Assistant configures a DNS zone specifically for that one server. This is great, but you may eventually need to change your server's Network preference to use a DNS service that offers a complete set of DNS records.

In this exercise you will replace the automatically created and limited DNS zone with a DNS zone for your larger organization: pretendco.com. You will create machine records for two additional servers, and Server Admin will automatically create reverse DNS records for you. You will configure your Open Directory master (10.1.17.1) to host the DNS service, and you will configure your other Mac OS X servers to use the DNS service offered by your Open Directory master. If you already have a DNS service available on your network, or if you have only one server, simply read through this exercise.

1   On your Mac OS X computer, open Server Admin to connect to your Open Directory master at 10.1.17.1 as ladmin (password: `ladmin`).

2   Select DNS in the list of services for 10.1.17.1.

3   Click Zones in the toolbar.

4 At the warning, select the "Do not show this message again" checkbox.

Be extra cautious with this exercise. Click OK.

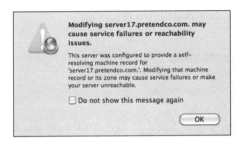

5 Click the Add Zone pop-up menu, and choose Add Primary Zone (Master).

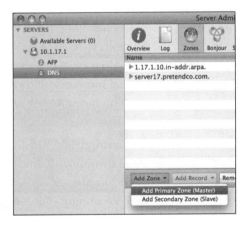

6 In the Primary Zone Name field, enter `pretendco.com`.

If you omit the trailing dot, Server Admin automatically adds it for you.

7 Click the Add (+) button next to the Nameservers field.

The Zone and Nameserver Hostname values are populated automatically.

Click Save to save the information for your new pretendco.com. zone.

8 With pretendco.com. still selected in the top pane, click Add Record and choose Add Machine (A).

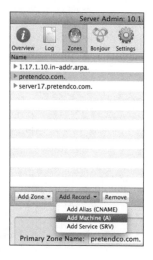

9 In the Machine Name field, enter server17, and then press Tab.

Press Tab again to move to the IP Addresses field.

10 In the IP Addresses field, press Return to edit the IP address.

11 Change the IP address to `10.1.17.1`, and then press Return to stop editing the IP address.

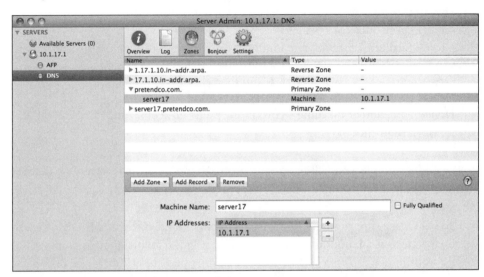

12 Click Save to save this new DNS record.

13 Ensure that pretendco.com. is still selected in the top pane. Click Add Record and choose Add Machine (A).

14 In the Machine Name field, enter `server18`, and in the IP Addresses field, enter `10.1.18.1`.

15 Click Save to save this record.

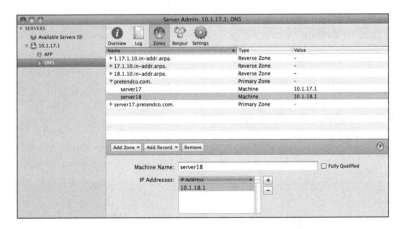

Note that Server Admin automatically created a new reverse DNS zone, 18.1.10.in-addr.arpa. This is necessary to translate 10.1.18.1 to server18.pretendco.com.

16 Click Add Record and choose Add Machine (A). Create a record for `server19.pretendco.com` at `10.1.19.1`, and then click Save.

17 Finally, add another machine record in the pretendco.com. zone for `xseclient` at `10.1.17.2`, and click Save.

To keep things simple, you will remove the primary zone and the reverse zone that Server Assistant automatically created when you set up the server at 10.1.17.1.

1 To help make sure you remove the correct item, use the disclosure triangle next to each zone to display *less* information, as shown in the following figure.

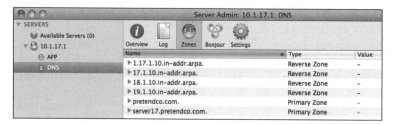

2 Select the server17.pretendco.com. zone. Be sure that you select the server17.pretendco.com. *zone*, not the server17 machine record (which should be hidden if you performed the previous step).

3 With server17.pretendco.com. selected, click Remove.

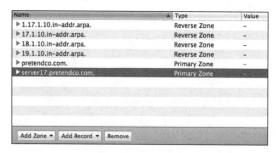

4   Select the 1.17.1.10.in-addr.arpa. zone (not 17.1.10.in-addr.arpa.), and click Remove.

This removes the reverse DNS zone that Server Assistant automatically created when you set up the server at 10.1.17.1.

5   Click the disclosure triangles next to each zone to show more information.

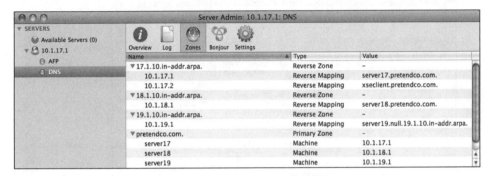

6   Confirm that you have the same zones and records as shown in the preceding figure.

Now that you have configured your Open Directory master to also offer DNS services for pretendco.com, you need to configure your Mac OS X client and your other servers to use that DNS service.

1   On your Mac OS X computer, open Server Admin. Choose Server > Add Server, and connect to 10.1.18.1 as ladmin.

2   In Server Admin, select 10.1.18.1 and choose Server > Share Server's Screen. Authenticate as ladmin to connect.

3   On 10.1.18.1, open System Preferences and open the Network preference.

4   Select the Ethernet interface, and in the DNS Server field, replace 127.0.0.1 with 10.1.17.1, and then click Apply.

Your server at 10.1.18.1 now relies on the DNS service offered by 10.1.17.1.

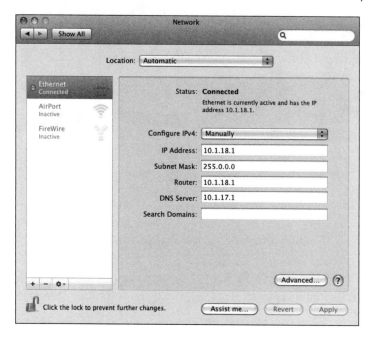

5   Log out of your server as ladmin.

6   Close the Screen Sharing window.

7   Repeat the preceding steps with the server at 10.1.19.1, with the result shown in the figure below.

Configure Mac OS X with a Static IP Address

1   On your Mac OS X computer, open System Preferences.

2   Open the Network preference.

3   From the Location pop-up menu, choose Edit Locations.

4   Click the Add (+) button, and name the new location Static.

Click Done to dismiss the new location pane.

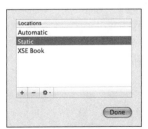

5   In the left column, select your Ethernet port.

6   From the Configure IPv4 pop-up menu, choose Manually.

Set the following values:

▶   IP Address: 10.1.17.2

▶   Subnet Mask: 255.255.0.0

▶   Router: 10.1.17.1

▶   DNS Server: 10.1.17.1

▶   Search Domains: pretendco.com

Click Apply.

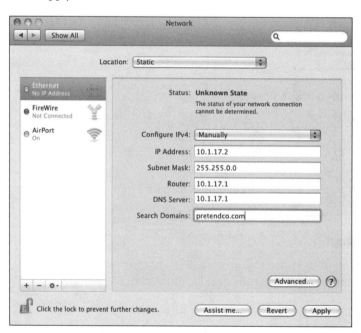

7   For each additional network interface, click the Action pop-up menu (labeled with a gear and a down arrow) and choose Make Service Inactive.

8   Click Apply, and then close the Network preference.

Now your Mac OS X computer uses the DNS service offered by the server at 10.1.17.1. There are now valid forward and reverse DNS entries available to your Mac OS X client and the servers.

What You've Learned

▶ Directory services centralize system and network administration and simplify a user's experience on the network.

▶ Open Directory is Apple's extensible directory-services architecture.

▶ Directories store information in a specialized database that is optimized to handle a great many requests for information and to find and retrieve information quickly. Information may be stored in one directory or in several related directories.

▶ The Open Directory service uses OpenLDAP to provide the LDAP standard to use for a common language for directory access, enabling you to maintain information in a single location on the network rather than on each computer. It also uses Kerberos to provide secure authentication, and for those applications that do not yet use Kerberos, the Open Directory service provides the Password Server service.

▶ The Open Directory service window of Server Admin lets you configure how Mac OS X Server works with directory information.

▶ Workgroup Manager enables you to create both local and network user accounts.

▶ The Accounts preference is the primary application for setting up a Mac OS X computer's connections with directories. To edit advanced options, use Directory Utility, which is available in /System/Library/CoreServices on both Mac OS X and Mac OS X Server.

References

The following documents provide more information about offering directory services with Mac OS X Server. All these and more are available at http://www.apple.com/server/macosx/resources/.

Mac OS X Server Administration Guides

Open Directory Administration

Upgrading and Migrating

User Management

Apple Knowledge Base Documents

You can check for new and updated Knowledge Base documents at http://www.apple.com/support/.

Document HT3186, *Mac OS X Server v10.5, 10.6: Enabling Directory Service debug logging*

Document TA24015, *Mac OS X Server 10.4.6 or later: changeip now requires fully qualified domain names*

Books

Carter, Gerald. *LDAP System Administration* (O'Reilly Media, Inc., 2003)

Bartosh, Michael, and Faas, Ryan. *Essential Mac OS X Panther Server Administration* (O'Reilly Media, Inc., 2005)

Dreyer, Arek, and Greisler, Ben. *Mac OS X Directory Services v10.6* (Peachpit Press, 2009)

White, Kevin. *Mac OS X Support Essentials v10.6* (Peachpit Press, 2009)

Garman, Jason. *Kerberos: The Definitive Guide* (O'Reilly Media, Inc., 2003)

URLs

Kerberos: The Network Authentication Protocol: http://web.mit.edu/kerberos/www/

Designing an Authentication System: A Dialogue in Four Scenes: http://web.mit.edu/kerberos/www/dialogue.html

OpenLDAP: community developed LDAP software: http://www.openldap.org/

Lightweight Directory Access Protocol (v3): Technical Specification:
http://www.rfc-editor.org/rfc/rfc3377.txt

SASL: Simple Authentication and Security Layer: http://asg.web.cmu.edu/sasl/

Chapter Review

1. What is the main function of directory services?

2. What standard is used for data access with Open Directory? What version and level of support is provided for this standard?

3. In terms of Open Directory, what four roles can Mac OS X Server play?

4. What are the two methods of applying password policies, and where are they located?

Answers

1. Directory services provide a central repository for information about the computers, applications, and users in an organization.

2. Open Directory uses OpenLDAP and the Lightweight Directory Access Protocol (LDAP) standard to provide a common language for directory access. Open Directory uses LDAPv3 to provide read and write access to the directory data.

3. Open Directory master, standalone server, connected to a directory system, and Open Directory replica.

4. Per-user policies are defined in Workgroup Manager, and global policies are defined in Server Admin.

4

Chapter **4**
Using File Services

This chapter addresses the topic of using Mac OS X Server to share files across a network. It begins by exploring the challenges associated with file sharing and the issues to consider when setting up file sharing. The main focus of the chapter covers setting up share points with appropriate access settings, and configuring the specific sharing protocols that Mac OS X Server will use. This chapter also addresses automatic network mounts and general file-sharing troubleshooting issues to consider when enabling file services on Mac OS X Server.

Mac OS X Server has many different ways to manage share points and permissions. This chapter takes you through using Server Preferences, Server Admin, and Workgroup Manager to set up and maintain file sharing.

Challenges of File Sharing

When setting up file services, there are a number of issues to consider. The obvious ones are what types of clients will be accessing your file server, what protocols they will be using, and what access levels they will need.

At first glance, these questions might seem relatively easy to answer, but the true requirements can get very complex. For example, a network share point might require access by Windows and Mac users, using their native protocols, where both platforms might be reading and writing to the same files at the same time. In other cases, you might need to support a complex workflow, such as in a print production environment, where the traditional UNIX permissions model is not sufficient to support the workflow. In other cases, you might have a large number of users and the challenge is managing their appropriate access over a period of time, as user and departmental needs change.

Historically, Mac OS X Server supported multiple platforms, but the experience may not have been optimal. Whereas Mac OS X Server implemented the UNIX permissions model, Windows NT servers later implemented a much different permissions model based on ACLs. In the past, accessing a server from a nonnative client, such as a Windows XP client accessing a Mac OS X v10.3 server, might have led to a confusing interpretation of the permissions available to that user, because the Windows client would have expected the more granular permissions model. Mac OS X Server v10.4 addressed this issue and others by supporting new features, such as ACLs, at both the file system and service levels.

The challenge also lies in the setup of the share points themselves. Careless layout of share points results in a more complex permissions matrix than necessary.

Different Protocols for Different Clients

Mac OS X Server includes a number of ways to share files. The method you select depends largely on the clients you expect to serve (although security is another factor to consider). Mac OS X Server provides the following file-sharing services:

▶   Apple Filing Protocol (AFP): This protocol is useful mainly for sharing files with Mac clients, both older Mac OS 9 clients and the latest Mac OS X clients.

▶   File Transfer Protocol (FTP): This file-sharing protocol is lightweight in the sense that it is simple and does not have all the features available in the other file-sharing services in Mac OS X. FTP allows you to transfer files back and forth between client and server, but you cannot, for example, open a document over an FTP connection. The primary benefit of FTP is that it is ubiquitous: It is hard to find a Transfer Control Protocol (TCP)–capable computer that does not support FTP.

▶ Network File System (NFS): NFS is the traditional method of file sharing for UNIX-based computers. NFS has its heritage in research facilities and academia in the 1980s. While it can be very convenient and flexible, it can suffer from some security holes that do not affect the other protocols. The primary use for NFS is to provide files to UNIX or Linux computers. Although Mac OS X has a core based on UNIX, you should normally use AFP for Mac clients.

▶ Windows file service: This service uses the Server Message Block (SMB) protocol (version 1), also sometimes called the Common Internet File System (CIFS). SMB is the native file-sharing protocol for Windows but is also used widely in UNIX environments. Mac OS X Server can appear to be a Windows server, even showing up in the Windows Network Neighborhood just as a Windows server would.

You can share a folder over several different protocols simultaneously.

Planning File Services

When setting up file services on Mac OS X Server, proper initial planning can save you time in the long run.

Setting Up File Services

Follow these guidelines when you first start planning to implement file services.

Plan Your File-Server Requirements

Determine your organizational requirements:

▶ How are your users organized?

▶ Is there a logical structure to follow for assigning users to groups that best address workflow needs?

▶ What types of computers will be used to access your file server?

▶ What share points and folder structures will be needed?

▶ How will users interact with one another when accessing these share points?

These answers will dictate the file services you configure, as well as how you might organize groups and share points.

> **NOTE** ▶ One of your early considerations is whether to use the access-control features available in Mac OS X Server. This decision will dictate how you proceed with setting user and group access rights to share points and folders, as well as how files and folders created over time on your server will be shared.

Use Workgroup Manager to Configure Users and Groups

The main goal is to end up with a group structure that best matches your organizational needs and allows easy maintenance over time. Setting up users and groups at the beginning is trivial. Setting up users and groups that continue to work as the organization goes through natural changes over time is not as simple as it first appears. Nevertheless, having a logical group structure that can be used to allow and deny access to your server file system will save you from continually adjusting file-service access later on. Mac OS X Server supports groups within groups, using groups as owners of a folder, and setting access-control lists on folders. Additionally, since Mac OS X Server v10.4, users can be members of more than 16 groups.

> **TIP** ▶ For testing of groups, share points, and ACLs, you do not need to have all users entered. You may decide to test with a skeletal set of users and groups that meet the business requirements of your organization. After verifying the groups and share points, you can then enter or import the full set of users.

Use Server Admin to Configure and Start the Services

Server Admin is the main application you use to configure share points, file permissions, and specific file services—AFP, FTP, NFS, Windows (SMB/CIFS). You first configure the settings for each service, addressing such options as maximum number of clients, guest access, logging levels, and other service-specific settings. Once the services are configured, set and test appropriate access for users to the specific services. For example, you may have one group of users that needs access from both Windows and Mac clients, while another group is using only Linux clients. For security reasons, you might limit the first group's access to the AFP and Windows services while limiting the Linux users' access to NFS or FTP services. Next, you define which folders should be shared by your file-sharing services, and what permissions each folder should have. Once everything has been properly secured, then you can use Server Admin to start each of the services you will be using and let users start accessing their appropriate file service.

> **NOTE ▶** Service ACLs should not be confused with file-system ACLs, which were covered in Chapter 2, "Authenticating and Authorizing Accounts." Service ACLs will be covered in depth later in this chapter.

Adjust Settings over Time and Monitor Your File Server for Problems

There are several ways to monitor your server services and manually adjust user and group settings:

▶ Use Server Admin to monitor logs and queues for specific services, to fine-tune any service-configuration settings, and to modify folder permissions and any service ACLs as required.

▶ Use Workgroup Manager to adjust users and groups.

▶ Use other appropriate applications for either monitoring or securing the server.

Once a server is deployed, you'll need to perform regular maintenance. This includes monitoring service usage to determine if it is addressing the needs of the organization, as well as looking for any security issues or unexpected activity. You might use additional software, such as Console, Terminal, or even third-party security software. As organizations change, use Workgroup Manager and Server Admin to adjust groups, users, and access to file systems and services.

Creating Share Points and Setting Access Permissions

After determining server and user requirements and entering at least a sample set of users and groups that represents the organizational structure, the next step in sharing files is to create your share points. A *share point* can be any folder, drive, or partition that is mounted on the server. When you create a share point, you make that item and its contents available to network clients via the specified protocols. This includes deciding what items you want to give access to and organizing the items logically. It requires using your initial planning and knowledge of your users and their needs. You might decide that everything belongs in a single share point and use permissions to control access within that share point, or you might set up a more complex workflow. For example, you could have one share point for your copywriters and a separate share point for the copy editors. Perhaps you would have a third share point where both groups could access common items or share files. Setting up effective share points requires as much knowledge of your users and how they work together as it does the technology of share points.

Remember that Mac OS X Server supports different file-sharing protocols for different clients. When you create a share point in Server Admin, you have the option of sharing it via any combination of AFP, FTP, SMB, or NFS. By default, any new share point is shared via AFP and SMB. If you want to share it over FTP or NFS, you must explicitly enable that service for that share point. For each protocol, you should review the Server Admin settings for items such as allowing guest access, creating a custom share-point name, Spotlight searching, and deciding whether service-specific inheritance is to be configured for that service. It is also important to keep in mind that different protocols will handle issues like filename case-sensitivity and extended file permissions differently. For this reason, it is usually best to limit your file-sharing protocols to those needed by the clients that are connecting to your server. For example, if you have only Mac OS X clients connecting to your server, it will simplify things to only use the AFP service and disable the SMB service for that share point.

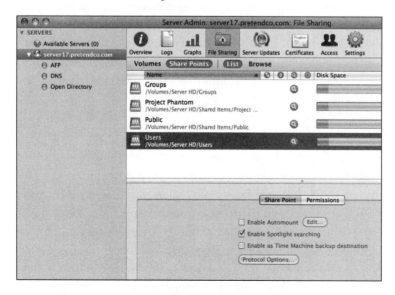

Ultimately, how a share point is configured for access, combined with the access settings for each file-sharing service, determines whether users are able to log in via a file-sharing protocol, and if so, what share points they are able to see upon login.

Using Apple Filing Protocol

Apple Filing Protocol (AFP) has been the default file-sharing protocol for Mac OS X and its predecessors for quite some time. As Apple moves forward with an ever-widening set of options when dealing with permissions, it is important to understand the basics of POSIX permissions and their role in Mac OS X and Mac OS X Server.

Understanding POSIX Permissions with AFP Share Points

When you share files over AFP, you should understand the POSIX permissions model. In the POSIX permissions model, permissions depend on whether an item is *new* or a *copy* of an existing item.

Here's the easy part: When you copy an item within a single volume, that item always retains its original ownership and permissions. In contrast, when you *create* a new item on a mounted volume, or *copy an item from one volume to another volume*, Mac OS X and Mac OS X Server use the following rules for ownership and permissions for the new file or folder:

▶ The owner of the new item is the user who created or copied the item.

▶ The group is the group associated with the enclosing folder; in other words, the newly copied item inherits its group from the enclosing folder.

▶ The owner is assigned read and write permissions.

▶ The group is assigned read-only permissions.

▶ "Others" is assigned read-only permissions.

The variable that controls the permissions for newly created files is called the *umask* (changing the umask from the default of 022 is outside the scope of this book). Under this model, if you create an item in a folder in which the group has read/write permission, the item will not inherit that permission. If you want to let other group members edit the new item, you must change its permissions manually, using the Finder's Get Info command, or using chmod in the command line. This is one reason you may decide to use ACLs.

Setting Access to Share Points and Folders

Once you've created a share point and determined the protocols you will use, you can begin to address levels of access within that share point. You need to consider POSIX privileges (ownership and permissions) as well as file-system access permissions (set via ACLs), both of which were discussed in Chapter 2, "Authenticating and Authorizing Accounts." Using this very flexible system, you can apply access settings to any folder within your share points through inheritance or explicit support.

> **TIP** You do not need to make a folder a share point to set its access level, because Server Admin allows you to browse the file system on your server. Also, you cannot set complex ACLs via the Finder using the Get Info command; you must use Server Admin for settings beyond the standard read/write, read-only, and none permission settings.

To configure access settings for share points or folders, use the Permissions pane when viewing that share point or folder in Server Admin. The standard POSIX settings are listed as Owner, Group, and Others in the bottom half of the pane; access settings using ACLs are set in the top half. You can use Server Admin to create and edit an ACL for a folder, but not for a file. Remember that POSIX privileges always exist for every file and every folder.

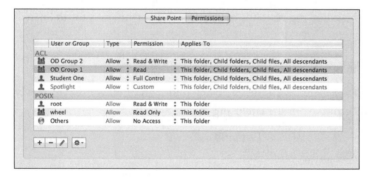

To see the result of access-control settings, you can use the Effective Permission Inspector, available from the Action pop-up menu (labeled with a gear and a down arrow) in the lower-left corner of the Permissions pane.

> **TIP** The best way to validate permissions is by logging in from client computers and testing access from valid user accounts.

Enabling Service Access with Server Preferences

You can use Server Preferences to quickly enable the default file-service protocols and share points. If you enable file sharing during your initial server setup, regardless of how you choose to manage your users and groups, your server will automatically offer AFP and SMB services, with a set of preconfigured share points. Here is a list of the share points and the paths to the share points:

Users (/Users)

Groups (/Groups)

Public (/Shared Items/Public)

You can easily add another share point, remove a share point, and edit basic access to the share point for network user accounts with Server Preferences.

Removing and Adding Share Points with Server Preferences

It is easy to remove or add a share point with Server Preferences, but Server Preferences doesn't let you create a folder. If you want to create a new folder to use for a share point, you must first use the Finder, Server Admin, or command-line tools to create a folder on your server.

To keep the example simple, rather than create another folder to share, you will use Server Preferences to remove the Public share point, then add the Public share point again.

1   On your Mac OS X computer, open Server Preferences and authenticate to your server with Local Administrator credentials.

2   Click File Sharing.

3   Select the Public share point.

4   Click the Remove (–) button and verify that you want to remove the share point.

You have just removed the Public share point. It is no longer accessible over AFP or SMB file sharing.

5   Add Public as a share point again.

Click the Add (+) button.

6   Navigate to /Shared Items/Public on your boot disk, then click Share.

Note that this enables the share point for both AFP and SMB access.

Editing Share Point Permissions with Server Preferences

You can adjust basic access to your share point with Server Preferences.

You have the choice of allowing read and write access to the share point for all users, or specifying a limited list of network user and group accounts. You can also enable or disable guests to have read-only access. Keep in mind that this enables and disables guest access for *both* AFP and SMB.

If you click Edit Permissions for a share point, you will see the following pane, which displays only network users and groups. When you select "Allow read and write access for," "Only these registered users and groups," this adds an allow ACE for the users you select, followed by a deny ACE for the group named Workgroup (all network users), to the ACL of the folder.

> **NOTE** ▶ When you use Server Preferences to create a new user, it automatically adds the new user to the group Workgroup. However, Workgroup Manager does not do this, so if you use both Server Preferences and Workgroup Manager to create new users, you should remember to add users you create with Workgroup Manager to the group Workgroup, or only use one tool to manage network users.

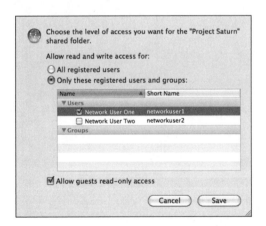

Note that there is a checkbox labeled "Allow guests read-only access." This checkbox affects both AFP and SMB services, so when you use Server Preferences to enable guest access for AFP, you also enable guest access for SMB.

Because Server Admin gives you much more flexibility in creating and enabling file-sharing services, the rest of this chapter focuses on using Server Admin.

Creating and Enabling Service Access with Server Admin

Server Admin offers you more options in configuring file-sharing services than Server Preferences.

The General and Access settings you configure for each service in Server Admin are part of the basic configuration steps you need to take regardless of which sharing protocols you decide to use. However, a few additional configuration settings are available for each share point from the pop-up menu in the Protocol Options pane in Server Admin. Here is the General pane under Settings for the AFP Service.

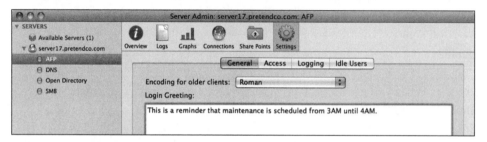

The Login Greeting field lets you specify a message to be displayed when a user connects. The message appears even when a user connects to his or her home folder.

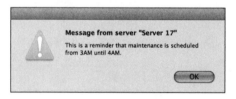

When you enable the AFP service, users of Mac OS X computers will see your server's Computer name (as defined in the Sharing preference) in the Finder sidebar by default. Here is Server 17's Sharing preference:

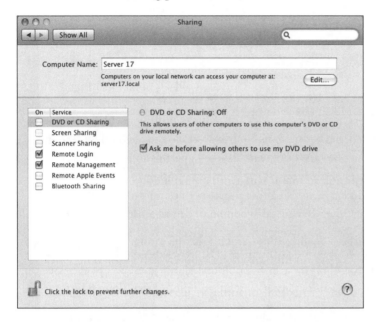

Here's what the Finder looks like for a Mac OS X computer on the same network as the Mac OS X Server with the AFP service enabled.

Controlling Access

AFP gives you the option to use either Kerberos or standard authentication as a method of authenticating users. If you choose Any Method in the Authentication pop-up menu, AFP will first try to authenticate using Kerberos; if the connection cannot be established using Kerberos, it will use standard authentication.

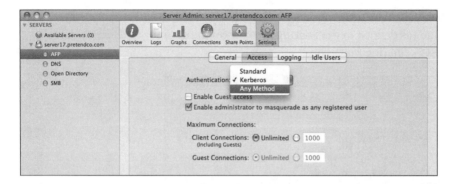

Once the user is authenticated, file permissions control access to the files and folders on your server. One setting should be called out with respect to permissions: the Others permissions. When you set Others permissions, those permissions apply to everyone who can see the item (either a file or folder) who is neither the owner nor part of the default group. You need to understand how Others permissions combine with another feature, guest access. As the name implies, guest access lets anyone who can connect to your server use its share points. A user who connects as Guest is given Others permissions for file and folder access. If you give read-only access to Others on a share point that allows guest access, everyone on your network (and possibly the entire Internet) can see and mount that share point.

If a folder is buried deep within a file hierarchy where guests can't go (because the enclosing folders don't grant access to Others), then guests can't use the Finder to browse to that folder. The Others permissions apply only to users who have been granted permission to see the enclosing folders but have not been granted permission to see that folder via their user and group settings.

Guest access can be very useful, but before you enable it, be sure you understand its implications in your permissions scheme.

Enabling Access

File ACLs control file-system access. Service ACLs (SACLs) control which service a user can access and provide an extra level of control when configuring your server. You can set SACLs per service or globally for the entire server. It is important to understand the ramifications when enabling SACLs across all services. Therefore, as a cautionary measure, it is best to enable SACLs per service to reduce the amount of confusion for your users.

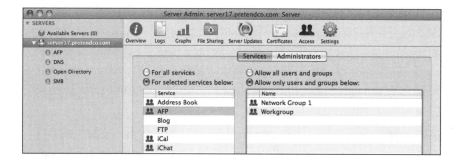

Logging Activity

Are you concerned that a user is accessing items that he or she should not have access to? Are you getting complaints from your users that their documents are disappearing or that they can't access things they should have access to? For troubleshooting these issues and more, logging is an invaluable resource.

AFP can keep two types of logs: the error log, which is always open by default, and the access log, which you must enable on the server using Server Admin (also used to view the logs). Enable the access log only when needed. Every action taken by a user is logged to this file, so it can become large very quickly and fill the available space in the file system. Logging all of these events for a busy server with a couple of hundred users can quickly result in a large log file that will be difficult to read through when attempting to diagnose the source of the issue. Alternately, you can configure the logging settings to save only certain events to the log, including Login, Logout, Open File, Create File, Create Folder, and Delete File/Folder. Another disk space–saving feature available to you is log archival. This will save (and compress) each log file after the specified period of time.

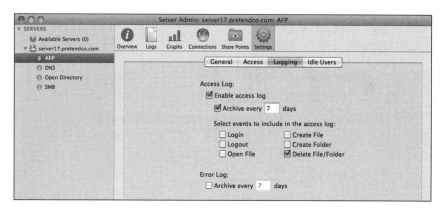

Troubleshooting and Monitoring Usage

In addition to the logs, Server Admin gives you graphical information about the current state of your server. You can view the number of connections, which users are currently connected, what protocol they used to connect, and how long they have been connected. In addition, the Graphs pane gives you a historical view of the amount of overall activity that the server has seen recently.

Monitoring server usage is a valuable tool to keep track of workflow. You can view graphs and watch for usual traffic patterns, usage spikes, and low-usage periods that you could use to plan backups or perform server maintenance.

Configuring Apple File Service

Use Server Admin to make a folder on your server computer and share it via AFP.

Set Up a Folder for Sharing

Before a folder can be shared via any protocol, you must set it up for sharing.

1   On your Mac OS X computer, open Server Admin, connect to your server with its DNS name, server17.pretendco.com, as ladmin (password: ladmin).

2   Select the AFP service for your server in the left column.

3   Click Share Points in the toolbar.

4   Click Volumes, then click Browse.

5   On your boot volume, navigate to Shared Items, click New Folder, name the folder Apple File Services, then click Create.

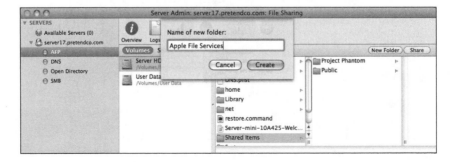

6   Select the Apple File Services folder.

Be sure to click the right folder before you set it as a share point in the next step.

7   Click the Share button in the upper-right corner, then click Save.

This item is now shared. By default, Mac OS X Server shares items over AFP and SMB only. Because you want this item to be viewable only by your Mac clients, you'll modify the default setting so that the item is shared only via AFP.

8   Click the Protocol Options button in the Share Point pane at the bottom of the window, and under AFP make sure that "Share this item using AFP" is enabled (it should be enabled by default).

9   Select the checkbox labeled "Allow AFP guest access."

This allows users to connect anonymously, provided the AFP service is configured to allow guest users.

10   Change the AFP name to `Corporate AFP Server`.

This is the name that will be given to the volume when client computers connect to it, while preserving the original folder name when viewed from the server. On your server, you'll want to be sure to choose names for the shares that correlate to their use. You may also want to retain the original folder name as the AFP name to avoid confusion between the name of the folder when viewed from the server versus when remotely connected from a client computer.

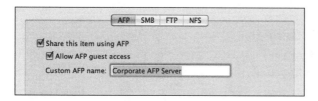

11 Click the SMB tab next, and deselect the "Share this item using SMB" checkbox.

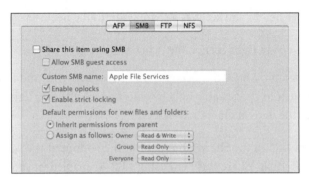

12 Click the FTP tab next, and confirm that the checkbox labeled "Share this item using FTP" is deselected.

Click OK to dismiss the pane, then click Save in the main Server Admin window.

Now your shared folder named Apple File Services is visible only to Mac clients using AFP. No action needed to be taken in the FTP and NFS panes because share points are not exported as FTP or as NFS shares by default.

Configure and Start AFP Service

Because you want to share this folder using AFP, you must configure AFP service with Server Admin, and then start the AFP service.

1 In Server Admin on your Mac OS X computer, select the AFP service, then click the Settings button in the toolbar.

If the AFP service isn't listed, you must first add it by choosing Add Service from the Action pop-up menu in the bottom-left corner of Server Admin.

2   Click the Access tab, choose Any Method from the Authentication pop-up menu, and select the "Enable Guest access" option. Click Save.

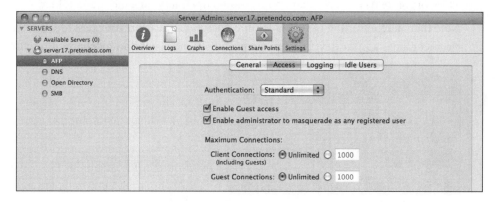

3   AFP should already be running from previous exercises. If it isn't, start it by clicking the Start AFP button.

4   On your Mac OS X computer, switch to the Finder and use Connect to Server to connect to your server at server17.pretendco.com.

5   Connect as a guest user.

6 Select the Corporate AFP Server share point and click OK.

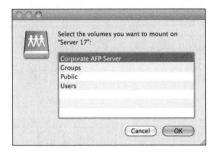

The Corporate AFP Server share point should open in your Finder as a folder.

Note that an icon for the network volume does *not* appear on your desktop, but an eject icon does appear next to your server in the Finder window sidebar.

7 Unmount the Corporate AFP Server share point.

Restrict Access to Files

Now that you have shared the Apple File Services folder, modify the permissions to restrict access to the files.

1 On your Mac OS X computer in Server Admin, click the File Sharing button in the toolbar, and then click the Share Points button, followed by the Browse button. Select the Apple File Services share point.

2 Click the New Folder button in the upper-right corner of Server Admin and create a folder inside Apple File Services called Press Releases. Click Save.

You can create folders and share points using Server Admin without actually going to your server computer.

3 Create a second new folder inside Apple File Services called Snow Leopard Development. Click Save.

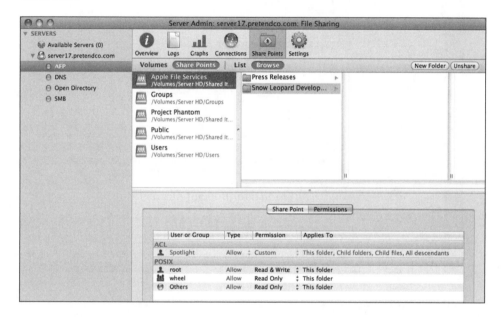

4 Click the Snow Leopard Development folder in Server Admin.

5 In the Permissions pane, change the POSIX permissions as follows:

▶ Owner: student1, Read & Write

▶ Group: admin, Read & Write

▶ Others: No Access

6 Click Save.

Set Other AFP Options

You now have a basic AFP share ready for use. However, it's possible you may need to set some additional settings. Next, you're going to look at the various other options you can configure for an AFP share.

1 In Server Admin, select the AFP service and click the Settings button in the toolbar.

2 In the General pane, type some text in the Login Greeting box.

This message will be displayed to each user who connects to the Apple File Service on your server. If users don't have to see the message every time they connect, you can configure the Apple File Service to display it just once for each user.

3 Select the checkbox for "Do not send same greeting twice to the same user."

Users will now see the message the first time they connect. They won't see a message again until you change the greeting.

4 Click Save.

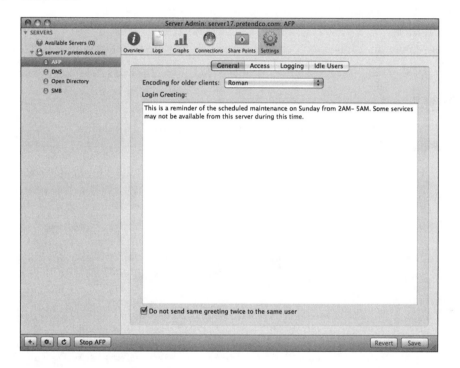

5 Click the Access tab.

6 Select "Enable administrator to masquerade as any registered user" if it isn't already selected.

With this option enabled, you can simulate another user's access: You can authenticate to the AFP service by providing the other user's name, then providing any administrator's password. This is helpful when troubleshooting permissions issues.

Limit Concurrent Users

In some cases, it may be useful to put limits on the number of users who can be connected to your server at any one time. This can be particularly useful if your server isn't very powerful, or if you have a very slow network connection. In most cases, you'll always want to set the number of maximum connections to a number higher than the number of guest connections to leave room for real users to connect to your server.

1   Under Maximum Connections, change the setting for Guest Connections from Unlimited to 3.

2   Change the setting for Client Connections to 10.

This limits the number of users who can be connected to the Apple File Service simultaneously to 10.

Of the 10 possible users who can be connected at one time, only 3 of them can be connected anonymously.

3   Click Save.

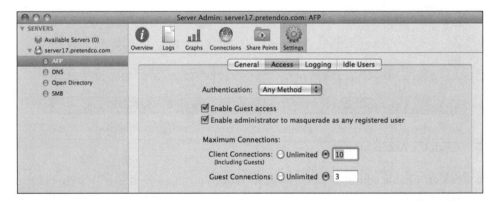

Keep Error and Access Logs

Logs are critical assets for diagnosing any problem, including AFP issues. Certain laws or company policies may also require you to keep logs of activity on your server. Configuring your server to create error and access logs is done through Server Admin as well.

1   Click the Logging tab.

2 Select every checkbox.

3 Click Save.

This will enable all the possible logs, including both access and error logs. This will save information about such actions as when a user connects to your AFP server (Login), disconnects (Logout), reads or copies a file (Open File), creates a new file or folder, or deletes a file or folder. Additionally, there is a setting to archive the logs after a specified number of days. This is useful on a high-traffic server where the logs would otherwise grow too large and possibly fill your disk.

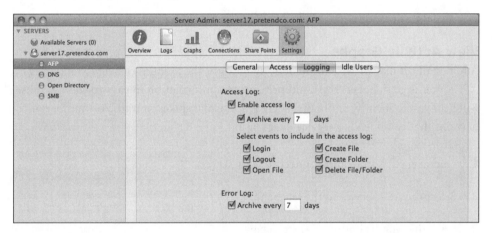

Use Your Server for Time Machine Backups

Normally, for Mac OS X you would configure Time Machine to back up to a second hard drive directly connected to a given computer. However, you can use a remote AFP share for this purpose as well by selecting the "Enable as Time Machine backup destination" option in a share point's Share Point pane.

Monitoring AFP Activity

Earlier in this chapter, you configured the AFP service to log everything. Your settings indicated that the logs would record when a user connects to your AFP server (Login), disconnects (Logout), reads or copies a file (Open File), creates a new file or folder, or deletes a file or folder. Additionally, the logs will show more general information such as when the AFP server was stopped or started.

View Access and Error Logs

You can view both the Access and Error logs using Server Admin.

1 Open Server Admin and connect to your server.

2 Select the AFP service in the left pane.

3 Click the Logs button in the toolbar.

4 Select the Access or Error log using the View menu at the bottom of the window.

The log will auto refresh while it is being displayed on your screen.

View Activity Graphs

Additionally, it may be wise to proactively monitor the amount of activity and usage your AFP server is getting. Server Admin presents this information in easy-to-view graphs. This will help you to identify anomalies such as abnormal spikes in traffic or number of connections that could lead to service degradation.

1 Open Server Admin and connect to your server.

2 Select the AFP service in the left pane.

3 Click the Graphs button in the toolbar.

4 Select whether you want to view the network throughput (bytes per second) at a given time, or the total number of connected users at a given time by using the pop-up menu at the bottom of the window.

5 Change the time period you wish to monitor using the other pop-up menu at the bottom of the window.

Using Windows File Service

Mac OS X Server permits you to share files over the SMB protocol. Sometimes referred to as CIFS, this is the primary protocol used by Windows clients to access files on a remote file server. It has some differences from AFP that you will explore. Understanding the fine differences between the two will lead to better integration when sharing folders.

Windows Share Points

As shown in the following figure, when you use Server Admin to configure a share point for use with Windows service (SMB), you can specify:

▶   Whether or not to make this share point available over SMB

▶   Whether or not to allow guest access to this share point

▶   How the SMB service handles file locking

▶   How the SMB service assigns permissions for newly created files and folders

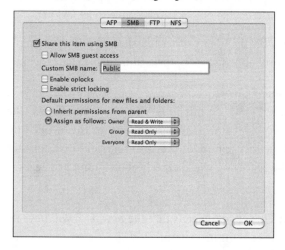

SMB File Locking

File locking prevents multiple clients from writing changes to a file simultaneously. The choices you make for file locking depend on what kinds of file-sharing clients you have, and which protocols you use to your share points. In order to make an appropriate decision, you need to understand the significance of oplocks and strict locking:

▶   *Oplocks* are opportunistic locks, a client-side performance enhancement that requires cooperation between a Windows client and the SMB service. If SMB service supports oplocks, the client can request to cache a file locally, in order to perform read and write operations on the cached file rather than directly on the server. This saves network bandwidth and increases performance for the SMB client. If another SMB client requests access to the file, the SMB service notifies the holder of the oplock, and that client should write changes from its cache back to the SMB service. The SMB service does not let another client have access to the file until the first client has finished writing.

▶ *Strict locking* requires the SMB client to request a lock for an entire file, as opposed to only a portion of the file. Without strict locking, two SMB clients can simultaneously edit different portions of the same file, which is a nice feature for certain environments and workflows, but could cause data loss if any other file-sharing protocol is involved. Strict locking causes the SMB service to check for an existing file lock with every read and write request.

What does this mean for you? If your server shares a share point via the SMB protocol only, and you have "well-behaved" SMB clients (which check for file locks appropriately), then for better SMB performance, you may want to enable oplocks and disable strict locking.

However, if you share a share point via SMB and any other file-sharing protocol, then to prevent data corruption, you should probably disable oplocks and enable strict locking.

Default Permissions for New Files and Folders

Recall from the section "Understanding POSIX Permissions with AFP Share Points" that the operating system assigns to new files read and write permissions for the owner, but read only for the group and others. One nice feature of the SMB service is that, for each share point, you have the choice of the following two methods of assigning privileges to newly creates files and folders:

▶ Inherit permissions from parent: This option means that the new item will have the same permissions as the folder that contains that item.

▶ Assign as follows: The default choice is read and write for the owner, but read only for the group and Others. However, you can use the pop-up menus to specify "Read & Write," "Read Only," "Write Only," or "No Access" for the owner, for the group, and for Others. If you specify "Read & Write" for the group, you can enable all the members of a group to edit files without first changing permissions.

Server Name and Workgroup

The Windows service has a number of configuration options available in Server Admin. Just as Mac computers can browse for servers using Bonjour, Windows clients have their own way to find servers on the network, based on a protocol called Network Basic Input/Output System (NetBIOS). The Computer Name field in the General pane of the Settings pane defines the server's NetBIOS name. It is set automatically, but it is always best to make sure your server's Windows NetBIOS name matches the host name and the

DNS name for your computers. That way, there is no chance for a client computer to get conflicting information if it tries to get the server name using different protocols.

Workgroups are another feature of NetBIOS. The workgroup name is an arbitrary text string used to group servers together. You often see descriptive workgroups, such as MARKETING, RESEARCH, and so on. Your server's Windows service will join whatever workgroup you specify. If you type the name of a workgroup that doesn't exist on your network, your server creates its own workgroup, and Windows computers will see that group.

This is also the location where you choose the role of your Windows service on the server. A standalone server provides file service, but does not provide any Windows authentication services. Configuring the server as a domain member will provide file service by authenticating the user against an external domain controller. You can configure an Open Directory master to take the role of a primary domain controller (PDC); you can configure an Open Directory replica as a backup domain controller (BDC). If your server is a domain controller, not only can you provide file service, but Windows clients can also authenticate directly against your server.

Advanced Windows Services

The Advanced pane of the Settings pane lets you set other Windows configuration options:

▶   The Code Page pop-up menu refers to the character set supported by Windows service on this server. The default setting (Latin US) is correct for U.S. English. Other language settings can be chosen from the list.

▶ The Workgroup Master Browser option means your server can become a local master browser. It doesn't mean the server necessarily will be the local master browser, just that it will participate in the election process to determine who will serve as the local master browser.

▶ The Domain Master Browser option is similar to the Workgroup Master Browser option, but selecting its checkbox will now result in a possible election between your domain master browser and the Windows domain master browser.

Browsing is a key element of a Windows network. Users can find shared resources on the network by using Network Neighborhood, a Windows utility. A Windows network maintains a list of all the computers connected to it by using central repositories known as workgroup master browsers (or simply master browsers) and domain master browsers.

How do you know whether to select the browser options? You should consult with your Windows administrator. Generally speaking, if you are in a workgroup with a Windows server acting as a domain controller, you should not make Mac OS X Server the domain master browser. In that case, the Windows server is the domain master browser, and adding another domain master browser will result in an election process that the Windows administrator may not want to happen. When computers capable of acting as master browsers come online, they automatically elect a computer to be the master browser for a given network. Some Windows administrators may not feel comfortable with a non-Windows computer acting in such a role.

▶ Windows Internet Name Service (WINS) is Microsoft's implementation of NetBIOS Name Service (NBNS). WINS resolves NetBIOS names to IP addresses. You can distribute this information using the DHCP service in Mac OS X Server.

How do you know if WINS needs to be configured? Again, you should consult the administrator who is responsible for your Windows computers. Selecting "Enable WINS server" makes your Mac OS X Server a WINS server. Selecting "Register with WINS server" allows you to become the client of an existing WINS server by specifying its IP address or name.

▶ Finally, if you want to host home folders for Windows users on your Mac OS X Server, make sure that the "Enable virtual share points" option is selected.

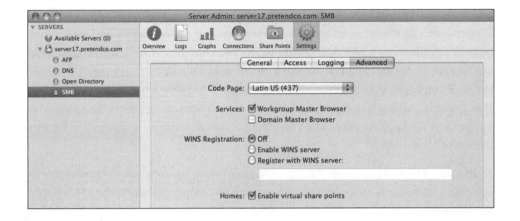

Browsing from a Windows Client

Once you configure your name, your workgroup, and—if necessary—the Advanced settings, Mac OS X Server can be browsed just like any other Windows server on the network. The following figure depicts Mac OS X Server showing up on a small network with no WINS service. A Windows server is creating the Example workgroup, and Mac OS X Server is creating the workgroup named Workgroup.

From a Windows computer, once you have chosen the Mac OS X Server as a share point, the Windows service in Mac OS X Server provides support for authentication via the protocols LAN Manager, NT LAN Manager (NTLM), and NTLMv2 and Kerberos (the last two being one option simultaneously).

SMB Activity Monitoring

Windows service logs are configurable in Server Admin; however, configuration is not quite as flexible as with AFP. Server Admin lets you configure three levels of detail—low, medium, or high—but you can choose a much more verbose level of logging by editing the SMB configuration file directly. Unless you are debugging a particular problem with Windows file sharing, you'll probably want to choose Medium from the Log Detail pop-up menu in the Logging pane. The lower the Log Detail setting, the better you preserve the server's resources.

As with the AFP service, Server Admin contains an easy-to-use graph feature that will show how many users are connected for any period of time. To access the SMB graphs, do the following:

1   Open Server Admin and connect to your server.

2   Select the SMB service on the left side of the window.

3   Click the Graphs button in the toolbar.

4   Change the time period, if desired, using the menu at the bottom of the window.

This exercise demonstrates some of the more useful features of Windows file service on Mac OS X Server. After creating a Windows share point, you will explore the Windows browsing features and browse to your Windows services using the Connect to Server command in Mac OS X.

Configuring Windows File Service

You use Server Admin to share a folder over SMB. This process is very similar to how you created an AFP share point, but it will be using the SMB (also known as CIFS) protocol to make the share point available to Windows clients.

1   On your Mac OS X computer in Server Admin, click the File Sharing button in the toolbar, then click the Volumes button, followed by the Browse button. Navigate to and select the Shared Items folder on your boot volume.

2   Click the New Folder button in the upper-right corner of Server Admin to create a folder inside Shared Items called Windows Services. Click Save.

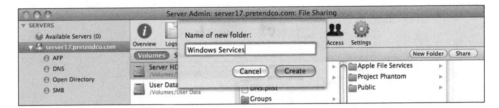

3   Select the Windows Services folder from the list. Click the Share button, and then click Save.

4   In the Share Point pane at the bottom of the window, click the Protocol Options button, and deselect the "Share this item using AFP" checkbox.

5   In the Protocol Options pane, choose SMB, and be sure the "Share this item using SMB" checkbox is selected.

6   Select "Allow SMB guest access."

This allows SMB connections to be made to this share point without providing a user name if the SMB service has been configured to allow guest access.

7   In the "Custom SMB name" field, type Windows.

This is the name that clients see when they browse for and connect to the share point using SMB.

If you append the dollar symbol ($) at the end of the Custom name, the share point will be hidden from Windows clients.

8   Select "Enable oplocks" and "Enable strict locking."

9 Change the permissions model to "Assign as follows:"

▶ Owner: Read & Write

▶ Group: Read & Write

▶ Everyone: Read Only

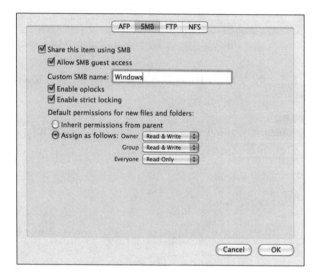

10 Click OK to close the Protocol Options dialog.

11 Click Save.

Configuring Access and Starting Windows File Services

Now it's time to configure access and start the Windows file service.

1 Select the SMB service on the left side of Server Admin, and then click the Settings button in the toolbar.

If the SMB service isn't listed, you must first add it by clicking the Add (+) button and Choosing Add Service from the pop-up menu.

2 In the General pane, enter server17 in the Computer Name field and WG_SEVENTEEN in the Workgroup field.

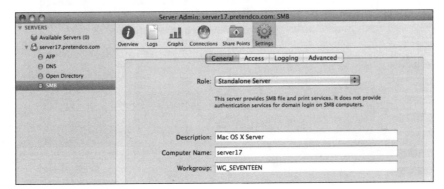

3 Click the Access tab, and select the "Allow Guest access" checkbox.

4 Set the maximum number of client connections to 15.

5 Leave the default authentication models selected ("NTLMv2 & Kerberos" and NTLM).

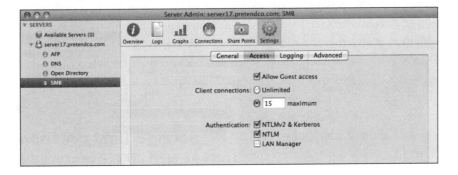

6 Click the Advanced tab. Select "Enable WINS server" from the WINS Registration options.

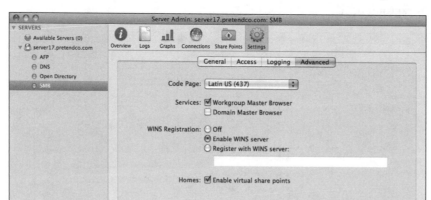

7 Click Save.

8 Start the SMB service by clicking the Start SMB button in the bottom-left corner.

Using NFS Share Point Access

Network File System (NFS) is one of the oldest shared file systems. Because of its deep roots among UNIX platforms, it is still used in a number of situations today. It is considerably different from either the AFP or SMB service. The most outstanding difference is that NFS does not support user logins. When you try to connect to Windows or Apple services without a valid Kerberos ticket, the first thing you do is identify yourself with a user name and password. In the absence of a Kerberos ticket, NFS does not give access to users; it gives access to computers. More accurately, it gives access to particular IP addresses. If your computer has one of these IP addresses, the NFS service lets you connect. Without a Kerberos ticket, it won't prompt you for a user name or password.

Starting with Mac OS X Server v10.3, NFS file and file-range locks (standard POSIX advisory locks) are enabled by default. This means that two users can safely edit the same file concurrently, as long as they are not editing the same section of the file. If two users attempt to modify the same section of a file, one is locked out in read-only mode until the other is done saving changes.

Mac OS X Server v10.5 and v10.6 use NFSv4, which adds the ability to use Kerberos v5 for identification and authentication for NFS.

NFS Trusts the Client for User Authentication

If NFS doesn't prompt you for a user name and password, how can it deal with permissions? If you sit down at a client computer and start using an NFS volume, how does it know if you're a member of the group that has access? Who does it assign as the owner of a file you create?

The server simply believes what the client tells it, based upon the user ID provided by the client. The client tells the server that user Jim is creating a folder or deleting a file, and the server believes it. If Jim has access to that file or folder, the operation is allowed. In Mac OS X, the user that the client reports to the server is normally the user who logged in at the login window. Two issues arise with this method of user identification:

▶ User mismatch: Maybe the user really is Jim, and your client is correctly reporting his identity to the server. What if the server doesn't know who Jim is? Or what if there are different Jims—one on the server and one on the client? Remember that each Mac OS X client has a list of users (configured in Accounts preferences), and Mac OS X Server has its own list of users (configured in Workgroup Manager). The two lists may not have any common users, or they may have users who appear to be the same but only coincidentally have the same information. NFS can't keep this straight on its own.

▶ Identity theft: Imagine you are a standard user on the server, but you are the administrator of your own MacBook running Mac OS X. Because you control that MacBook, you can create any user you want locally and thus pretend to be anyone you want to be. You can now see why NFS is a security concern.

NFS Options to Increase Security

One response to the problem of identity theft is to map NFS users. Rather than accept what the client reports, the server can simply pretend that the user is "nobody," and hence the user gets the permissions that are assigned to everyone. You'll almost certainly want to select this mapping for the root user—the all-powerful superuser who can delete any item on a volume. It is just as easy to steal the root user's identity as it is any other user's. Beyond this, you can map all users to nobody and just ignore altogether what the client is reporting for a user. Checking both these options is similar to giving guest access under AFP.

The Minimum Security pop-up menu offers a number of options to increase the level of security for sharing files over NFS:

▶ Standard—Use only IP address to grant access to the NFS service

▶ Any—Accept any method of authentication

▶ Kerberos v5—Accept only Kerberos authentication

▶ Kerberos v5 with data integrity—In addition to accepting only Kerberos authentication, checksum the data transfer

▶ Kerberos v5 with data integrity and privacy—In addition to accepting only Kerberos authentication, checksum and encrypt the data transfer

If you need to provide NFS services only to computers with Mac OS X v10.5 or Mac OS X v10.6, it is recommended that you choose an option that includes Kerberos for the Minimum Security setting for NFS service.

Configuring NFS

Setting up NFS share points is similar to setting up AFP and SMB share points.

1   On your Mac OS X computer in Server Admin, click the File Sharing button in the toolbar, and then click the Volumes button, followed by the Browse button. Navigate to and select the Shared Items folder.

2   Click the New Folder button in the upper-right corner of Server Admin to create a folder inside Shared Items called NFS Services. Click Save.

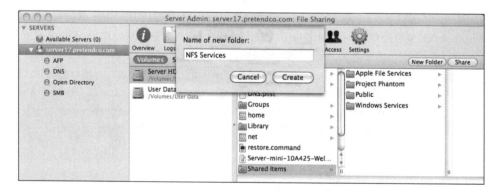

3   Click the Share button, and then click Save.

4   In the Share Point pane at the bottom of the window, click the Protocol Options button, and disable AFP, SMB, and FTP services for this folder.

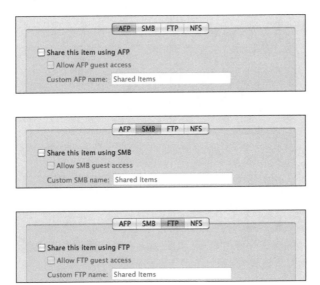

5   In the Protocol Options pane, click NFS.

6   Select "Export this item and its contents to" and leave World chosen in the pop-up menu.

This setting allows any computer (unless blocked by a firewall) access to this NFS share, regardless of its IP address.

7   Set the Mapping pop-up menu to Root to Nobody.

This setting blocks users from using the root user account (UID=0) to get unlimited access to the file on the share point. Anyone using a root user account will be treated the same as the nobody, or guest, user on the server.

8   Select the "Read only" option.

Because of the security deficiencies with NFS, many people choose to offer file services via NFS in a read-only manner.

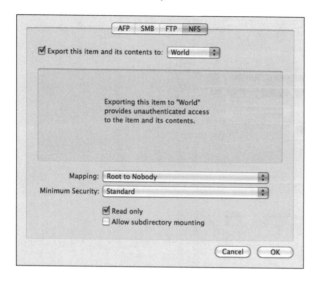

9   Click OK to dismiss the Protocol Options dialog.

10 Click Save.

Starting the NFS Service

The NFS service Settings pane contains only a few options, which can safely be left at their defaults for basic NFS file servers. You start the NFS service in the same manner as other services.

1   In Server Admin, click the Add (+) button and choose Add Service from the pop-up menu.

2   Select the checkbox for NFS, and click Save.

3   Select the NFS service in the left column.

4 Click the Start NFS button.

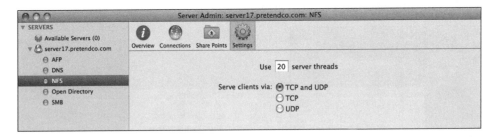

Connecting to an NFS Share

NFS has one major difference over other file-sharing protocols that comes up when you mount an NFS share from your client computer. With most sharing protocols, you connect to the share point without knowing where it is on the file server's file system. With NFS, you must specify the full path of the share point as it exists on the server. Also unlike other protocols, you won't be given a list of share points to choose from. If you need to know what shares exist on a server, you can type showmount -e nfs.server.name in a Terminal window.

1 In the Finder on your Mac OS X computer, choose Go > Connect to Server.

2 Enter this URL: nfs://server17.pretendco.com:/Shared Items/NFS Services.

3 Click Connect.

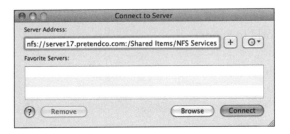

A new Finder window will appear, and a new entry for the server will appear in the sidebar.

Note that you were not prompted for any user name or password. Also note the Read-Only icon in the corner of the Finder window; it is shown because the volume is read only, as you configured it to be earlier. Depending on your use of NFS, you may have a read-write NFS share, or you may limit NFS to read only but also share the same folder using another protocol for any write actions.

Setting Other NFS Share Options

Usually for NFS you don't want to export (share) the folder to the entire world, but rather restrict it to a certain subnet or list of IP addresses.

1　In Server Admin, click the name of your server on the left, followed by the File Sharing button in the toolbar.

2　Click the Share Points button just below the toolbar.

3　Click the NFS Services share point, then click the Share Point tab.

4　Click the Protocol Options button.

5　Click the NFS tab.

6　Change the pop-up menu from World to Subnet.

7　Enter a Subnet address of 10.1.0.0.

8　Enter a Subnet mask of 255.255.0.0.

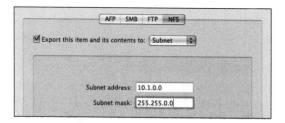

For even better security, if you have only a few computers that will be connecting to your NFS server, you would want to limit connections to just those IPs.

9 Change the pop-up menu at the top from Subnet to Client List.

10 Click the Add (+) button.

127.0.0.1 (localhost) appears in the list. You probably want to leave that IP there so the server can talk to itself.

11 Click the Add (+) button again.

12 Type an address of 10.1.17.2 (or use the IP address assigned to your Mac OS X computer).

Modify some additional NFS settings that might be appropriate for your use:

13 Change the Mapping to "All to Nobody."

This setting will ignore any user names on the client side, and treat any NFS clients as if they were using the Nobody (guest) account on the server.

14 Change the Minimum Security setting to "Kerberos v5 with data integrity and privacy."

This setting requires that clients must possess a Kerberos ticket, and it will authenticate both the client and server as well as encrypt all the NFS network traffic.

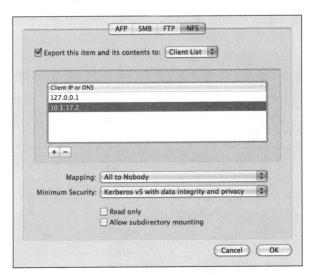

15 Click OK.

16 Click Save.

Using FTP File Service

FTP is a well-known cross-platform method for transferring files. Mac OS X Server supports FTP as a way to transfer files to and from your server. However, keep in mind that FTP is not known for its good security. Because of this, you should only use FTP when it is absolutely necessary. One such use might be to distribute your product documentation or drivers to everyone on the Internet. Such a situation would not fit well with other file-sharing mechanisms because you wouldn't know what platforms they are using and wouldn't want to create accounts for everyone.

Enabling FTP

You configure the FTP service in much the same way as you configure the AFP and SMB services—using Server Admin. The General pane of the Settings pane of Server Admin lets you control the number of users who can connect to the FTP service, the authentication protocol they use for connecting, and whether to let anonymous users connect. Anonymous FTP users are similar to guest-access users under AFP or SMB.

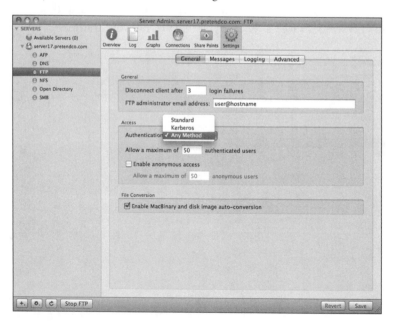

NOTE ▶ Although FTP service supports Kerberos authentication, neither the Finder nor the command-line FTP clients support Kerberos authentication.

By default, all share points you create in Server Admin are shared via AFP and SMB, but FTP needs to be allowed. Once allowed by checking off FTP in the Protocol Options of the share point, simply turning on the FTP service gives access to these share points. The Advanced pane of the FTP service lets you modify this behavior. By enabling Home Directory with Share Points from the "Authorized users see" pop-up menu, you can force users to see only their home folders. FTP share points appear as a subfolder inside users' home folders. This is a good way to prevent users from having access to other users' home folders. The most restrictive option is "Home Directory Only." This selection gives users access only to their own home folders. If you have FTP share points set up, anonymous users have access to those share points.

When providing access via FTP, passive FTP can be a useful option. *Passive FTP* is commonly used to access an FTP server behind a firewall. If your network administrator doesn't allow any FTP access through your firewall, this option will not help you, but a common firewall configuration is to allow passive FTP but not active FTP. This is a client-side option. You do not need to configure anything on the server, but you may need to explain to your users that they must use passive FTP to connect to your server.

Understanding FTP File Conversions

One hidden, but useful, feature of the Mac OS X Server FTP service is its ability to perform automatic file conversions. The FTP server can automatically compress, archive, and encode files on the fly at the time they are requested. There are a few situations in which this comes in particularly handy:

▶ MacBinary: Some legacy applications use a special type of file called a *forked* file. This type of file can cause difficulties with FTP, so the server encodes the file in MacBinary format before sending it. To request this type of encoding, simply add the extension .bin to the file you are requesting. For example, if the FTP server has a copy of SimpleText, you can ask for SimpleText.bin, and the server will encode and send the SimpleText file in MacBinary format. MacBinary can be combined with both .tar and .gz compressions.

▶ Automatic archiving: If you need an entire folder of documents, just ask for the folder with .tar added at the end before the transfer. The server creates a single archive file of the folder, and you can expand it after you have downloaded it. Be aware that this feature doesn't perform compression.

▶ Disk-image creation: When you include the .dmg extension in the URL, the FTP server converts the download into a disk-image file. This also works when downloading an application that has .app in the filename. In this case, the server automatically creates a .dmg file for the downloaded application.

▶ Automatic compression: If you are copying a large document, you can compress it by adding .gz to the end. This uses a UNIX-style gzip program. A useful shortcut is to chain archiving and compression. If you want a folder called bigfolder, you can ask for bigfolder.tar.gz, and the folder will be archived and compressed before it is sent.

Monitoring FTP Activity

The FTP server has a log that you configure in the Logging pane of the Settings pane. You can have the log keep track of uploads or downloads. You can view the activity in the FTP Log pane by clicking the Logging tab in the Server Admin toolbar.

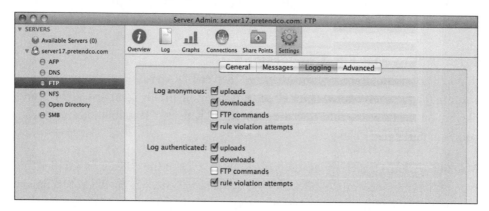

Configuring FTP Service

You use Server Admin to share a folder over FTP. As you've done previously with SMB and NFS shares, you'll create a folder and make it available to others using the FTP protocol.

1   With Server Admin on your Mac OS X computer, select your server, then click File Sharing in the toolbar.

2   Click Volumes, then click Browse.

3   Navigate to the Shared Items in your boot volume.

4   Click New Folder and create a folder named FTP Services.

5   Select the FTP Services folder, click Share, and click Save.

6   With FTP Services selected, click Protocol Options, and confirm that the checkboxes are deselected for sharing this item using AFP and SMB.

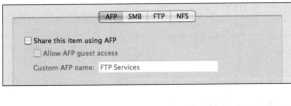

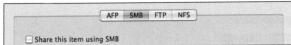

7   Click the FTP tab and select the checkbox for "Share this item using FTP."

8   Deselect the "Allow FTP guest access" checkbox.

9   Click OK to dismiss the Protocol Options pane, then click Save.

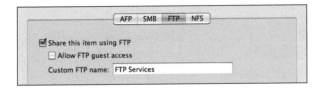

Now your shared folder is visible only to FTP clients.

Allow Access for Selected Users

Next, you'll start the FTP service and allow access to FTP for certain users and groups.

1   On your Mac OS X computer, open Server Admin and select your server in the left column.

2   Click the Add (+) button and choose Add Service from the pop-up menu. Select FTP and click Save.

3   Select the FTP service, then click Settings.

4   Click General.

5   Choose Any Method from the Authentication pop-up menu.

6   Deselect the "Enable anonymous access" checkbox.

7   Click Save.

8   Click the Start FTP button in the bottom-left corner.

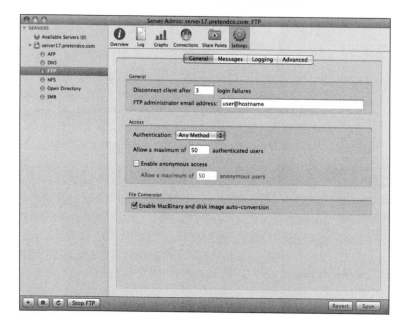

9   Select your server (rather than the FTP service) in the left column of Server Admin.

10 Click Access in the toolbar.

11 Select "For selected services below."

12 Select FTP from the list.

13 Select "Allow only users and groups below" and click the Add Group Members (+) button.

14 Drag users Student One and Student Two from the Users and Groups window to the list of allowed users.

15 Click Save.

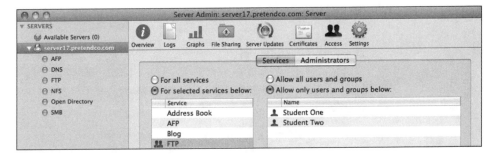

Connect to Server via FTP

Finally, you'll use the client computer to connect via FTP on the server.

1   On your Mac OS X computer, switch to the Finder, and choose Go > Connect to Server.

2   Type ftp://server17.pretendco.com and click Connect.

3   Authenticate as student3 (password: network) and click Connect.

4   Because the SACL you just created for the FTP service does not include student3, you will see an error. The authentication may have succeeded, but the authorization to use the FTP service failed, and you should see a message that you entered an invalid user name or password. Click OK.

5   Authenticate as student1 (password: network) and click Connect.

A Finder window should appear with the share points that are available via the FTP service.

Note which folders you have access to in the mounted share point.

6   Unmount the FTP volume from your client computer: Close the Finder window that just appeared, then click eject next to your server in the sidebar.

Although it can be useful to restrict connections per service group user, it will interfere with future exercises.

1   On your Mac OS X computer, open Server Admin and authenticate if necessary.

2   Select your server.

3   Click the Access tab, and do the following:

▶   Select the "Allow all users and groups" option.

▶   Select the "For all services" option.

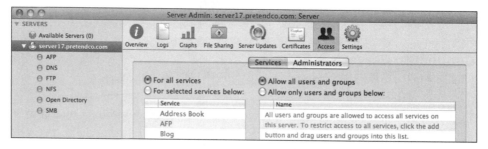

4   Click Save.

Network-Mounted Share Points

You'll often need to make files and folders on a server available to users on client computers. One way to do that is to tell users to connect to the server from the Finder. Connecting from the Finder is easy, but it requires users to remember which server to connect to and where to find the files on that server.

For frequently accessed resources, such as applications, libraries, or fonts, you might want to simplify your users' experience even more. If so, you can make a folder, disk, or partition on a server mount automatically on some or all of the client computers in a domain. You do this by configuring network-mounted share points.

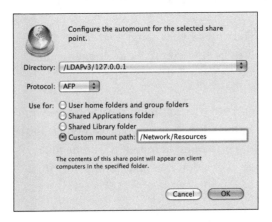

For example, suppose you want to have a specific set of applications available to every user in a given LDAP directory. You could create a share point containing the desired applications and then set the share point to automatically mount into a /Network/Applications folder on client computers that can utilize either the AFP or the NFS protocol. To do this, you configure the share points using Server Admin, and then select the Enable Automount checkbox and click the Edit button to configure those share points to automatically appear in a folder in the Finder windows of supported client computers. Information about these automatically mounted share points is stored in the LDAP directory.

Preparing for a Network Home Folder

You also can set up a share point to automatically be available for a network home folder for a network user. The user's home folder can reside in any AFP or NFS share point that the user's computer can access. The share point must be automountable—it must have a network mount record in the directory domain where the user account resides. An automountable share point ensures that the home folder is automatically visible in /Network/Servers when the user logs in to a Mac OS X computer configured to access the shared domain. Because AFP is the native file-sharing protocol for Mac OS X, and allows Mac OS X clients to reconnect to the AFP service after a temporary network disconnection, without errors, Apple recommends storing home folders in AFP share points.

NOTE ▶ The home folder doesn't need to be stored on the same server as the directory domain containing the user's account. In fact, distributing directory domains and home folders among various servers can help you balance your workload.

When a network user logs in to a Mac OS X computer, the computer retrieves the account information from a shared directory domain on the accounts server. The computer uses the location of the user's home folder, stored in the account, to mount the home folder, which resides physically on a home folder server. If you don't set up a home folder for a network user account, the user cannot log in.

Configuring Network Mounts

Next, you'll configure the /Users folder to be used for network home folders. This is required for your users to log in to local computers using network accounts maintained on the server.

1   If you have turned on Fast User Switching, you may encounter errors, which will prevent users from logging in to the Network account if they switch from a local account. Log off all users on your Mac OS X computer except your initial administrator account.

2   On your Mac OS X computer, open and authenticate as ladmin to Server Admin.

3   Click the File Sharing button in the toolbar, click the Share Points button, and then click the List button.

4   Select the Users folder, and then click Share Point.

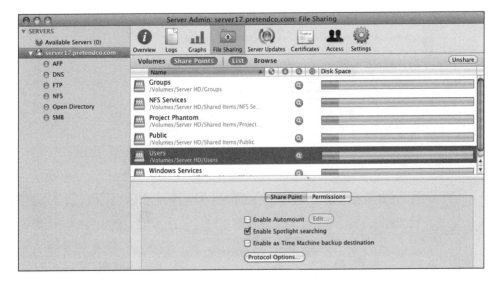

5   Select the Enable Automount checkbox.

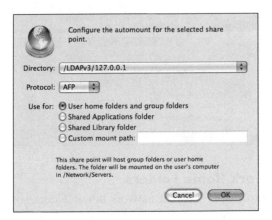

6   Confirm that AFP is chosen in the Protocol pop-up menu.

7   Select "User home folders and group folders."

8   Click OK.

9 Authenticate as diradmin if prompted (password: diradmin).

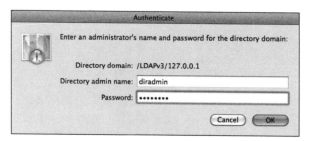

10 Click Save.

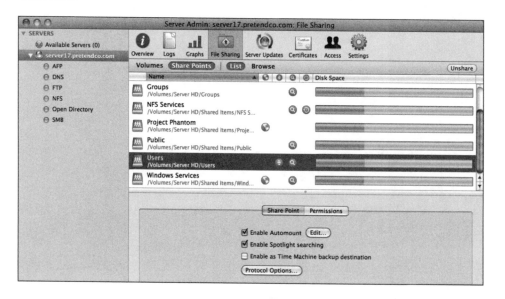

Configuring Users to Use Network Home Folders

In addition to configuring the file server to share /Users for network home folders, you must also use the Home pane for a user account in Workgroup Manager to select the Users automount share point as the location for the user's home folder.

When storing home folders on a server, the disk space can be used up very quickly. You can use the Disk Quota field to limit the disk space a user can consume to store files in the partition where the user's home folder resides.

For example, when user Sharon places files in user Rafael's folder, the size of the files affects either Sharon's or Rafael's disk quota, depending on the protocol Sharon uses to transfer the files:

▶ If Sharon uses AFP to drop files in Rafael's drop box, Rafael's quota is affected because the owner of the drop box (Rafael) becomes the owner of the files.

▶ If Sharon uses NFS to copy the files to Rafael's folder, Sharon is still the owner, and so copying affects Sharon's quota, not Rafael's.

You must set each user account record to indicate the server and share point that contains their home folder. To set up a home folder for a network user in Workgroup Manager, follow these steps:

1   On your Mac OS X client computer, open Workgroup Manager.

2   Connect to your Open Directory server as diradmin (password: `diradmin`).

3   Click the Accounts button in the toolbar, and make sure you are viewing the LDAP Directory, not the Local Directory. Authenticate if prompted.

This is the shared Open Directory domain you created in Chapter 3. User accounts defined in this domain are accessible from your Mac OS X computer via the network.

4   Click the Users button in the toolbar, and select all the users except Directory Administrator. Click the Home tab and select the Users share point for your server.

5   Enter a Disk Quota of 200 MB for all of the selected users.

6 Click Save.

If you do not click Create Home Now before clicking Save, the home folder is created the next time the user restarts the client computer and logs in remotely. The home folder has the same name as the user's first short name. When having Windows users connect, the home folder must be created in advance of the Windows users' initial login.

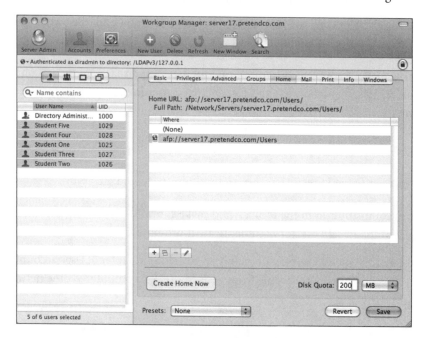

7 Click Student One and verify that the values for Home URL and Full Path look like the values in the figure below:

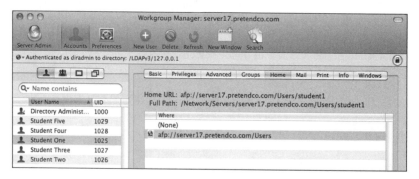

8 On your Mac OS X computer, open the Accounts preference, then click Login Options to verify that you are still bound to your server.

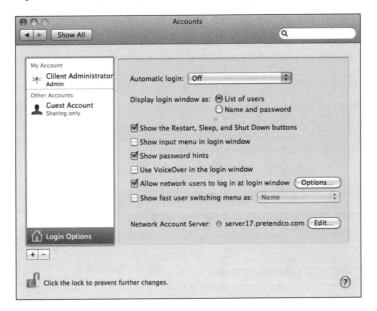

9 Click Edit, then click Open Directory Utility.

10 In Open Directory, click Search Policy, and verify that your server is still listed in the Authentication path for your Mac OS X computer.

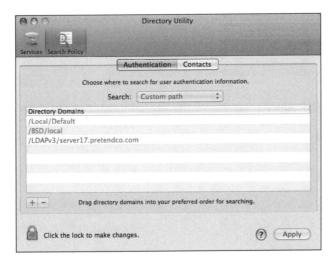

11 On your Mac OS X computer, log out as ladmin.

12 On your Mac OS X computer at the login window, click Other, then log in as student1 (password: network).

13 After you log in, the Finder should display a window with student1's network home folder.

Option-click the student1 proxy icon in the title bar of the Finder window, and verify that the hierarchy displays that your home folder is located on the network share point rather than directly in the /Users folder on your Mac OS X computer, as shown in the figure below:

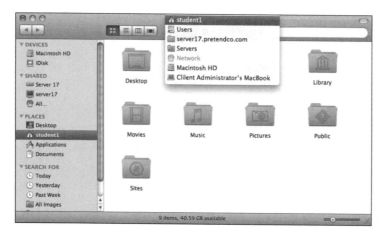

14 Log out as student1.

Verify that a new home folder is created in the /Users folder on your server computer.

15 Log in to your Mac OS X computer as cadmin (password: cadmin).

16 Open Server Admin, connect to your server and authenticate as ladmin (password: ladmin).

17 Select your server, click File Sharing in the toolbar, click Share Points, then click Browse.

18 Select the Users share point, then select the student1 home folder.

19 Verify that the name of the new home folder matches the short name of the user (in this case, student1).

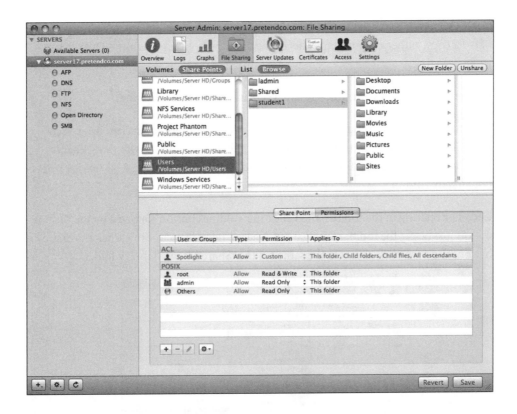

Using Automounts for Other Folders

Automounts can be used for more than just user home folders. Presets exist for creating shared Applications and Library folders, but any folder can be set to automount at any path. Next, you'll create a new folder, copy some applications into it, and share its contents as a network mount.

1   On your Mac OS X computer, use Server Admin to create two new folders in /Shared Items. Name the folders Applications and Library.

  To create new items in /Shared Items, click File Sharing, click Volumes, then click Browse. Navigate to /Shared Items, and click New Folder to create a new folder.

2   Choose Server > Share Server's Screen.

3   Authenticate as ladmin (password: ladmin). Log in on your server as ladmin.

4   Copy Calculator and Stickies from /Applications to /Shared Items/Applications. Make a copy, rather than moving the application, by holding down the Option key while dragging.

5   Log out as admin on your Mac OS X Server, and quit Screen Sharing.

6   On your Mac OS X computer, in Server Admin's Computers & Services list, select AFP. Click the Settings button, and then click the Access tab to verify that "Enable Guest access" is selected; if it isn't, select it and click Save. Start the AFP service if it is not already running.

7   Click File Sharing in the toolbar, then click the Volumes button followed by the Browse button just below the toolbar. Navigate to /Shared Items/Applications, click the Share button, and then click Save. Do the same for the /Shared Items/Library folder.

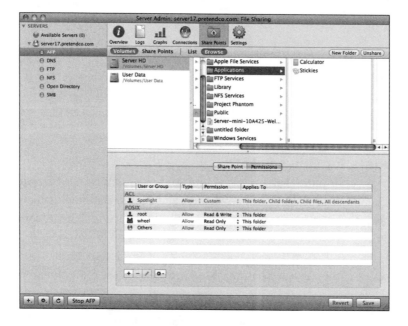

8   Reselect the Applications folder. In the Share Point pane at the bottom, select the Enable Automount checkbox.

9   Choose your LDAP directory in the pop-up menu. If your server were bound to several other servers, you would see them in the Directory pop-up menu. In this case, all you see is the /LDAPv3/127.0.0.1 directory.

10 Confirm that AFP is chosen in the Protocol pop-up menu, and select "Shared Applications folder."

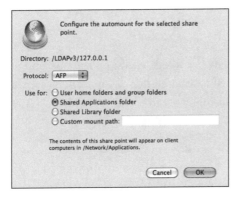

11 Click OK. Authenticate to your directory if prompted.

12 Click Save.

13 Select the /Shared Items/Library folder. In the Share Point pane at the bottom, select the Enable Automount checkbox.

14 Select your LDAP directory in the pop-up menu, confirm that AFP is chosen in the Protocol pop-up menu, and select "Shared Library folder."

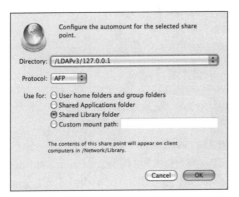

15 Click OK. Authenticate to your directory if prompted.

The shared Library folder can be used for giving your client computers access to a shared set of fonts, preferences, or other objects that normally reside in your Library folder.

16 Click Save in Server Admin to save the changes to the automount.

17 On your Mac OS X computer, switch to the Finder.

18 Chose Go > Go to Folder and type /Network.

19 The Finder opens a new window. In the Network folder, click Applications, and note that the two sample applications you copied to /Shared Items/Applications are visible here. The applications you place in this folder are available to all Mac OS X and Mac OS X Server computers bound to the Open Directory service.

Note that these resources are available to local users as well as network users; you should be logged in as Client Administrator, a local user account on your Mac OS X computer, and see the two applications you made available in /Network/Applications.

Controlling Access to Shared Folders

In many cases, you won't want everyone to have access to your file services. There are a few simple steps that can be followed to greatly increase the security of your file server.

Reduce the Number of File-Sharing Services

First and foremost is reducing the number of services itself. Every service that's running on your server represents a potential point of entry for an unwanted visitor. Reducing the number of services on your server will also reduce this risk. For example, if you have only Mac OS X computers connecting to your server, you probably don't need the SMB or FTP services running. Similarly, if you're only providing services to Windows computers, the AFP and FTP services likely won't be used and can be stopped. In most cases, the FTP service should only be used when you need to provide access to the broadest set of computers external to your organization.

Remove Guest Access for Every Share Point

The next thing to consider is guest access. If you are sharing files only with members of your organization who have accounts on your server, or if everyone is bound to the same directory server, you should consider removing guest access. Remember that there are a few places you can set this. Follow these steps to remove guest access for every protocol on every share point:

1   Open Server Admin and connect to your server.

2   Click the File Sharing button in the toolbar.

3   Click the Share Points button just below the toolbar.

4   Select a share point.

5   Click the Share Points pane in the bottom half of the window.

6   Click the Protocol Options button.

   A dialog will appear with options for each of the protocol options that apply to that share.

7   For each protocol, deselect "Allow guest access."

8   Click OK.

9   Click Save.

10 Repeat for every share point on your server.

Remove Guest Access for Each Protocol

Remove guest access for each protocol itself. Though disabling guest access for each share point, or for the entire protocol itself, will accomplish what you're looking for, it's best to disable it in both places to minimize the risk of reactivation.

1   In Server Admin, click the AFP service in the left column.

2   Click the Settings button in the toolbar.

3   Click the Access tab.

4   Deselect "Enable Guest access."

5   Click Save.

6   Repeat the same steps for the FTP and SMB services.

Set Up SACLs

Review who has access to connect to each of your file-sharing services. This access is controlled through the use of SACLs, a topic described in more detail in Chapter 2, "Authenticating and Authorizing Accounts." SACLs require explicit permission to connect to your file server. Each user, or a group the user belongs to, will need to be registered as being allowed to use a given service. You can set up SACLs using these steps:

1   In Server Admin, select your server name in the left column.

2   Click Access in the toolbar.

3   Select the services you wish to restrict.

4   Determine which users and/or groups should have access to that service.

5   Click Save.

Once complete, review the file system permissions on the folders that are your share points. The permissions of the folders that are your share points will control what share points are listed on the client when they connect to your server. In many cases, you should also review the permissions of the enclosed folders because a larger group will often have access to the share point than will have access to all of its subfolders.

Troubleshooting File Services

Whether you're using AFP, SMB, NFS, or FTP, troubleshooting file services on Mac OS X Server typically involves the following considerations.

▶ User access: What users or groups should have access to the specific files and folders on the server, and are their appropriate permissions set correctly?

▶ Platform and protocol access: From what clients are users trying to access the server, such as Mac OS X, Mac OS 9, Windows, or Linux systems? What protocols are they using when accessing the server?

▶ Special needs: Are there any special circumstances, such as users' needing concurrent access to files or access to files in a nonnative format to the system they are using?

▶ Concurrent access: Is there a possibility that in your users' workflow, there could be multiple clients simultaneously accessing the same files, regardless of the file-sharing protocol(s) being used?

For troubleshooting access settings, you will want to test access by using the Effective Permissions Inspector and by logging in from remote clients. Here the biggest issue will be starting with an appropriate logical group structure and maintaining it over time.

While the different sharing protocols (AFP, SMB, FTP, NFS) support multiple platforms, it can be tricky to provide concurrent access to the same files or when platform-specific issues come into play. Concurrent access means that multiple users are trying to access or modify the same files at the same time. Many times this is dependent on the specific cross-platform applications knowing how to allow multiple users to access the same file. Because Mac OS X Server includes support for ACLs and these ACLs are compatible with ACLs from the Windows platform, permissions mapping between Windows clients will be in line with what Windows users expect to see. Prior to Mac OS X Server v10.4, this was not necessarily the case.

Another consideration is if the clients will be storing forked files on the share point. If you use Mac OS Extended for an SMB share point or an NFS export, files created or copied onto the server from the client side will have shadow files instead of resource forks. These files will not look right when viewed from the server. Conversely, files created from the server side will look wrong from the client, which cannot see the resource forks.

Case-Sensitivity Issues in File Sharing

Case sensitivity becomes an issue if you are copying files between two computers and only one of them has a case-sensitive file system. Beginning with Mac OS X Server v10.3, drives can be formatted as Hierarchical File System Plus (HFS+) case-sensitive volumes. Suppose you have two files, Makefile and makefile, in the same folder on a case-sensitive Mac OS X server. If you were to copy those files to a Mac OS X client computer, which is by default not case sensitive, you would run into problems. The operating system would attempt to overwrite one file with the other. When you copy files from a case-insensitive file system to a case-sensitive file system, you might have a problem with executable files. For example, suppose you had an executable script called Runscript on your case-insensitive file system. If you were to copy that file, without altering its name, to a case-sensitive file system, users would be able to run it from the command line only by typing `Runscript`. This could be problematic if the documentation called for typing `runscript` (all lowercase).

You need to be aware of the issues associated with case sensitivity now that Mac OS X Server can easily be configured to be case sensitive, while the Mac OS X client cannot. Not much can be done to synchronize case-sensitive and case-insensitive systems. You need to work around the incompatibility. Given that NFS, FTP, and AFP are case-sensitive protocols, mounting a share point using any of these protocols enables you to see the different case-sensitive files and download whichever one you'd like.

More specifically, SMB does not seem to be a case-sensitive protocol, but it has a distinct preference for uppercase filenames. For example, if your share point contains the files Runscript and runscript, and you use SMB to download either of these files to the client, only Runscript is downloaded, whether you asked for Runscript or runscript. Similarly, if you try to move runscript to a different folder in the share point, Runscript is moved, not runscript. Also, if you upload a local file named runscript to an SMB share point that already contains Runscript and runscript, you are prompted to replace the existing file, but then the operation fails and Runscript is deleted.

Here's what happens: When you attempt to copy runscript to the server, SMB detects the existence of a file with the same name and asks if you want to replace it. Once you click OK, SMB deletes the file Runscript and then attempts to copy runscript to the server. However, that operation fails because runscript still exists on the server. If you try the upload again, however, it succeeds, because now there is only one runscript on the server. When you tell the server to replace the file, it does so without confusion.

A Comparison of File-Sharing Protocols

This table gives a short comparison of the file-sharing protocols you have seen thus far. There really isn't one best protocol. Instead, think of the protocols as different tools at your disposal to give different types of access.

	AFP	**SMB**	**NFS**	**FTP**
Native platform	Mac OS	Windows	UNIX	Multi-platform
Security	Authentication is normally encrypted	Authentication is normally encrypted	Authentication only if using Kerberos	Uses clear text passwords
Browsable	Bonjour	NetBIOS	Bonjour	Bonjour
Example URL	afp://server17. example.com/ SharePoint	smb://server17. example.com/ Share	nfs://server17. example.com/ Volumes/Data/	ftp://server17. example.com nfs_share

AFP and SMB are both full-featured file-sharing protocols with reasonably good security.

NFS (without Kerberos) is not as secure as the other protocols, but it is very convenient for UNIX clients. Be careful before you "export" (share) a volume over NFS. With a Mac OS X server and a Mac OS X client, NFS volumes are browsable in Connect to Server; that is, a user can find them by browsing through a list of servers in the Connect to Server window.

FTP is useful because it offers maximum compatibility. However, FTP also offers a minimal feature set, and its passwords are sent over the network as clear text unless you are using the Kerberos option and a supported Kerberos FTP client—something the Mac OS X Finder lacks.

Mac OS X supports secure File Transfer Protocol (SFTP), a secure alternative for FTP that uses SSH to encrypt the FTP connection. Of the four file-sharing protocols, only AFP has simple built-in support for encrypting connections. If you're in a fully Kerberized environment, you can also use NFS in an encrypted fashion, but you still must deal with its other shortcomings.

What You've Learned

▶ The first step when implementing file-sharing services is to plan out the shared services needed.

▶ A share point is any folder, drive, or partition that you make available to network clients. Share points are created and configured in Server Admin. A share point can be shared over AFP, SMB, NFS, or FTP. Access control lists can be used to set very flexible restrictions on share points and folders.

▶ Mac clients normally access share points over AFP, which is configured in Server Admin.

▶ Windows service allows share points to be accessed by Windows clients over SMB.

▶ NFS provides UNIX systems with access to share points. Unlike AFP and SMB, NFS relies upon the IP address of the computer for authentication (unless you're using Kerberos).

▶ Mac OS X Server provides FTP access for share points as well. Mac OS X Server's FTP service provides the additional feature of automatically encoding, archiving, or compressing a file on the fly, based upon the extension that the client adds to the filename.

▶ Automount share points and network home folders also can be configured on Mac OS X Server.

References

Apple's support page for file sharing is at: http://www.apple.com/support/macosxserver/filesharing

Mac OS X Server Administration Guides

The following documents provide more information about installing Mac OS X Server. All of these and more are available at http://www.apple.com/server/macosx/resources/documentation.html.

Getting Started

Upgrading and Migrating

File Services Administration

Windows Services Administration

User Management

Command-Line Administration

Apple Knowledge Base Documents

You can check for new and updated Knowledge Base documents at http://www.apple.com/support.

Document HT1822, "Mac OS X Server: Admin Tools compatibility information"

Document TA23008, "Mac OS X 10.4 Tiger: 'Connection failed' error when connecting to an AFP server"

Document HT2202, "Mac OS X Server 10.5: Setting a custom umask"

Document TA24986, "Mac OS X Server 10.5: About Kerberized NFS"

URLs

Mac OS X Server File-Sharing Issues: http://www.afp548.com

Network File System (NFS) version 4 Protocol: http://www.ietf.org/rfc/rfc3530.txt

AFP Reconnect/Timeout Definitions and Behavior: http://support.grouplogic.com/?p=1568

Chapter Review

1. Name four file-sharing protocols supported by Mac OS X Server and their principal target clients.

2. How does Mac OS X Server support browsing for Windows clients?

3. What is the primary security concern with NFS?

4. What does FTP file conversion do?

Answers

1. AFP for Mac clients; SMB for Windows clients; NFS for UNIX clients; and FTP for multiple cross-platform client access are four file-sharing protocols supported by Mac OS X Server.

2. On smaller networks, Mac OS X Server uses NetBIOS to advertise its presence. On larger networks, Mac OS X can be a WINS server, or it can use an existing WINS server. If there are no other servers on the network, Mac OS X Server can be a workgroup master browser or a domain master browser.

3. Normally, NFS has no user-authentication process: NFS trusts that the client is who it claims to be. Beyond a security concern, this can also be a management issue if the client and server aren't working with a unified user list. If you're using Kerberos with NFS, you can authenticate the connection process, however.

4. FTP file conversion is a feature of the FTP server that automatically encodes a file or folder requested by an FTP client. The client appends .tar, .bin, or .gz to the end of the filename, and the server does the appropriate encoding.

5

Time	This chapter takes approximately two hours to complete.
Goals	Learn how Internet email travels from the sender's computer to the recipient's computer
	Configure the Mac OS X Server mail service
	Protect your mail service from spam and viruses
	Secure your mail service
	Restrict email abuse using quotas
	Create mailing lists for email distribution

Chapter **5**

Hosting Mail Services

Electronic mail, or email as it is more commonly known, is one of the fundamental services on the Internet. Mac OS X Server includes a feature-rich email service that you can use to send, receive, and store email for your organization. Aside from the obvious reason of hosting an email server to gain an Internet identity, there are a number of other factors that make hosting your own mail service advantageous. If you have a small office with a slow Internet connection, you may find that keeping all of your email within the building rather than using external email servers makes better use of your network bandwidth. This is especially true if typical messages within your organization include large attachments. Additionally, many organizations are required to keep the information held in their email messages secure for regulatory or competitive reasons. Hosting your own email server in-house can keep confidential data from falling into the wrong hands. You may also find that various third-party email services don't offer the exact services you want. By running your own mail servers, you can customize various options to meet the needs of your organization.

The mail service in Mac OS X Server is based on two open source email packages:

▶ Postfix handles acceptance and delivery of individual messages.

▶ Dovecot accepts connections from individual users downloading their messages to their mail client. Dovecot replaces Cyrus, found in earlier versions of Mac OS X Server.

In addition to these programs, the mail service in Mac OS X Server makes use of a number of other packages to provide features, such as webmail, spam and virus scanning, and mailing lists. Each of these will be discussed in-depth throughout this chapter, but first you must learn how Internet email works.

Understanding Internet Mail

Although email is one of the oldest and simplest systems on the Internet, it is composed of a number of different protocols. The primary protocol is the Simple Mail Transfer Protocol (SMTP). SMTP is responsible for delivering a message from the sender's email server to the recipient's email server. When a message is sent, the outgoing mail server first looks up the address of the destination's Mail eXchange (MX) server using DNS. A given Internet domain can have multiple MX servers to help balance the load and provide redundant services. Each MX server is assigned a priority. The highest-priority servers are assigned the lowest number and are tried first when delivering mail via SMTP.

To look up information about a domain's MX servers, you can use the Network Utility found in /Applications/Utilities on a Mac OS X computer.

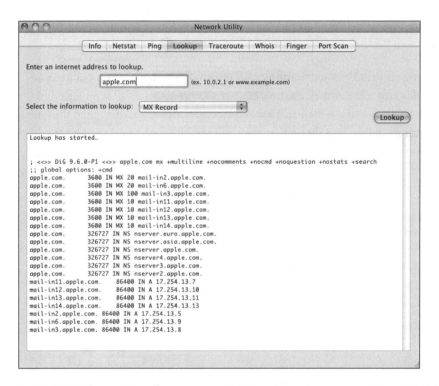

An individual email message may travel through many servers while en route to its final destination. Each server that a message passes through will tag a message with the name of the server and the time it was processed. This is done to provide a history of which servers handled a given message. To examine this trail using the Mail application, you can choose View > Message > Long Headers while viewing the message.

> **Received:** from cooper ([127.0.0.1]) by localhost (cooper.pretendco.com [127.0.0.1]) (amavisd-new, port 10024) with ESMTP id 09379-03 for <david.pugh@pretendco.com>; Sat, 21 Sep 2002 15:31:32 -0400 (EDT)
> **Received:** from mail-out4.apple.com (mail-out4.apple.com [17.254.13.23]) by cooper (Postfix) with ESMTP id 5D5B9B7C672 for <david.pugh@pretendco.com>; Sat, 21 Sep 2002 15:31:32 -0400 (EDT)
> **Received:** from relay14.apple.com (relay14.apple.com [17.128.113.52]) by mail-out4.apple.com (Postfix) with ESMTP 292BD251CA2; Sat, 21 Sep 2002 15:31:31 -0700 (PDT)
> **Received:** from relay14.apple.com (unknown [127.0.0.1]) by relay14.apple.com (Symantec Mail Security) with ESMTP 0E96B20A4C; Sat, 21 Sep 2002 15:31:31 -0700 (PDT)
> **Received:** from [17.09.21.02] (sep21-2002.apple.com [17.09.21.02]) (using TLSv1 with cipher AES128-SHA (128/128 bits)) (No client certificate requested) by relay14.apple.com (Apple SCV relay) with ESMTP id E1B20A24685; Sat, 21 Sep 2002 15:31:30 -0700 (PDT)

Once the email message is delivered to the recipient's mail server, it will be stored there until the recipient retrieves the message using either of two available protocols:

▶ Post Office Protocol (POP) is a common email retrieval protocol used on mail servers where disk space and network connections are at a premium. POP is preferred in these environments because a mail client will connect to the server, download the email, remove it from the server, and disconnect very quickly. Although good for the server, POP mail servers are typically less user-friendly because they don't support server-side folders and may cause difficulties for a user connecting from multiple computers.

▶ Internet Message Access Protocol (IMAP) is commonly used by mail services that want to provide more features to the user. IMAP allows the storage of all email and email folders on the server, where they are generally backed up. Additionally, a mail client will often remain connected to the mail server for the duration of the user session. This can result in quicker notification of new messages. The downside to using IMAP is that it puts more load on the resources of the mail server.

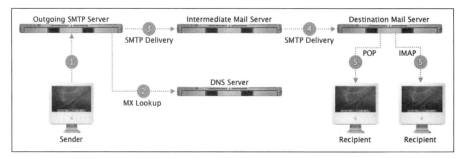

Setting Up Mail Service

Setting up the Mac OS X Server mail service requires configuring a few different pieces that all work together. You need to have the MX records configured in DNS, your SMTP service configured to deliver outgoing mail and to accept incoming mail, and your IMAP or POP service configured to allow mail clients to retrieve their email. Additionally, you'll need to enable the mail service for each user. Later in the chapter, you'll take steps to refine your mail service by providing spam and virus filtering, along with setting other options.

Enabling the Mail Service

Now that DNS is configured correctly for mail delivery to your domain, we need to configure the Mac OS X Server mail service to process mail messages. This, like most other services, is done through Server Admin.

1   Open Server Admin and connect to your server.

2   Select the mail service in the left column.

    NOTE ▶ If the mail service isn't listed, you can add it by selecting your server name in the left column, clicking the Settings button in the toolbar, clicking the Services tab, selecting the mail service in the list, and clicking Save. After you've added the mail service to your server, select it in the left column.

3   Click the Settings button in the toolbar.

4   Click the General tab if it's not already selected.

5   Configure the settings as follows:

    ▶   In the Domain name field, type `pretendco.com`.

    ▶   In the Host name field, type `server17.pretendco.com`.

    ▶   Select the option Enable SMTP.

    ▶   Select the option Enable IMAP.

    ▶   Select the option Enable POP.

    The option to "Allow incoming mail" should already be selected.

6   Click Save.

7 Click Start Mail in the lower-left corner of Server Admin.

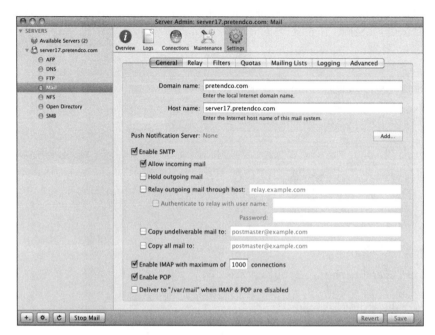

Configuring Users on Your Mail Server

Although you have a fully functional Internet email server running now, none of your users are configured to use it yet. There are two steps to follow. The first is to allow a user to receive email on your email server. The second is to define your Mail application presets so when a client computer binds to your directory server, that user's Mail application will be automatically configured to use your mail server and the chosen protocol, IMAP or POP, for accessing his or her email.

1 Open Workgroup Manager and connect to your server.

2 Select all your users except any administrative accounts.

3 Click the Mail tab.

4 Click Enabled.

This option allows those users to receive email on your server.

5   Configure the settings as follows:

▶   Set the Mail Server to `server17.pretendco.com`.

▶   Set the Mail Quota to 500 MB.

▶   Set Mail Access to "Both POP and IMAP."

6   Click Save.

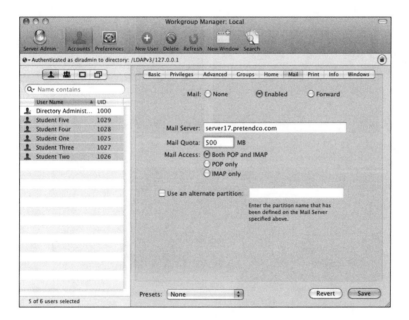

Enhancing Mail Service

Now that your users can use your mail server, there are a number of adjustments you can make to increase performance, add features, and secure your mail server.

Setting Server Connection Options

To conserve system resources, you can limit the number of concurrent IMAP connections that are allowed. It's best to base this number on actual usage to ensure that you have the proper balance between allowing all your users to be logged in at the same time and not overwhelming your server.

Some Internet service providers require that all outgoing email be routed through their SMTP server rather than being delivered directly to the destination. This could be for security, efficiency, or spam-prevention reasons. Additionally, some providers may require you to provide a user name and password to relay mail through their SMTP server. You can enter these here as well. These settings and requirements can be obtained from your ISP.

1   On the Server Admin Mail Settings General pane, change the maximum number of IMAP connections to 50.

2   Select the option "Relay outgoing mail through host," and enter relay.pretendco.com as the host.

3   Click Save.

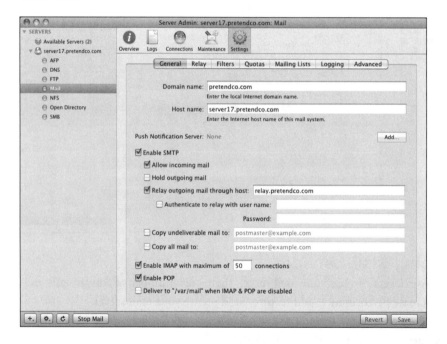

4   Click the Relay tab.

5   Under "Accept SMTP relay only from these hosts and networks," click the Add (+) button and add a network: 10.1.0.0/16.

6   Click OK.

7   Click Save.

Server Admin automatically adds your subnet to the list, but your organization may be made up of other networks. To allow all of your computers to send outgoing email through your mail server, make sure to add all of your organization's subnets here.

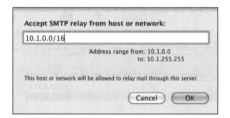

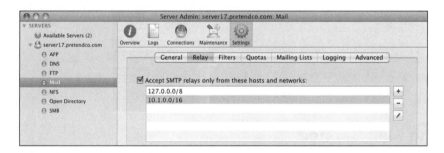

Accessing Mail on the Web

In addition to using an email client with POP or IMAP to access email, Mac OS X Server includes a webmail service that permits users to log in to a webpage to access their email. Once you've configured your web server, you can enable this feature by selecting the Webmail option in the Web Services pane of a given website.

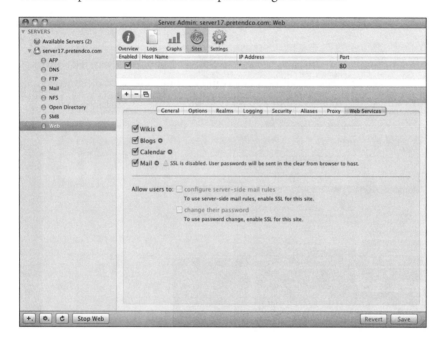

Securing Mail Service

Email is arguably one of the most used services available on the Internet. Along with significant use comes significant abuse. Mail, like any other Internet-enabled service, has numerous options that can increase the security of it and reduce or eliminate the risk for abuse. In this portion of the chapter, we'll focus on three primary areas of abuse and what can be done to reduce their impact on your users.

▶   Password security focuses on ensuring that your users' passwords are safe and that frequent checking of email does not expose their passwords.

▶ Spam prevention actually has two components. First, you want to keep other users from using your server for delivering their spam to others, and second, you want to reduce the amount of spam your users receive.

▶ Virus detection is used to protect the integrity of your users' computers by keeping known viruses out of their email.

Protecting User Passwords

Any time a user must authenticate to a service over the Internet, particularly over an insecure wireless network, his or her password is at risk. You can reduce this risk by taking advantage of higher levels of password hashing and by enabling encryption.

The mail service in Mac OS X Server offers a number of different authentication mechanisms. They have different levels of security, but more important, they are not all supported by every email client. When selecting authentication methods, it's important to determine which email clients your users will be running and what authentication methods they support. Authentication methods range from Clear or PLAIN, which send passwords over the network completely unencrypted, all the way to Kerberos, which is considered one of the most secure because passwords are never sent over the network. If none of your users will be using a particular authentication method, you should disable that method. Additionally, if you want to force your users to only use more secure methods, you should disable the less-secure mechanisms, such as Clear and PLAIN, or require the connection to use SSL.

1 Open Server Admin and connect to your server.

2 Select the mail service in the left column and click the Settings button in the toolbar.

3 Click the Advanced tab.

4 Click the Security tab.

5 In the SMTP column, select the CRAM-MD5 option.

6 In the IMAP/POP column, leave CRAM-MD5 selected.

7 In the IMAP/POP column, leave APOP selected.

NOTE ▶ APOP is a very weak form of password security, though still better than Clear, which offers no encryption. For more protection, you should only use these when combined with SSL.

8 Click Save.

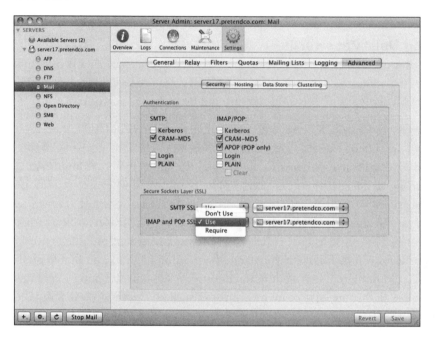

The authentication options protect only the user's password. To further protect the user's password and protect the message content from eavesdropping as well, you can also take advantage of SSL encryption. This provides the same level of protection used by secure websites, and can either be offered to compatible clients by choosing Use from the SSL menus or be required by selecting the Require option instead. Unless you have incompatible clients or don't want to manage SSL certificates for your server, you generally will want to set both of the SSL options to Require.

Preventing Spam

Spam, or unsolicited junk email, is a growing problem on the Internet. Although spam is nearly impossible to eliminate altogether, there are steps you can take to reduce it. There are two main components to this. First, you want to keep your server from being misused, and second, you want to reduce the amount of spam your users receive.

Keeping Your Server from Being Misused

Now that you're running your own email server, you want to take steps to ensure that your server can't be misused by spammers to send their messages. Spammers make use of unprotected servers to send thousands of messages to lists of recipients. When this happens, users outside of your organization are using your server as their outgoing email server, thus providing an extra layer of anonymity to them. Servers that allow anyone to send messages through them are typically referred to as *open relays*. Fortunately, protecting your server from being used as an open relay is very simple. You can either require authentication for your SMTP server, or you can limit the networks that are allowed to relay through your server.

1   In Server Admin's Mail settings, click the Relay tab.

2   Be sure "Accept SMTP relays only from these hosts and networks" is selected.

3   Click the Add (+) button to add any individual IP address or subnets that should be allowed to relay messages through your server.

    The entries in this list can be a single IP address; a network/netmask pattern such as 192.168.10.0/24; a host name, such as mail.pretendco.com; or an Internet domain name, such as pretendco.com.

    In the following example, the highlighted entry was added so that relays would be accepted from hosts that had an IP address that started with 10.1.

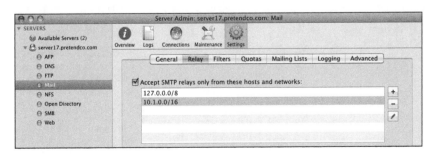

This list should always include the server itself by using the loopback address of 127.0.0.1 so the server can send error emails, and can also include any networks that are part of your organization. The 127.0.0.0/8 subnet is automatically populated and includes the 127.0.0.1 address.

4 Click Save.

Once you've configured your server to prevent open relays, you'll want to confirm that it is, in fact, blocking open relaying. There are a number of websites that can verify this for you. A quick Internet search for "open-relay test" will bring up many third-party sites that can verify that your server is sufficiently protected.

Reducing Incoming Spam Using Known Sources

Now that your server can't be used to deliver junk mail to others, you should take steps to reduce the amount of junk mail your users receive. There are some key ways to accomplish this. The "refuse all messages from these hosts and networks method" method blocks known sources of junk mail. Although this method is guaranteed to stop junk mail coming from known spam servers, you also run the risk of blocking legitimate messages delivered through a server that was misidentified as a spam server.

1 In Server Admin's Mail settings, click the Relay tab.

2 Select the option to "Refuse all messages from these hosts and networks."

3 Click the Add (+) button.

4 In the dialog, type 10.54.199.3.

That address is a fictitious source of spam. In a real-world situation, you'd have to examine the headers of your spam messages to determine the origin of the spam.

5 Click OK.

6   Click Save.

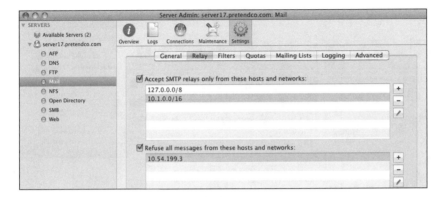

Reducing Incoming Spam Using a Blacklist Service

Examining every spam message to try to determine its source would be a very tedious, and probably not very successful, method of spam prevention. An alternative is to take advantage of one of the many blacklist services that exist. A *blacklist service* publishes and updates a list of known open-relay servers.

You can configure your Mac OS X Server to reference such a service for determining whether you should accept mail from a given host. If, for example, there was a blacklist service offered by a server named blacklist.pretendco.com, you would follow these steps:

1   In Server Admin's Mail settings, click the Relay tab.

2   Select the option to "Use these junk mail rejection servers (real-time blacklist)."

3   Click the Add (+) button.

4   In the dialog that appears, type `blacklist.pretendco.com`.

Note that this will cause a delay in receiving any emails if the server cannot be resolved. This can become an issue if the blacklist server goes offline.

5 Click OK.

6 Click Save.

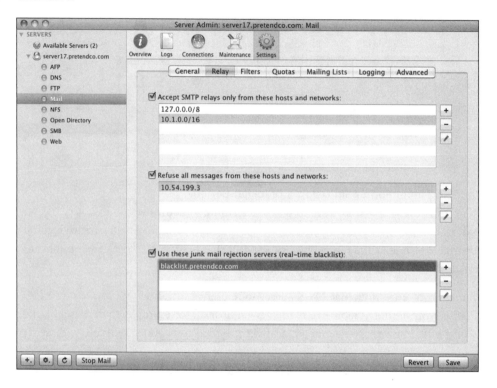

Reducing Incoming Spam Using Filters

Another type of spam reduction involves inspecting every incoming message. This method relies on recognizing patterns of text that are commonly seen in spam junk mail.

There are four choices for what to do with mail tagged as junk:

▶ Bounced—Will attempt to reject a message and attempt to send it back to the sender. Note, however, that many spammers use fake addresses, so this may add extra load to your server.

▶ Deleted—Emails will be discarded. This is risky because no spam system is perfect and valid email could be lost.

▶ Delivered (with a subject tag or the message attached)—The mail will come through but the subject or message will be changed so that it is obviously spam. A user can check the subject to evaluate if the mail is really spam and respond accordingly. It can also be used to filter email at the client level.

▶ Redirected—Spam emails can be sent to another address for evaluation or a honeypot.

1 In Server Admin's Mail settings, click the Filters tab.

2 Select the option to "Enable junk mail filtering."

3 Adjust the "Minimum junk mail score" to 20 hits.

This setting may need to be adjusted depending on the types of email your users are supposed to receive. If you set the number too high, your users will continue receiving spam. However, if you set the number too low, legitimate messages will be tagged as spam and may not be seen by their intended recipient. You may also find that you'll want to start with a high number, and then, once your server has received a sufficient amount of training, you can reduce the setting.

4 Set the option to indicate that "Junk mail messages should be Delivered" and "Encapsulate junk mail as MIME attachment."

As with the previous option, this setting can either make life easier for your recipients by not delivering their spam messages or cause problems by not delivering messages misidentified as spam. Additional options include the ability to bounce messages identified as spam, which may tell the spam originator that the email address they sent to was bad (even though it wasn't) and may result in a reduction of spam. You can also redirect all spam messages to another email address for collection. This may be handy for spam server training or a honeypot project.

5   Click Save.

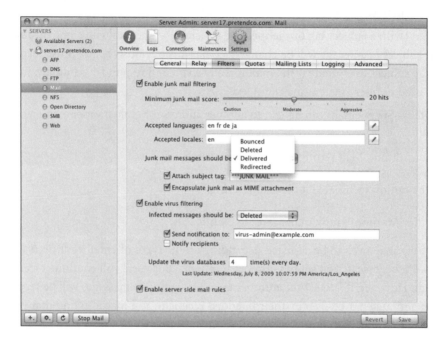

Detecting Viruses

As with spam, no user wants to receive a virus in his or her email. Mac OS X Server includes virus scanning as well. This is enabled on the same settings pane as spam filtering.

1   In Server Admin's Mail settings, click the Filters tab.

2   Select the option to "Enable virus filtering."

3   Select the option to indicate that "Infected messages should be Deleted."

4   Deselect the option to "Send notification to virus-admin@example.com."

5   Select the option to "Notify recipients."

This option will send an email to the intended recipients telling them a message was detected as having a virus and was deleted. This can be useful if a legitimate attachment was misidentified as a virus so that users know why they never received it.

6 Set the option to "Update the virus databases 4 times every day."

Updating more often will catch new viruses sooner but also add extra load to your server and your network.

7 Click Save.

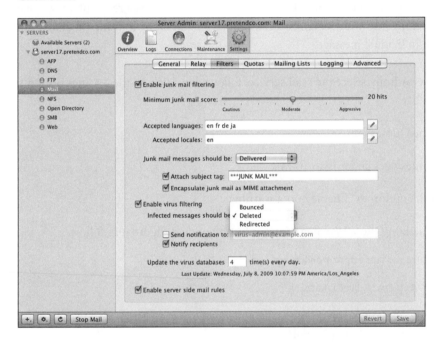

Maintaining Mail Service

Now that you have your mail server configured with settings helpful to the users, you'll want to make some further adjustments that are helpful to you, the system administrator. These settings include options that will keep your server healthy, aid in diagnosing problems, distribute mail to multiple users, as well as help you adhere to any regulatory requirements.

Saving Disk Space

The most important settings to be aware of are those that affect disk consumption. Every message that arrives at your server will take up disk space. If your server runs out of free disk space, you won't be able to receive any more messages. There are two main methods to keep this from happening. The first method is by establishing mail quotas for your users. We set this number earlier in the chapter using Workgroup Manager when we enabled each user's mail access. This setting will control the total amount of disk space a given user can occupy with all his or her email that is stored on the server. The other item to keep in mind is the possibility of running out of disk space as a result of a few huge messages coming into your server. You can reduce this threat by limiting the maximum size of each individual message.

1   In Server Admin, select the mail service, followed by clicking the Settings button in the toolbar.

2   Click the Quotas tab.

3   Refuse messages larger than 10 MB.

4   Select the option to "Enable quota warnings."

5   Click the Edit Quota Warning Message button and configure it as follows:

▶   From: `postmaster@pretendco.com`

▶   Subject: `Email Quota Warning`

▶   Body: `You are approaching your email storage quota. Please delete some messages soon to avoid blocked messages.`

6   Click OK.

7   Select the option to "Disable a user's incoming mail when they exceed 100% of quota."

8   Click the Edit Over Quota Error Message button and configure it as follows:

▶   From: `postmaster@pretendco.com`

▶   Subject: `Email Over Quota`

▶   Body: `You have exceeded your email storage quota. Until you delete some messages, you will no longer receive new email.`

9 Click OK.

10 Click Save.

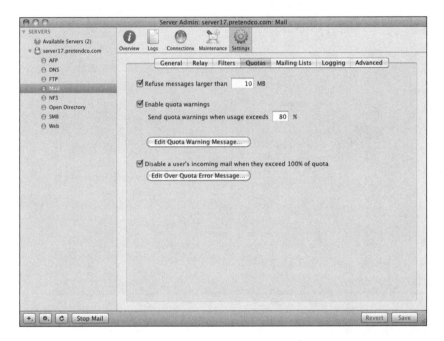

Redirecting Messages

Because of company policy or in order to adhere to certain regulations, you may need to save copies of every message sent through your server, whether delivered or undelivered to a final recipient. Mac OS X Server offers easy configuration to meet these needs. You'll probably want to create a new user with no quota for these delivery email addresses and periodically archive the mail so it doesn't fill your mail server.

1 In Server Admin's Mail settings, click the General tab.

2 Select the option to "Copy undeliverable mail to: postmaster@server17.pretendco.com."

3 Select the option to "Copy all mail to: postmaster@pretendco.com."

4 Click Save.

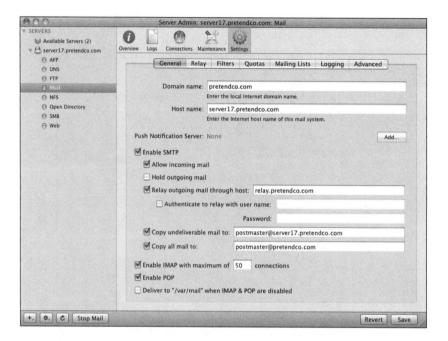

Creating Mailing Lists

You can also use Server Admin to set up mailing lists. This functionality is based on an open-source project called Mailman and allows you to create an email address on your server that will distribute a copy of every message it receives to all of the members of that list.

1 In Server Admin's Mail settings, click the Mailing Lists tab.

2 Select the option to "Enable mailman mailing lists."

3 A dialog will appear. Configure it as follows:

▶ Master password: Mail4Apple

▶ Administrators: student1@pretendco.com student2@pretendco.com

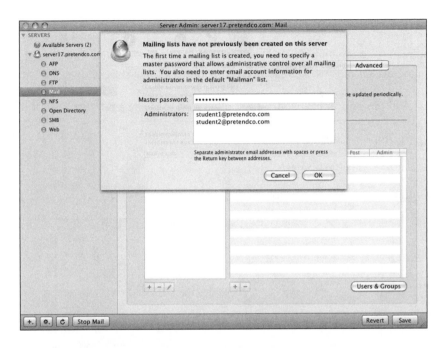

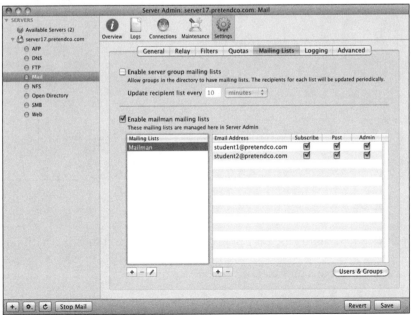

4   Click OK.

The Mailman master mailing list will be created. This is just a systemwide list for tracking the master password. We'll be creating our mailing list next.

5   Click the Add (+) button below the Mailing Lists list to create a new list.

6   A dialog will appear. Configure it as follows:

▶   List Name: PretendcoTraining

▶   Admin User: student1@pretendco.com

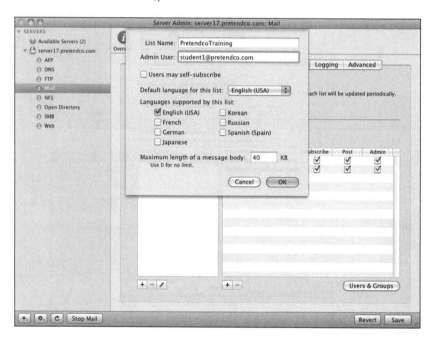

7   Click OK.

The new PretendcoTraining list has just been created. We'll add members to it now.

8   Click the Users & Groups button.

9 Drag the user names of Students Two, Three, and Four at Pretendco to the list of Email Address members of the PretendcoTraining Mailing List.

Note that Student One is already a member because she was designated as an administrator of that mailing list earlier.

10 Click Save.

Now any messages sent to PretendcoTraining@pretendco.com will be distributed to all of the students who were added to the mailing list.

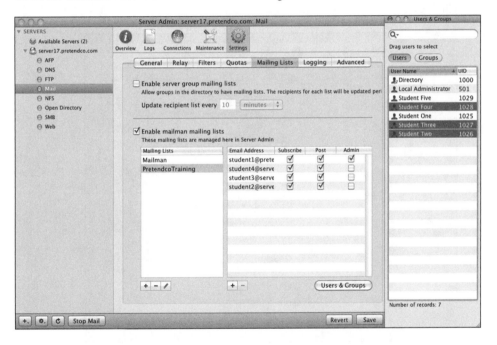

Configuring Mail Logs

As with all services, logs play a big part in diagnosing and troubleshooting any mail issues. In the case of email, logs may also be used for confirmation of message delivery if a dispute arises. Configuration of the mail server logs is done through Server Admin. Depending on the scenario, you may be adjusting the various log levels. Because email is received in such great quantity, you probably don't want verbose mail-service logging when operating under normal conditions.

1   In Server Admin's Mail settings, click the Logging tab.

2   Set the "SMTP log level" to Warning.

3   Set the "IMAP/POP log level" to Warning.

4   Set the "Junk Mail/Virus log level" to Warning.

5   Select the option to "Archive logs every 1 day."

6   Click Save.

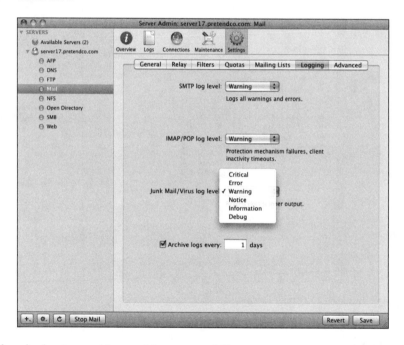

If you're having problems with message delivery, you may want to increase the level of SMTP logging to Information or Debug. If users are having problems with their mail clients, you'll want to increase the level of IMAP/POP logging to Information or Debug. Lastly, if messages are being incorrectly tagged as junk mail or containing a virus, you can increase the logging level for that service.

Once your mail service is running, you can use your logs to diagnose problems that your users are having. The logs will be able to identify if email addresses are mistyped or if the user is over quota. If the user is having problems retrieving his or her mail, you'll recognize failed authentication attempts in the logs.

What You've Learned

▶ Mac OS X Server includes a robust email server that handles SMTP, IMAP, and POP communication.

▶ Internet email messages travel from server to server based on MX record information in DNS.

▶ Numerous mail authentication options are available and can be enabled or disabled as needed.

▶ You should configure your server so it does not act as an open-relay server.

▶ You can configure the mail service to filter spam and virus-infected messages.

▶ Quotas should be enabled to control disk consumption.

▶ You can create mailing lists to distribute a message to multiple recipients.

References

The following documents provide more information about installing Mac OS X Server. (All of these and more are available at www.apple.com/server/documentation.)

Mac OS X Server Administration Guides

Mac OS X Server Getting Started

Mail Service Administration

Network Services Administration

Apple Knowledge Base Documents

You can check for new and updated Knowledge Base documents at http://www.apple.com/support.

URLs

Clam AntiVirus: http://www.clamav.net

Dovecot: http://www.dovecot.org

MacEnterprise: http://www.macenterprise.org

Mailman: http://www.list.org

Postfix: http://www.postfix.org

SpamAssassin: http://spamassassin.apache.org

SquirrelMail: http://www.squirrelmail.org

Chapter Review

1. What is an open relay?

2. What is an MX record?

3. What is SMTP?

4. What are the main differences between POP and IMAP?

5. What is a mail cluster?

6. What are the two methods to limit the amount of disk space used on a mail server?

Answers

1. An open relay is a mail server that allows anyone on the Internet to anonymously send email messages through it. It is the primary tool used by spammers on the Internet.

2. An MX record is a DNS record that indicates the priority and host name of a domain's email server.

3. Simple Mail Transfer Protocol defines how messages travel from one computer to another on the Internet.

4. IMAP maintains a persistent connection between the client and server, allows folder access, and supports higher security authentication methods. POP requires fewer server resources.

5. A mail cluster is a group of Mac OS X Server computers attached to a common Xsan file system to provide distributed and redundant mail services.

6. Two methods to control disk consumption by users are user quotas and maximum message size limits.

6

Time　This chapter takes approximately three hours to complete.

Goals　Define Mac OS X Server's web engine

Understand how to manage the web service

Configure multiple websites and locate site files

Examine website log files

Locate and use secure certificates for websites

Use WebDAV for users and groups

Understand the ramifications of folder listings on websites

Manage web service modules

Define realms as they relate to websites

Differentiate the various file-sharing protocols as they relate to WebDAV

Chapter **6**

Managing Web Services

This chapter helps you understand, manage, and secure the various aspects of Apple's web services, including managing high-bandwidth connections, sharing files, and locating log files for access, viewing, and troubleshooting.

Mac OS X Server's web service is based on Apache, open source software used on a variety of operating systems. Apache can be enhanced by the use of modules (think of them as plug-ins), and Apple has included several additional modules with Mac OS X Server to extend the abilities of Apache. As of this writing, the version installed on Mac OS X Server is Apache 2.2.11.

Understanding Basic Website Concepts

Before you manage any websites, it is important to know where critical Apache and website files are stored. All Apache and Apple configuration files for web services are located in /private/etc/apache2/, which is normally hidden from view in the Finder. Apache modules—including Apple-specific modules—are located in /usr/libexec/apache2/, which is also normally hidden from view in the Finder. The default location for Mac OS X Server's website is located in /Library/WebServer/Documents/. Each user added to Mac OS X Server, regardless of whether they are added to the local directory or the shared LDAP directory, has a home folder created and receives a folder with a default webpage that anyone can access when web services and appropriate modules are enabled. The location of these individual websites resides inside the Sites folder in each user's home folder. The URL to reach a Mac OS X Server's webpage is its IP address or fully qualified domain name (FQDN), such as http://10.1.17.1 or http://server17.pretendco.com. To access any user's website, a forward slash, a tilde (~), and the short name of the user are added to either the IP address or the FQDN. New for 10.6 is that user sites are off by default and the appropriate modules need to be turned on to activate them.

Also, all website files and the folders in which they reside normally must be at least read only for Everybody or the www user or group, otherwise users won't be able to access the files displayed by their web browsers when they visit your site. Later in this chapter, there are examples of when restrictions should be placed on read-only access and how to implement this feature. Therefore, any location described in the preceding paragraph must have at the very least read-only access in order for the pages to be seen by all.

Enabling Websites

When managing websites on Mac OS X Server, you use the Server Admin tool. You also use the Server Admin tool to manage file and folder permissions, thus allowing or restricting access to folders that are to be seen by web browsers, such as Safari.

Because Mac OS X Server has preconfigured web services for the default website, all you need to do to start exploring is turn on the web service.

Enabling the Web Service in Server Admin

To start the web service, you must first enable it as a service in Server Admin.

1 Open Server Admin and select your server in the list of servers on the left.

2 Click the Settings button in the toolbar, click the Services tab, select the web service, and click Save.

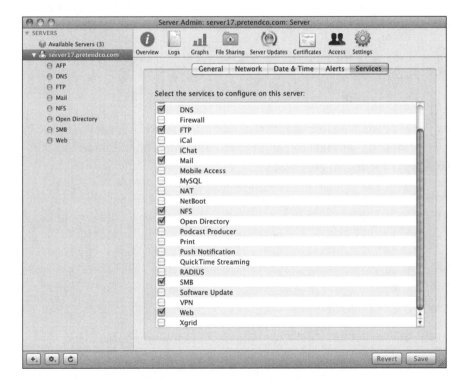

Starting the Web Service in Server Admin

Now that you have enabled the web service, you can simply start the service.

1 Select the web service in the list of services displayed under your server on the left side of Server Admin.

2 Click the Start button in the lower left of Server Admin to start the web service.

3 Open Safari on Mac OS X and connect to `http://10.1.17.1`. Observe the page, and then enter the FQDN (`http://server17.pretendco.com`) and make sure you can observe the page again. Refresh the page if necessary.

> **NOTE** ▶ Notice that you did not configure the website in any way. Mac OS X Server's web service is set to serve up the default webpages automatically.

4 Select the web service in Server Admin and go to Settings, then Modules. Turn on the apple_userdir_module by checking the box, then restart the web service.

> **NOTE** ▶ Unlike in prior versions of OS X, user websites are not on by default. It is necessary to turn on this module to allow user websites. The change was made in an effort to increase security and limit access to user information.

5 Enter a tilde (~) and the short name `tina` after http://server17.pretendco.com/ and view that user's personal default webpage. The entry should appear like this: *http://server17.pretendco.com/~tina.*

> **NOTE** ▶ Again, notice that you did not configure the personal website in any way. Mac OS X Server, like Mac OS X's web service, is set to serve up the default user webpages automatically once the web service is started.

> **NOTE** ▶ It is important to note that the preceding exercises showcase the default behavior of Mac OS X and Mac OS X Server with respect to starting web services without any other configuration.

6 Quit Safari by using Command-Q or choosing Quit from the Safari menu.

You will now examine some basic options for managing websites on Mac OS X Server.

Managing Websites

You can manage many websites with Mac OS X Server. Each website can be distinguished by a different IP address, domain name, or port over which everyone accesses the site. Before you change any parameters on your existing site or add a new site, it is worth learning how Apple configures the defaults for the original site.

Viewing Default Website Parameters

Understanding what parameters Mac OS X Server sets for default websites is important, as you will often want to adjust or change some of them.

1 Select the web service in the list of services displayed under your server on the left side of Server Admin.

2 Click the Sites button in the toolbar, and then click the General tab to view the general parameters for the default website.

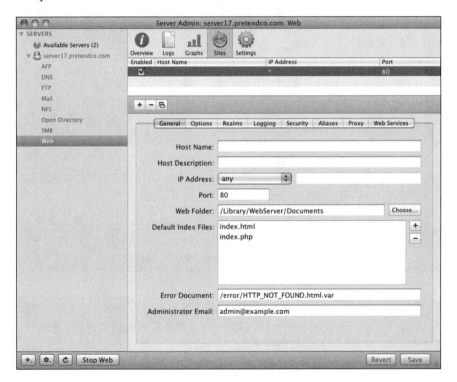

Notice the domain name is not listed, even though you were able to reach it with the FQDN.

3   Enter the fully qualified name, `server17.pretendco.com`, choose your IP address from the pop-up list beneath the domain name, and save the changes.

Notice the site is enabled via the Enabled checkbox in the Sites pane.

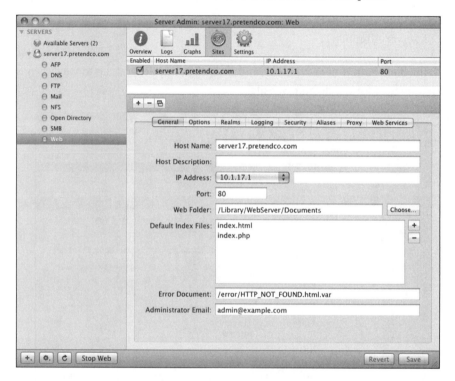

4   Open Safari on Mac OS X and connect to `http://10.1.17.1`. Observe the page, and then enter the FQDN (`http://server17.pretendco.com`) and ensure you can observe the page again. Refresh the page if necessary.

NOTE ▶ All you did was specify a domain name and IP address. Mac OS X Server can have multiple IP addresses on a single interface, or, in the case of Mac Pros and Xserves, more than one Ethernet interface. Therefore, it is important to distinguish IP addresses as mapped to certain sites. Entering this information limits the site to just the entered parameters.

5 View the other general parameters for websites managed under Mac OS X Server:

▶ Host Name: Fully qualified domain name

▶ Host Description: Definition of the site

▶ IP Address: IP address of the site

▶ Port: Logical port value that users visiting the site may need to know in order to access the site. Ports 80 and 443 are known by most browsers and do not require additional typing when entering the address.

NOTE ▶ Port 443 assumes SSL access to a site, which we will enable later.

▶ FQDN, IP address, and port are used to separate sites from one another. For example, you can have two sites on the same IP address as long as their ports are different. You can also have two sites with the same IP address and different domain names. By editing and ensuring that one of these three parameters is unique, you are logically separating your sites.

▶ Web Folder: The location of the files served up by the selected site

▶ Default Index Files: Initial file that is loaded when a user visits the site. Depending on how complex the site is, the default file may be an executable file or code that interacts with a language, such as WebObjects, Hypertext Preprocessor (PHP), or Perl.

▶ Error Document: Path to the page that visitors see if they are misdirected or attempt to access a page that does not exist

▶ Administrator Email: Email address of the site administrator

Creating a Website

Now that you have viewed the general parameters, you will create a secondary website based on a second IP address.

1 On your server, create a folder in the User Data volume named Library.

2   Use the Finder to navigate to /Library/WebServer and drag a copy of it over to /User Data/
Library. This recreates the boot volume's path structure on your User Data volume.

3   Use the Finder to navigate to /User Data/Library/WebServer.

4   Select the Documents folder and choose File > Duplicate to duplicate the folder.
Rename it MySite.

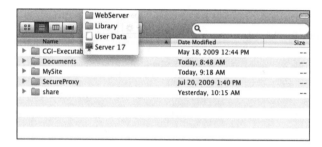

5   Open the MySite folder and locate the index.html file. Open it with TextEdit, and in
the first line change Mac OS X Server to MySite. Save the change and quit TextEdit.

You have now edited a file you will use for a second website.

6   Open Server Admin, select the web service in the list of services, select the Sites button from the toolbar, and click the General tab.

7   Click the Add (+) button to create a new site, and enter the following information:

▶   Host Name: `mysite.pretendco.com`

▶   IP Address: `10.1.17.1`

▶   Port: `8080`

▶   Web Folder: Click Choose and navigate to /User Data/Library/WebServer/
MySite/.

This tells Apache to look in the chosen location for the files to be used on this particular site.

▶   Default Index Files: Because you edited the default line, leave this value alone.

▶   Error Document: Leave this value alone.

▶   Administrator Email: `tina@pretendco.com`

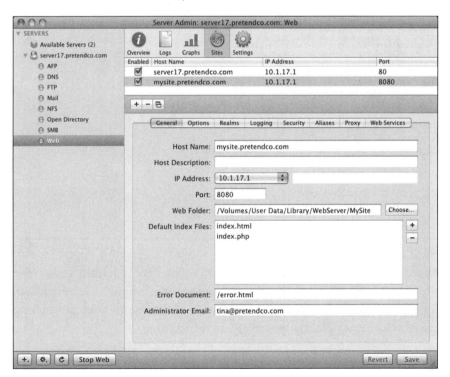

8   Enable the site via the checkbox and click Save.

9   Within Safari on your Mac OS X computer, enter `http://10.1.17.1:8080` in the address bar and press Return to contact the site.

You should see your edited webpage from your directory over the port you chose, 8080.

NOTE ▶ You will not be able to locate the site by using the fully qualified domain name because you did not add that record to your DNS entries.

10   If you try accessing http://www.pretendco.com, you will see it defaults back to the original Mac OS X Server default page, indicating that it has a DNS record, whereas mysite.pretendco.com doesn't. If you can't access the website via www.pretendco.com, add an alias for www pointing to server17.pretendco.com.

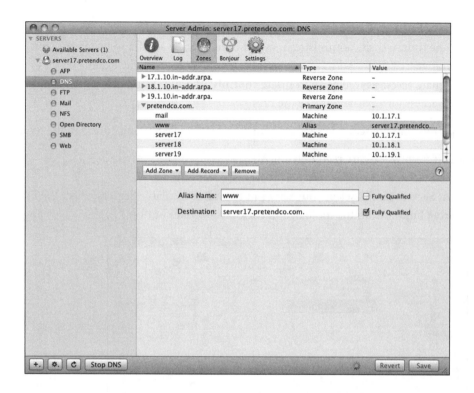

11 Within Server Admin, deselect the Enable checkbox for mysite.pretendco.com and click Save, thus disabling the site (as you would for maintenance, for example).

12 Attempt to contact http://10.1.17.1:8080 again. Notice you cannot access the site because you disabled it in Server Admin.

13 Enable the mysite.pretendco.com site and attempt to contact http://server17. pretendco.com:8080.

Notice it goes to the MySite folder. This is because you are asking for this website over port 8080, not the standard port 80. You have two unique sites defined by the port over which they are accessed. The IP address is the same and the FQDN works for one of the sites, but not for the other at this time. It is therefore the port number that is the defining factor.

14 Quit Safari.

Verifying Folder Access

Most of the time, website administrators want users to view all of a website's content. So it's imperative that folder permissions (and file permissions, to some extent) be set up with adequate access as well as appropriate controls. At a minimum, the www group must have read access for Apache to serve the files.

Folder permissions are set up via Server Admin under the File Sharing button in the toolbar.

To check if permissions are read only for All:

1 Open Server Admin, select your server in the list of Available Servers, select the File Sharing button from the toolbar, and click the Volumes button.

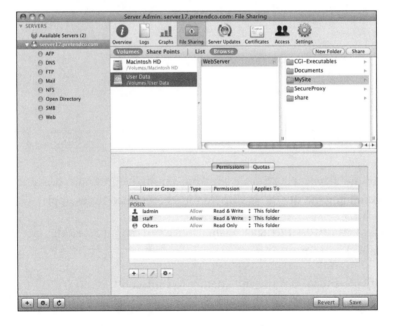

2 With your volume selected, navigate through /User Data/Library/WebServer/MySite/.

3 View the POSIX permissions on the MySite folder in the lower half of the window. Notice that for Others, permissions are set to Read Only. If during the copy of data from one location to the other it was set to Read & Write, change it to Read Only.

This is why you were able to view your index.html page in your MySite folder.

Using Aliases

Website aliases are a way of having a website respond to more than one name. This is often done when site administrators want to cover a gamut of names that lead back to one site.

Prior to enabling aliases, DNS should be configured to point the website to the aliased domains.

To enter a web alias:

1   Select the web service in the list of services displayed under your server on the left side of Server Admin.

2   Click the Sites button in the toolbar, select the server17.pretendco.com site in the sites list, and then click the Aliases tab.

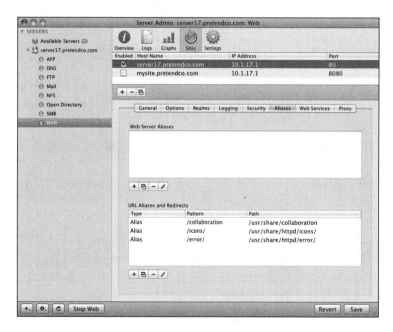

3   If there's an asterisk in the list, select it and click the Minus (–) button to remove it from the list.

The asterisk is a wildcard that, when removed, permits the entry of additional names for your website.

4   Click the Add (+) button and enter www.pretendco.com. Click OK, then click Save.

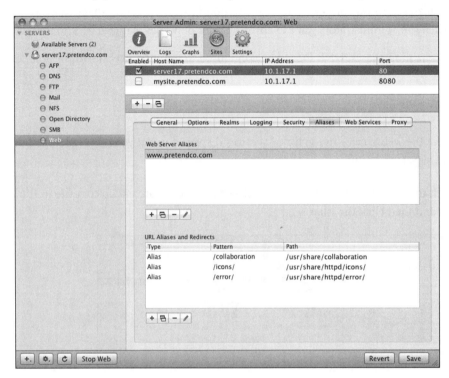

5   You can now test the alias from your Mac OS X computer. Because there is a DNS record for www.pretendco.com, the alias will work.

Redirects work by sending the visitor to a site, folder, or page that differs from the originally requested page. This is common when certain portions of a website are being upgraded. A redirect does not cause any other links on the site to break but instead silently forwards the visitor(s) to other locations.

Setting Advanced Website Options

There are additional options for websites on Mac OS X Server that can enhance file viewing, provide security, increase functionality, and handle file-sharing duties similar to those of other protocols, such as AFP or SMB. Additionally, when administering a website, it is important to understand how Mac OS X Server handles Apache log files, where they are stored, and how to view them.

Managing Apache Modules

Functionality is extended to Apache via modules, which can be enabled or disabled via Server Admin. Mac OS X Server ships with 70 modules, 41 of which are already enabled. Eight of these modules are Apple-specific modules. A module extends the capabilities of Apache by allowing interaction with the web browser and the web server. Some examples of this are allowing secure connections via the ssl_module, permitting Kerberos authentication via the spnego_auth_module, or enabling execution of PHP code via the php5_module.

For security reasons, several modules that enable working with scripting languages are disabled by default in Mac OS X Server.

To enable, disable, or edit a module:

1   Select the web service in the list of services displayed under your server on the left side of Server Admin.

2   Click the Settings button in the toolbar, and then click the Modules tab.

3   Click the Enable column header to sort the module list by those that are enabled and disabled by default.

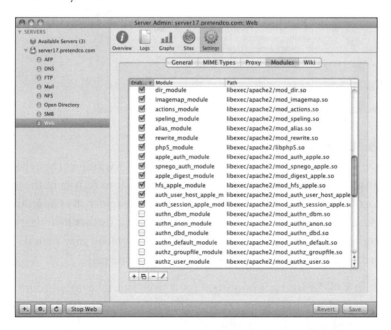

TIP ▶ It is important that you keep a record of which modules Apple enables by default. This way you can quickly revert to the standard Apple default module set if necessary.

4 Select the checkbox adjacent to the module you wish to enable or disable.

5 To edit the name or path to a module, select the module in the list and click the Edit (pencil) button beneath the module list.

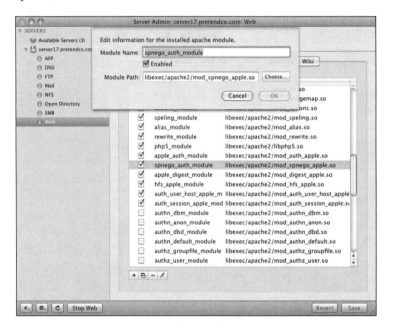

Managing Folder Listings

Websites are a collection of folders and files displayed via a browser window. The types of files vary, but in almost every case, a complex folder structure exists to restrict both web developers and visitors to the site to certain areas of the site. If the folder structure can be seen at any level, an attacker can decide which folders may merit further investigation. Conversely, a site that hosts files or applications for visitors to download may want its entire folder structure to be seen, which makes navigation of the site easier.

When deciding whether a folder listing is important for a given site, take into account the type of data stored in the folders and the names of the folders themselves. This will help in making the correct decision about folder listings.

Folder listings, unlike modules, are site-based, meaning they can be enabled or disabled per site, whereas modules are enabled or disabled for the entire web service.

To manage folder listings:

1   Select the web service in the list of services displayed under your server on the left side of Server Admin.

2   Click the Sites button in the toolbar, select the server17.pretendco.com site from the sites list, and then click the Options tab.

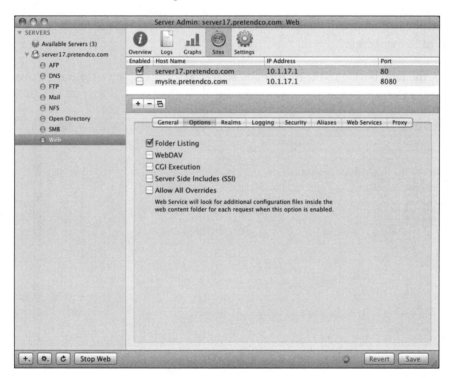

3   Select the Folder Listing checkbox and click Save.

4   From your Mac OS X computer, open Safari and enter `http://server17.pretendco.com`.

You are presented with a folder listing instead of the standard index.html page.

Viewing Apache Log Files

Apache has excellent logging capabilities and uses two main files when logging website information: the Access log and the Error log. The log files can store all kinds of information, such as the address of the requesting computer, amount of data sent, date and time of transaction, page requested by the visitor, and a web server response code, just to name a few.

Log files, named access_log and error_log, are located inside /var/log/apache2/ and are readable via the Server Admin tool.

To view Apache log files for a given site:

1   Select the web service in the list of services displayed under your server on the left side of Server Admin.

2   Click the Logs button in the toolbar and select the server17.pretendco.com Access log from the Domain Name list to view that log.

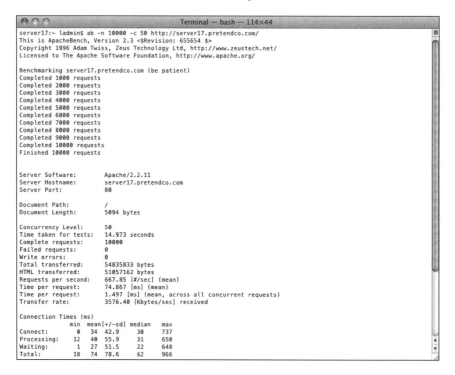

```
server17:~ ladmin$ ab -n 10000 -c 50 http://server17.pretendco.com/
This is ApacheBench, Version 2.3 <$Revision: 655654 $>
Copyright 1996 Adam Twiss, Zeus Technology Ltd, http://www.zeustech.net/
Licensed to The Apache Software Foundation, http://www.apache.org/

Benchmarking server17.pretendco.com (be patient)
Completed 1000 requests
Completed 2000 requests
Completed 3000 requests
Completed 4000 requests
Completed 5000 requests
Completed 6000 requests
Completed 7000 requests
Completed 8000 requests
Completed 9000 requests
Completed 10000 requests
Finished 10000 requests


Server Software:        Apache/2.2.11
Server Hostname:        server17.pretendco.com
Server Port:            80

Document Path:          /
Document Length:        5094 bytes

Concurrency Level:      50
Time taken for tests:   14.973 seconds
Complete requests:      10000
Failed requests:        0
Write errors:           0
Total transferred:      54835833 bytes
HTML transferred:       51057162 bytes
Requests per second:    667.85 [#/sec] (mean)
Time per request:       74.867 [ms] (mean)
Time per request:       1.497 [ms] (mean, across all concurrent requests)
Transfer rate:          3576.40 [Kbytes/sec] received

Connection Times (ms)
              min  mean[+/-sd] median   max
Connect:        0   34  42.9     30     737
Processing:    12   40  55.9     31     650
Waiting:        1   27  51.5     22     648
Total:         18   74  78.6     62     966
```

3   On your Mac OS X computer, open /Utilities/Terminal and type

```
ab -n 10000 -c 50 http://server17.pretendco.com/
```

then press Return.

This is an Apache test tool that tells your Mac OS X computer to ask for 10,000 (the -n parameter) requests run concurrently by 50 (the -c parameter) pretend users' concurrent connections.

4   Click the Refresh button to see the number of requests increase.

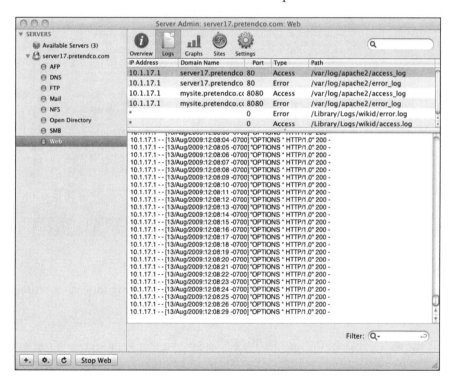

5   On your Mac OS X computer, open Safari and type

```
http://server17.pretendco.com/hollyg.html.
```

This page does not exist; therefore, it will log an error.

6   Using Server Admin, check the error_log for server17.pretendco.com. You will see an error generated by the bad request.

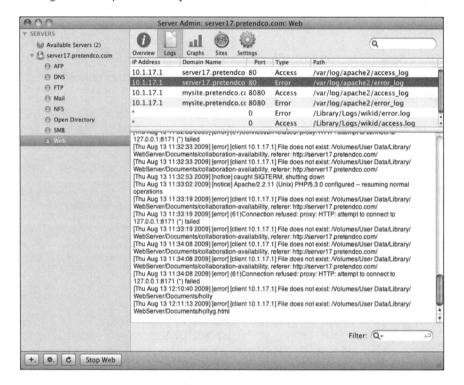

Disabling Apache Log Files

You can also disable and/or archive both the access and the error log for each website. To do so:

1   Select the web service in the list of services displayed under your server on the left side of Server Admin.

2   Click the Sites button in the toolbar, select the server17.pretendco.com site in the sites list, and then click the Logging tab.

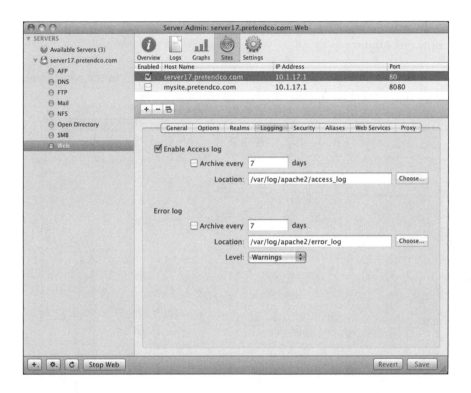

3 Notice the possible configurations for disabling and archiving the log files and the location and formatting for the access log. You can also change the level of logging for the error log, depending on the development and operational parameters of your site.

Graphing Web Traffic

Mac OS X Server permits you to view web traffic coming to your server. You can view both the number of requests and the throughput, although both are cumulative, not site-based. If your Mac OS X Server hosts many services, it is worthwhile to watch the traffic generated by your website(s) and compare that with the CPU and RAM usage on your server. It may be that your website(s) generate enough traffic to warrant a server of their own. When viewing the graphs, you can choose a time for the x (horizontal) axis. It can be as short as one hour and as long as the past seven days of usage.

1   Select the web service in the list of services displayed under your server on the left side of Server Admin.

2   Click the Graphs button in the toolbar and choose Throughput in the pop-up menu. Choose a time period in the adjacent pop-up menu.

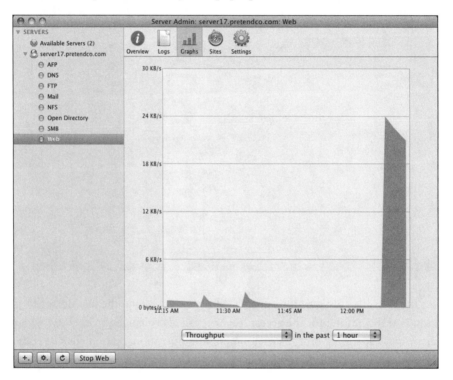

Managing Website Realms and WebDAV

Mac OS X Server provides realms, which are essentially directories or locations—such as other URLs—that can only be accessed by certain users or groups. Additionally, Mac OS X Server makes use of another open standard called WebDAV, which allows sharing capabilities similar to that of other protocols.

Using Realms

Realms are incredibly useful when dealing with websites that contain sensitive information or sections of a site that should only be accessible to one person or group. For example, you could set up a website so that only those users in a given group can access the site. You could also set up a realm on a portion of the site so that only a department has access to those particular pages. In most cases, realms are set up after users and groups are created, because the access to certain web directories is based on users and/or groups.

1 Select the web service in the list of services displayed under your server on the left side of Server Admin.

2 Click the Sites button in the toolbar, select the server17.pretendco.com site in the sites list, and then click the Realms tab.

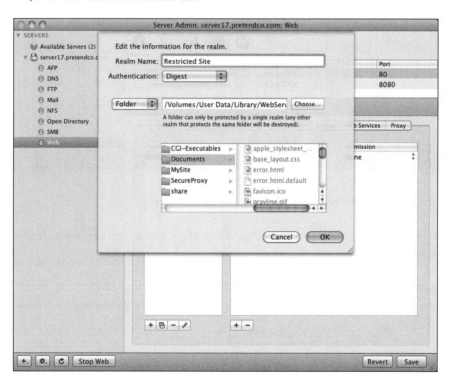

3 Click the Add (+) button under the Realms pane and give the realm a name. Then choose Digest as the authentication type. Leave the directory path at the default.

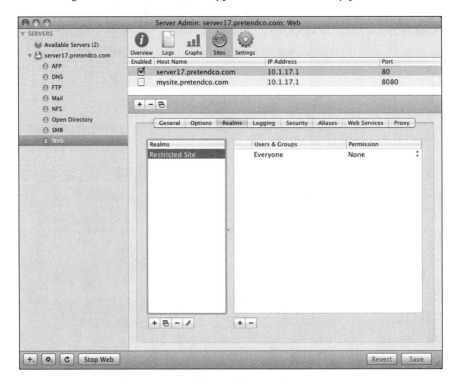

4 Click Save to save the realm. Click the realm to select it.

NOTE ▸ When you create a realm, no one has access to the realm by default. You must now add users and/or groups to have access to the realm.

5 Click the Add (+) button under the Users & Groups pane and add a group to the list. Once added, change the permissions to Browse Only for the group and click Save.

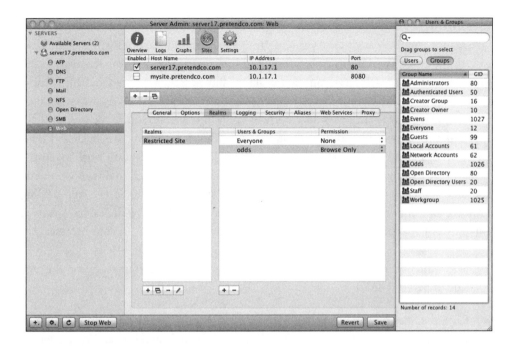

6   On your Mac OS X computer, open Safari and type `http://server17.pretendco.com`.

You are presented with an authentication dialog.

7   Enter a user within the group you added and click the Log In button.

You are now authenticated to view the site.

Enabling WebDAV

Like realms, WebDAV restricts users and groups to certain directories with regard to web servers. However, WebDAV is a bit different in that a user or group can actually mount the directory of the web server on their desktop, allowing them to read and copy from the server or actually change files and write to the directory. WebDAV is extremely useful when using third-party web development applications that require the user of that application to upload files to the web server. Instead of transferring files back and forth, a WebDAV-enabled server and associated web development application work together to allow live editing of files directly on the server, without the need to download them and then subsequently upload them again. When using Connect to Server, Apple Filing Protocol uses afp:// as a precursor to the server address, and Samba uses smb:// as its precursor. WebDAV uses http://, just as it would if you were to type it in your browser.

1 Select the web service in the list of services displayed under your server on the left side of Server Admin.

2 Click the Sites button in the toolbar, select the server17.pretendco.com site in the sites list, and then click the Options tab. Select the WebDAV checkbox and click Save.

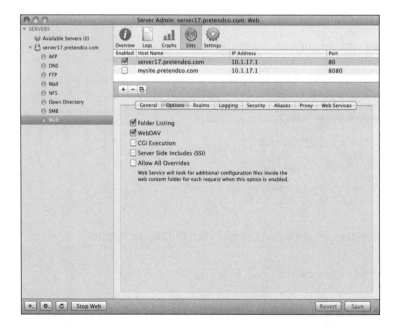

WebDAV is now enabled for that particular site.

Once you enable WebDAV, you must ensure that the folder within your website has the correct permissions for the user or group in your realm. Use Server Admin to check permissions and change them if necessary. If these files are going to be seen by all visitors to the site, it is important to allow read-only access for all other users.

NOTE ▶ Even though Server Admin allows you to change permissions on the WebDAV realm folder from within the web service, ultimately it is still the effective permissions of the web server that determine what is accessible over WebDAV.

To check or change permissions on a folder for WebDAV usage:

1 Select your server in the list of Available Servers, select the File Sharing button from the toolbar, and click the Volumes button.

2 Click Browse to navigate to the /UserData/Library/WebServer/Documents folder and click the New Folder button. Call the new folder data and click Save.

3 Select the web service in the list of services displayed under your server on the left side of Server Admin.

4 Click the Sites button in the toolbar, select the server17.pretendco.com site in the sites
list, and then click the Realms tab.

5 Double-click the realm you created earlier and view the path to the folder that holds
those documents. In this case, it is /User Data/Library/WebServer/Documents/.

6 Click the Ellipsis (...) button and change the realm path to /User Data/Library/
WebServer/Documents/data. Click OK.

7 Click the realm to select it and edit the odds group's permissions to Browse and
Read/Write WebDAV. Change the Everyone group's permissions to None.

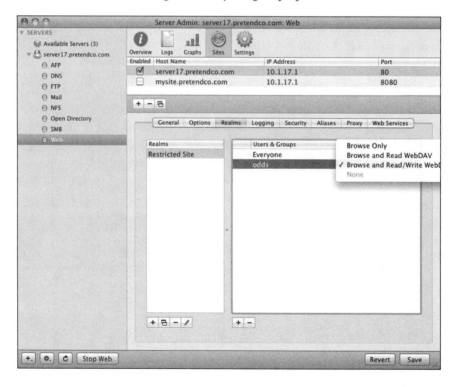

8 Click Save.

9 Select your server in the list of Available Servers, select the File Sharing button from
the toolbar, and click the Volumes button.

10 Click Browse to navigate to the /Library/WebServer/share/httpd folder and view the POSIX permissions at the bottom of the window.

11 Within the Documents folder, scroll down and locate the data folder, select it, and view the permissions. This is the folder we want to restrict.

12 Change the POSIX permissions on the data folder as follows.

▶ _www: Allow Read & Write, This folder

▶ _www: Allow Read & Write, This folder

▶ Others: Allow No Access, This folder

13 Click Save.

14 From the Go menu, choose Connect to Server and enter `http://server17.pretendco.com/data`, then click Connect.

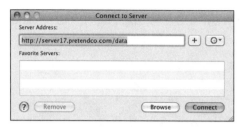

15 You are presented with an authentication dialog. Enter the user name and password of a member of the odds group and click OK.

16 You are shown a Finder window that permits you to edit files, add files, and delete files from this folder, just like you would any other file-sharing protocol.

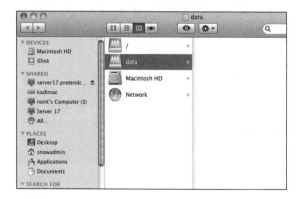

17 Eject the share point.

Comparing File Sharing

Now that you have learned how WebDAV can be implemented, you should understand the basic differences between and uses of the other file-sharing protocols with respect to WebDAV.

Table 6.1 File-Sharing Comparison

	AFP	SMB	FTP	NFS	HTTP
Native	Mac OS X	Windows	Multiple	UNIX	Multiple platform
Security	Kerberos or standard	Kerberos or NTLMv2	Kerberos or clear text	Kerberos or none	Kerberos, digest, or basic
Browsable	Yes	Yes	No	Yes	No
Example URL	afp://server17.pretendco.com	smb://server17.pretendco.com	ftp://server17.pretendco.com	nfs://server17.pretendco.com	http://server17.pretendco.com

Securing Your Website

Most web traffic travels across the network in clear text, meaning that the content can be viewed by anyone who captures the web traffic. For many situations this is acceptable, but any time sensitive information is sent across the wire a method of protection is required.

It is very easy to encrypt the web traffic using SSL (Secure Sockets Layer) and a certificate.

Using SSL

OS X Server makes it very easy to turn on SSL for a website. During the process of turning on SSL, the default port of the website changes from 80 to 443.

1   Select the web service in the list of services displayed under your server on the left side of Server Admin.

2 Click the Sites button in the toolbar, select the server17.pretendco.com site in the sites list, and then click the Duplicate button.

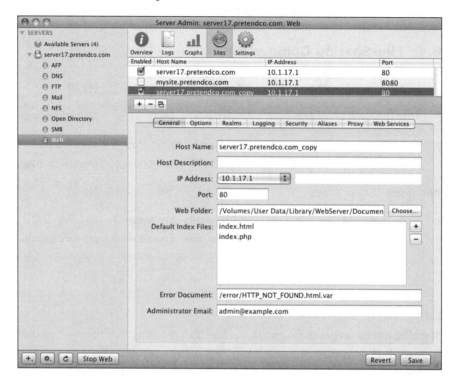

3 Select the server17.pretendco.com_copy site and click the Security tab. Select the Enable Secure Sockets Layer (SSL) checkbox. A warning will appear notifying that port 443 will be used. Click OK.

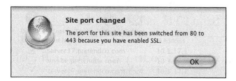

4   Choose the server17.pretendco.com certificate. Click Save and answer No to restarting
the service.

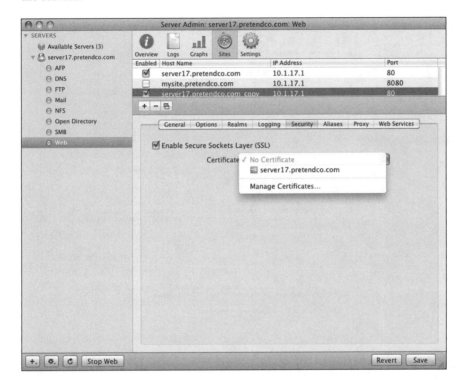

5 Click the General tab and remove *_copy* from the end of server17.pretendco.com in Host Name. Click Save and let Web restart.

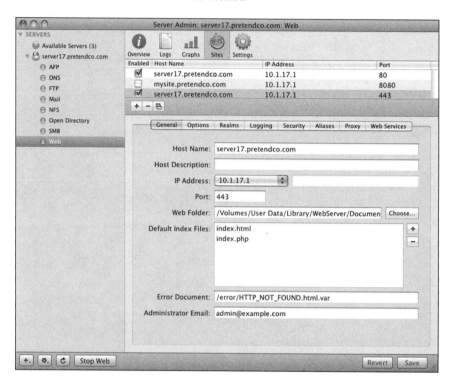

6 Open Safari and enter https://server17.pretendco.com. A warning that Safari can't identify the identity of the website will appear. Click Show Certificate and examine the contents. When done, click Continue. Notice the lock symbol in the upper-right corner of the Safari window indicating a secure site.

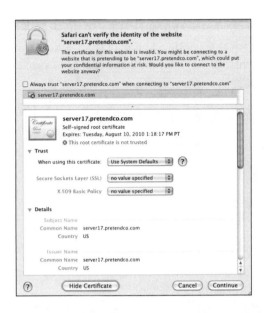

7 In Server Admin, select the web service, the secure site, and then the Web Services tab. Select the "configure server-side mail rules" and "change their password" checkboxes.

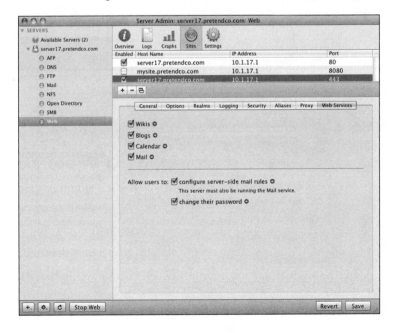

8 Open Safari and return to https://server17.pretendco.com. Notice that the default webpage includes links for configuring vacation notices and mail rules, and changing passwords. Both of these services use sensitive information that needs to be protected.

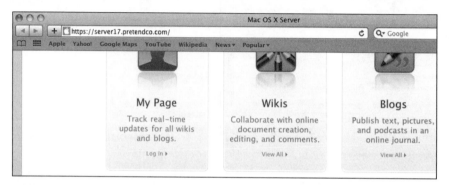

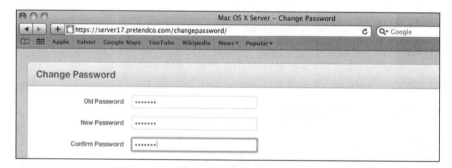

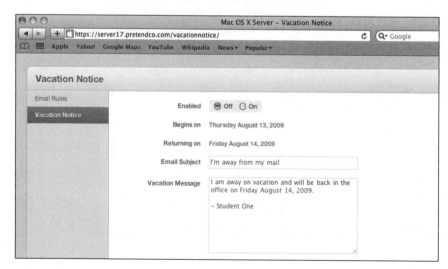

9   Select the nonsecured port 80 site server17.pretendco.com and click the Aliases tab.

10 Click the Add (+) button under URL Alias and Redirects. Choose Redirect and enter
/ in the Pattern box and `https://server17.pretendco.com` in the Path box. Click Save.

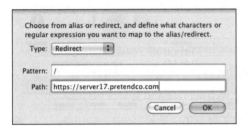

11 Open Safari and go to `http://server17.pretendco.com`. Notice you are immediately redirected to the secure https version of the site. This is a handy way of forcing users to
use a secure web connection.

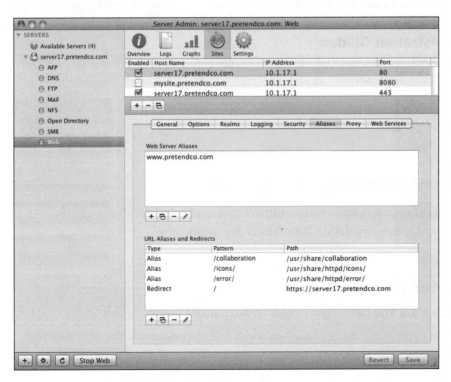

What You've Learned

▶ Mac OS X Server's web service is based on Apache, as is Mac OS X's web service.

▶ Apache uses modules to extend its functionality.

▶ Permissions on website folders are crucial to visitors gaining access to portions of the site.

▶ Realms can be used to restrict areas of a site to certain users or groups.

▶ Mac OS X Server can host multiple websites over a single IP address.

▶ Server Admin is used to manage both the web service and folder permissions.

▶ You can graph the throughput and number of requests for your websites.

References

The following documents provide more information about installing Mac OS X Server. (All of these and more are available at http://www.apple.com/server/macosx/resources/.)

Administration Guides

Web Technologies Administration (http://images.apple.com/server/macosx/docs/Web_Tech_Admin_v10.6.pdf)

File Services Administration (http://images.apple.com/server/macosx/docs/File_Server_Admin_v10.6.pdf)

URLs

Apache Organization site: http://httpd.apache.org

Apache log formatting information: http://httpd.apache.org/docs/2.2/logs.html, http://httpd.apache.org/docs/2.2/mod/mod_log_config.html

Chapter Review

1. On what is Mac OS X Server's web service based?

2. What permissions are necessary on a web folder so visitors to the site can access the pages?

3. What are realms?

4. How do you enable folder listings and WebDAV, and can you do so for more than one site?

5. Where is the default location for the Apache log files?

6. What is the advantage of using SSL on a website?

Answers

1. Mac OS X Server's web service is based on Apache, the open source web server software.

2. The www group must have read access to the web files.

3. Realms are paths to folders or URL locations that can be restricted based on user and/or group.

4. You enable folder listings and WebDAV options by selecting your site and clicking the Options button. They can be enabled on a site-by-site basis. Modules are enabled or disabled for the entire web service.

5. The default location for Apache log files is /var/log/apache2/access_log and /var/log/apache2/error_log.

6. SSL helps protect the traffic traveling to and from the website by encrypting the data.

7

Time

This chapter takes approximately three hours to complete.

Goals

Set up the wiki service on Mac OS X Server

Allow users and groups to manage a wiki

Enable the iCal service

Secure an iCal service connection

Use the iChat service on Mac OS X Server

Log iChat service transcripts

Permit users and groups to use the iChat service

Permit the joining of two iChat service servers

Configure the Address Book service to store users' contacts

Configure Mac OS X to use the Address Book service

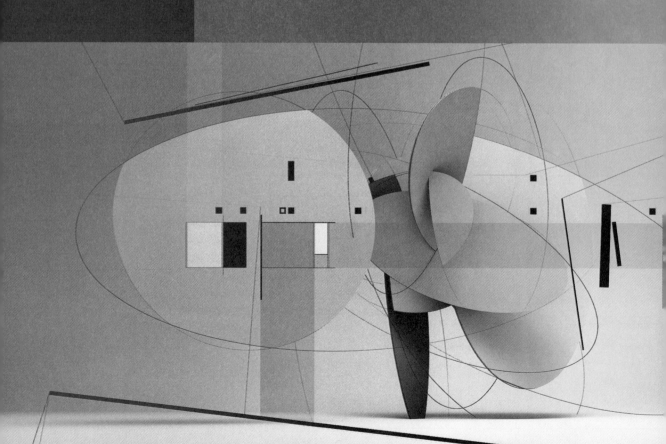

Chapter **7**
Using Collaborative Services

Mac OS X Server has several services that offer a true collaborative environment for users. These services allow for the sharing of contacts, information, events, and schedules, as well as chatting and blogging. They form the core of what is known as collaborative services. They are the:

▶ iChat service

▶ Wiki service

▶ iCal service

▶ Address Book service (new in v10.6)

With these services, users can chat in approved groups in a secure environment about internal projects, schedule appointments and meetings and permit others to manage their calendars, set up a wiki to document the progress of projects, and blog about their projects. They can access these services from multiple computers and devices, and create projects with the wiki service without your intervention.

Choosing Administrative Tools

In Mac OS X Server v10.6, you can use Server Preferences with the Address Book, iCal, iChat, and Web services for basic management, but you may decide to use Server Admin and Workgroup Manager since they offer more management options.

For the Web Server service, you can use Server Preferences to start or stop the service. You can also define the default home page and enable or disable Wikis, Calendar, Blogs, and Webmail.

In the Custom Sites pane, you can add additional sites, but be sure that you have DNS records that support the DNS name you use for the custom site. Be aware that while you can use Server Preferences to choose the domain name, the port number, and the folder in which to save the site files, you cannot choose to enable SSL for sites.

For the iCal service, you can use Server Preferences to start or stop the service and to specify limits for calendar sizes.

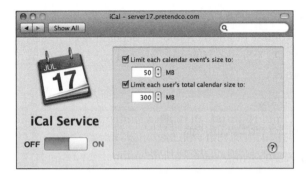

For the iChat service, you can use Server Preferences to start or stop the service, to enable logging, and to enable server-to-server communication.

For the Address Book service, you can use Server Preferences to start or stop the service and to specify a limit for each user's total address book size.

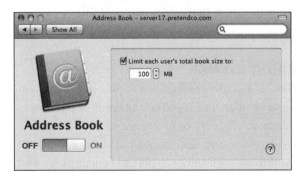

For any service, be sure to test your workflow if you intend to use Server Preferences in addition to Server Admin to configure services. In general, if you intend to use Server Admin, it is best not to go back to Server Preferences to change settings.

Changing the Data Stores

Each service stores its data on the boot volume or another volume, depending on your choices during your initial setup of Mac OS X Server. However, you can use Server Admin to specify where each service's data store is.

The default folder for each service is as follows.

Address Book: /Library/AddressBookServer/Documents/

iCal: /Library/CalendarServer/Documents/

iChat (archives): /var/jabberd/message_archives/

Wiki: /Library/Collaboration/

While using Server Assistant to perform the initial setup of your server, if you choose "Create Users and Groups" or "Import Users and Groups," you have the opportunity to select a volume on which to store service data. If you chose a volume named User Data, for example, the locations for service data would be:

Address Book: /Volumes/User Data/ServiceData/AddressBook/Documents

iCal: /Volumes/User Data/ServiceData/Calendar

iChat (archives): /Volumes/User Data/ServiceData/Jabber

Wiki: /Volumes/User Data/ServiceData/Web/Documents/Collaboration

Specify the location for service data before you start a service. Changing location and migrating data after a service has already been used is beyond the scope of this book.

Understanding and Managing a Wiki

A wiki is a collaborative web-based tool that allows users and groups to post information in a manner that promotes the logical progression of an idea, a project, a theme, or any other focal point of discussion within an organization. Wikis are central to the idea of all users within a given group being able to post, edit, review, and discuss material without interference from other groups or departments within an organization. This can benefit the group whose wiki is hosting a secret project or sensitive information. Mac OS X Server wikis also keep a detailed history of a group's wiki, so you can retrieve older information if necessary.

There are a few layers of access control. You can administratively control the users and groups you allow to create wikis. Once a user creates a wiki, he or she can specify who can read it and who can edit it, all without any intervention from an administrator.

Once users have access to a wiki, they can post articles, images, and files for downloading, link pages together, and format the pages to their liking. Quick Look is a new feature in the wiki service. It allows users to view the contents of a document without downloading the document—they just click the Quick Look icon next to an attachment and view the contents.

Similar to wikis are blogs. Blogs permit users and groups to catalog their experiences surrounding a project or theme. Whereas wikis are collaborative, blogs tend to be singular in nature and organized in a chronological format; however, with group blogging, shared experiences are posted together.

Enabling a Wiki in Server Admin

Enabling the wiki service on Mac OS X Server is a simple task. In Chapter 6, "Managing Web Services," you enabled and started the Web service for server17.pretendco.com. Now, you will use Server Admin to configure and enable the wiki service.

In this exercise, you will change the location of the data store for the wiki service, and then limit who can create wikis. You will ensure that your site uses SSL and that wikis, blogs, and calendar services are enabled for your site. If you do not have a separate volume for your data store, skip steps 4–7.

1   Open Server Admin and select your server in the list of servers on the left.

2   Select Web in the list of services under your server on the left side of Server Admin, and ensure the service is running, as noted by the green status indicator next to the service.

3   Click Settings in the toolbar, and then click the Wiki tab.

4   Click Choose to change the data store.

5   Select your User Data volume, and then click New Folder.

6   Name the folder Collaboration, and then click Create.

7   Select the Collaboration folder, and then click Choose.

8 Under the Wiki Creators list, click the Add (+) button, which opens the Users & Groups window.

9 Drag the group Odds to the Wiki Creators list. This group includes student1, student3, and student5, so these users will be able to create wikis.

10 For the SMTP Relay, click Configure.

11 In the Sender Address field, enter ladmin@server17.pretendco.com, and then click Done.

12 Click Save to save your wiki settings.

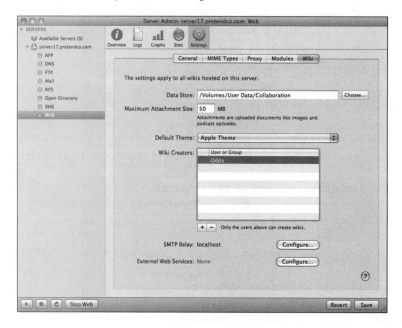

13 Click Sites in the toolbar.

14 Confirm that the checkbox is selected for your default site.

15 Choose your default site, and then click the Security tab.

16 Confirm that the Enable Secure Sockets Layer (SSL) checkbox is selected.

17 Choose the certificate server17.pretendco.com, and then click Save. If you are asked, click Restart to restart the Web service.

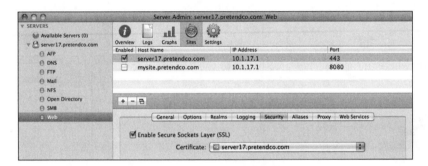

18 Click the Web Services tab, and then select the checkboxes for Wikis, Blogs, and Calendar.

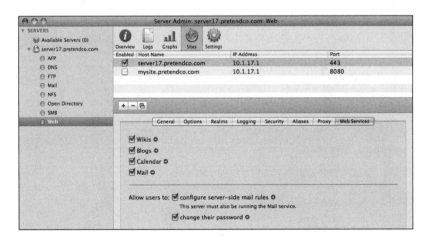

19 Click Save.

You have now enabled the option to allow the members of the Odds group to create wikis.

Creating Wikis

Users that you authorized to create wikis can begin the process of creating a wiki. Because wikis are web based, you can use any browser on any platform to authenticate users to start the process of wiki creation. In this exercise, you will use network user credentials to create a wiki, manage access to it, create some content, and use Quick Look to view an attachment.

1 From your Mac OS X computer, open Safari, enter `https://server17.pretendco.com`, and then press Return.

The default webpage for your Mac OS X Server appears.

2 Click anywhere in the My Page area to get to the login window.

3 Log in as `student1` with the password `network`.

4   Click "wikis."

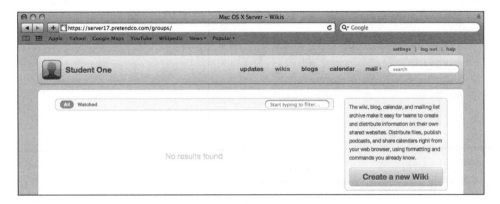

5   Click "Create a new Wiki."

6   Enter the name Project A. In the Description field, enter This is the wiki for
Project A.

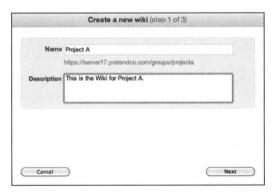

7   Click Next.

8 Choose the default Apple Theme, and then click Next.

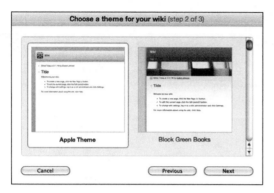

9 In the "Set wiki access" window, you could make the site public, yet still require users to log in to read or log in to write or both. However, you will make this site private and accessible only to some users and groups.

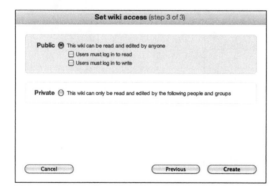

Click Private.

10 In the "Type a user or group name here" field, you must type a name and select from the list that appears. Enter Odds, and then choose Odds <odds>.

Be sure to choose the group, not just type its name.

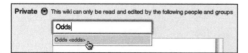

11 In the text field, enter student4, and then choose Student Four <student4>.

Be sure to choose the user, not just type the name.

12 Change student4's permission to "Read only."

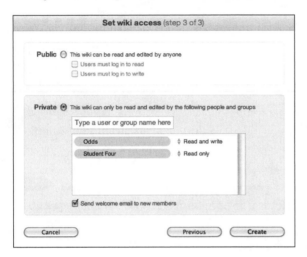

13 Click Create.

14 Click Go to Wiki.

15 You should see the page for the Project A wiki.

16 Click the Edit button (a pencil icon).

17 Click at the end of the existing text, press Return for a new line, and then click the Attachment icon (a paper clip).

18 Click Choose File, navigate to your Documents folder, select the About Stacks.pdf file, and then click Choose.

19 Click Attach to attach the file.

20 In the Comment field, enter Uploaded attachment.

21 Click Save to save the edits to the page.

22 Click the Quick Look icon next to the attachment to quickly view the contents of the file.

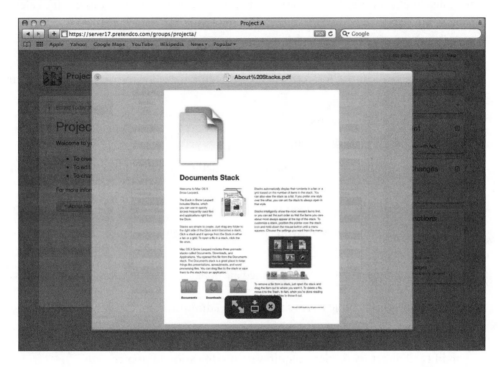

23 Close the Quick Look window.

24 Click "log out," and then quit Safari.

In this section, you used Server Admin to control which users and groups have permission to create wikis, and then you used Safari as a user to quickly set up a wiki. You used Safari to enable a group to edit that particular wiki, and set read-only permission for a user. You can experiment with this to confirm your expectations and to try out all the features of the wiki service.

The wiki service integrates with the iCal service, which the next section covers.

Using the iCal Service

Mac OS X Server v10.6 contains a calendaring service based on several open source initiatives, mainly the Calendar Server Extensions for WebDAV (CalDAV) calendaring protocol. The iCal service uses HTTP for access to all of its files. Users who want to use the calendaring service can take advantage of several handy features:

▶ Scheduling rooms or items that can be checked out, such as projectors

▶ Enabling access control for delegation of scheduling and/or restricted viewing of your calendar(s)

▶ Allowing multiple calendars per user

▶ Permitting the attachment of files to events

▶ Sending invitations to events, regardless of whether or not the recipient is a user on the iCal server

▶ Checking to see if users or meeting locations are available for a certain event

▶ Privately annotating an event with comments that only they and the event organizer can access

▶ Using Push notification to support immediate updates for computers and mobile devices

And these under-the-hood features should make administrators happy:

▶ Integration with Open Directory in Mac OS X Server, Microsoft's Active Directory, and LDAP directory services, requires no modification to user records.

▶ Service discovery makes it easy for users to set up iCal when you choose "Create Users and Groups" or "Import Users and Groups" during your initial server setup.

▶ Server-side scheduling frees up client resources for better client performance.

▶ Optimization for the Xsan clustered file system makes it easy to add new iCal servers as the demand for calendaring services grows.

Once the iCal service is started, users can create and manipulate their events and schedules with iCal 4.0 (which comes with Mac OS X v10.6), Calendar for iPhone and iPod touch, and wiki calendar pages. There are third-party applications that also work with the iCal service; you can locate them by doing a web search for CalDAV support.

Configuring and Starting the iCal Service

You can use Server Admin to start and manage the iCal service. The parameters that you can adjust are:

▶ Location of the data store

▶ Maximum attachment size and user quota

▶ Address for Push notification server

▶ Wiki server and whether or not it uses Secure Sockets Layer (SSL)

▶ Enabling or disabling of email invitations and various related settings

▶ Authentication for service that can be Kerberos (tried first if you choose Any Method from the menu) or Digest

▶ Name of calendaring server (if you have more than one name for your server in DNS)

▶ Port for access to service

▶ Ability to use SSL

Before you configure your iCal service with Server Admin, prepare a separate location for the data store. If you do not have a separate volume, do not perform these steps, just read through them. Configure the iCal service, and then start it.

1   Open Server Admin and select your server in the list of servers on the left.

2   Click the Settings button in the toolbar, click the Services tab, select the iCal service, and then click Save.

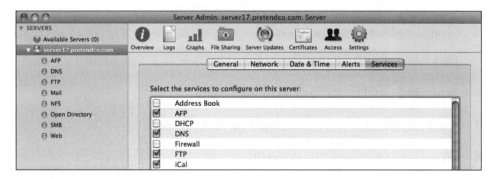

3 Select the iCal service in the list of services under your server on the left side of Server Admin.

4 Click Settings in the toolbar, and then click General.

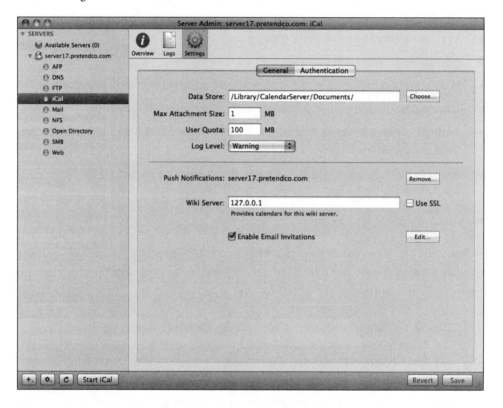

5 Change the location of the data store.

Click Choose, open the User Data volume, and then click New Folder.

6 Name the new folder iCal, and then click Create.

7 Select the folder you just created, and then click Choose.

8 Set the Max Attachment Size to 50 MB.

9   Change the User Quota to 300 MB, and then click Save.

You set user quotas to prevent users from attaching extremely large files to every event they have. For example, if users attach a large file to one event, they are probably under the maximum attachment size. However, if they have many events, each with an attachment, they may run into the user quota limit and thus be prevented from attaching any more files to events. If users reach the quota limit, they will be able to create events, but they will not be able to add any attachments; you could suggest that they remove attachments but leave the underlying events intact.

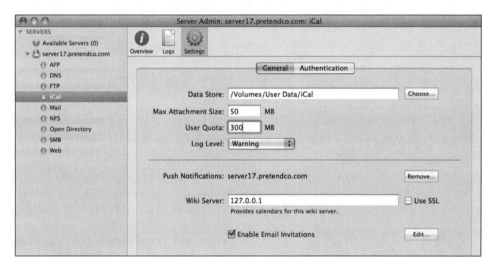

10   Click the Authentication tab.

11   You can leave the Host Name field blank, and the iCal service will use the local host name.

NOTE ▶ If you decide to use a different host name in order to make it easier for users to specify the calendar server—for instance, icalserver.pretendco.com—make sure you have forward and reverse DNS settings for the alternate host name and, if appropriate, a valid SSL certificate for the alternate host name.

12   Choose Use from the SSL pop-up menu, and then choose the server17.pretendco.com certificate.

Note that the SSL port changes to port 8443.

13 Click Save.

14 Click the Start iCal button to start the service.

Using iCal Server Utility to Add Resources and Locations

If you have an Open Directory server, you can use it to store resources (like a projector or a set of speakers) and locations (such as a building or a meeting room), and then your users can attempt to schedule an event with a location and resources. The iCal service automatically accepts the invitation for the location or resource if it is free, and makes the free/busy information available to users.

iCal Server Utility allows Open Directory users to create and manage resources and locations. You need a Kerberos ticket in order to create items with iCal Server Utility.

You add locations and resources with iCal Server Utility; you add users and groups with Server Preferences or Workgroup Manager.

To add a location and a resource with iCal Server Utility:

1 On your Mac OS X computer (with the Server Admin tools installed), open iCal Server Utility, which is in /Applications/Server.

2 Click the Add (+) button, and then choose New Location from the pop-up menu.

3 If prompted for a Kerberos identity, enter `student1@SERVER17.PRETENDCO.COM`, and then click Continue.

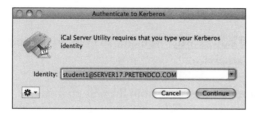

4   If prompted to authenticate for a Kerberos ticket, provide student1's password (network), and then click Continue.

5   Enter and/or change the following data for your new location:

▶   The name of the Location should be Conference A.

▶   Enter 3 for the Building.

▶   Enter 2 for the Floor.

▶   Enter 200 for the Capacity.

▶   Leave the contact as Student One.

▶   There are no maps to choose from at this point.

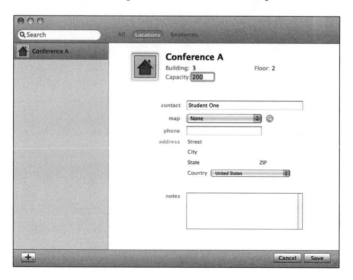

6   Click Save to save the changes to the location.

You have now added a location that you can see when you add an event to or modify an event on a calendar hosted by the iCal service.

7   Click the Add (+) button, and then choose New Resource from the pop-up menu.

8   Enter and/or change the following data for your new resource:

▶   The name of the resource should be Projector A.

▶   Choose Projector for the Resource type.

▶   Leave the owner as Student One.

▶   In the notes field, enter the text Bulb type 251.

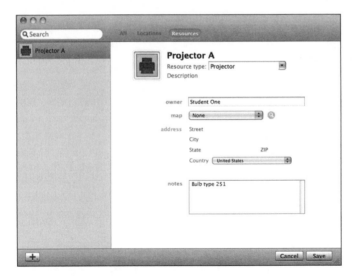

9   Click Save to save the changes to the resource.

You have now added a resource that you can invite to an event.

10   Quit iCal Server Utility.

Accessing the iCal Service as a User

Users can create and modify events with iCal, a web browser, and mobile devices. In this exercise, you will open iCal, add a network iCal account, change who can access the account as a delegate, create an event with a location and a resource, and then create one more event and access the free/busy feature.

1   On your Mac OS X computer, open iCal (in /Applications).

2   Choose iCal > Preferences, and then click Accounts.

3   Click the Add (+) button to add an iCal service account, and enter the following data:

▶   For the Account type, choose Automatic.

▶   For the Email address, enter student1@server17.pretendco.com.

▶   For the Password, enter network.

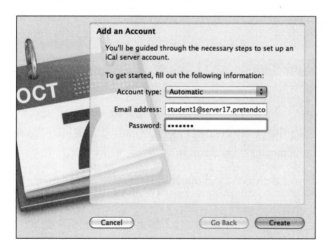

4   Click Create to add the account.

5   Delegate other users to access your calendar to edit and review your events. Click the Delegation tab.

6   Click Edit.

7   Click the Add (+) button.

8   Enter Student Four, and then choose Student Four from the list. Make sure you click the name to choose it.

9   Click the Add button, enter Student Five, and then choose Student Five from the list.

10   Select the Allow Write checkbox for Student Five. This allows Student Five to edit events on behalf of Student One, and Student Four to view Student One's events.

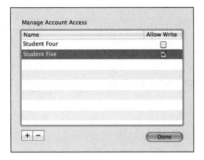

11   Click Done to close the Delegation pane.

12   Close the Preferences window.

13   In the Calendars column, select the newly created calendar named "calendar" so that when you create a new event, iCal uses this calendar.

You could press Return to change the calendar name, but leave it as "calendar" for now.

14   Choose File > New Event.

15   Choose Edit > Edit Event.

16   Replace "New Event" with the text Status Update.

17   Press Tab to move to the location field, and then enter only the first few characters of Conference A.

18 Click Conference A in the list that iCal displays, and then press Return to choose it.

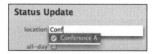

19 Click Add Invitees, and then enter only the first few characters of Student Two.

20 Click Student Two in the list that iCal displays, and then press Return to choose it.

21 While still in the invitees field, enter only the first few characters of Projector A.

22 Click Projector A in the list that iCal displays, and then press Return to choose it.

23 Click Add File, navigate to your Documents folder, select About Stacks.pdf, and then click Open.

24 Click Send to save the changes to this event. This will cause Projector A to automatically accept the event, and Student Two will get an invitation to the event.

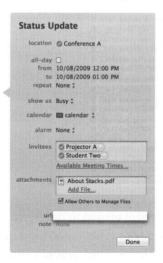

25 Click the event you just created. Choose Edit > Duplicate, which should create a new event at the same time as your original event.

26 Choose Edit > Edit Event.

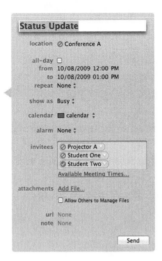

27 Note that the Conference A location has an unavailable icon, because you already scheduled an event for this location. Because Student Two has not yet replied to the invitation, this is the only participant listed without the unavailable icon.

Click Available Meeting Times to choose a new meeting time that works for the location and invitees (which includes people and resources).

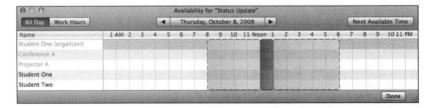

28 Note that free/busy information is listed for each participant invited to the event, including the location, people, and resources. The unavailable times are blocked out in gray, and the available times are displayed with the color assigned to your calendar.

Click Next Available Time, and note that the event moves to the next time that is not busy for each of the invitees.

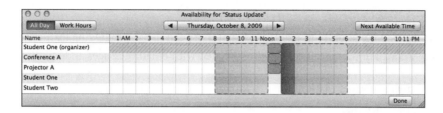

29 Click Done to close the Availability window and use the new time selected.

30 Click Send to save the changes to the event and notify the invitees of the event. Locations and resources automatically accept invitations.

31 Quit iCal, or try out some of the other features. One starting point could be to use screen sharing, control your Mac OS X Server, and configure iCal for student2.

Even though you used iCal in this exercise, you could also use the calendar link from your wiki pages. Of course, the iCal service works with Calendar for iPhone and iPod touch through the CalDAV configuration option.

Managing the iChat Service

iChat allows users to collaborate in real time. iChat users can use the following features to quickly share information without the delay associated with email messages and wiki posts:

▶   Exchange text messages instantly.

▶   Send files to each other.

▶   Set up an instant audio conference (including the microphone built into many Macs).

▶   Initiate a face-to-face video conference using video cameras (including the iSight camera built into many Macs).

▶   Allow another iChat user to take control of their Mac (using screen sharing).

▶   Use iChat Theater to share many kinds of documents, including text files, PDFs, photos, QuickTime movies, Keynote slide shows, and iPhoto albums.

Unlike a telephone call, which you must either answer or allow to go to voicemail, you can accept an instant text message but answer it after a delay, when you are ready to process it. Chat encompasses all the features listed above.

Users who chat with each other can use the iChat service to keep those chats within their organization and control the text of the chats. Like many other services on Mac OS X Server, the iChat service can be restricted to certain users or groups, permitting chats to be private and controlled. Chats can also be secured through encryption and logged, permitting them to be searched later. The iChat service is based on the open source Jabber project. The technical name for the protocol used is the Extensible Messaging and Presence Protocol (XMPP).

Setting Up the iChat Service

You use Server Admin to enable the iChat service like all the other services on Mac OS X Server. Once enabled, the service is managed in a fashion similar to that of the other services.

In this exercise, you will create a folder and change the owner and group associated with that folder. If you do not have a separate volume, do not perform these steps, just read through them.

1   Open Server Admin and select your server in the list of servers on the left.

2 Click File Sharing, and then Volumes, and then Browse.

3 Select your User Data volume, and then click New Folder.

4 Name the new folder Jabber, and then click Create.

5 Select the Jabber folder you just created, and then click Share.

6 Click Permissions.

7 Double-click root in the owner row, and then change the User to _jabber. Click OK.

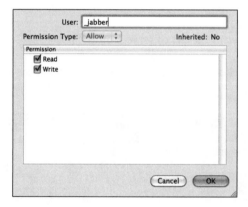

8 Double-click admin in the group row, and then change the Group to _jabber.

9 Deselect the checkbox for the Write permission.

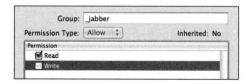

10 Click OK to dismiss the User and Permission pane.

11 Change the Permission for Others to No Access.

12 Click OK to dismiss the Group and Permission pane.

13 Click Save.

Now that you have a folder ready to hold the iChat service data, configure the iChat server, and then start it.

1 Open Server Admin and select your server in the list of servers on the left.

2 Click the Settings button in the toolbar, click the Services tab, select the iChat service, and click Save.

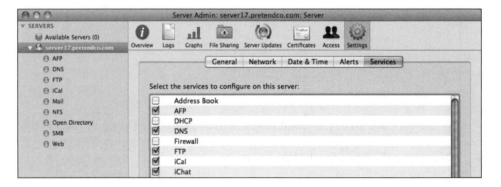

3 Select iChat in the list of services displayed under your server on the left side of Server Admin.

4 Click the Settings button in the toolbar to view the iChat service options.

5 From the SSL Certificate pop-up menu, choose server17.pretendco.com.

6 Choose Any Method from the Authentication pop-up menu. By designating Any Method, when users join the iChat service, Kerberos will be tried first, and then Digest. You can also specify that just Kerberos or Digest authentication will be used.

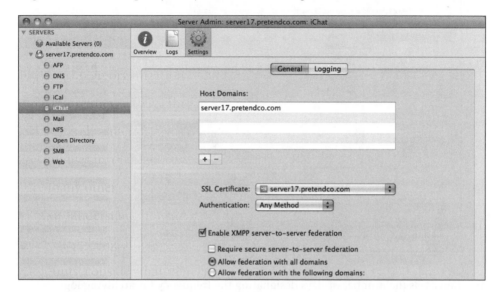

Managing iChat Service Logs

The iChat service can be used for all sorts of purposes, among them group chatting related to projects. Often a member of the group will want to review the chat logs of a conversation, perhaps to follow up or to gather notes relating to future meetings.

The iChat service can log all chat messages and save them in a directory of your choosing. The default directory is located in /var/jabberd/message_archives/. If you do not have a second volume on which to store the data, skip the step to change the location.

To enable iChat service logging and to change the location of those logs:

1 Select iChat in the services listed under your server on the left side of Server Admin, and then click the Settings button in the toolbar.

2 Click the Logging tab.

3 Ensure that the "Automatically save chat messages" checkbox is selected.

4 If you have a second volume for data storage, click Choose, navigate to the Jabber folder on your User Data volume, and click Choose to select that folder.

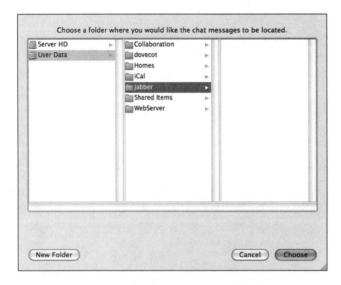

5 Enter 7 as the number of days designating the frequency for archiving logs.

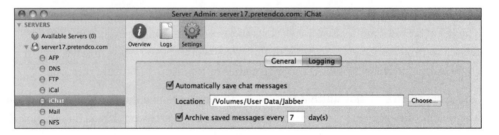

6 Click Save.

7 Click Start iChat.

To view any logged messages, you must be the root user and navigate to /var/jabberd/message_archives/. You can then use any text editor to view the log files and search them for relevant keywords.

Configuring iChat Service Users

After the iChat service has been set up, you can permit users to join the iChat service (called Jabber in the interface). The iChat service account is a user's short name, the @ symbol, then an iChat service's host domain. For example, the user student5 would set up the iChat application as student5@server17.pretendco.com.

To enable an iChat account to use the iChat (Jabber) service:

1   On your Mac OS X computer, select the iChat icon in your Dock and click past the introduction screen.

2   Choose Jabber from the Account Type pop-up menu.

3   Enter student1@server17.pretendco.com in the Account Name field, and enter the password network in the Password field.

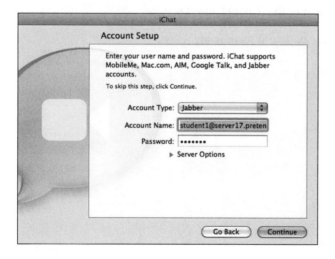

4   Click Continue, and then click Done.

iChat will open, and you will see your iChat (Jabber) service buddy list. iChat displays the full name of the user that is logged in on Mac OS X. Even though you are logged in to the iChat service as student1, iChat displays Client Administrator because you are logged in to Mac OS X as Client Administrator.

You can add buddies (other users with whom you want to chat and whose names you want to appear in a list so you can frequently open a chat with them) to your buddy list as you normally would when using iChat for any other account. You can optionally add a buddy who exists in your Open Directory database. Be sure to include the full name when adding an iChat (Jabber) service buddy.

Once you add a buddy, that person receives a notice when he or she logs in to iChat (Jabber) asking if he or she would like to be added to your buddy list. If another user attempts to add student1 as a buddy, you would see the following window appear.

Once you have authorized the listing of your name in that person's buddy list, he or she will see you every time you log in to the iChat (Jabber) service.

You can of course communicate back and forth using iChat.

Restricting iChat Service Users

You can also restrict who is permitted to use the iChat service by using service access controls. As with many other services discussed in this book, you can restrict user and/or group access.

To restrict users or groups from chatting with others on the iChat service:

1 Open Server Admin and select your server in the list of servers on the left.

2 Click the Access button in the toolbar and click the Services tab.

3 Select the "For selected services below" option, and select the iChat service.

4 Select "Allow only users and groups below."

5 Click the Add (+) button and drag over any users or groups you want to use the iChat service, and then click Save.

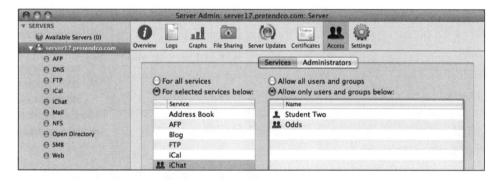

Using iChat Federation to Join Services

Your organization may have more than one Mac OS X Server. If both of those servers use the iChat service, it is possible to join them together, allowing users and groups in both Open Directory masters to engage each other in instant messaging. The process of joining different iChat service servers together is called federation. Federation not only allows two Mac OS X Servers running iChat services to join, it also allows any other XMPP chat service, such as Google Talk, to join as well. The iChat service federation is enabled by default.

> **NOTE** ▶ You can enable secure encryption for the federation if you are already using an SSL certificate. This forces all communications between the servers to be encrypted, similar to the way the communications between iChat and the iChat server are encrypted when using that certificate. For archiving purposes, messages are always decrypted on the server.

By default, you allow federation with any other iChat service running on any other Mac OS X Server. However, you can restrict the iChat service federation to approved iChat servers only. To do so, select the "Allow federation with the following domains" option and click the Add (+) button to add only those domains that you want to participate within the federation.

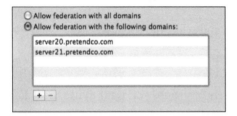

Viewing iChat Service Logs

As an administrator, you have access to various iChat service log files. These files permit you to see who is currently logged in to the iChat service, and the ports used during an iChat session. These parameters are recorded in the iChat service log, which can be accessed by choosing that log file from the pop-up menu under the Logs button in the toolbar after selecting the iChat service in the services list of Server Admin. Once there, simply enter session started in the search field, and you will see all users, dates, and times that sessions have begun.

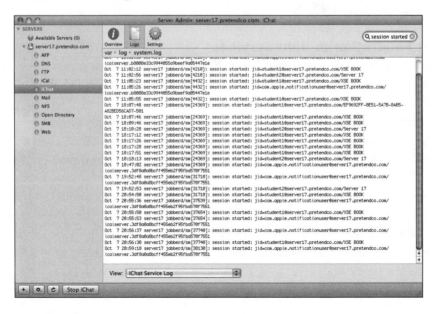

The iChat service log can also log any errors that may occur, and you can search for them using the search field in the toolbar in a fashion similar to the way you locate users who have started an iChat session. Typical troubleshooting involves ensuring valid DNS entries, network configuration, Network Address Translation (if the servers are on networks with NAT), and firewall configuration. See the article "'Well known' TCP and UDP ports used by Apple software products" (link at the end of the chapter) to help troubleshoot potential firewall issues.

You must have root access to view the jabberd_user_messages.log file, which contains all the messages your users have exchanged using your server's iChat service.

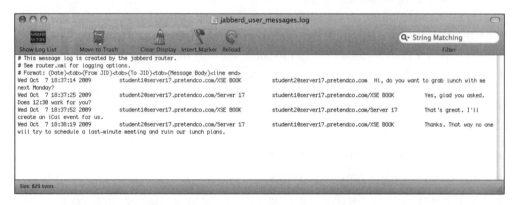

Understanding the Address Book Service

The Address Book service is new to Mac OS X Server v10.6. It enables users to store contacts on the server and to access those contacts with multiple computers and devices. The following applications in Mac OS X v10.6 are compatible with the Address Book service:

▶   Address Book 5

▶   Mail 4

▶   iChat 5

You can enable the Directory Gateway to allow the Address Book service to provide LDAP searches of the directory servers that your Mac OS X Server is bound to, so your users do not have to configure their Address Book preferences to include various LDAP servers.

You can also enable the Directory Gateway to allow users to search public contacts that were created with the utility named Directory in Mac OS X v10.5 (there is no utility named Directory for Mac OS X v10.6).

The Address Book service uses open source technologies including CardDAV (an extension to WebDAV), HTTP, and HTTPS, as well as vCard, a file format for contact information. You must use Open Directory user accounts to access the Address Book service, so your server must either be an Open Directory server or be bound to one.

When you create a contact with the Address Book service, you use CardDAV, not LDAP, to copy the changes to the server.

Configuring the Address Book Service with Server Admin

Although Server Preferences allows you to configure only the maximum size of each user's total Address Book, Server Admin allows you to configure:

▶ The data store

▶ User quota

▶ Log level (Error, Warning, Info, or Debug)

▶ A Directory Gateway for user accounts

▶ A Directory Gateway for shared accounts (from the utility named Directory in Mac OS X v10.5)

▶ Authentication method (Digest, Kerberos, or Any Method [Kerberos and then Digest])

▶ Host name for the Address Book service

▶ Port

▶ Whether or not to use SSL for CardDAV

In this exercise, before you start the Address Book service, you will change the data store, enable the Directory Gateway, and specify an SSL certificate for the service to use. If you do not have multiple volumes, skip the steps to choose a different data store.

1   On your Mac OS X computer, open Server Admin and connect to your Mac OS X Server as ladmin.

2   Click the Add (+) button, and choose Add Service from the pop-up menu.

3   Select the checkbox for Address Book, and click Save.

4   Select Address Book in the left column.

5   Click the Settings button in the toolbar.

6   Click the General tab.

7   For the data store, click Choose.

8   Select your User Data volume, and then click New Folder.

9   Name the new folder AddressBook, and then click Create.

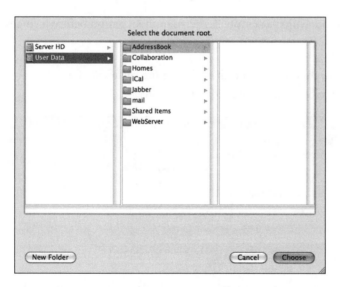

10 In the selection window, make sure the folder you just created is highlighted, and then click Choose.

11 Select the checkbox labeled "Search for user accounts."

12 Click the Authentication tab.

13 Leave Type as Any Method, which attempts Kerberos authentication before trying the Digest method.

14 In the SSL pop-up menu, choose Use, and then choose the certificate for server17.pretendco.com. Note that the SSL port used is 8843.

15 Click Save.

16 Click Start Address Book.

Configuring Mac OS X to Use the Address Book Service

The Address Book application in Mac OS X v10.6 is designed to work with the Address Book service on Mac OS X Server v10.6. Before you do any configuration, perform a search for a network user's contact information, and then configure Address Book to use student1's account, create a few test contacts, and perform a few searches.

1 On your Mac OS X computer, open Address Book (in /Applications).

2 Select Directory Services in the Group column of Address Book. This applies to all directory services that this Mac OS X computer is bound to. In this case, your Mac OS X computer is bound to server17.pretendco.com.

3 In the search field in the upper-right corner, enter three.

4 The record for Student Three is returned immediately. Note that there is no extra information stored with this user record, because you have not edited any extra information with Workgroup Manager. Also note that you cannot edit any information for Student Three.

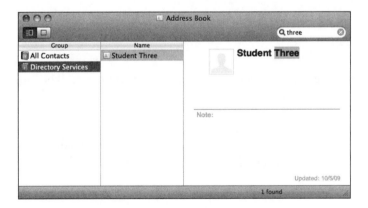

5 Choose Address Book > Preferences.

6 Click Accounts.

7 Click the Add (+) button.

8 Leave the Account type as CardDAV, as the Address Book service implements CardDAV.

9 In the User name field, enter student1.

You must use the user's short name.

10 In the Password field, enter network.

11 In the Server address field, enter server17.pretendco.com.

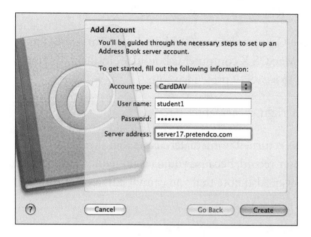

12 Click Create.

13 If a Verify Certificate dialog appears, click Show Certificate, select the checkbox for "Always trust," and authenticate as cadmin (password cadmin).

Of course, in a production environment, you would populate client computers to trust your known-good SSL certificates, and then train users to alert an administrator when they see an unknown-certificate message.

14 You should see the new account appear in the Accounts list.

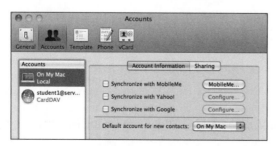

15 Select the On My Mac entry.

16 Click the "Default account for new contacts" pop-up menu, and choose student1@server17.pretendco.com.

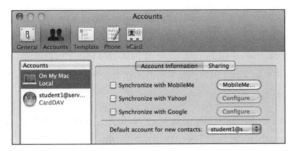

Now when you create a new contact, it will automatically be created on the server.

17 Close the Accounts window.

18 Select All Contacts.

19 Click the Add (+) button under the Name list (not the Group list) to create a new contact that will be stored on the server.

20 Enter sample information for a user, including email and Jabber addresses. You can use the following values:

First: Masayuki

Last: Nii

Email (work): nii@example.com

Jabber (work): nii@jabber.example.com

21 Click Edit to save your changes.

The contact you just created is synced locally on your Mac OS X computer, and it is also stored with the Address Book service, so you can access it from other computers and devices.

Use the following steps to confirm that the Mail 4.0 application in Mac OS X v10.6 uses the Address Book Server account you have configured with the Address Book application.

If you haven't already configured the Mail service and application, refer to Chapter 5, "Hosting Mail Services."

1   Open Mail (in /Applications).

2   Choose File > New Message

3   In the To field, start entering the name of the contact you just created. Enter Masa, and the Mail application should automatically enter the full name and email address for this contact.

    This contact appears because Mail automatically accesses your Address Book Server account, not because you are bound to server17; you could unbind your Mac OS X computer from the Open Directory server on your server, and Mail would still use your Address Book Server account.

4   Press Return to accept the address. Note that Mail now displays the user name.

5   Because you are on an isolated network and cannot actually send mail to this sample contact, choose File > Close, and then click Don't Save.

6   Quit Mail.

iChat 5.0, which comes with Mac OS X v10.6, also supports your Address Book Server account. Use the following steps to demonstrate that you can use your Address Book Server account with iChat. If you haven't already configured iChat with your network user account, refer to Managing the iChat Service in this chapter.

1   If iChat is not already running, open iChat (in /Applications).

2   If the Jabber List window is not already displayed, choose Window > Jabber List.

3   Click the Add (+) button in the lower-left corner, and choose Add Buddy.

4   Click the Disclosure button to reveal additional choices.

5   Click the entry you created (Masayuki).

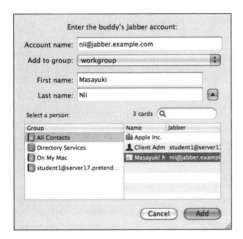

6   Click Cancel.

In a production environment, you would click Add to add this user to your buddy list. Do not click Add now, because this would create an authorization request for the foreign Jabber server, and you are on an isolated network.

7   Quit iChat.

The contacts you create with your Address Book Server account are available to you on other Mac OS X v10.6 computers, as long as you configure Address Book with your Address Book Server account. You can also access your contacts with any application that uses CardDAV.

What You've Learned

▶   Setting up the wiki service involves running the Web service with at least one web server running on Mac OS X Server.

▶   A wiki can contain files, graphics, text, and links.

▶   The iCal service is based on CalDAV, an open source initiative.

▶   The iChat service uses the XMPP protocol and is also based on an open source initiative, in this case Jabber.

▶ iChat service servers can be joined together in a process called federation.

▶ The new Address Book service uses such open source technology as CardDAV, an initiative based on WebDAV; vCard; and HTTP and HTTPS.

References

The following documents provide more information about the Mac OS X Server collaboration services. All of these and more are available at http://www.apple.com/server/macosx/resources/.

Administration Guides

Web Technologies Administration

Wiki Server Administration

Wiki Tools Deployment Guide

iCal Service

iChat Service

Address Book Server Administration

User Management

Getting Started

Advanced Server Administration

Upgrading and Migrating

URLs

Wiki site: http://www.wiki.org

CalConnect site: http://www.calconnect.org

CardDAV: http://www.ietf.org/id/draft-ietf-vcarddav-carddav-07.txt

Jabber site: http://www.jabber.org

"'Well known' TCP and UDP ports used by Apple software products": http://support.apple.com/kb/TS1629

Chapter Review

1. What protocol is used for the iChat service?

2. How would you enable a wiki on Mac OS X Server?

3. What tools can an administrator use to specify users that are allowed to create wikis? How does a network user specify which users and groups are allowed to edit a wiki?

4. How would you enter the iChat name for the user Holly Gleason (short name holly) on server17.pretendco.com?

5. What application do you use to create resources and locations for use in iCal events?

6. What new open source protocol does the Address Book service use?

Answers

1. The iChat service uses the Extensible Messaging and Presence Protocol (XMPP).

2. The following steps are executed to enable a wiki:

    1. Authenticate to Server Admin.

    2. Enable the Web service.

    3. Click the Sites button.

    4. Select the appropriate website.

    5. Click the Web Services tab.

    6. Select the checkbox for wikis (and optionally select the checkboxes for blogs, calendar, and mail).

3. Administrators can use the Wiki Creators list in the Wiki tab of the Web service settings in Server Admin. When creating a wiki with a web browser, a user can specify permissions for users and groups to access and edit the wiki.

4. The iChat name format for Holly Gleason on server17.pretendco.com is holly@server17.pretendco.com.

5. iCal Server Utility (located in the /Applications/Server folder on Mac OS X computers with the Server Admin tools installed) is used to create resources and locations for use in iCal events.

6. The Address Book service uses CardDAV.

8

Time This chapter takes approximately six hours to complete.

Goals Learn the advantages of Apple's network-based deployment solutions

Create NetBoot and Network Install images

Configure the server to allow NetBoot and Network Install

Boot from a NetBoot image

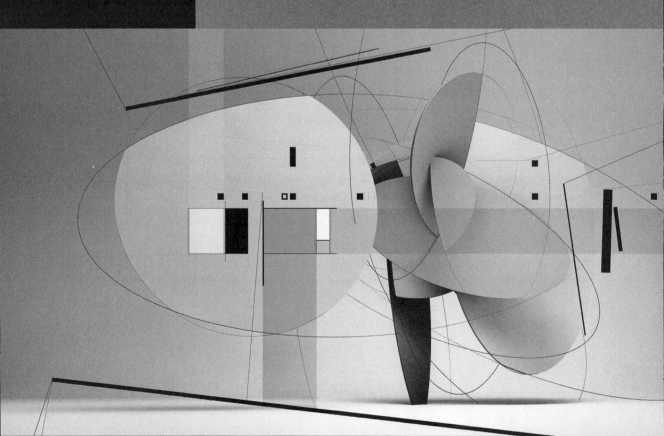

Chapter **8**

Implementing Deployment Solutions

Knowing how to use time efficiently is a very important aspect of an administrator's job. When managing several hundred Mac OS X computers, an administrator needs a solution that is both speedy and flexible for performing day-to-day management of computers. When computers need to be set up for the very first time, what software should be installed? Should they have the latest software updates? Should they have a full complement of non-Apple software, such as Adobe Creative Suite or Microsoft Office? What about shareware programs and the necessary work-related files? Safety videos? Mandatory PDFs?

Before you can push out data to a computer, you must decide *how* to push out that data and in what state. Apple has several applications to assist you with this process, and there are several third-party tools that also complete the tasks of image creation and deployment. Apple has several applications—including System Image Utility, Apple System Restore (ASR), Apple Remote Desktop (ARD), and NetBoot—to help you with this process.

With the advantage of these deployment software tools, you can build an automated system that needs very little user interaction to function. This chapter will focus primarily on the NetBoot service provided by Mac OS X Server.

Creating NetBoot images can be a lengthy process, but most of it is just waiting for the image to be processed. Because this chapter includes creation of two images, you may wish to split this chapter over a couple days or over a dinner break at either of the two image-creation steps.

Deployment Issues

One significant challenge for Mac OS X administrators today is the deployment of software to multiple computers. Whether it is operating system (OS) releases and updates or commercial applications, installing the software manually is a labor-intensive process. Mac OS X Server provides services and technologies to aid in this deployment. The NetBoot service simplifies OS rollout and upgrades.

Managing Computers with NetBoot

Think about the ways you boot your computer. Most often, your computer starts up from system software located on the local hard drive. This local startup provides you with a typical computer experience of running applications, accessing information, and accomplishing tasks. Sometimes when you perform OS installations or system upgrades, you need to boot from a CD-ROM or DVD-ROM disc.

Managing a single standalone computer isn't much of an inconvenience. However, imagine managing a lab of computers. Every time you need to upgrade the operating system or install a clean version of Mac OS X, you would need to boot each computer in the lab from the installation CD or DVD disc. Even with a set of installation discs for each computer, it would still be time-consuming to update or refresh the entire lab.

Mac OS X Server provides the NetBoot service, which simplifies the management of operating systems on multiple computers. With NetBoot, client computers start up using system software that they access from a server instead of from the client's local hard drive. With NetBoot, the client obtains information from a remote location. With other startup methods, the client boots off a local source, such as the internal hard drive, DVD, or other device.

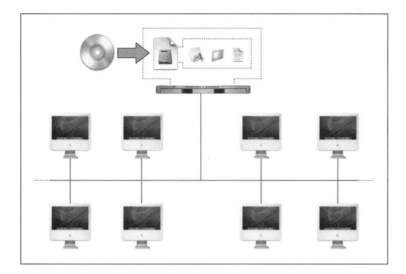

NetBoot is most effective in situations where there is a high frequency of user turnover and where a large number of computers are being deployed with a common configuration. The ability to deploy standard configurations across multiple computers makes NetBoot ideal for computing environments such as:

▶ Classrooms and computer labs: NetBoot makes it easy to configure multiple identical desktop systems and repurpose them quickly. With NetBoot, you can reconfigure systems for a different class simply by restarting from a different image.

▶ Corporate workstations: Using NetBoot to install system software allows you to reimage, deploy, and update workstations very quickly by not having to use a DVD to load each workstation individually. Also, because installation is done over the network, it can even be done in place at the user's desk. A creative way to take advantage of this technology is to create a NetBoot image with various computer diagnosis and disk recovery software. Booting into a NetBoot rescue image at a user's desk could save a lot of time for a frustrated user.

▶ Kiosks and libraries: With NetBoot, you can set up protected computing environments for customers or visitors. For example, you can configure an information station with an Internet browser that connects only to your company's website, or set up a visitor kiosk that runs only a database for collecting feedback. If a system is altered, a simple restart restores it to its original condition.

▶ Computational clusters: NetBoot is a powerful solution for data centers and computational clusters with identically configured web or application servers. Similarly purposed systems can boot from a single NetBoot image maintained on a network-based storage device.

Hardware Requirements

For NetBoot to function properly certain minimum hardware requirements must be met:

▶ 512 MB RAM on the client computer

▶ 100Base-T Ethernet (up to 10 clients)

▶ 100Base-T switched Ethernet (10 to 50 clients)

▶ 1000Base-T switched Ethernet (beyond 50 clients)

Apple has no official test results for configurations beyond 50 clients. Apple does not support the use of AirPort wireless technology with NetBoot clients.

Understanding NetBoot Startup Types

There are three types of NetBoot startup:

▶ A standard NetBoot startup (using a NetBoot boot image) provides a fairly typical experience, because clients start up using software that they access from a server.

▶ A Network Install startup sequence (using a NetBoot Install image) enables you to quickly perform fresh installations of your operating system (much like installing from a DVD), install applications or updates, or install configured disk images. The terms *Network* Install and *NetInstall* are used interchangeably in this chapter.

▶ A new choice for Mac OS X Server v10.6 is NetRestore. This choice is aimed at deploying existing volumes, similar to the volume source choice in the previous version of System Image Utility. Another defining choice is the ability to define a restore image source other than the disk image embedded in the NetInstall set. This allows you to host the image on other servers, much like DeployStudio.

Keep these three types of NetBoot startup in mind while you work through the remainder of this chapter.

With NetBoot, you create disk images on the server that contain Mac OS X or Mac OS X Server system software. Multiple network clients can use each disk image at once. Because you are setting up a centralized source of system software, you need to configure, test, and deploy only once. This dramatically reduces the maintenance required for network computers.

When you start up from a NetBoot image, the startup volume is read-only. When a client needs to write anything back to its startup volume, NetBoot automatically redirects the written data to the client's shadow files (which are discussed later in this chapter, in the section "Understanding Shadow Files"). Data in shadow files is kept for the duration of a NetBoot session. Because the startup volume is read-only, you always start from a clean image. This is ideal in lab and kiosk situations where you want to ensure that users never alter the startup volume.

Stepping Through the NetBoot Client Startup Process

When a client computer boots from a NetBoot image, it performs a number of steps to start up successfully:

1. The client places a request for an IP address.

   When a NetBoot client is turned on or restarted, it requests an IP address from a DHCP server. While the server providing the address can be the same server providing the NetBoot service, the two services do not have to be provided by the same computer.

2. After receiving an IP address, the NetBoot client sends out a request for startup software. The NetBoot server then delivers the boot ROM (read-only memory) file ("booter") to the client using Trivial File Transfer Protocol (TFTP) via its default port, 69.

3. Once the client has the ROM file, it initiates a mount and loads the images for the NetBoot network disk image.

   The images can be served using Hypertext Transfer Protocol (HTTP) or network file system (NFS).

4. After booting from the NetBoot image, the NetBoot client requests an IP address from the DHCP server.

   Depending on the type of DHCP server used, the NetBoot client might receive an IP address different from the one received in step 1.

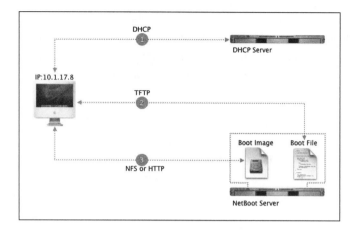

Using Home Folders with NetBoot

When you restart a client computer from a NetBoot image, the client computer receives a fresh copy of the system software and the startup volume. Users cannot store documents or preserve preferences on this startup volume because it is a read-only image. If the administrator denies access to the local hard drive or removes the hard drive, users might not have any place to store documents. However, if users log in using a network user account, they can store documents and preserve preferences in their network home folders.

When a user logs in to a NetBoot client computer using a network user account, the client computer retrieves his or her home folder from a share point. Typically, this share point resides on a server other than the NetBoot server, although with a small number of clients, one could perform both duties from the same server.

> **TIP** The NetBoot service places high demands on a server. To prevent performance degradation, store home folders on a different, preferably dedicated home directory server.

Creating Images with System Image Utility

System Image Utility is the tool you use to create Mac OS X NetBoot and Network Install images. It replaces the Network Image Utility of previous releases. Located in the /Applications/Server folder on your Mac OS X server computer, System Image Utility uses files on a Mac OS X Install DVD, mounted volume, or disk image to create a NetBoot image.

Each image requires an image ID, or index, which client computers use to identify similar images. If, when a client lists the available NetBoot images in the Startup Disk pane of System Preferences, two images have the same index, the client assumes that the images are identical, so it displays only one entry. If only one server will serve an image, assign it a value between 1 and 4095. If multiple servers will serve the same image, assign it a value between 4096 and 65535. In the System Image Utility that comes with Mac OS X Server v10.6, the index is chosen automatically for you unless you customize the install.

When creating an image, you specify where to store it. For the NetBoot service to recognize the image, it must be stored in /<volume>/Library/NetBoot/NetBootSP*n*/*imagename.nbi*, where *n* is the volume number and *imagename* is the image name you entered when you created the image. If you have already configured the NetBoot service, the Save dialog includes a pop-up menu listing the available volumes. If you choose a volume from that pop-up menu, the save location changes to the NetBootSP*n* share point on that volume.

TIP ▶ In a NetBoot environment, many clients booting from the same NetBoot server can place high demands on the server and slow down performance. To improve performance, you can set up additional NetBoot servers to serve the same images.

System Image Utility also enables you to customize your NetBoot, NetRestore, or Network Install configurations by instituting the following:

▶ Add Packages and Post-Install Scripts, which allows you to add third-party software or make virtually any customization you desire automatically.

▶ Add User Account, which will include additional users in your image. These users could include accounts such as system administrator accounts or teacher accounts.

▶ Apply System Configuration Settings, which allows you to automatically bind computers to LDAP Directory servers, along with applying basic preferences such as the computer's host name.

▶ Automated Installation, which can assist in doing speedy deployments where you're dealing with identical configurations and want to do hands-off installations.

▶ Disk partition support, which is built in to System Image Utility so you can add a partition automatically in your deployments.

▶ View the Automator Library for other available customizations.

System Image Utility contains a feature called Filter Computer Models that enables you to determine which system the image will boot. You can specify which model of hardware will be booted off which image. For example, if you wanted to configure a portable or desktop image, you could choose those models from a list for each image.

Creating NetBoot Image Types

With System Image Utility, you can create two distinct types of NetBoot images:

▶ A *boot image* is a file that looks and acts like a mountable disk or volume. NetBoot boot images contain the system software needed to act as a startup disk for client computers on the network. When creating a boot image, you can specify a default user account that the client can use to access the network disk image. You must specify a user name, short name, and password.

▶ An *install or restore image* is a special boot image that boots the client long enough to install software from the image, after which the client can boot from its own hard drive. Just as a boot image replaces the role of a hard drive, an install image is a replacement for an installation DVD.

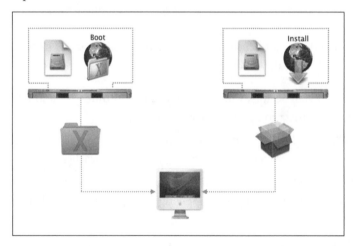

NOTE ▶ There is no real difference between the NetBoot, Net Restore, and Network Install processes: A boot image starts up and runs either the Finder or the Installer. The distinction is how the image file is tagged. The tag allows the user to visually differentiate between image file types in utilities such as Startup Disk in System Preferences.

Using Network Install

Like a bootable DVD-ROM, Network Install is a convenient way to reinstall the OS, applications, or other software onto local hard drives. For system administrators deploying large numbers of computers with the same version of Mac OS X, Network Install can prove very useful. Network Install does not require the insertion of a DVD into each NetBoot client, because all startup and installation information is delivered over the network. You can perform software installations with Network Install using a collection of packages or an entire disk image (depending on the source used to create the image).

TIP ▶ For installing small packages and not entire disks, it might be easier to use ARD because not all packages require a restart. If NetInstall is chosen to deploy a package, the client system has already been restarted once to actually boot off the NetBoot server.

When creating an install image with System Image Utility, you have the option to automate the installation process to limit the amount of interaction from anyone at the client computer. Keep in mind that responsibility comes with this automation. Because an automatic network installation can be configured to erase the contents of the local hard drive before installation, data loss can occur. You must control access to this type of Network Install disk image, and you must communicate to users the implications of using these images. Always instruct users to back up critical data before using automatic network installations. When configuring your NetBoot server, you will be warned about this even if you aren't doing automated installs.

NOTE ▶ Set the default NetBoot image on every server. Images that normal users can select should probably be NetBoot images, not Network Install images. You may also turn off the NetBoot service when you don't need it.

Creating NetBoot Images

When creating NetBoot images, specify a source for the image in System Image Utility. System Image Utility can only build images of Mac OS X v10.6. If you wish to make images of earlier Mac OS X versions, you should use the respective version of Mac OS X Server to build the image. You can create images using installation DVDs, hard drives, or disk images as sources:

▶ DVDs: You can use System Image Utility to build a new NetBoot image from a Mac OS X Install DVD. Startup images created using installation discs contain a "clean" version of the operating system and require minimal configuration. Install images created using the install disc replicate the experience of starting from the install disc to install the OS.

▶ Mounted volumes: When a mounted volume is selected as a source, the entire contents of the volume—including the operating system, configuration files, and applications—are copied to the image. When a client computer starts up from an image created from a mounted volume, the boot experience is similar to that of starting up from the original source volume. A copy of the source volume is written to the client computer's disk drive. A benefit of using volumes for image sources is that the image creation is much faster than when using discs. In addition, installations that use images created from volumes are faster than installations that use disc-created images.

▶ Disk images: Instead of using a configured hard drive as a source, you can use Disk Utility to create a disk image of a configured hard drive, and then use the disk image as a source for creating NetBoot images.

When creating the images, you have the option of adding additional software to the image. For example, you may need to include an update to the operating system with an image created from the installation discs. You specify additional software to be installed, in the form of an installer package, in the Other Items field.

TIP Use the latest version of the operating system when creating NetBoot images to ensure backward compatibility.

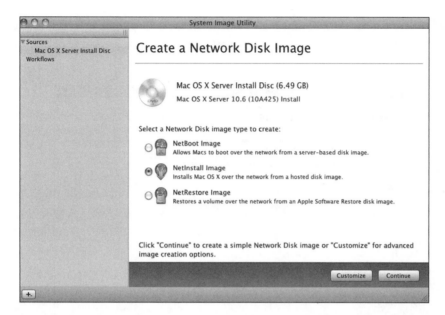

When adding new computers to the NetBoot environment, you may need to update the NetBoot image to support them. Check the OS software version that accompanied the new computer.

To create a Network Install image from a Mac OS X Install DVD, follow these steps:

1   Insert the Mac OS X Install DVD in your Mac OS X server computer.

2   Launch /Applications/Server/System Image Utility.

3   In the Sources list on the left, select Mac OS X Install DVD.

4   Select the NetInstall Image radio button.

5   Click Continue.

6   Change the Image Name to My Install v1.

7   Change the Description to NetInstall of Mac OS X 10.6 Version 1.

TIP ▶ Give your images unique identifiers to help you keep track of which image is which. This process often involves multiple attempts and updates, and you want to be able to track them.

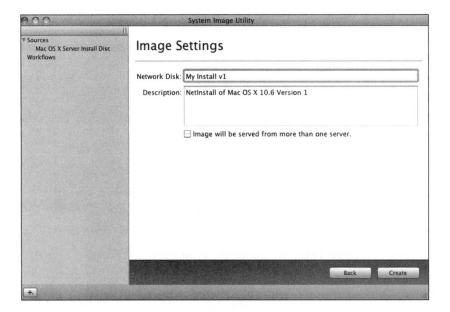

8   Click Create.

9   Agree to the software license agreement.

10 When prompted where to save the image, select your desktop and click Save.

Creating an image can take from 15 minutes to a few hours depending on the size of the source image and the speed of the computer. In the meantime, we'll continue by configuring your server.

Creating a NetRestore image is very similar to creating a NetInstall image, but you start with an existing machine image or by connecting a preconfigured machine via FireWire Target Disk Mode and picking it as the image source. This replaces the NetInstall from a volume used in previous versions of Mac OS X. For more information refer to the deployment guide available on the Apple website, or the Peachpit Deployment Training material.

Specifying a Default Image and Protocol

The NetBoot service is configured in Server Admin. Within Server Admin, the Images pane lists the available NetBoot images on the server, which can host up to 25 different disk images. Each image can be enabled, allowing client computers to use the image to boot, or each image can be disabled, preventing client computers from accessing the image. While you can have several images, you must specify one of the NetBoot images as the default image. When you press the N key on a client computer at startup, and the client has never started up from that NetBoot server before, the server will provide the default image to start up the client.

For each image, you can also specify which protocol, NFS or HTTP, is used to serve the image. NFS continues to be the default and the preferred method. HTTP is an alternative that enables you to serve disk images without having to reconfigure your firewall to allow NFS traffic.

> **TIP** ▶ Remember that image files can be very large and can take up a large amount of disk space on the server. Consider using a second volume to hold the images and keep them off the boot volume.

Understanding Shadow Files

Many clients can read from the same NetBoot image, but when a client needs to write anything (such as print jobs and other temporary files) back to its startup volume, NetBoot automatically redirects the written data to the client's *shadow files*, which are separate from regular system and application software files. These shadow files preserve the unique identity of each client during the entire time the client is running off a NetBoot image. NetBoot also transparently maintains changed user data in the shadow files, while reading unchanged data from the shared system image. The shadow files are re-created at boot time, so any changes that the user makes to the startup volume are lost at restart.

This behavior has important implications. For example, if a user saves a document to the startup volume, after a restart that document is gone. This preserves the condition of the environment the administrator set up, but it also means that you should give users accounts on a network server if you want them to be able to save their documents.

For each image, you can specify where the shadow file is stored using the Diskless checkbox in the NetBoot image configuration in Server Admin. When the Diskless option for an image is disabled, the shadow file is stored on the client computer's local hard drive at /private/var/netboot/.com.apple.NetBootX/Shadow. When the Diskless option is enabled, the shadow file is stored in a share point on the server named NetBootClients$n$ in /<volume>/Library/NetBoot, where n is the number of the client using the shadow file. With the Diskless option enabled, NetBoot enables you to operate client computers that are literally diskless.

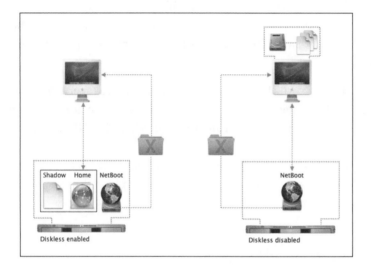

TIP Make sure you consider the storage need for shadow files when configuring your server. When running diskless, users may experience delays, since writes to the shadow files take place via the network and not locally.

Configuring a NetBoot Server

We need to configure your server to offer NetBoot images to your client computers. This, like many other services, is done through Server Admin.

1   Open /Applications/Server/Server Admin and connect to your server.

2   Select the NetBoot service in the left column.

If the NetBoot service isn't visible, add it by clicking the Add (+) button and choosing "Add Service" from the pop-up menu.

3   Click the Settings button in the toolbar.

4 In the General pane, enable the Ethernet port.

5 Select your server's storage hard drive to serve both Images and Client Data.

6 Click Save.

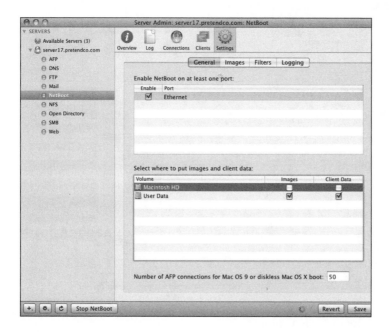

Verifying the Share Points

Your NetBoot service is now partially configured. The action of selecting a hard drive to serve the images from should have automatically configured two share points for you. You should verify this now. Running AFP is only needed if you will host diskless NetBoot.

1 Select your server name in the left column of Server Admin.

2 Click the File Sharing button in the toolbar.

3 Click the Share Points button just below the toolbar.

You should notice the addition of two share points, NetBootClient*n* and NetBootSP*n*. These share points are used for the shadow files and NetBoot images, respectively. However, only the NetBootClients0 share is available over AFP by default.

Additionally, this process does not start the file-sharing services, so you should do that now.

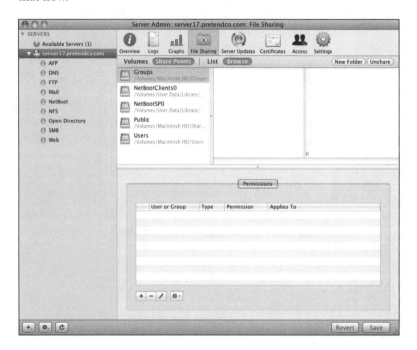

4 Select the AFP service in the left column.

If the AFP service isn't visible, add it by clicking the Add (+) button and choosing "Add Service" from the pop-up menu.

5 Click the Start AFP button in the lower-left corner of Server Admin.

Configuring NetBoot to Serve an Image

Before we can start the NetBoot service, it has to have an image it can serve, and be configured to use it.

1 After the image is created, copy your My Install NetBoot image (NBI) to the NetBootSP0 folder. Do so by dragging the entire My Install v1.nbi folder to the NetBootSP0 folder.

2 After it has copied over, return to Server Admin.

3   Select the NetBoot service in the left column.

4   Click the Settings button in the toolbar.

5   Click the Images tab.

You should see your My Install image listed. Note when you select it that it was assigned an image ID index, and that the description you typed when creating the image is visible in the bottom pane. This is the only place where the description is shown, and it can be useful to describe certain aspects of the image. Users will not see this description.

6   Enable the image by selecting the Enable and Default checkboxes.

7   Click Save.

8   Click the Start NetBoot button.

The NFS service will start automatically if it isn't already running. You may have to wait a few seconds and click the Refresh button to see this.

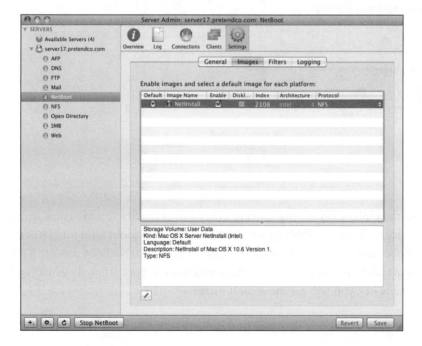

Configuring a NetBoot Client

As long as your client computer has the latest version of its firmware and is a supported client computer, you don't need to install any other special software. The Extensible Firmware Interface (EFI) (Intel) boot code contains the software used to boot a computer using a NetBoot image.

There are three ways to cause a computer to use NetBoot at startup:

► Press the N key on the keyboard until the blinking NetBoot globe appears in the center of the screen. This method allows you to use NetBoot for a single startup. Subsequent reboots return the computer to the previous startup state. Your client machine will then boot from the default NetBoot image hosted by the NetBoot server.

► Select the desired network disk image from the Startup Disk pane in System Preferences. The version of the Startup Disk pane included with Mac OS X v10.2 and later presents all available network disk images on the local network. Notice that NetBoot and Network Install disk images maintain unique icons to help users differentiate between the two types of images. With the desired network disk image selected, you can reboot the computer. The computer then attempts to use NetBoot on every subsequent startup.

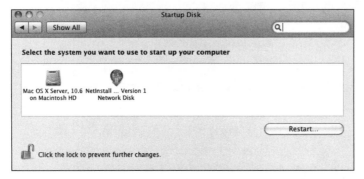

► Hold down the Option key during startup. This invokes the Startup Manager, which presents an iconic list of available system folders as well as a globe icon for NetBoot. Click the globe icon and click the advance arrow to begin the NetBoot process. This option doesn't allow you to pick which image you want to boot from. As when holding down the N key, you will get the default image.

It is important to note a couple of things that can upset the NetBoot process:

▶ If no network connection exists, a NetBoot client will eventually time out and look to a local drive to start up. You can prevent this by keeping local hard drives free of system software and denying users physical access to the Ethernet ports on a computer.

▶ Zapping the parameter random-access memory (PRAM) resets the configured startup disk, requiring you to reselect the NetBoot volume in the Startup Disk pane of System Preferences.

We'll try starting up your client computer with NetBoot now.

1 Shut down your Mac OS X computer.

2 Turn on the computer while holding down the N key on the keyboard until the blinking NetBoot globe appears.

It should boot into the Mac OS X Installer from the NetInstall image you just created and enabled. Because we don't actually want to reinstall your computer, just shut down the computer. We'll be booting the computer into Target Disk Mode in the next section, so just leave it turned off.

Configuring NetBoot Images

The NetInstall image you created is a very basic image used for the same purpose as the Mac OS X installation media. In most NetBoot situations where people are working off the network image, you will probably want to create a customized environment for them. In our example, we'll take the Mac OS X client computer you've been working on and use it as our template machine for creating a NetBoot image that hundreds of computers could boot and operate from.

1 Hold the T key on your client computer, and power it on. Release the T key once you see a FireWire logo on the screen.

This boots your client computer into Target Disk Mode, effectively turning the computer into an external FireWire disk enclosure.

2 Plug a FireWire cable between your client and server computers.

You should see your client computer's hard drive appear on your server's desktop.

3 On your server, open System Image Utility.

4 Click the Customize button.

This opens a window containing Automator Library actions related to System Image Utility. This is a feature that allows you to create complex workflows for creating NetBoot images, and save them for later repeated use if desired.

5 In the Define Image Source action that should already be in the window, select NetBoot, with the Source being your client computer's hard drive.

6 Drag the Add User Account action to the workflow.

7 Configure the Add User Account action as follows:

▶ Name: NetBoot Admin

▶ Short Name: nbadmin

▶ Password: nbadmin

▶ Allow user to administer this computer.

If desired, you could add additional local accounts by adding more Add User Account actions to the workflow.

8 Drag the Apply System Configuration Settings action item to the workflow and configure it as follows:

▶ Generate unique Computer Names starting with Chapter8.

▶ Change ByHost preferences to match client after install.

This last setting may or may not be desired in your environment. Certain settings are saved in preference list (plist) files that include the MAC (Media Access Control) address of your computer in the filename. If you'd like those files to be renamed to the MAC address of the target machine, you should use this option.

9   Drag the Create Image action to the bottom of the workflow and configure it as follows:

▶   Save To: NetBootSP0. Because we're on the server and it already knows we're running NetBoot, it allows you to save the image directly in the correct location, /Library/NetBoot/NetBootSP0.

▶   Image Name: *The Boot*

▶   Installed Volume: *The Boot*

▶   Description: This is the boot image made from a target mode computer.

▶   Index: Pick a number below 4095 that is different from the index of your first image, such as 432.

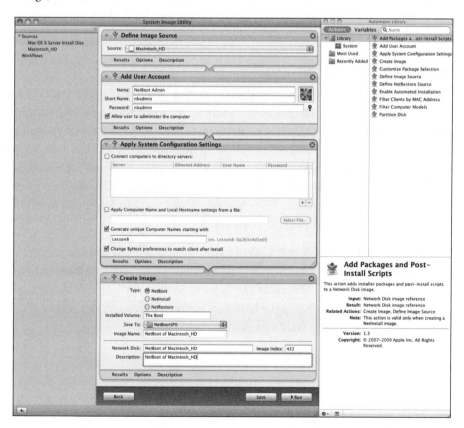

10 Click Run.

If you'd like to see more information about what is happening, you can choose View > Show Log.

After the image is created, you must enable it.

Configuring NetRestore Images

NetRestore image building is very much the same as making a NetBoot or NetInstall image. There are new features available, including external image sources such as a network share or ASR multicast streams. For more information refer to the deployment guide available on the Apple website, or *Apple Training Series: Mac OS X Deployment v10.6*.

Filtering NetBoot Clients

The NetBoot Filters pane permits you to allow or deny access to NetBoot services based on the client computer's hardware, or MAC, address. Once you enter a list of hardware addresses, you can either limit NetBoot access to just the listed computers or prevent the listed computers from using NetBoot (and allow all others to use it). This allows NetBoot and non-NetBoot clients to coexist in harmony. Filtering removes the risk of allowing non-NetBoot clients to access unlicensed applications or to accidentally perform a network installation. By maintaining accurate Filters settings, you can seamlessly integrate NetBoot into traditional network configurations.

NetBoot access is controlled through a list of hardware addresses. If you know a computer's hardware address, you can click the Add Hardware Address (+) button and type it in. Alternatively, if you enter a computer's DNS name in the Host Name field and click the Find button, Server Admin retrieves the hardware address, which you can add by clicking the Add (+) button next to the Hardware Address field.

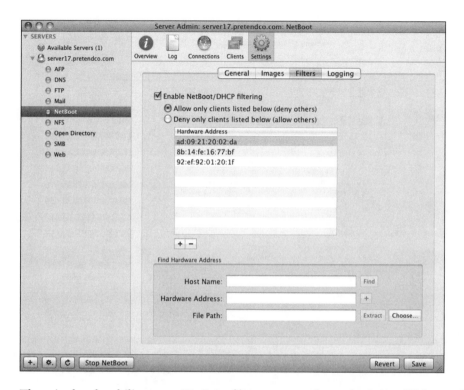

There is also the ability to set NetBoot filters on a per-image basis in addition to the per-server filters. This could be particularly useful if you have one server for multiple Mac classrooms. Each classroom could be configured with its own NetBoot image, and use per-image filters to limit which classrooms can access which image.

1   Open Server Admin on your server computer.

2   Click the Edit Image (pencil) icon at the bottom of the Images pane.

This pane allows you to perform per-image filters based on hardware type and/or specific Ethernet hardware addresses. It's important to differentiate between the per-image filters and the NetBoot servicewide filters.

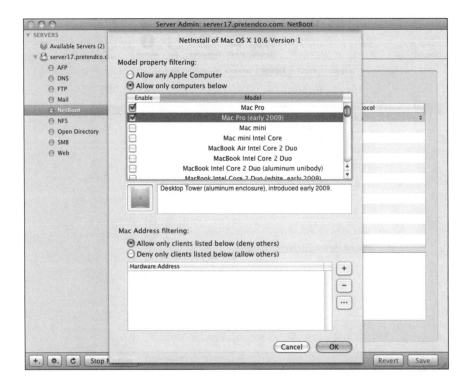

3   Select "Allow only clients listed below," and select your client computer hardware type in the list.

4   Click OK to dismiss the Edit Image dialog.

5   Click Save.

6   If you still have your client machine connected to the server, drag your client computer's drive icon to the Trash to eject it from your server.

7   Turn off your client computer and remove the FireWire cable attaching it to your server.

8   Boot your client computer normally and log in.

9   Open System Preferences.

10 Click Startup Disk.

11 Select NetBoot image with the filters.

12 Restart your client computer.

It should boot from the NetBoot image you just created. Try logging in using the nbadmin account you specified when creating the image.

Monitoring NetBoot Clients

You can monitor NetBoot usage with Server Admin. The NetBoot Clients pane provides a list of client computers that have booted from the server. Note that this is a cumulative list—a list of all clients that have connected to the server—not a list of currently connected computers only. By selecting a given computer in the list, you can also see additional information about that client, such as its system type, client name, the name and index of the NetBoot image it booted from, and the last time it booted.

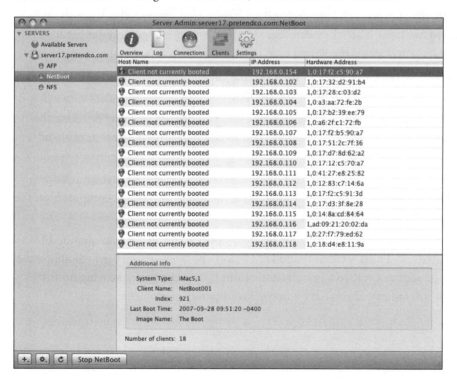

Additionally, the NetBoot logs can be useful when monitoring the progress of a NetBoot in action. You can access your NetBoot server logs using these steps:

1   Open Server Admin and connect to your server.

2   Select the NetBoot service on the left.

3   Click the Log button in the toolbar.

Troubleshooting NetBoot

NetBoot is a fairly straightforward process. If a client does not successfully start up from a NetBoot server, you can troubleshoot the issue by looking into the following areas:

▶   Check the network. The client needs an IP address obtained through DHCP.

▶   The underlying process that serves NetBoot is bootpd, so you can check the server logs for bootpd messages. These logs can also identify if you mistyped an Ethernet hardware address or selected the wrong type of hardware for a filter.

▶   Press and hold the Option key as you boot the client, which will indicate if you have a firmware password configured for the computer.

▶   Check the disk space on the server. Shadow files and disk images may be filling the server's hard drive disk space. You may want to add bigger hard drives or more of them to accommodate these files.

▶   Check for server filters. Do you have filters enabled for IP address, hardware address, and model type? If you do, you should disable the filters to allow all computers on the network to NetBoot or NetInstall.

▶   Check your server firewall configuration. NetBoot requires that a combination of DHCP/BOOTP, TFTP, NFS, AFP, and HTTP ports be open. Temporarily disabling the firewall or adding a rule to allow all traffic from the subnet you're starting up with NetBoot will indicate if you have a firewall configuration problem.

What You've Learned

▶ Deployment options are available to keep multiple desktops up-to-date.

▶ NetBoot, NetRestore, and Network Install are server-based methods of deploying.

▶ You can create images from optical media, hard drives, or disk images.

▶ You can add servicewide or per-image filters based on hardware type or Ethernet hardware address.

References

The following documents provide more information about installing Mac OS X Server. (All of these and more are available at http://www.apple.com/server/documentation.)

Administration Guides

Mac OS X Server Getting Started

System Imaging and Software Update Administration

Deploying Mac OS X Computers for K-12 Education

Apple Knowledge Base Documents

You can check for new and updated Knowledge Base documents at http://www.apple.com/support.

URLs

Mike Bombich, Mac OS X Deployment: http://www.bombich.com

MacEnterprise: http://www.macenterprise.org

Chapter Review

1. What are the advantages of using NetBoot?

2. What are three ways to configure the network startup disk?

3. What network protocols are used during the NetBoot startup sequence? What components are delivered over each of these protocols?

4. What is a NetBoot shadow file?

5. What are the major differences between NetBoot, NetInstall, and NetRestore?

Answers

1. Because NetBoot unifies and centralizes the system software that NetBoot clients use, software configuration and maintenance are reduced to a minimum. A single change to a NetBoot image propagates to all client computers on the next startup. NetBoot also decouples the system software from the computer, decreasing potential time invested in software troubleshooting.

2. A client must have selected a network disk image via the Startup pane within System Preferences, or the user must hold down the N key at startup to boot from the default NetBoot image, or use Remote Desktop Admin.

3. NetBoot makes use of DHCP, TFTP, NFS, and HTTP during the NetBoot client startup sequence. DHCP provides the IP address, TFTP delivers the boot ROM ("booter") file, and NFS or HTTP is used to deliver the network disk image.

4. Because the NetBoot boot image is read-only, anything that the client computer writes to the volume is cached in the shadow file. This allows a user to make changes to the boot volume, including setting preferences and storing files; however, when the computer is restarted, all changes are erased.

5. NetBoot allows multiple machines to boot into the same environment. NetInstall provides a convenient way to install operating systems and packages onto multiple machines. NetRestore provides a way to clone an existing image to multiple machines.

9

Time   This chapter takes approximately four hours to complete.

Goals   Create and configure home folders for network user accounts

Create and manage access to shared group folders

Manage user, workgroup, and computer preferences

View and edit an application's preferences

Configure a local software update server

Create mobile accounts and configure Mac OS X Server for mobile home folders

Chapter 9
Managing Accounts

If you run an organization with several hundred users, how can you make sure they all have the same items in their Dock? Their printers? Their Finder interface? In previous chapters you learned management techniques involving the user name, password, and home folder. There are many other aspects to user account management, and it is important to understand how these various aspects interact with each other. When applying other types of management to your user and group accounts, consider that there are also two other types of management—computer and computer group accounts—to add to your options. Careful planning will reveal the best way to implement your management, whether it is based on user accounts, group accounts, computer accounts, computer group accounts, or a combination of all four.

This chapter covers the following areas of account management:

▶ Concepts and tools—Describes account management and its main tool, Workgroup Manager.

▶ User, group, computer, and computer group accounts management—Describes how to use Workgroup Manager to manage users, groups, computers, and computer groups.

▶ Preference management—Describes how to use Workgroup Manager to customize and control the Mac OS X user experience.

▶ Software Update server—Describes how to get better network utilization and control over which updates are available to your users.

▶ Mobile accounts and mobile users—Describes challenges and solutions for home folders of users who work at multiple computers and computers that aren't always attached to the network.

▶ Troubleshooting preferences—Lists the top issues that cause problems with managed accounts.

Introducing Account Management

Account management encompasses everything from setting up accounts for network access and creating home folders to fine-tuning the user experience by managing preferences and settings for users, groups, and computers. The term *managed client* refers to a user, group, or computer whose access permissions and preferences are under administrative control.

With effective account management, you can:

▶ Provide users with a consistent, controlled interface while allowing them to access their documents from any computer

▶ Control permissions on mobile computers

▶ Restrict certain resources for specific groups or individuals

▶ Secure computer use in key areas such as administrative offices, classrooms, or open labs

▶ Customize the user experience using group folders

▶ Customize Dock settings

▶ Control access to software updates

Workgroup Manager

Workgroup Manager is an account management tool that, among other capabilities, provides centralized, directory-based management of users, groups, and computers from anywhere on your network. You can create standardized desktop configurations, set system preferences, establish and enforce password policies, and control access to hardware, software, and network resources. Your settings are automatically cached, so the preferences and user permissions you've defined remain in effect even when computers are offline. These caches are stored at /Library/Managed Preferences/ on a managed computer.

You can also configure systems to open predefined applications, mount resources on the desktop, and provide users with network-based home folders, allowing them to access their own personalized desktop, applications, and files from any computer on the network.

Workgroup Manager stores managed preferences for users, groups, and computers in their respective records in a shared directory. Typically, an Open Directory server is used, but other directory servers, such as Active Directory, can be used with the proper schema modifications.

Workgroup Manager Inspector

Workgroup Manager is a directory services editor, and the user interface is customized for entering data specific to managing user, group, computer, and preference records. The Workgroup Manager application enters the data into the directory in a known format, and other applications and utilities may also save data in the directory. Applications may also store preference-type XML data, which could be added to the attributes of user records, for example. When you need to dig deeper into the attributes and the associated values of those attributes, Workgroup Manager provides the Inspector for viewing and editing this raw data. The Inspector is enabled as a Workgroup Manager preference so that once it's enabled, you can click any specific record and select the Inspector to bring up the XML data stored for that entry.

Basic type casting is handled for you in the editor, and there is minimal error checking at this level. Manual editing using the Inspector is a power-user option. The Inspector is read-only, so it is a powerful debug tool.

Enable the Inspector now in Workgroup Manager:

1   Open /Applications/Server/Workgroup Manager and connect to your server.

2   Choose Workgroup Manager > Preferences from the menu bar.

3   Select "Show 'All Records' tab and inspector." A warning will announce that you can now do things that you should be very careful with. Click OK to acknowledge.

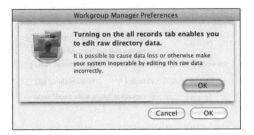

4   Click OK.

The Inspector is now visible as a new bull's-eye icon above your user list. Click it and explore the contents of various records. User records are shown by default, but others can be viewed using the pop-up menu above the user list. Be sure not to change any values here at this time.

Managing User, Group, Computer, and Computer Group Accounts

Mac OS X saves settings for four different types of accounts:

▶   User—Usually relates to a specific person. This is the account that the person identifies himself or herself with when logging in to the machine. A user's short name or UID number uniquely identifies the user on a system.

▶   Group—Represents a group of users, a group of groups, or a mixture of both.

▶   Computer—Similar to a user account, it's the singular entity that represents a given piece of hardware. Computer accounts are uniquely identified by their Ethernet ID.

▶ Computer Group—Represents a group of computers, a group of computer groups, or a mixture of both.

When you log in to a Mac OS X system using a local user account, both the user account information and the home folder are stored on that computer. This arrangement is difficult for an administrator to manage, because the user configuration on each computer has to be managed individually and locally. With Workgroup Manager, Mac OS X Server provides two additional types of user accounts with different user configurations:

▶ Network—A Mac OS X Server user account with the following characteristics:

The account information can reside in any Open Directory domain accessible from the Mac OS X server computer that needs to use the account. A directory domain can reside on a Mac OS X computer (for example, the LDAP directory of an Open Directory master), or it can reside on a non-Apple server (for example, an LDAP or Active Directory server). The user's home folder can be stored on the same server as the directory domain that contains the user's account, or it can be stored on another file server.

▶ Mobile—A Mac OS X Server user account with the following characteristics:

Two synchronized accounts. The main account resides in a shared directory domain. The second account is a copy of the main account and resides in the local domain of the user's computer. The user's home folder resides locally, on the user's computer, or, in the case of external accounts, on a removable drive.

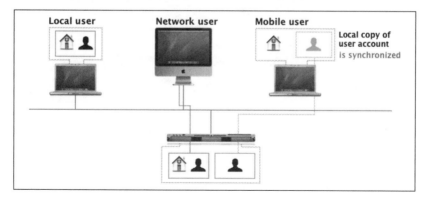

Setting Up a Network Home Folder Review

As discussed in Chapter 4, "Using File Services," you also use Workgroup Manager to set up a network home folder for a network user.

Set and create home folders for all users who do not yet have home folders.

1   On your Mac OS X computer, open Workgroup Manager and authenticate as necessary.

2   Click the Accounts button in the toolbar, and then click the globe icon below the toolbar. Choose /LDAPv3/127.0.0.1 from the pop-up menu.

3   Select all the users and deselect the Directory Administrator account.

4   Click the Home tab.

5   Select the path afp://server17.pretendco.com/Users.

6   Click the Create Home Now button, and then click Save.

If you already have home folders for some of the users, this will not change those settings.

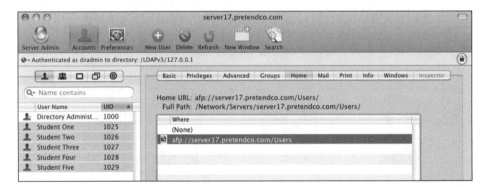

7   On your server, navigate to the /Users folder and verify that all the home folders were created.

8   Verify that you have a home folder for Student One by logging in as Student One from your Mac OS X computer, and then log out and log in as Local Administrator.

Managing Preferences for Users in a Workgroup

Although you can set up preferences individually for users with network accounts, it's more efficient to manage preferences for the workgroups to which they belong. Using workgroups allows you to manage users regardless of which computers they use. Using Workgroup Manager, you can provide all users in a workgroup with the same access permissions for media, printers, and volumes. A workgroup is group of users with managed preferences.

> **NOTE ▶** It is important to understand the difference between a workgroup and a group. A group is a file-system designation. It is used to handle access to the file system (as in owner, group, others). It is specific to the file system, server, or computer. A workgroup is a directory service record separate from any specific file system or server. It is used as a method of associating similar preferences for sets of user records.

A user can be assigned to one or more workgroups, and during login, the user is presented with a list of the workgroups to which he or she belongs. At login he or she can select which workgroup's settings should preside over that login session. The user then has all the permissions and access privileges assigned to that workgroup.

> **TIP** Administrative users are given an option to disable management. Once selected, this option is hidden but is visible again if the Option key is pressed during login.

Setting Up a Group Folder

You can use Workgroup Manager to set up a *group folder* for use by members of a particular workgroup. A group folder offers a way to organize documents and applications of special interest to group members and gives group members a way to pass information back and forth.

To set up a group folder in Workgroup Manager (you will do this in a later exercise):

1   Select the group and click the Group Folder tab.

2   Select a listed share point in which to set up a group folder.

If the predefined Groups share point or any other existing share point is not listed in the Group Folder pane, create an automount record for it in the File Sharing window in Server Admin.

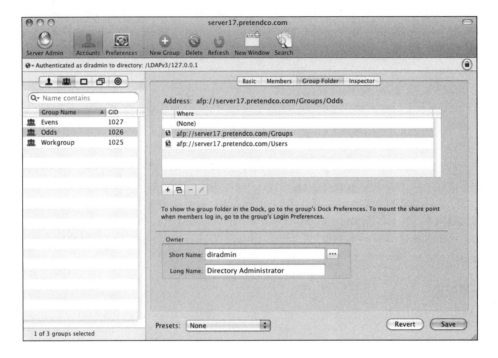

3   In the Short Name field, click the Browse (…) button to select an owner (diradmin) from a list of users in the current directory domain.

A common mistake is to not assign an owner to the folder. This will result in errors. The group folder owner is given read/write access to the group folder.

4   Click Save.

5   Create the group folder using the sudo CreateGroupFolder command in Terminal on the server.

NOTE ▶ You need to run CreateGroupFolder manually on the server containing the groups, because it is not automatically executed.

TIP There are at least two ways in which you can facilitate a group member's access to the group folder when the user logs in. You can set up Dock preferences to make the group folder visible in the Dock, or you can set up login preferences so that the share point in which the group folder resides appears on the desktop.

Managing Computer Group Accounts

A *computer group account* is set up for a group of computers that have the same preference settings and are available to the same set of users and groups. You create and modify these computer groups in Workgroup Manager. Computer groups that you set up appear in the searchable list on the left side of the window. Computer group settings appear in the panes on the right side of the window. In Mac OS X v10.5 and later a computer can be a member in multiple computer groups.

When you set up a computer group, make sure you have already determined how computers are identified. Use descriptions that are logical and easy to remember (for instance, the description might be the computer name). You must use the built-in Ethernet address for a computer's address information. For v10.5 and v10.6 machines you need to have the Hardware UUID, available via System Profiler. The Hardware UUID is not used for v10.4 clients. This information is unique to each computer. The client computer uses this data to find preference information when a user logs in. An easy way to add computers to a group is to use the Browse (…) button. When you select a computer from the browse list, Workgroup Manager automatically enters the computer's Ethernet address, Hardware UUID, and name for you. It is best to use a computer group for resources in a specific area, as well as for computers of a specific type, such as portables. For example, all kiosk computers might have the same login preferences, or all computers in a lab might have the same default printer preferences. Where preferences are associated with users, workgroups are more efficient.

When a computer starts up, it checks directory services for a computer record that contains its Ethernet address. If it finds one, it checks to see if that computer record is a member of any computer groups, and if so, it uses settings for that computer group. If no record is found, the computer uses settings for the default Guest Computer computer account. You can add up to 2000 computers to a computer group. A computer has the ability to belong to more than one group. You can even have computer groups that contain other computer groups.

NOTE ▸ Computer groups are not part of any ACLs. They should not be confused with user groups.

TIP ▸ Although you can add different types of computers (for example, iMac and MacBook computers) to computer groups, in some cases it is more effective to create homogeneous computer groups (for instance, one list for iMac computers and another for MacBook computers). In this way, you can avoid hardware incompatibilities when you configure computer groups.

Creating a Computer Account

The way to set up a computer account in Workgroup Manager is to follow these generic steps (you'll execute these steps in a later exercise):

1 Click Accounts.

2 Click the globe icon below the toolbar, and select the directory domain where you want to store the new account.

3 If the selected directory domain is still locked as shown by the lock icon, click the lock and enter your user name and password.

4 Click the Computer button (the square icon).

5 Choose Server > New Computer, or click the New Computer button in the toolbar.

6 Enter a computer name in the Name field.

7 Enter a short name in the Short Name field.

8 Enter a comment and assign keywords if desired.

9 Enter the Hardware UUID.

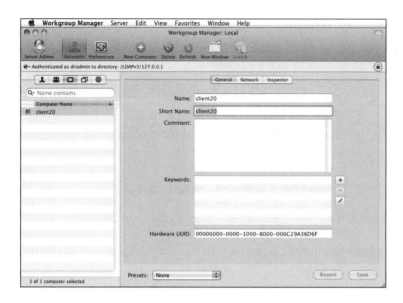

10 Click the Network tab.

11 Enter the Ethernet hardware address in the Ethernet ID field.

12 Click Save.

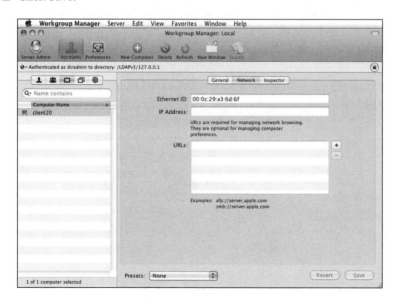

Creating a Computer Group

The generic steps for setting up a computer group account in Workgroup Manager are as follows (you'll execute these steps in a later exercise):

1   Click the Accounts button.

2   Click the globe icon below the toolbar, and open the directory domain where you want to store the new account.

3   If necessary, click the lock and enter your user name and password.

4   Click the Computer Group Name button (the multisquare icon).

5   Choose Server > New Computer Group, or click the New Computer Group button in the toolbar.

6   Enter a group name in the Name field.

A default group ID and a short name that is a derivative of the long name will automatically be inserted but can be changed if desired.

7   Click Save.

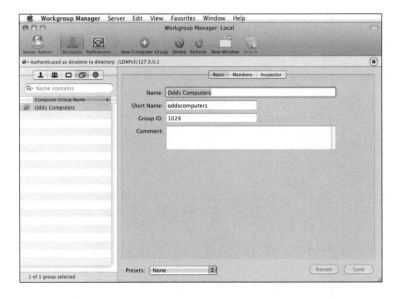

Adding Computers to a Computer Group

When adding computers to an existing computer group in Workgroup Manager, follow these steps (you'll execute these steps in a later exercise):

1   In the left column, select the computer group to which you want to add computers.

2   Click the Members tab.

3   Click the Add (+) button to add a computer to the list, and drag the desired computer into the Members list.

If the computer you're looking for is not in the list, you must either add a computer account for it, or you may be able to browse for it by clicking the Browse (...) button. If Workgroup Manager can see the computer in its browse list, you simply need to click the computer to create a computer account for it.

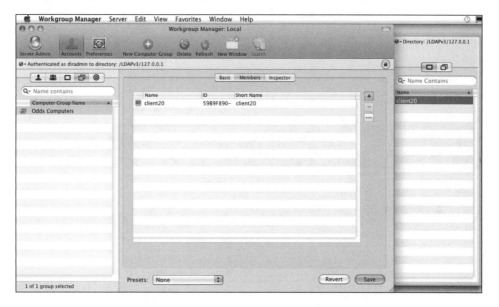

4   Click Save.

> **TIP** ▶ Even when there are only a few computers to manage, it is useful to enter them into a computer group or groups.

Creating a Guest Computer Account

A *guest computer* is one that does not have managed preferences via a computer or computer group account. Settings chosen for the guest computer account apply to these unknown or guest computers. Using a guest computer account (or just a single computer group) is not recommended for large numbers of computers. Most of your computers should belong to regular computer groups. This makes managing them easier.

To manage guest computers in Workgroup Manager, choose Server > Create Guest Computer. After the account is created, "guest" appears in the list of computer accounts. Each directory domain can have only one guest computer account. Depending on network organization and setup, you may not be able to create a guest computer account in certain directory domains.

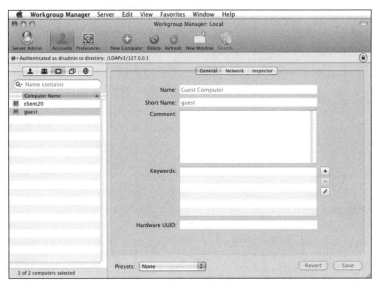

NOTE ▶ You cannot change the name, short name, Ethernet ID, IP address, or URLs associated with the guest computer account.

Managing Workgroups and Computer Accounts

Once you have computers assigned to your computer groups, you can limit which workgroups can access computers in each of the computer groups. Different sets of users may access the same sets of computers (for example, different shifts in a workplace or different classes in a computer lab, or any time you have multiple-use computers).

In the following figure, only members of the Marketing and WidgetMaster 3000 groups can access computers in the Marketing Computers list, which have sensitive information and special applications that no one else should have access to.

Similarly, only members of the WidgetMaster 3000 and Engineering groups can access computers in the Engineering Computers list.

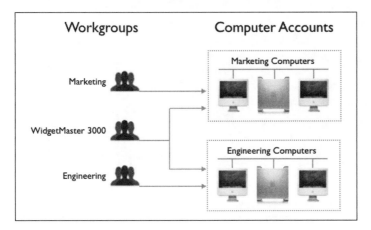

Managing Preferences

When you manage preferences, you centrally control the configuration of specific system settings. You also control users' ability to change those settings, as well as their ability to access applications, printers, removable media, or even certain computers. Information about preferences and their settings in user, group, computer, or computer group records is stored in a directory domain accessible to Workgroup Manager, such as the LDAP directory of an Open Directory master. In addition, a copy of group preferences is stored in the workgroup's folder and, at login, user preferences are stored in the local directory domain.

After user, group, computer, and computer group accounts are created, you can start managing preferences for them using the Preferences pane in Workgroup Manager. To manage preferences for Mac OS X clients, you should make sure that each user you want to manage has either a network or local home folder.

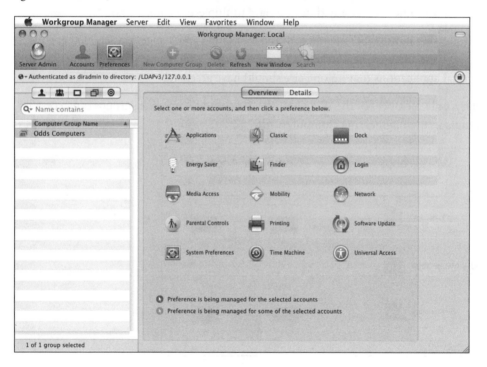

Which Preferences Can Be Managed?

In addition to various other settings for user, group, computer, and computer group accounts, Workgroup Manager provides control over the preferences listed in Table 9.1.

Table 9.1   Manageable Preferences

Preference	What You Can Manage
Applications	Applications and widgets available to users
Classic	Classic startup settings, sleep settings, and the availability of Classic items such as control panels
Dock	Dock location, behavior, and items
Energy Saver	Available only for computers and computer groups; sleep configuration for the computer
Finder	Finder behavior, desktop appearance and items, and availability of Finder menu commands
Login	Items that open automatically when a user logs in and automatically mounted volumes; additionally, for computers and computer groups, login window appearance, login and logout scripts, autologout, login access, including guest and external account availability
Media Access	Settings for CDs, DVDs, and recordable discs, plus settings for disk images, and internal and external disks such as hard drives
Mobility	Creation and management of mobile accounts, including their synchronization and FileVault configurations
Network	Configuration of proxy settings for Internet services; for computers and computer groups, disabling of Internet sharing, AirPort, or Bluetooth
Parental Controls	Website and time limits
Printing	Available printers and printer access
Software Update	Software Update server to connect for Software Update service
System Preferences	System preferences available to users
Time Machine	Available only for computers and computer groups; backup server and Time Machine configuration
Universal Access	Settings to control mouse and keyboard behavior, enhance display settings, and adjust sound or speech for users with special needs

When you manage preferences for a user, group, computer, or computer group, an arrow icon appears next to the managed preference in the Preferences pane to indicate that you're managing that preference. If the arrow is dimmed, it means that you have selected two or more accounts in the list at the left of the window, and that for some of the selected accounts this item is managed, while for others it is not.

When Do You Want to Manage Preferences?

In Workgroup Manager you have three common options for managing a preference:

► Never—If you don't want to manage settings for a particular preference, select Never in the management bar. If you provide users with access to an unmanaged preference, they can change settings as they wish. Never is the default management setting for all preferences.

> **NOTE** ► Even if you select Never, it is possible these settings will still get managed at a different level, such as if the user is a member of a workgroup for which these settings are managed.

> **TIP** ► If you do not manage a particular preference, the user and system preferences are set to default values until changed by the end user. For example, if you do not set any managed preferences for Dock placement, the Dock uses the default location at the bottom of the screen.

► Once—If you want to manage a preference initially for accounts but allow the user to make changes if he or she has that privilege, select Once in the management bar. When a user logs in, preference files in his or her home folder are updated and time-stamped with any preferences that are managed once. If you update settings for a preference that is managed once, Workgroup Manager applies the most recent version to the user's preference files the next time the user logs in. For some preferences, such as Classic preferences or Media Access preferences, Once is not available; you must select Never or Always.

► Always—You can force preference settings for an account by selecting Always in the management bar. The next time the user logs in, the preference settings are those selected by the administrator. A user cannot change a preference with a management setting of Always, even if the user is allowed access to that preference. In that case, the changes will just not be saved.

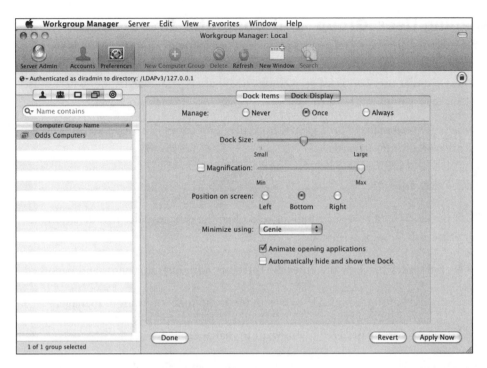

Not all settings make sense in all cases. For instance, the Once setting does not make sense for application access, as you typically want to maintain control over which applications are allowed.

There is also a fourth choice, Often. This persistent setting allows the user to change the preferences but resets them to the original settings the next time the computer boots or a user logs in.

> **NOTE** ▶ The Often option is available only via the Preference Manifest screen. This is available by clicking the Details tab on the main preferences screen and manipulating the key values.

Managing User, Group, and Computer Preferences

You might want to manage preferences at the user level only for specific individuals, such as students, teachers, or technical staff. You should also consider which preferences you want to leave under user control. For example, if you aren't concerned about where a user places the Dock, you might want to set Dock Display management to Never.

Follow these steps to manage user, group, computer, and computer group account preferences with Workgroup Manager:

1   Click Preferences.

2   Click the globe icon below the toolbar, and open the directory domain that contains the accounts you want to manage.

3   If necessary, click the lock and enter the directory administrator name and password.

4   Select the user, group, computer, or computer group that you want to manage.

5   Click the icon for the preference you want to manage.

6   In each pane for that preference, select a management setting (Never, Once, or Always), and then select preference settings or fill in the information you want to use.

7   Click Apply Now.

A more efficient way to manage user preferences is to do it at the workgroup level. Workgroup preferences are shared among all users in the group. Setting some preferences only for groups instead of for individual users can save time, especially when you have large numbers of managed users. In some cases, it may be more efficient to manage preferences for computers instead of for users or groups. An example of this would be printers, as they tend to be localized to the computers, but any user might utilize the computer. These options are all part of proper planning when preparing to manage accounts.

Managed Preference Precedence—Inherit

If you manage the same preference for user, group, computer, and computer group accounts, which preference setting takes precedence? This can be a complicated question, because in some cases the preferences override each other, while in others they are combined.

To simplify preference management, you might decide to manage certain preferences at only one level. For instance, you could set Login preferences only for workgroups, set Dock preferences only for computers, set Finder preferences only for computer groups, and set Applications preferences only for users. In such a case, if a user logs in at a managed computer that is a member of a computer group with a managed user account that is a member of a workgroup, the user will inherit each of the managed preferences from each of the managed accounts.

	Login	Dock	Finder	Applications
Workgroup	Address Book launch at login	"Not Managed"	"Not Managed"	"Not Managed"
Computer Group	"Not Managed"	"Not Managed"	Snap to grid	"Not Managed"
Computer	"Not Managed"	Right	"Not Managed"	"Not Managed"
User	"Not Managed"	"Not Managed"	"Not Managed"	Chess Allowed
Result:	Address Book launch at login	Right	Snap to grid	Chess Allowed

Managed Preference Precedence—Override

In cases where you have set managed preferences at more than one level and the preference setting can have only one value, the override rule applies: Managed user preferences override managed computer preferences, which override managed computer group preferences, which in turn override workgroup preferences. For example, if you are managing Dock preferences and decide to set the Dock position to the right for the workgroup the user belongs to, to the left for the computer the user is logging in at, and to the bottom for the computer group that computer belongs to, what does the user get when using that computer? Because computer preferences override computer group and workgroup preferences, the user will see the Dock on the left.

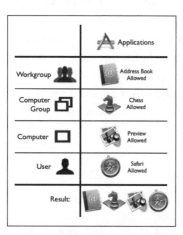

TIP In general, it's most efficient to manage preferences at the group level. Then you can use the override rule to grant additional privileges to specific users, or to set specific preferences on certain computers.

Managed Preference Precedence—Combine

If a preference can have more than one value and you set different values for it at the user, computer, computer group, and workgroup levels, Workgroup Manager combines these values. For example, suppose you configure managed Applications preferences to allow a workgroup to open the Address Book application, a user to open Safari, the computer the user is logging in at to open Preview, and the computer group that contains that computer to open Chess. When the user logs in, he or she will be able to open all four of the applications because the rules are combined.

Managing Preference Manifests

Applications store their preference data in specific formats, which are known only to the application developers. Therefore, Workgroup Manager has no way of determining or decoding these formats. In Mac OS X v10.4, Workgroup Manager introduced the notion of *preference manifests*, which are built into the application and list various options that can be managed for that application.

Applications that adhere to the manifest format can have their preference data imported and stored with user, group, computer, and computer group accounts. This allows management of preferences for items other than those that are already defined in Workgroup Manager. Workgroup Manager will do simple checking for the manifest format when you click the Add (+) button in the Details pane.

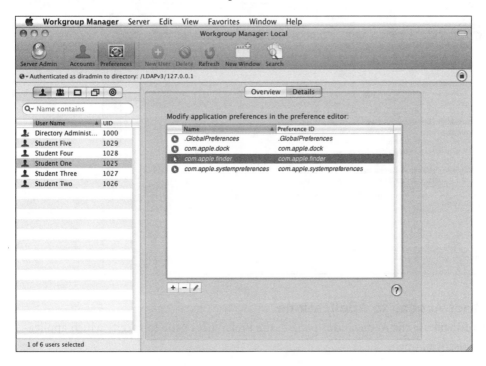

Edit Preference Manifests

All Workgroup Manager preferences (such as Dock, Finder, and System Preferences) are editable using the preference manifest edit function once they have been initially managed. Select the preference you want to view or edit, and an XML editor appears. You can edit entries here and set them to be managed always, often, or once. This is the only place where the Often setting is available. Workgroup Manager will attempt to display record types in known formats. Not all the options configurable may be displayed. Only those settings with values are displayed, and no error checking is applied to the fields (for example, it would be possible to set a font size to 240 instead of 24).

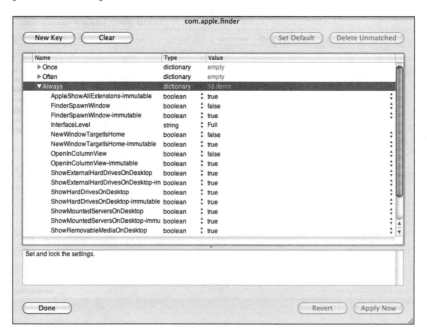

Restrict Access to Applications

Now you will use the Applications pane in the Preferences pane to specify which applications a user can open.

1   Open Workgroup Manager on your Mac OS X computer, and authenticate if necessary.

2   Select Student One in the Accounts list, and click the Preferences button in the toolbar.

3 Click the Applications tab in the Preferences pane, and select Always as the management choice.

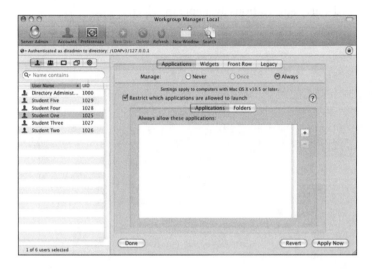

4 Select "Restrict which applications are allowed to launch."

5 Click the Add (+) button to add applications.

6 Select Calculator, Dictionary, Font Book, Mail, and Preview, and then click Add.

NOTE ▶ The applications listed are those found on your local computer. Therefore, it's best to do this from a computer configured similarly to your users' computers so you have the same third-party applications available to select.

7   Click Apply Now.

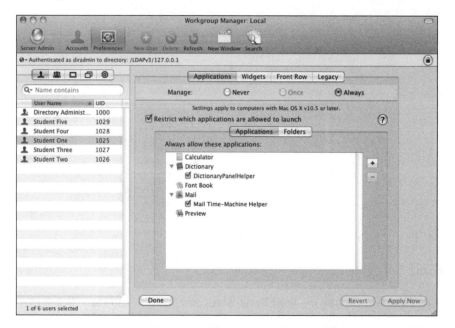

8   Log out of your Mac OS X computer, and log back in as Student One. (You can use fast user switching for this if you wish.)

9   Go to the Applications folder and double-click Dictionary. What happens?

10   Click System Preferences in the Dock. What happens?

Go to the Applications folder and double-click System Preferences. What happens?

In both instances, you can't open System Preferences.

NOTE ▶ System Preferences is an application. By not allowing access to this application, you have prevented Student One from viewing or changing any system preferences.

11 Attempt to open Disk Utility, which is located in /Applications/Utilities.

You cannot open Disk Utility.

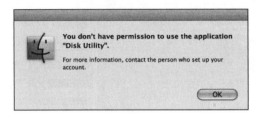

12 Log out as Student One.

NOTE ▸ Do not use fast user switching to switch out of the managed user's account during these exercises, because updated preferences take effect only when a user logs in, not when a fast user switching session is restored.

Restrict Access to Selected System Preferences

In the following steps, you will enable Student One to access a selected number of system preferences:

1 Log in as Local Administrator, open Workgroup Manager, and select Student One. Click the Preferences button in the toolbar, and click the Applications tab. (This view will still be open if you just used fast user switching in the previous exercise.)

2 Click the Add (+) button, select System Preferences in the list of applications, click Add again, and click Apply Now.

You must add the System Preferences application back to the list of applications that the user can manage. If you don't do this, attempting to manage various system preferences is pointless.

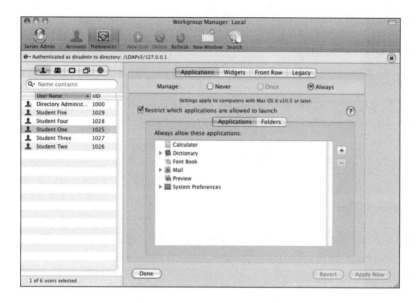

3 Click the Preferences button in the toolbar, and click the System Preferences icon in the Preferences pane.

4 Select Always as the management choice, and deselect the Accounts and Energy Saver preferences.

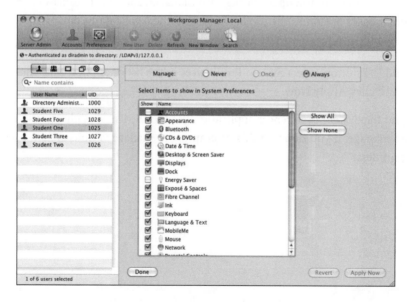

5   Click Apply Now.

6   Log out or use fast user switching and log back in as Student One.

This will reset the preferences for the user Student One. Preferences are configured when the user logs in to the system.

7   Open System Preferences.

In the System Preferences window, the Accounts and Energy Saver preferences are dimmed and cannot be changed by Student One.

8   Log out as Student One, and log back in as Local Administrator.

Managing Preferences on a Network

Next you will use Workgroup Manager to manage Login, Dock, and Finder preferences for given accounts.

Configure Login Preferences

These steps show you how to use the Login pane under Preferences in Workgroup Manager to make the Mail application open the first time a user logs in to a Mac OS X computer.

1   Back in the Local Administrator account's session, open Workgroup Manager if it's not already open.

2   Select the user Student Two, and then click the Preferences button in the toolbar.

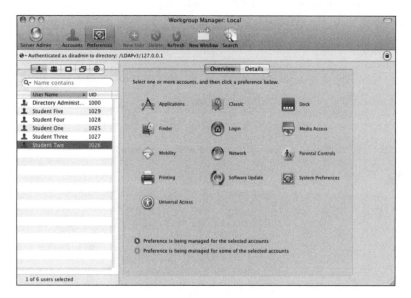

3   Click the Login icon in the Preferences pane.

4   Click the Items tab, and select Once as the management choice in the Items pane. Click the Add (+) button to add the Mail application (located in /Applications), and then click Apply Now.

The Mail application will always open automatically when Student Two logs in, unless that user changes the login options and removes Mail from the list of applications that open automatically at login.

5 Open System Preferences on your Mac OS X computer, click the Accounts preferences pane, click Login Options, and select the "Show fast user switching menu as" check-box if you have not already done so.

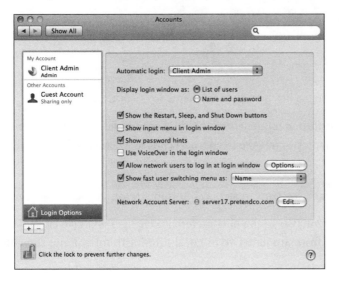

6 Use fast user switching to switch to the login window, and log in as Student Two.

Notice that Mail starts automatically.

7 Quit Mail by clicking the Cancel button.

8 Open the Accounts pane in System Preferences, select the Student Two account, and click Login Items.

Notice that Mail has been added to the list of items that open automatically when Student Two logs in.

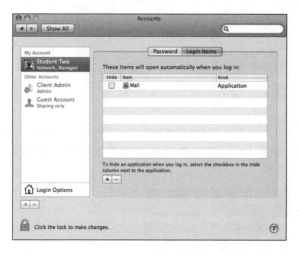

9 Select Mail in the Login Items list, and click the Remove (–) button.

Mail will not start the next time Student Two logs in, because the preferences were set to Once. Therefore, Student Two has the freedom to choose whether to keep Mail as a login item or not.

10 Log out as Student Two, and log back in as Local Administrator.

You must log out as Student Two so the next preference changes will take effect. Just doing fast user switching from Student Two to Local Administrator will not show the newer preferences.

Because you are using fast user switching, Workgroup Manager is still running, assuming you are running Workgroup Manager on your client machine.

Configure Dock Preferences

Use the Dock preferences pane to add three applications (Calculator, Stickies, and TextEdit), to add the Applications folder to Student Two's Dock, and to set the size of the Dock.

1   In Workgroup Manager, select the Student Two account, and then click the Preferences button in the toolbar.

Notice that because you previously managed Login preferences, it has an arrow next to the icon.

2   Click the Dock in the Preferences pane, select Always as the management choice, click the Add (+) button next to the Applications list, and add the following applications:

▶   Calculator

▶   Stickies

▶   TextEdit

3   Click the Add (+) button next to the Documents and Folders list, navigate to the Applications folder, click Add, make sure "Merge with user's Dock" is selected, and click Apply Now.

4   Click the Dock Display tab, select Always as the management choice, set the Dock Size to Large, select "Automatically hide and show the Dock," and click Apply Now.

When Student Two logs in, the Dock will contain Calculator, Stickies, and TextEdit; it will be large; and it will be hidden until the pointer is moved to the bottom of the screen.

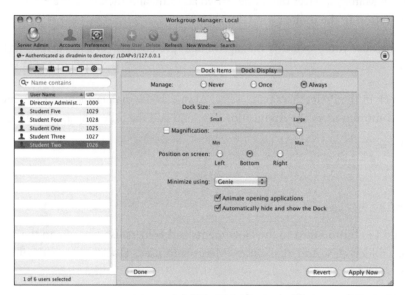

5   Use fast user switching, and log back in as Student Two.

Verify that the Dock settings you just defined in Workgroup Manager have taken effect. Verify that the change is persistent and that Student Two can't remove the contents of the Dock.

6   Log out as Student Two, and log back in as Local Administrator.

Because you are using fast user switching, Workgroup Manager is still running.

Configure Finder Preferences

Next you will use Workgroup Manager to configure Finder preferences to restrict the views and remove some menu commands.

1   In Workgroup Manager, select the Student Two account and click the Preferences button in the toolbar.

Notice that because you previously managed Login preferences and Dock preferences, they have arrows next to the icons.

2   Click the Finder icon in the Preferences pane.

3   Click the Views tab, and select Always as the management choice.

4   Set the Icon Size to Large in three places: Desktop View, Default View, and Computer View.

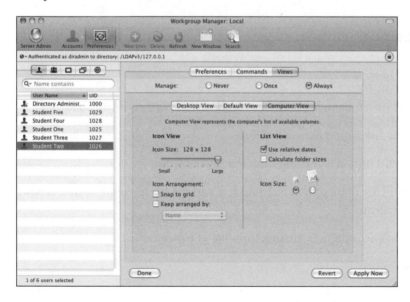

5   Click the Commands tab, select Always as the management choice, and deselect the following checkboxes:

▶   Go to iDisk

▶   Burn Disc

▶ Go to Folder

▶ Restart

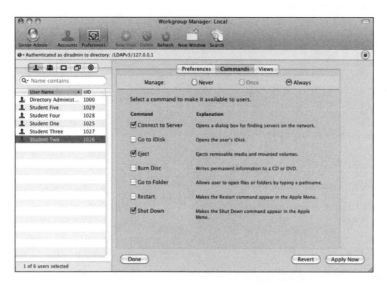

6 Click Apply Now.

7 Use fast user switching to log back in as Student Two, and verify the following:

▶ The hard disk icon is extremely large.

▶ The Restart option is missing from the Apple menu.

▶ The Go to My iDisk option is deselected, and the Go to Folder option is removed from the Go menu.

▶ The Burn Disc option is missing from the File menu.

8 Log out as Student Two, and log back in as Local Administrator.

Because you are using fast user switching, Workgroup Manager is still running.

Managing Workgroup Accounts

You will use Workgroup Manager to configure Applications preferences, Dock preferences, and Finder preferences for a group. You will then log in to the Mac OS X computer and observe how group preferences work with user preferences.

Create Groups with Workgroup Manager

First, you will create a group to share preferences.

1 In Workgroup Manager on your Mac OS X computer, choose the /LDAPv3/127.0.0.1 domain from the Directory pop-up menu.

2 Click the Accounts button in the toolbar, and then click the Groups button. Click the New Group button, and create a group called Odds.

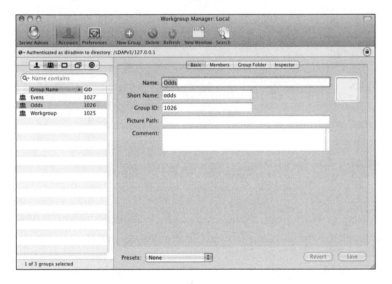

3 Add the three members:

▶   Student One

▶   Student Three

▶   Student Five

4 Create another group called Evens with Students Two and Four .

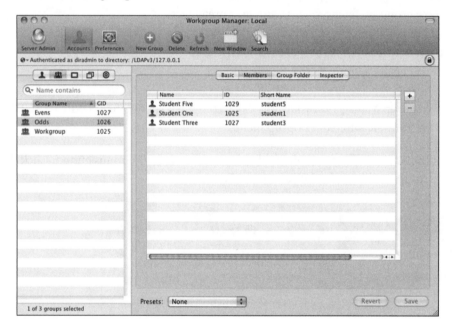

Specify Preferences for Groups

Configure preferences for the Odds group.

1 Select the Odds group in Workgroup Manager, click the Preferences button in the toolbar, and then click the Applications icon in the Preferences pane.

2 Select Always from the Manage options, and select "Restrict which applications are allowed to launch."

3   Click the Add (+) button and add the following applications to the approved list:

▶   Console (located in /Applications/Utilities)

▶   Image Capture (located in /Applications)

▶   Keychain Access (located in /Applications/Utilities)

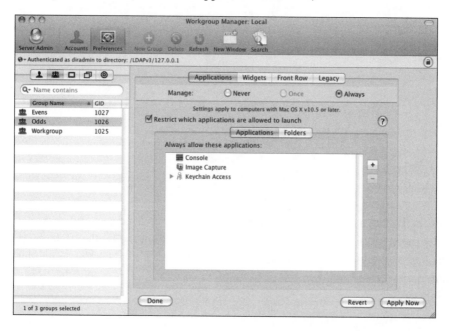

4   Click Apply Now.

5   In Workgroup Manager, click the Preferences button in the toolbar and click the Dock icon. Click the Dock Items tab.

6   Select Always from the Manage options, and click the Add (+) button to add the following applications to the Dock:

▶   Image Capture (located in /Applications)

▶   Console (located in /Applications/Utilities)

▶   Keychain Access (located in /Applications/Utilities)

7   Click Apply Now.

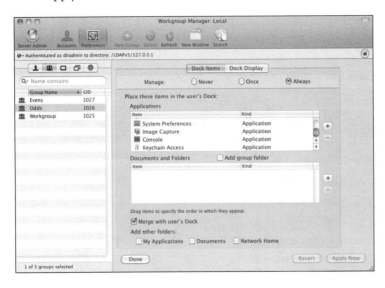

8   Click the Preferences button in the toolbar in Workgroup Manager, and click the Finder preferences icon. Click the Preferences tab that is in the Finder preferences pane, select Always from the Manage options, and select the "Always open windows in column view" checkbox.

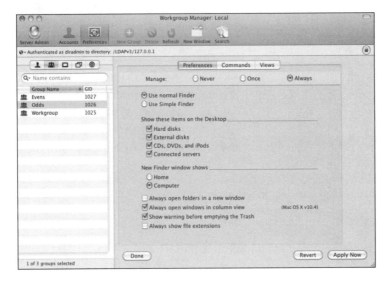

9   Click the Views tab, select Always from the Manage options, click Desktop View, and
set Icon Size to Small.

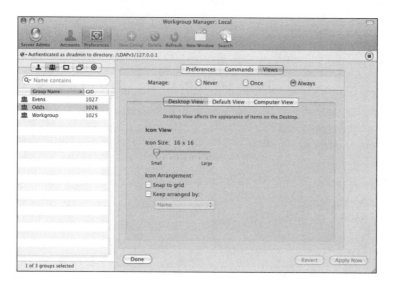

10   Click Apply Now.

Check Group Preferences Against User Preferences

Now you will learn how group preferences work with user preferences.

1   In Workgroup Manager, select Student One, click Preferences in the toolbar, click the
Dock icon, click the Dock Display tab, select Always from the Manage options, set
"Position on screen" to Left, and then click Done.

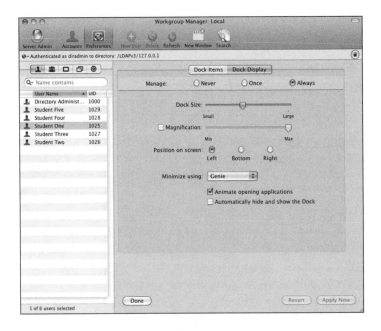

2   In Workgroup Manager, click the Groups button, select Odds, click Preferences, click the Dock icon, click the Dock Display tab, set Always as the Manage option, set "Position on screen" to Right, and then click Done.

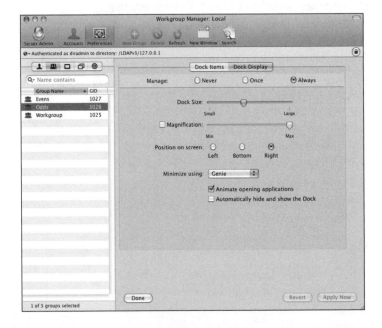

3 Log in as Student One and notice that that user's Dock is on the left even though Student One's group preference is set for the right. This shows how the user preference overrides the group preference.

4 Log out as Student One, and log in as Student Three. Notice that Student Three's Dock appears on the right in accordance with the Odds group preference.

Create Group Folders

Now you will use the CreateGroupFolder command to manually create group folders.

1 Open Server Admin and connect to your server.

2 Click the File Sharing button, click the Share Points button, and select the Groups folder in the list. In the Share Point pane, select the Enable Automount checkbox.

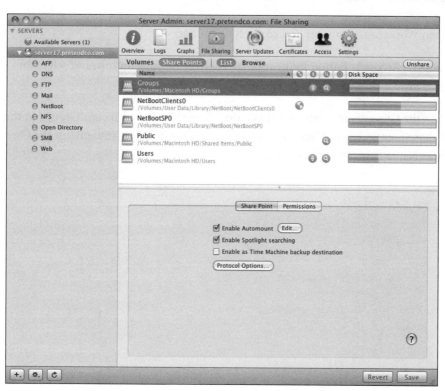

3 Set the Protocol to AFP, and select "Use for: User home folders and group folders."
Click OK, and then click Save.

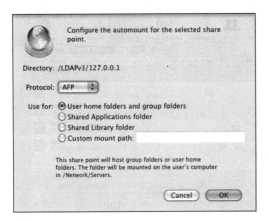

4 Open Workgroup Manager and connect to your server.

5 Click the Accounts button in the toolbar, click the Groups button, and select the
Odds group.

6 Click the Group Folder tab, and select afp://server17.pretendco.com/Groups in the list
of share points shown. Click the Browse (...) button to select student1 in the Owner
Short Name field, and then click Save.

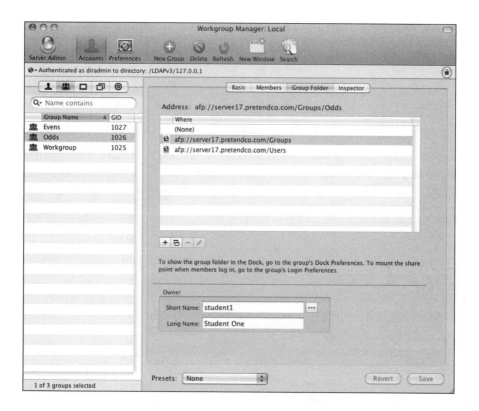

7 On your Mac OS X computer, open the Terminal application (located in /Applications/Utilities), enter ssh ladmin@10.1.17.1, and press Return.

If this is the first time you have connected to your server via Terminal (exactly what you are doing here), enter yes at the prompt about the RSA Fingerprint and press Return.

8 Enter the password for ladmin (root's password on Mac OS X Server is initially the same as the administrator's during the setup process).

9 Enter sudo CreateGroupFolder and press Return.

In the Finder on your server, notice that a new group folder is created in /Groups called Odds.

10 Enter exit in Terminal and press Return to exit the SSH connection, and then quit the Terminal application.

Configure the Group Folder to Be Available to Members

You can make the group folder automatically available to members of the group when they log in to their computers by changing the Login and Dock preferences.

1 In Workgroup Manager on your Mac OS X computer, choose the /LDAPv3/127.0.0.1 domain from the Directory pop-up menu.

2 Select the Odds group in Workgroup Manager, click the Preferences button in the toolbar, and click the Dock icon in the Preferences pane. Then click the Dock Items tab, select the "Add group folder" checkbox, and click Apply Now.

3 Click the Preferences button in the toolbar, click the Login icon to reveal the Login preference options, and then click the Items tab.

4 Select Always from the Manage options, and select "Add group share point." Then select the share point Groups from the Login Items window, and select the "Authenticate selected share point with user's login name and password" checkbox. Click Apply Now.

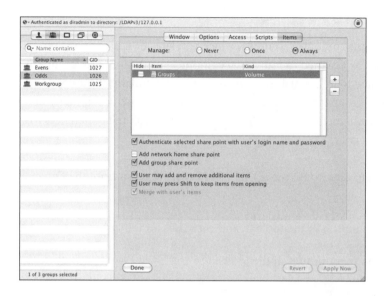

5 Log back in as Student One. Verify that the Odds folder is in the Dock, that the Groups share point is mounted on the desktop, and that you have access to the Odds group folder.

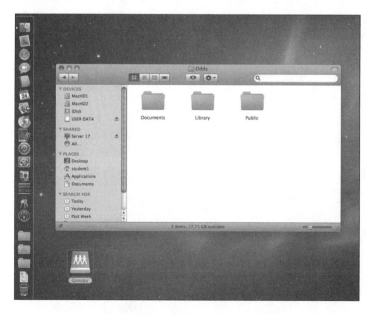

6 Log out as Student One.

Creating Computer Accounts

Now you will create some computer accounts, which will later be added to a computer group. Preferences can be assigned to individual computers or to computer groups, just like they can be assigned to individual users or workgroups. Similarly, it's usually best to make use of computer groups that mimic your organizational structure so that you only have to manage the group membership rather than reassigning all the preferences to each computer as it enters service.

1   In Workgroup Manager, choose the /LDAPv3/127.0.0.1 domain from the Directory pop-up menu.

2   Click the Accounts button in the toolbar, and click the Computer button.

3   Click the New Computer button in the toolbar.

4   In the Name field, enter One's Machine.

5   In the Short Name field, enter onemachine, and then click Save.

6   In a regular situation you would go to System Profiler, find the Hardware UUID in the Hardware Overview, copy the number, and paste it in the Hardware UUID field. In this example we will make up the UUID as 00000000-0000-1000-8000-AD09212002DA.

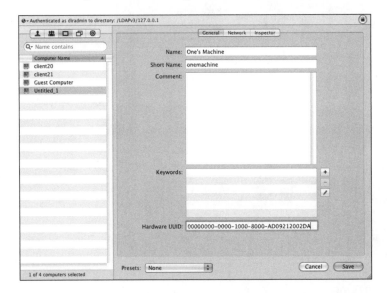

7 Click the Network tab.

8 In the Ethernet ID field, enter `ad:09:21:20:02:da`, and then click Save.

This Ethernet ID is a fictitious one used for this exercise. Normally you would use the actual Ethernet ID for the computer for which you're creating a computer account.

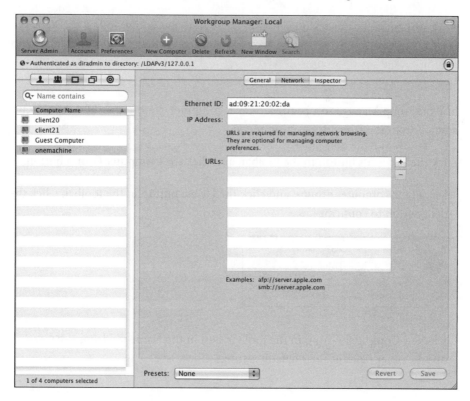

9 Repeat these steps to create another computer with these attributes:

  ▶ Name: `Two's Machine`

  ▶ Short Name: `twomachine`

  ▶ Hardware UUID: `00000000-0000-1000-8000-EDEA15AABEEF`

  ▶ Ethernet ID: `ed:ea:15:aa:be:ef`

Managing Computer Access

Now you will create a computer group, add a computer to it, and configure its Applications, Dock, and Finder preferences. You will then log in to the client and observe how computer group preferences work with group and user preferences. Finally, you will enable automatic logout for the computer group.

> **WARNING** ▸ While this lesson is nondestructive, if you do not follow the steps exactly, you may not be permitted access to your applications again. If you have not already backed up, do so now.

1   In Workgroup Manager on your Mac OS X computer, choose the /LDAPv3/127.0.0.1 domain from the Directory pop-up menu.

2   Click the Accounts button in the toolbar, and click the Computer Group button.

3   Select all the computer groups, and click the Delete button in the toolbar. Click the Delete button to confirm.

4   Click New Computer Group in the toolbar, and in the Name field, enter XSE Course. Leave the other fields at their default settings. Click Save.

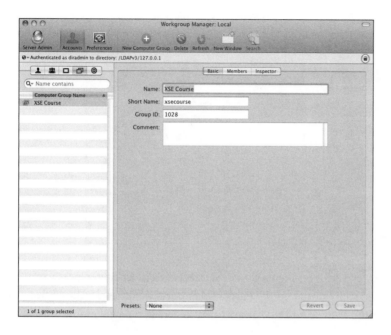

5   Click the Members tab, click the Browse (…) button, select your Mac OS X computer in the list, and click Add.

6 Click Save.

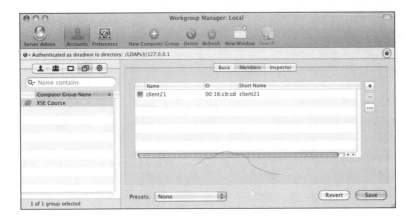

7 Click the Preferences button in the toolbar, and select the Finder preferences icon. Click the Preferences tab located in the Finder preferences pane, select Always from the Manage options, and then select the "Always open folders in a new window" checkbox.

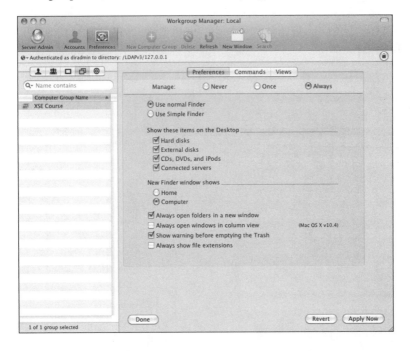

8 Click Apply Now.

9 Click the Preferences button in the toolbar, and select the Login preferences icon.

10 Click the Access tab located in the Login preferences pane, and then select Always from the Manage options.

11 Click the Add (+) button and add the Odds group to the access control list. Click Apply Now.

Only members of the Odds group have access to the Mac OS X computer.

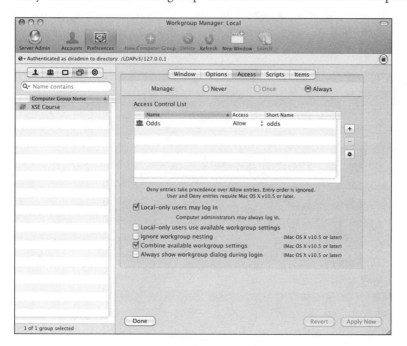

12 Attempt to log in as Student Two.

You cannot log in because Student Two is not part of the Odds group.

13 Attempt to log in as Student One, and verify that restricted access allows login because Student One is part of the Odds group.

14 Log out as Student One, and log back in as Local Administrator.

Configuring Computer Group Preferences

Configure the Applications preferences for the XSE Course computer group to allow users to open the Chess application.

1   In Workgroup Manager on your Mac OS X computer, choose the /LDAPv3/127.0.0.1 domain from the Directory pop-up menu.

2   Select XSE Course in the Computer Group list, and click the Preferences button in the toolbar.

3   Click the Applications icon in the Preferences pane, select Always from the Manage options, and allow users to open only the Chess (located in /Applications) and Workgroup Manager (located in /Applications/Server) applications.

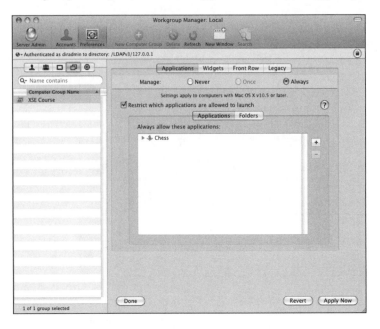

4   Click Apply Now, and then click Done.

Clicking the Done button is another way to get back to the main Preferences pane of Workgroup Manager. Using this button is optional.

5 Click the Dock icon in the Preferences pane, and then click the Dock Items tab. Select Always from the Manage options, and click the Add (+) button to add Chess to the list of applications in the Dock. Click Dock Display, and select Bottom for "Position on screen."

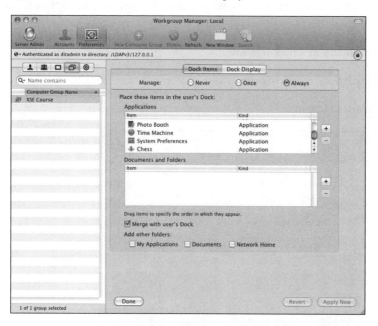

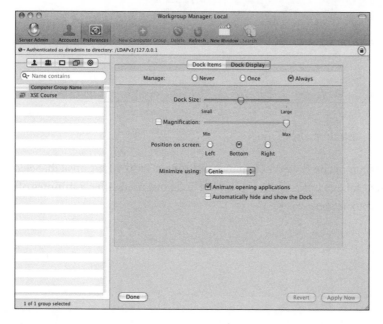

6 Click Apply Now, and then click Done.

7 Click the Finder icon in the Preferences pane, and then click the Preferences tab located in the Finder preferences pane. Select Always from the Manage options, and select the following:

> ▶ Always open folders in a new window

> ▶ Show warning before emptying the Trash

> ▶ Always show file extensions

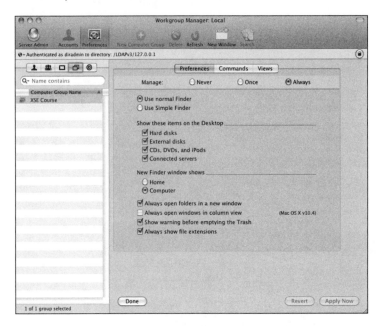

8 Click Apply Now, and then click Done.

9 Click the Login icon in the Preferences pane, and then click the Options tab. Select Always from the Manage options, and select the "Log out users after x minutes of inactivity" checkbox (where x is 5).

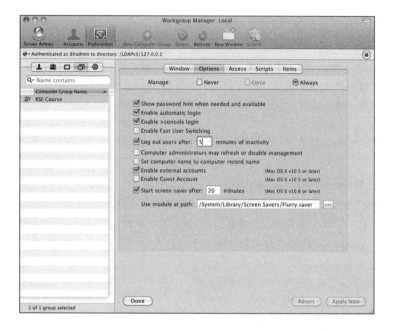

10 Click Apply Now, and then click Done.

11 Log back in as Student One, and observe how computer group preferences interact with group and user preferences.

Notice that Student One's Finder preferences, which specify that the Dock location be set to Left, take precedence over the workgroup preferences, which are set to Right. Also notice that Student One can open only the Chess application, which now shows up in that user's Dock.

12 Log out as Student One, and log in as Student Five (another member of the Odds group).

Notice how Student Five's Dock is located on the bottom. This is because the computer group takes precedence over the workgroup.

13 Log out as Student Five, and log in as Local Administrator. Open Workgroup Manager, navigate to the XSE Course computer group's Dock preferences and remove the preference by changing Manage to Never.

14 Log out as Local Administrator, and log in as Student Three (another member of the Odds group).

Notice how Student Three's Dock shows up on the right, as defined by the Odds group preference. This is because Student Three does not have a preference for Dock location set, and thus the workgroup preference becomes active.

15 Log out as Student Three, and log back in as Local Administrator.

Customizing the Preference Choices

You can use preference manifests to add additional preference management choices to Workgroup Manager. For example, if you wanted all the users in your company to have their Safari homepages set to http://www.pretendco.com/, you would follow these steps:

1 In Workgroup Manager on your Mac OS X computer, choose the /LDAPv3/127.0.0.1 domain from the Directory pop-up menu.

2 Select XSE Course in the Computer Group list, and click the Preferences button in the toolbar.

3 Click the Details tab.

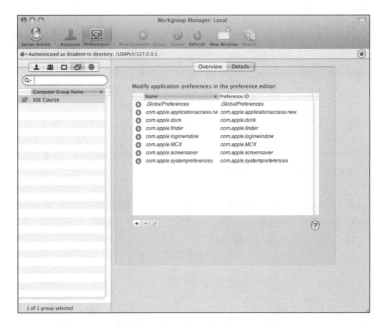

4   Click the Add (+) button at the bottom of the window.

5   Navigate to and select the Safari application.

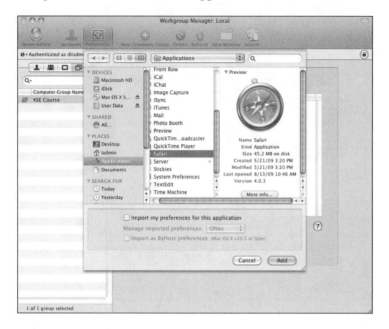

6   Deselect the "Import my preferences for this application" checkbox.

This option would be used in cases where you want to preconfigure an entire user experience for an application by configuring the application to your liking and then importing your preferences.

7   Click Add.

8 Find Safari in the list, select the com.apple.Safari entry, and then click the Edit icon (a pencil).

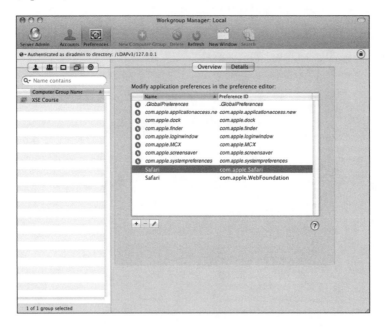

9 Click the disclosure triangle next to Once.

10 Select the Once entry so it's highlighted.

11 Click the New Key button.

12 Click New Item when it appears. A menu builds with the preference choices for Safari found in its preference manifest.

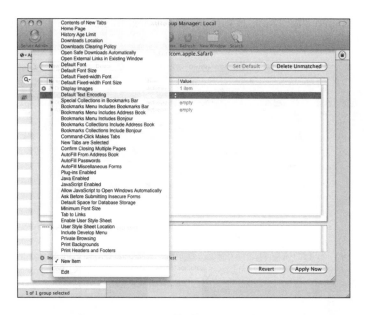

13 Choose Home Page from the menu.

Notice that the Value field is prepopulated with an example setting.

14 Double-click the Value field, and change it to `http://www.pretendco.com/`.

15 Click Apply Now, and then click Done. Notice the arrow next to Safari indicating it has a managed preference.

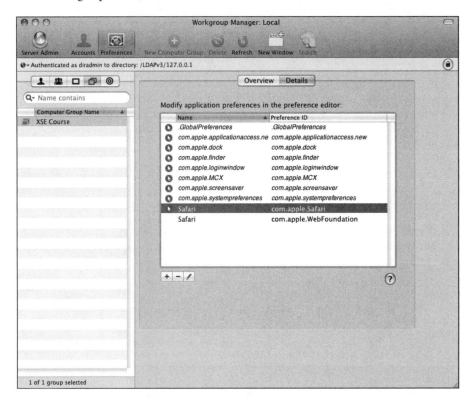

16 Click the Overview tab to return to the main Preferences pane.

17 Click the Applications icon, and add Safari to the list of allowed applications for the XSE Course computer group.

18 Log back in as any user who has rights to log in to the machine, as we are managing the Safari preference at the machine level, and then open Safari. Notice how it attempts to load http://www.pretendco.com/ as its homepage.

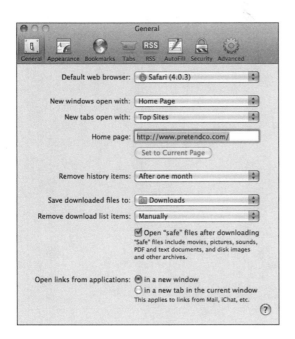

Managing Software Updates

With Mac OS X Server, you have the option of mirroring Apple's Software Update servers on your local server. This has two distinct advantages. The first is that you can save Internet bandwidth. All of your client computers will retrieve their software updates from the server on your local network rather than over the Internet, which will also result in faster downloads for your users. The second advantage is that you can control which updates are downloaded and which are available to your users. This can be particularly useful when a software update might be incompatible with some software you're using.

Setting up your software update server is easy. Here's how:

1 From your Mac OS X computer, open Server Admin and connect to your server.

2 Click the Add (+) button in the lower-left corner, and choose Add Service to add the Software Update service on your server. Click Save.

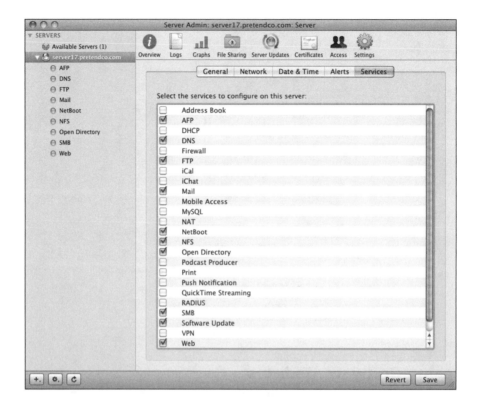

3 Click the Software Update service on the left side of the Server Admin window.

4 Click the Settings tab.

5 Configure the settings as follows:

▶ Set "Provide updates using port" to 8088 (the default).

▶ Select "Copy all updates from Apple."

▶ Select "Automatically enable copied updates."

▶ Select "Delete outdated software updates."

▶ Do not select "Limit user bandwidth to."

TIP If you have a slow network between your client and server machines, or if you have a large number of clients, you may want to limit the user bandwidth.

TIP You can change the location of the update packages. You may want to consider doing this, as the default location is on your boot drive and the updates can take a considerable amount of room on the volume. If you have another storage volume, you might want to use it.

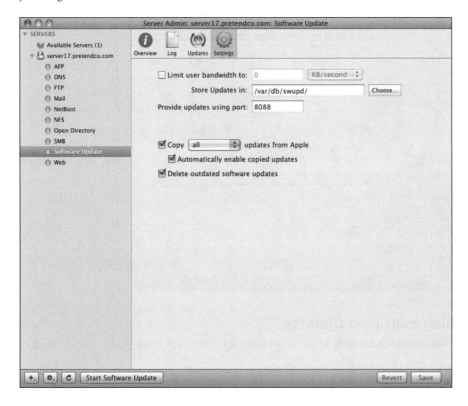

6 Click Save.

7 Click the Start Software Update button at the bottom of Server Admin.

8 Click the Updates button in the toolbar.

9 Click the Update List button.

This will begin mirroring the software updates from Apple. If you have a slow Internet connection, this initial sync will take quite some time, possibly a number of hours.

Enabling Individual Updates

You can select which updates to make available to your users from within the list of updates.

1   In Server Admin, select the Software Update service on the left.

2   Click the Settings button in the toolbar.

3   Click the Updates tab.

This screen lists all the updates currently available from Apple's servers.

4   Select which updates you want to be enabled.

If the list of updates is empty, it is still being copied down from Apple.

NOTE ▶ The update must be copied down before you can enable it.

5 Click Save.

If you aren't copying all the updates automatically, this is the same screen where you would choose which updates you wanted to copy.

Configuring Computers for Your Software Update Service

As with other settings, you'll be using managed preferences to tell your computer to utilize your local software update server instead of Apple's. This preference can be set at the user, group, computer, or computer group level. This example sets the preference at the user level.

1 Open Workgroup Manager and connect to your server.

2 Select Student Four in the Accounts list.

> **NOTE ▶** You could also assign this preference to a workgroup, computer, or computer group.

3 Click the Preferences button in the toolbar.

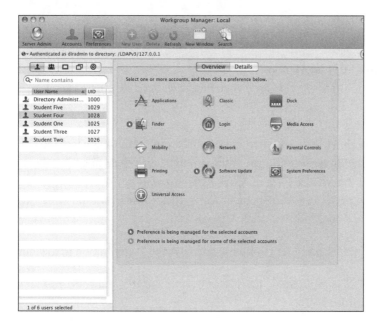

4   Click the Software Update icon.

5   Select the Always management setting.

6   In the "Software Update server to use" field, enter `http://server17.pretendco.com:8088/index.sucatalog`.

7   Click Apply Now.

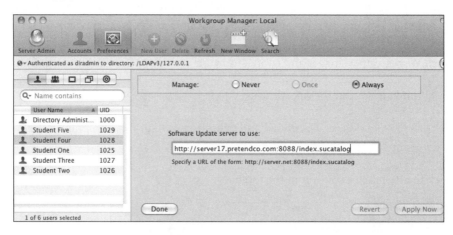

Restoring the Default Settings

We want to make sure to undo the managed preferences we set up in these exercises, so follow these steps:

1   Log in as Local Administrator, and then open Workgroup Manager. Select the Odds account list, click the Preferences button in the toolbar, click the Applications icon, and select Never in the Manage option. Click Apply Now. If any other management arrows exist next to preference management icons, click those icons and select Never from the Manage options, and then click Apply Now.

2   Select XSE Course in the Computer Group list, and click the Delete button in the toolbar.

3   Restart the Mac OS X computer, log in as Local Administrator, and confirm that you can access all applications.

Managing Mobile User Accounts

Network user accounts provide a great deal of administrative control, but they are useful only for computers that are constantly connected to the network. If a computer is disconnected from the network, it no longer has access to network user accounts or home folders. To help manage accounts on computers that are not always connected to the network, such as portables, Mac OS X Server v10.3 and later provides the Mobile Accounts managed preference, which allows you to create mobile user accounts.

A *mobile user account* is a Mac OS X Server user account that resides in a shared domain but is copied to the local computer. This allows a user to log in to a portable computer using the network account even when the computer is not connected to a network. Mac OS X Server v10.4 added the ability to do file synchronization with the server account. Files can be set through Workgroup Manager to be automatically copied from the user's network home folder.

When a computer is connected to the network and the mobile user logs in, the operating system authenticates the user using the account information stored in the shared domain to which the computer is bound. The mobile account on the computer is updated automatically, including any managed preferences. When the computer is disconnected, the user logs in using the local account, which provides the same level of administrative control as the network account does. In either case, whether the computer is connected to the network or not, the home folder is stored locally on the computer.

Because this will also work if a mobile user logs in to multiple computers, it's possible that the user may get a mobile account created on dozens of computers. Mac OS X Server v10.5 added account expiry as an option to help clean up stale mobile accounts.

Mac OS X Server v10.5 also added a new type of mobile account, known as an *external account*. This type of account stores the user's account information and files on a removable drive such as a FireWire drive. This allows mobile users to take their accounts with them, rather than relying on a network connection to the main server to copy everything down each time they log in to a new computer.

Mac OS X Server v10.6 adds the ability to host external accounts on MS-DOS (FAT) formatted drives. This extends compatibility with a wider range of preformatted drives and reduces the need to reformat the drive. It also allows the drive with an external account on it to be plugged into a Windows-based PC and to have data transferred from it.

Creating and Deleting Mobile User Accounts

After creating an account, you can follow these generic steps to convert it into a mobile account. This option, like other account management options, is set through Workgroup Manager's Preferences options.

1 Open Workgroup Manager, select a network user account, and then click Preferences in the toolbar.

2 Click Mobility and select the Always management setting.

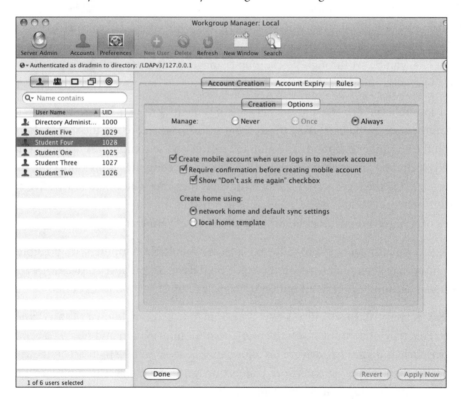

3 Select "Create mobile account when user logs in to network account."

4   Select "Require confirmation before creating mobile account" if you want to allow the user to decide whether to create a mobile account at login.

If this option is selected, the user sees a confirmation dialog when logging in. The user can click Create to create the mobile account immediately, or click Continue to log in as a network user without creating the mobile account.

5   Click Apply Now.

> **TIP** If you manage only the creation of a mobile account for a network user, the user's local home folder becomes the default home folder. Any files that were stored in the network home folder are not copied to the local home folder. There is no file synchronization unless you set up rules for automatically copying files.

You can also create mobile user accounts by managing the Mobility preference for a workgroup, computer, or computer group. For example, if you manage the Mobility preference for a workgroup, all members of the workgroup become mobile users. This can be very useful in a large setting of portables, such as a school full of MacBook computers. Similarly, if you manage this preference for a computer group, all users of the computers become mobile users.

If a user no longer requires a mobile account, you should select Never as the Mobility preference in Workgroup Manager. In addition, you might want to delete the local copy of the account. Both the mobile account and its local home folder are deleted. You must have a Local Administrator account and password to delete a mobile account.

When you want to delete a mobile account from a computer where the user has logged in before:

1   Open System Preferences on the client computer.

2   Click Accounts.

3   Select the account you want to delete.

The mobile account should have the word *Mobile* beneath it.

4 Click the Remove (–) button, and then click OK.

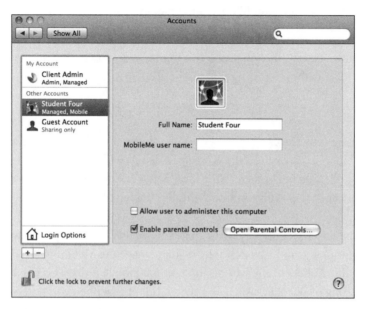

Synchronizing Accounts

Creating a mobile account is useful because a user can authenticate with the network information, and the owner of the files on the local and network folders is the same. You can set up rules for automatically copying files. For each preference set, you can establish which files can be synchronized at login and logout. These files are copied only from the home folder path.

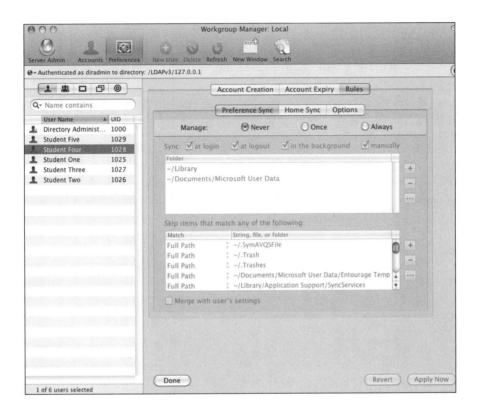

NOTE ▶ While you can set up mobile accounts for your Mac OS X v10.3 users, only users of Mac OS X v10.4 or later can take advantage of the synchronization rules.

Synchronizing Account Preferences and Home Folders

The Rules pane lets you designate which files you want synchronized. Mac OS X Server v10.6 changed the syncing options to separate preference and home folder syncing. This is reflected in the Preference Sync and Home Sync tabs under the Rules tab of Mobility preferences. These local files will be synchronized with the corresponding folders and preference files on the server. Because the mobile account is a duplicate of the network account, all the permissions and ownership are identical. You can set up folders to copy and decide whether the copy takes place in the background. You can also determine which files should not be copied.

Because preference files tend to be small, you might want to consider setting them to sync at login and logout, and setting the larger data files of the home sync to sync in the background to help prevent delays during login and logout.

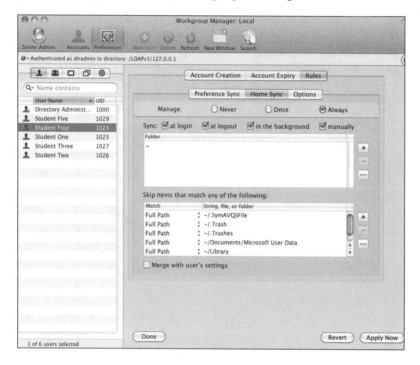

TIP Cache files, temporary files, and settings specific to the mobile account such as printer settings can be set to never be cached. Limit what is synchronized to essential files and important data. Network administrators may want to exclude music and photos as a rule, but be aware that this could break certain project files for GarageBand or iMovie.

Setting Account Synchronization Options

The Options tab lets you set the timing for the synchronization of files. This can be done at set time intervals or manually. This option is only for the file synchronization in the background and is set at 20 minutes by default.

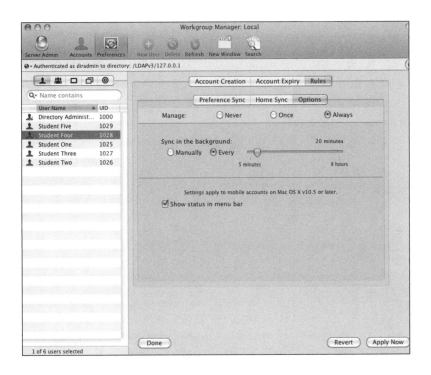

Configuring Mobile Computing

Now you will use one of the accounts you set up previously and set up a synchronized mobile user account for that person.

1   In Workgroup Manager on your Mac OS X computer, choose the /LDAPv3/127.0.0.1 domain from the Directory pop-up menu.

2   Select Student Four in the Accounts list, and click the Preferences button in the toolbar.

3   Click the Mobility icon. In the Account Creation pane, select Always from the Manage options, and select the following checkboxes:

▶   Create mobile account when user logs in to network account

▶   Require confirmation before creating mobile account

▶   Show "Don't ask me again" checkbox

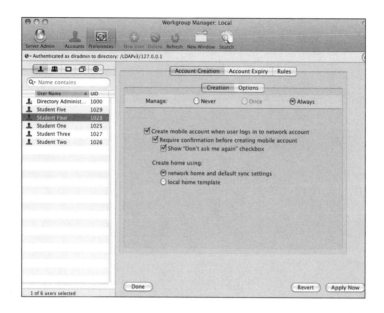

4   Click the Rules tab, click the Preference Sync tab, and select Always from the Manage options. Deselect the "in the background" checkbox, and leave the others selected.

The default is to copy the entire ~/Library and ~/Documents/Microsoft User Data paths except those folders listed in the Skip pane.

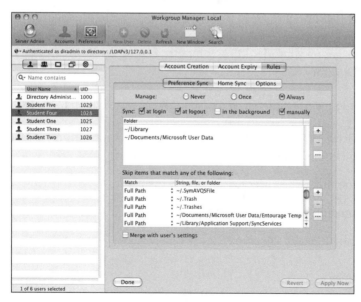

5   Select the ~ in the Folders pane. Click the Remove (–) button next to the Folder pane, and remove ~.

6   Click the Add (+) button, and enter ~/Documents so you are synchronizing just the Documents folder.

7   Deselect the "at login" and "at logout" checkboxes. This will force the sync to happen in the background, reducing the delay during login and logout while large files get pushed across the network.

8 Click the Options tab, select Always from the Manage options, and verify that the timing slider is set to 5 minutes. Click Apply Now.

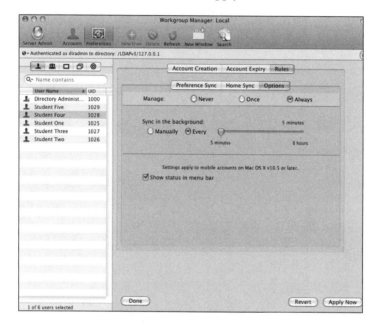

Configuring Account Expiry

1 Click the Account Expiry tab.

2 Select Always from the Manage options.

3 Select "Delete mobile accounts: 2 Days after user's next login."

4 Leave "Delete only after successful sync" selected.

This option ensures that there's no data loss from data that may not have been synchronized back to the server prior to the account's deletion.

5 Click Apply Now.

6 Quit Workgroup Manager and restart your Mac OS X computer.

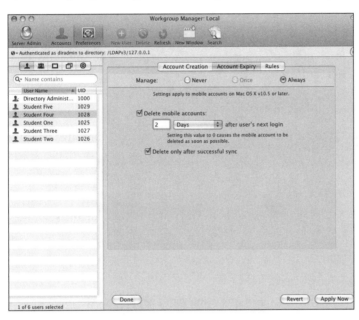

Verifying a Mobile Account from the Client

The Student Four account is now configured to exist locally on each system successfully logged in to, and files stored in ~/Documents will be synchronized with the network account.

1 On the Mac OS X computer, log in as Student Four.

2 Click the Create Now button when the confirmation dialog asks if you want to create a mobile account with a portable home directory.

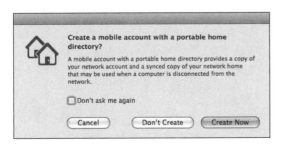

3   Open TextEdit, create a text file, and save it to the ~/Documents folder.

4   Wait five minutes.

5   On the server, view Student Four's Documents folder type with Terminal by entering
    `sudo ls -al /Users/student4/Documents/`.

6   Enter the ladmin password when asked.

    This will show all of Student Four's documents without actually logging in as Student
    Four on the server.

    The file should appear after about five minutes.

7   On your Mac OS X computer, log out as Student Four, and then log in as Local
    Administrator.

Configure External Accounts

You will use one of the accounts you set up previously and set up an external user account
for that person.

1   In Workgroup Manager on your Mac OS X computer, choose the /LDAPv3/127.0.0.1
    domain from the Directory pop-up menu.

2   Select Student Two in the Accounts list, and click the Preferences button in the toolbar.

3   Click the Mobility icon. In the Account Creation pane, select Always from the Manage
    options, and select the following checkboxes:

    ▶   Create mobile account when user logs in to network account

    ▶   Require confirmation before creating mobile account

4   Click the Options tab, and select Always from the Manage options.

5   Set the home folder location to "user chooses any external volume."

6   Click Apply Now.

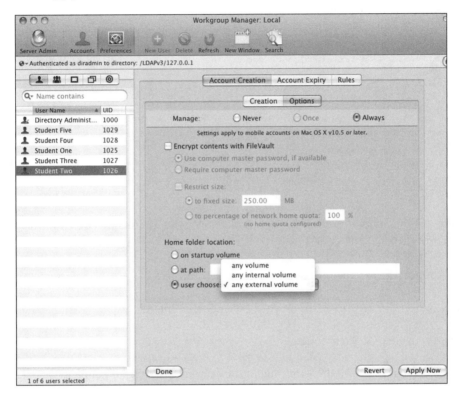

Verify an External Account from the Client

The Student Two account is now configured to exist on an external drive. If you have an Mac OS Extended or MS-DOS (FAT) formatted external drive available to you, you can try logging in as Student Two with the drive attached.

1   Open System Preferences, click Accounts, and click Login Options, and then set your login window to display as "List of users."

2   Log out as Local Administrator, and then log in as Student Two.

3   If the desired external device isn't already chosen, choose it from the pop-up menu that appears.

4 Click the Create Now button when the confirmation dialog asks if you want to create a mobile account with a portable home directory.

5 After logging in as Student Two has completed, log out as Student Two and shut down your Mac OS X computer.

6 Disconnect the external drive you saved the account on.

7 Disconnect the network cable on your Mac OS X computer.

8 Start your Mac OS X computer.

9 After the login window appears, plug in the external drive. What happens?

Because all of Student Two's account information and files are stored on the external drive, that account appears in the list when you connect the drive. Because the account information, including the password, is stored on the drive, you can log in without a network connection.

10 On your Mac OS X computer, log in as Student Two.

11 Log out as Student Two, and then log in as Local Administrator.

12 Plug your network cable back in, and eject your external drive.

Troubleshooting

The majority of problems encountered arise from users not being able to connect. This happens primarily at login. When troubleshooting account management issues, do the following:

▶ Check that the client bound to the correct directory.

▶ Check that the user and/or group home directories exported correctly.

▶ Check the user, group, computer, and computer group settings. Are the settings too restrictive? For example, is guest access denied and a new computer online?

▶ Check the preferences by logging in as a similar user. This works best if preferences are shared by a group.

▶ Use the Inspector in Workgroup Manager to view the raw preferences. It is especially useful if settings are set manually and copied into the user records. The Details function can also serve as a quick check for a set of preferences.

What You've Learned

▶ Account management encompasses everything from setting up accounts for network access and creating home folders to fine-tuning the user experience by managing preferences and settings for users, groups, and computers.

▶ Workgroup Manager is an account management tool. It provides centralized directory-based management of users, groups, and computers—from anywhere on your network.

▶ The account information for a network user resides in a shared domain, and the user's home folder resides on a home folder server. Network users can log in from any client on the network and have access to their home folders.

▶ A group folder offers a way to organize documents and applications of special interest to group members and gives group members a folder where they can pass information back and forth.

▶ A computer group is a list of computers that have the same preference settings and are available to the same users and groups. You can create and modify computer groups in Workgroup Manager.

▶ Preferences can be set for many built-in Mac OS X options for users, workgroups, computers, or computer groups. Other preferences can be managed if a preference manifest is provided with an application.

▶ Running a local software update server can control what updates are available to users and make more efficient use of the network for downloading software updates.

▶ A mobile user has many synchronized accounts. The main account resides in a shared domain, and a copy of the main account resides locally on the user's computer or an external disk. You can configure the user's files to be synchronized.

References

The following documents provide more information about managing accounts on Mac OS X Server. All these and more are available at http://www.apple.com/server/documentation.

Administration Guides

Getting Started

System Imaging & Software Update Administration

User Management

Apple Knowledge Base Documents

You can check for new and updated Knowledge Base documents at http://www.apple.com/support/.

Chapter Review

1. What is the difference between a local user account and a network user account?

2. How is a mobile user different from a network user?

3. Can a user be a member of more than one workgroup?

4. Can a computer be a member of more than one computer group?

5. What is the difference between a group and a workgroup?

6. In Workgroup Manager, how can you configure preferences for user, group, computer, and computer group accounts to avoid overrides?

7. Name two ways to review raw preference data in Workgroup Manager.

8. What folders are synchronized in a mobile account?

Answers

1. In the case of a local user account, the home folder and account information are stored locally. But in the case of a network user account, the home folder is stored on a remote home folder server, and the account information resides in a shared domain.

2. A mobile user is a network user whose Mobility preference is managed. When you manage this preference, the next time the user logs in, Mac OS X Server creates two things: a copy of the user's account in the local domain of the user's computer, and a local home folder, which becomes the user's default home folder.

   Important: Any documents that were stored in the network home folder are not copied to the local home folder.

3. Yes.

4. Yes, in v10.5 and later.

5. A group is a file-system designation. It is used to handle access to the file system (as in owner, group, others). It is specific to the file system, server, or computer. A workgroup is a directory service record separate from any specific file system or server. It is used as a method of associating similar preferences for sets of user records.

6. You can avoid overrides by setting each preference for only one type of account. For example, you could set printer preferences only for computers, set application preferences only for workgroups, and set Dock preferences only for users. In such a case, no override occurs for these preferences because the user inherits them without competition.

7. The Inspector and the Details pane of the preference management screen.

8. Only those in the home folder hierarchy are synchronized in a mobile account.

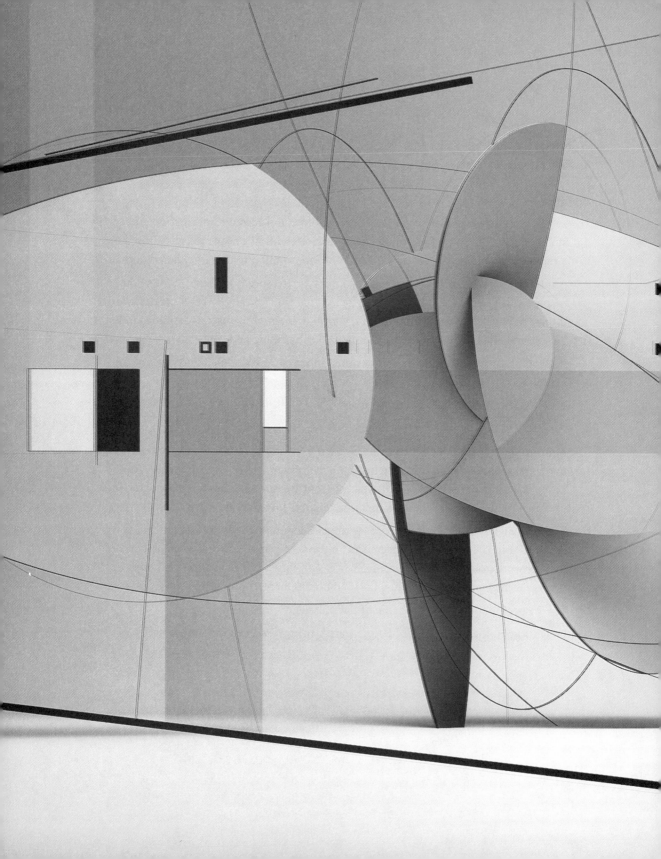

Index

The Apple Pro Training Series

The official curriculum of the Apple Pro Training and Certification Program, the Apple Pro Training books are comprehensive, self-paced courses written by acknowledged experts in the field. Focused lessons take you step by-step through the process of creating real-world digital video or audio projects, while lesson files on the companion DVD and ample illustrations help you master techniques fast. In addition, lesson goals and time estimates help you plan your time, while chapter review questions summarize what you've learned.

Final Cut Pro 7
0-321-63527-2

Cut a scene from the TNT television series *Leverage*, create a promo for Sea-World's *Believe* documentary, master effects as you edit a segment of Playing for Change. In this bestselling guide, Diana Weynand starts with basic video editing techniques and takes you all the way through Final Cut Pro's powerful advanced features. You'll learn to mark and edit clips, mix sound, add titles, create transitions, apply filters, and more.

Final Cut Pro 7 Advanced Editing
0-321-63679-1

This Apple-authorized guide delivers hard-to-find advanced editing and finishing techniques. Director and editor Michael Wohl shows how to create polished transitions, fix screen direction errors, edit multi-camera projects, work with nested sequences, create fantastic effects, use filters creatively, and composite like a pro.

Motion 4
0-321-63529-9

Create sophisticated Motion projects including a 3D show promo, a network-style title sequence, a complex motion menu, and an actual temp effect used in Overture Film's *Traitor*. Mentor trainer Mark Spencer shows you how to harness Motion's behavior-based animations, particles, filters, effects, keying, tracking, and 3D capabilities to create professional animations, show opens, promos, text treatments, and more.

Sound Editing in Final Cut Studio
0-321-64748-3

Your guide to audio post-production with Final Cut Pro 7 and Soundtrack 3.

Color Correction in Final Cut Studio
0-321-63528-0

This guide to color grading and finishing starts with the basics of color correction in Final Cut Pro 7 and moves on to the fine points of secondary grading in Color 1.5

DVD Studio Pro, Third Edition
0-321-53409-3

Learn to author professional DVDs with this best-selling guide. Use striking real-world footage to build four complete DVDs

Logic Pro 9 and Logic Express 9
0-321-63680-5

Record, edit, mix, and polish music files using Apple's pro audio software.

Compressor 3.5
0-321-64743-2

Author Brian Gary teaches you real-world techniques for audio and video compression, batch-encoding, test-clip workflows, and more.

Final Cut Server 1.5
0-321-64765-3

Covers everything from tools for tracking, reviewing, and approving jobs to automating complex sequences of tasks in a busy post environment.

Final Cut Pro 7 Quick-Reference Guide
0-321-69468-6

Ideal for students and editors on the go, this is the quick look-up guide you've been hunting for.

Motion 4 Quick-Reference Guide
0-321-63677-5

Designed as a desktop companion for both editors and motion graphics artists, this is the perfect at-a-glance guide to Motion 4.

Apple Pro Training Series: Shake 4
0-321-25609-3

Apple-certified guide uses stunning real world sequences to reveal the wizardry of Shake 4.

Encyclopedia of Visual Effects
0-321-30334-2

Ultimate recipe book for visual effects artists working in Shake, Motion and Adobe After Effects.

Encyclopedia of Color Correction
0-321-43231-2

Comprehensive training in the real-world color correction and management skills editing pros use every day in the field.

Aperture 2
0-321-53993-1

The best way to learn Aperture's powerful photo-editing, image retouching, proofing, publishing, and archiving features.

Final Cut Express 4
0-321-53467-0

The only Apple authorized guide to Final Cut Express 4 has you making movie magic in no time.

Final Cut Pro for Avid Editors, Third Edition
0-321-51539-0

This comprehensive "translation course" is designed for professional video and film editors who already know their way around Avid nonlinear systems.

Final Cut Pro for News and Sports Quick-Reference Guide, Second Edition
0-321-56406-5

This easy look-up guide provides essential techniques for broadcast studios using Final Cut Pro to edit news and sports.

Shake 4 Quick Reference Guide
0-321-38246-3

This compact reference guide to Apple's leading compositing software offers a concise explanation of the Shake interface, workspace, and tools.

QuickTime Pro Quick-Reference Guide
0-321-44248-2

An invaluable guide to capturing, encoding, editing, streaming, and exporting media.

Xsan 2 Administration: A Guide to Designing, Deploying, and Maintaining Xsan
0-321-61322-8

This Apple-certified reference provides invaluable guidance in planning, designing, configuring, deploying, and maintaining an Xsan network.

The Apple Training Series

Apple Training Series: Mac OS X Server Essentials v10.6
ISBN: 0-321-63533-7

Apple Training Series: Mac OS X Support Essentials v10.6
ISBN: 0-321-63534-5

Apple Training Series: Mac OS X Deployment v10.6
ISBN 0-321-63531-0

Apple Training Series: iLife 09
0-321-61850-5

Apple Training Series: Mac OS X Directory Services v10.6
ISBN: 0-321-63532-9

Apple Training Series: Mac OS X Security and Mobility v10.6
ISBN: 0-321-63535-3

Apple Training Series: iWork 09
0-321-61851-3

Apple Training Series: AppleScript 1-2-3
0-321-14931-9

Apple Training Series: Garageband 3
0-321-64852-8

Apple Training Series: A Teacher's Guide to Digital Media in the Classroom
0-321-59143-7

To order books or view the entire Apple Pro Training Series catalog , visit: www.peachpit.com/appleprotraining